D1297294

SUPERFUND

The
Political
Economy of
Environmental Risk

SUPERFUND

JOHN A. HIRD

THE JOHNS HOPKINS UNIVERSITY PRESS   BALTIMORE AND LONDON

© 1994 The Johns Hopkins University Press
All rights reserved. Published 1994
Printed in the United States of America on acid-free paper

03 02 01 00 99 98 97 96 95 94   5 4 3 2 1

The Johns Hopkins University Press
2715 North Charles Street
Baltimore, Maryland 21218-4319
The Johns Hopkins Press Ltd., London

LIBRARY OF CONGRESS CATALOGING-IN-PUBLICATION DATA

Hird, John A.
    Superfund : the political economy of environmental risk / John A. Hird.
        p.   cm.
    Includes bibliographical references and index.
    ISBN 0-8018-4806-7 (hc, acid-free paper). — ISBN 0-8018-4807-5 (pbk., acid-free paper)
        1. Hazardous waste sites—Cleaning—Finance—Government policy—United States.
2. Hazardous waste sites—Government policy—United States.   3. Hazardous wastes—
United States—Risk assessment.   I. Title.
HC110.P55H57   1994
363.73'84'0973—dc20   93-44891
    A catalog record for this book is available from the British Library.

Published in cooperation with the Center for American Places,
Harrisonburg, Virginia

For my parents, Doris and John

Contents

Preface

Perhaps nowhere has the fear of chemical hazards been more pronounced and publicized than with the disposal of hazardous wastes. Public opinion polls show that Americans routinely rate hazardous waste sites as the most important environmental problem. The solution would appear to be simple: clean up the waste sites littering the country. But the issue is not as simple as it might seem. In fact, most experts who study chemical hazards rate the environmental and human health risks from hazardous waste sites well down on the list of environmental and public health priorities. Moreover, the cost of remediating thousands of abandoned and inactive waste sites has been estimated to be as high as $500 billion over 50 years. Therefore, considerable disagreement persists over the allocation of scarce funds for what experts believe to be a relatively minor environmental and public health threat.

In spite of these disagreements, and motivated by the public outcry over sites like Love Canal, a federal Superfund program was established in 1980 to remediate abandoned hazardous waste sites. The multibillion-dollar program set out with high expectations from legislators and the public, but hopes for rapid site cleanups were quickly dashed by an Environmental Protection Agency that showed little willingness to comply with congressional intent. The Superfund program was hurriedly pieced together with little apparent concern for important policy issues such as fairness, the appropriate level of government to implement the cleanup program, acceptable site cleanup levels, and so on. As a result, Superfund has been racked by more controversy than any other domestic environmental program, and EPA officials have witnessed irate citizens, physical threats, and kidnappings. The program went through a politically wrenching reauthorization in 1986 and is scheduled for another round in 1994. How should Superfund be reformed, and more importantly, how should governments resolve environmental risk decisions that pit the views of experts against those of the public? This study examines Superfund in the broader context of environmental risk management and concludes that significant changes are necessary to improve hazardous waste cleanup policy, principles that can be applied to other environmental risk management decisions.

This book examines the fundamental controversy that Superfund needs to resolve: the difference between the public's view of hazardous waste site risks and the perception of experts. The argument expressed here is that both perspectives—that Superfund sites pose significant risks (the public) and that they generally do not (experts)—are, oddly enough, accurate. They are both accurate because the definitions of risk used by the public and the experts are distinct. Experts view risks technically, as the likely environmental and health threats posed by individual toxic chemicals, and although the scientific evidence is sketchy, most agree that these risks are relatively small at Superfund sites. The public, on the other hand, views risks far more expansively. Many elements can affect the public's view of risk, including the environmental and health threats, the origin of the risk (natural or manufactured?), the distribution of risk (are some individuals particularly exposed or susceptible?), the voluntariness of exposure (is the risk avoidable?), and so forth. These seemingly irreconcilable views of risk need not result in the policy impasse that has gripped Superfund for the past dozen years. Virtually no participants in the cleanup of hazardous waste sites are satisfied with the progress of Superfund, yet the differing views of the risks from Superfund sites preclude a reasonable discussion of reforms: most reform proposals implicitly favor one perspective over the other.

This book is intended to serve several purposes. First, it is an analysis of the political and economic factors that shape, and are shaped by, Superfund. These include analyses of the relative risks posed by Superfund sites compared with other environmental problems, Superfund's effectiveness in reducing risks, several views of equity and fairness, the extent to which political institutions have forged Superfund's course, and finally a political analysis of why the Superfund program has evolved the way it has. Second, the book recommends significant policy reforms in the Superfund program that would improve its efficiency, effectiveness, equity, and perhaps most importantly, encourage meaningful public participation in managing environmental risks. Finally, and most broadly, I argue that creative public institutions can be crafted to address environmental risk-management disputes, even ones as contentious as that over Superfund. Policymakers must recognize the multiple perspectives of managing risks and build political institutions to translate those views into public policy. The failure to do so will doom controversial programs like Superfund that address environmental risks. My hope is that these proposed reforms will not only improve Superfund policy but also stimulate some creative thinking about how governments manage risks to public health and the environment.

1 Assessing and Managing Risks

1 Introduction to Superfund

The language of environmental policy was until recently dominated by words like "conservation" and "stewardship," and environmentalists like John Muir, Aldo Leopold, and dozens of others less prominent spent most of their time outdoors admiring, studying, and chronicling a wilderness that has for the most part vanished from the United States. The great political successes of the environmental movement in years past included the establishment and preservation of extensive national park and national wildlife refuge systems, and protection of wilderness areas that served both human and ecological needs. In the last twenty years or so, however, the terms of the environmental debate have been altered dramatically. Most of the major pieces of environmental legislation enacted since 1970—the Clean Air Act of 1970, the Federal Water Pollution Control Act of 1972, the Safe Drinking Water Act of 1974, the Resource Conservation and Recovery Act of 1976, the Toxic Substances Control Act of 1976 (TSCA), the Federal Insecticide, Fungicide, and Rodenticide Act of 1978 (FIFRA), and the Comprehensive Environmental Response, Compensation, and Liability Act of 1980—have been motivated not by threats to distant and wild lands but almost exclusively by concerns about risks to human health. To be sure, conservation issues are still a central element in any comprehensive environmental policy, and legislation like the Endangered Species Act of 1973 and land-use controversies, like those over grazing and mining rights, remain important issues to environmental organizations. Nevertheless, the terms of the environmental policy debate—driven by public concerns—are increasingly based on human health risks, chiefly from chemical products and wastes.

Chemical Risks and the Scope of the Hazardous Waste Problem

Chemical risks have received considerable media attention, particularly in the wake of Rachel Carson's 1962 book *Silent Spring*, which first alerted the American public to the risks from pesticides. Greater media attention was fueled in part by poor government and industry responses to such incidents as the discovery of seeping hazardous wastes in Love Canal, New York, the methyl isocyanate leak at Bhopal, India, fears about food additives like cyclamates and Alar, and the nuclear accident at Chernobyl in the former Soviet Union. Additional media attention is now paid to common environmental issues as well. One calculation showed that comparing environmental news coverage in 1986 with that in 1954, the *New York Times* devoted three times as much space to stories on air pollution in 1986, six times as much to water pollution, and twelve times as much to solid waste.[1] Less well publicized incidents, such as two companies in South Carolina being recently accused of mixing toxic heavy metals with fertilizer for export to Australia and Bangladesh,[2] have fueled a growing public concern that chemical risks are more widespread than industry or government have revealed. Finally, overlying all of these factors is the vastly increased sensitivity of Americans to environmental concerns generally, as indicated by the increasing percentage who call themselves "environmentalists," more who believe that the federal government is spending too little on environmental protection, increasing numbers who believe environmental protection should be pursued "regardless of cost," and growing membership in environmental organizations.[3]

The public's perception of rapidly increasing risks from chemical contamination also stems from the sensational growth of the U.S. chemical industry since World War II, which ushered in thousands of new synthetic chemicals. The chemical industry's growth—an industry that now employs more than 800,000 workers with annual sales exceeding $260 billion—fueled productivity advances in agriculture, manufacturing, pharmaceuticals, and many other fields.[4] However, the surge in chemical production was ultimately met by public concern about the effects on human health and the environment, leading to the passage of federal legislation, such as TSCA and FIFRA, to monitor and regulate the use of new and existing chemicals and pesticides.

A final source of public concern about chemical contamination is the increasing ability of scientists to measure chemical risks. Where twenty years ago scientists could detect chemicals in parts per thousand, today they can be identified in amounts smaller than one part per quadrillion. This has led to a bewildering flurry of information regarding whether or not a chemical is "carcinogenic," as if it were a simple yes-no determination. The Delaney Clause to the Food, Drug, and Cosmetic Act, which requires that food additives pose no carcinogenic risk, may have once seemed a reasonable protection. However, scientists' ability to measure ever more minute risks means that strict adherence to a "zero risk" policy would prohibit the consumption of dried basil, peanut butter, apple juice, and hundreds of other natural and processed foods that contain suspected carcinogens.

Americans have come to fear hazardous wastes like no other environmental problem, no small matter when one considers that Americans are annually responsible for generating more than one metric ton of hazardous waste per person.[5] Be it a fear of unknown consequences, the possibility that hazardous wastes could be located in their "back yards," the invisibility of hazardous waste, or an understandable aversion to anything labeled "hazardous,"fully 66 percent of respondents to a recent poll rated the danger of hazardous waste sites as "very serious,"ahead of nuclear accident radiation, pesticide residues, contaminated tap water, ozone layer destruction, acid rain, and every other environmental problem listed.[6] Hazardous wastes, which EPA has defined as either toxic, corrosive, ignitable, or reactive, can be transmitted through all environmental media—air, water, biota, and land. Approximately 10 to 15 percent of all wastes produced in the United States are considered hazardous.[7] Although there are hundreds of thousands of hazardous waste generators, about two percent of the generators produce about 95 percent of the waste.[8] Most hazardous wastes have been generated by the chemical and petroleum industries, with chemicals and allied products alone accounting for an estimated 48 percent of the total waste generated in 1983.[9] Industrial byproducts are not the sole source of hazardous wastes, however. Individuals regularly—and sometimes carelessly—use these materials themselves as a matter of everyday routine, in products such as batteries, used motor oil, swimming pool chemicals, bleach, pesticides, paints, and wood preservatives. Approximately 95 percent of hazardous waste is stored at the site where it was produced, while the remainder is disposed of off-site or treated.[10] Of course, hazardous waste problems, or programs to clean them up, are not unique to the United States. Hazardous waste problems affect both developed and relatively undeveloped countries. However, only wealthier countries have been able to direct significant resources to cleaning up the wastes. Germany, for example, will finance the cleanup of uranium mines with a $3.6 billion cleanup fund.[11] The international trafficking in hazardous waste has been the subject of much controversy between developed and developing countries as well.[12]

Public concern over hazardous wastes from industrial sources has been translated into a myriad of state and federal agencies and regulations. In addition to many state agencies concerned with hazardous wastes, more than a dozen federal agencies are involved in regulating the production, transport, disposal, and cleanup of hazardous wastes, including the Coast Guard, the Departments of Justice, Interior, Transportation, Energy, Defense, and of course the Environmental Protection Agency. The three principal federal laws addressing hazardous materials are the Toxic Substances Control Act of 1976, which regulates the introduction and use of new hazardous chemicals; the Resource Conservation and Recovery Act (RCRA) of 1976, which restricts the disposal of hazardous wastes into the air, water, and land (prior to RCRA, only air and water were protected under the clean air and water statutes) and imposes a "manifest" tracking system for all hazardous wastes; and the Comprehensive Environmental Response, Compensation, and Liabilities Act (CERCLA, otherwise known as Superfund) of 1980, which is intended to clean up abandoned hazardous waste sites. RCRA and CERCLA were amended significantly in 1984 and 1986, respectively. While the RCRA and Superfund hazardous waste programs are related—for example, current RCRA sites can become Superfund sites, and the Superfund liability scheme affects the operation of active waste sites—RCRA generally regulates current disposal of hazardous wastes, while Superfund addresses inactive or abandoned waste sites.

Because RCRA is mostly a regulatory program, EPA's expenditures on RCRA are relatively small compared with its total impact on the economy. While budgetary costs are relatively modest, RCRA hazardous waste regulation is estimated to impose annual costs on the U.S. economy of over $2 billion currently and over $12 billion annually by the year 2000 (both in constant 1986 dollars).[13] Superfund, on the other hand, is both a regulatory and a public works program. The bulk of the program requires private parties to remediate existing waste sites, which makes it essentially a public works project that is privately financed. But Superfund also causes hazardous waste producers to exercise great care in disposing of hazardous wastes for fear of creating a future Superfund site, and in that respect it operates much like a regulatory program. Estimates of Superfund's costs vary considerably, but all are significant. EPA estimates that Superfund expenditures will exceed $8 billion annually (in 1986 dollars) by the turn of the century.[14] The Office of Technology Assessment has estimated that present cleanup efforts of Superfund sites are dwarfed by future potential costs, which they estimate to be as high as $500 billion over the next fifty years.[15] A more recent Superfund cost estimate by researchers at the University of Tennessee shows that the ultimate cleanup cost for the most threatening sites, based on current cleanup policy requirements, will range from $106 to $302 billion, depending on whether 2100 or 6000 sites need to be remediated, excluding administrative and transactions costs. The study estimated that less stringent cleanup policies could reduce costs to between $63 and $180 billion, although more stringent standards could push costs to between $246 and $704 billion.[16] Because EPA estimates approximately 2000 sites will be on the National Priorities List (NPL) by the year 2000, more conservative cost estimates place the cleanup figure at around $100 billion.

Not only is the ultimate cost of the Superfund program uncertain, but even the number of sites that need to be remediated is unknown. The General Accounting Office (GAO) had earlier estimated that as many as 425,000 potential waste sites exist in the United States, compared with EPA's inventory of approximately 31,000 sites at the time. Even though better estimates followed GAO's, the specter of the federal government financing the cleanup of even a small fraction of the potential 425,000 hazardous waste sites posed a tremendous financial obligation and emphasized the importance of setting priorities in cleaning up waste sites. Even if the federal government financed only a quarter of the cleanups and contributed only $10 million to each (a conservative estimate), the cost would exceed $1 trillion, or approximately 160 times EPA's total annual budget. Even GAO's lower estimate of 130,000 sites, using the above assumptions, would cost the federal government $325 billion. If the federal government bears the direct cleanup costs, all Americans will still to varying degrees ultimately bear the burden through higher taxes, higher product prices, reduced output, and unemployment. Thomas Grumbly, president of Clean Sites, believes "It is not too much to say that we will be spending between $10 billion and $20 billion per year in hazardous waste cleanup by the year 2000."[17] The importance of identifying the correct number of priority sites also can be appreciated on a smaller scale by recognizing that one preliminary site assessment costs on average $6,000, while a site inspection costs an average of at least $35,000. Thus, preliminary assessments and site inspections (done at only 50 percent of the sites covered by preliminary assessments) would cost $10 billion for the 425,000 potential sites identified by GAO, more than the total amount allocated to Superfund by Congress between 1986 and 1991.

Although Superfund is an expensive program, its scale is better appreciated in relation to the magnitude of other environmental programs managed by EPA. Comparing Superfund with other EPA programs in terms of budgetary expenditures (as is so often done) is misleading, largely because most other EPA programs are predominantly regulatory—forcing private industry and individuals to finance pollution con-

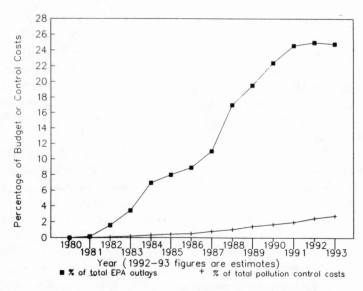

Figure 1.1 Superfund's portion of total EPA budget and total pollution control costs.

Sources: OMB, Budget of the United States Government, various years; and U.S. EPA, "Environmental Investments: The Cost of a Clean Environment." (Washington, D.C.: U.S. EPA, December 1990).

trol with little impact on the federal EPA budget—while Superfund contains a significant public works component paid for by the federal government. EPA's budget therefore appears to be lopsided in favor of Superfund expenditures rather than other environmental programs such as air protection, water protection, and pesticide controls (see figure 1.1); Superfund commands around one-fourth of all operating expenditures. Viewed from the perspective of Superfund's portion of all pollution control costs, however, figure 1.1 shows that Superfund expenditures are far more modest, peaking at around 3 percent of expenditures. While EPA estimates that Superfund costs will be over $8 billion annually by 2000, it estimates that air pollution programs will cost $44 billion and water programs another $64 billion. Indeed, EPA estimates that total annualized pollution control costs will be $160 billion by the turn of the century, with Superfund's share amounting to just 5 percent (all in 1986 dollars).[18] Superfund remains a large and significant program, but it is not projected to even approach the cost of EPA's air, water, and RCRA programs.

Program History

The 1978 Love Canal incident has come to symbolize for many the tremendous public outcry over toxic waste disposal. Scenes on national television of terrified families, as well as reports of plummeting housing values, sent waves of fear throughout the population, many of whom were concerned about the possibility of "ticking time bombs" in their own communities. The EPA had estimated that by 1980 enough hazardous waste was being produced to fill the New Orleans Superdome from floor to ceiling daily, with an estimated 90 percent of it disposed of improperly. Residents of many communities across the country began to clamor for action, and Congress responded with legislation.

In fact, the federal government already had enacted a number of laws and regulations to deal with hazardous wastes, well before the incident at Love Canal reached the headlines. Chief among them was the 1976 Resource Conservation and Recovery Act (RCRA), which although designed mostly as a regulatory program to monitor the disposal of hazardous waste from "cradle to grave" also contained provisions whereby the federal government could order responsible parties to clean up the hazardous waste they dumped. (It was no small source of congressional embarrassment that Love Canal came on the heels of the RCRA legislation intended to control the problem.) The problem with RCRA was that in many instances liable parties could not be found, in which case nothing could be done since no cleanup fund existed. Section 311 of the Clean Water Act allowed EPA to respond to oil spills and hazardous substances dumped into navigable waters using an annual $35 million appropriation,[19] and Section 504 authorized a $10 million fund to clean up any hazardous substance, though the latter had been little used.[20] The fund provided by the Clean Water Act dealt only with navigable waterborne spills, however, and was far too small to address a hazardous waste problem of this magnitude. In short, while significant legislation addressed existing hazardous waste generation and disposal, little could be done about the thousands of *abandoned* dumps reportedly scattered across the country. And because they were abandoned, the fear that a waste site could be in one's "backyard" was all the more compelling and resulted in even higher levels of public concern.

There had been general congressional interest in a hazardous waste cleanup program to plug these statutory gaps, but not until congressional Democrats saw the specter of an incoming conservative Republican president late in 1980 were significant program concessions made to secure Superfund's passage. (Had President Carter been reelected, many observers believe that Superfund would not have passed in 1980.) A lame-duck Democratic Congress, with the help of a lame-duck Democratic president, passed the Comprehensive Environmental Response, Compensation, and Liability Act (Public Law 96-510) in December 1980. CERCLA added to existing laws two central components: first, a $1.6 billion fund, financed by taxes on petroleum products and forty-two chemicals, which could be used to clean up land-based sites pending cost recovery actions against responsible parties; and second, liability provisions to compel responsible parties to finance cleanup costs. Where possible, the responsible parties were to pay for the potential damage caused.[21] The fund, to be administered by the EPA, was to be used primarily if no party could be held liable or if the responsible party could not afford restitution.[22] Chief among the Democrats' concessions were a smaller fund (an earlier Senate version called for a $4.1 billion fund over six years) and the deletion of a victims compensation provision for individuals injured by chemical accidents. The latter was strongly supported by environmental groups, who later called its omission from the final bill "a tragic loss."[23] In addition, House Democrats compromised by permitting weaker liability standards than they favored, and the Act failed to cover oil spills, in large measure due to a threatened filibuster by Senate Republicans. President Carter signed the CERCLA legislation on 11 December 1980.[24]

Initially, EPA officials spoke enthusiastically of a "shovels first, lawyers later" Superfund policy. However, the new legislation met with substantial resistance from a Reagan White House and EPA appointees favoring a diminished federal regulatory role.[25] The battle between environmentalists and EPA over hazardous waste policy came to a head when EPA—on White House orders, claiming "executive privilege"—refused to turn over its enforcement files to a congressional subcommittee. Congressional investigators had found in 1983 that EPA negotiated settlements favorable to polluters instead of litigating, which critics claimed significantly slowed Superfund's remedial efforts. The agency was charged with making "sweetheart deals" with industry for partial cleanups, and particularly galling to the Democratically controlled House, Superfund money was used in 1982 to aid Republican congressional candidates. One such example involved incumbent California Governor Brown's campaign against Republican challenger Pete Wilson. EPA Administrator Anne Burford reportedly had planned to award Superfund money to finance the cleanup of California's widely publicized Stringfellow Acid Pits site, but she later reneged for political reasons and reportedly said, "I'll be damned if I'm going to let Brown take credit for that Stringfellow cleanup."[26]

One commentator later reflected that EPA's "shovels-first, lawyers-later strategy was replaced by one of lunch now, lawyers maybe, but shovels never."[27] From the start, Rita Lavelle, the EPA official in charge of RCRA and Superfund who reportedly secured her job through connections in the White House to Edwin Meese, was viewed by many as out of her league in charge of a highly technical and political program. In the words of one former EPA official, "Rita screwed it up."[28] EPA Administrator Burford finally came to the same conclusion,[29] but when Burford tried to oust Lavelle, she refused to resign. President Reagan finally fired Lavelle directly, causing a public scandal that eventually forced Burford out of office after being cited for contempt of Congress. Burford had earlier signaled that she would not seek Superfund's renewal in 1985, steadfastly refusing to acknowledge the need for what she called a "son of Superfund." William Hedeman, an EPA official who had served under and had gained the respect of Burford, subsequently testified that there existed an "implicit policy to curtail the progress of the [Superfund] program."[30] The effects of this period on Superfund's political trajectory are conspicuous and enduring; one observer notes that "Superfund was nearly destroyed at the beginning due to the politicization . . . and in some ways it has never worked itself out of that politicization."[31]

William Ruckelshaus, EPA's first administrator (in 1970) returned after Burford's departure to improve internal morale—then at an all-time low—and to restore outside confidence in EPA. Many credit him with succeeding in that effort. He confronted a Superfund program that was badly mismanaged and faced numerous complaints about its accomplishments from Congress and others. Perhaps the most widely publicized criticism was that EPA had successfully remediated only six sites in four years, which led Democratic Representative James Florio, a chief Superfund sponsor from New Jersey, to claim that at that rate it would take EPA fifteen hundred years to clean up the two thousand sites it projected required remediation.[32]

Many in Congress were convinced that EPA needed prodding to quicken the pace of cleanups. They also recognized that the problem had grown larger than was initially estimated and that additional resources were needed as a result. Even Representative Florio, never one to understate the magnitude of the problem (particularly since New Jersey has more Superfund sites than any other state), testified in 1985, "Although those of us who worked on the original legislation suspected that a second installment of the program would be necessary, few imagined the actual scope of the additional funding needs which face us today."[33] In addition, the political foundation for renewal was clearly identified in Republican Representative Guy Molinari's statement, "There isn't a congressional district in this country that doesn't have this kind of problem."[34] In large measure due to election-year pressures from environmentalists, President Reagan had shifted his stance on Superfund in his 1984 State of the Union address by pledging to support its reauthorization, a full year before its taxing authority was to expire. He carefully avoided sending his own bill to Congress, however, in hopes of appearing to support Superfund without committing to anything specific, particularly because of his "no new taxes" campaign pledge. The Democrats, on the other hand, hoped to force President Reagan to sign a Superfund law in the middle of an election year. Democratic Representative Dennis Eckart of Ohio summarized their hasty political strategy succinctly: "I can't think of a better bill to lay on Ronald Reagan's desk as he speaks so piously of his new, reborn concern with the environment. I can't think of a worse bill to put on his desk when he isn't facing re-election."[35] The Democrats' ambitious plan to pass controversial Superfund legislation during the 1984 election year succeeded in the House but died in the Senate. The House passed H.R. 5640, calling for a fund increase to $10.2 billion over five years to be financed by increased general revenues and additional taxes on chemical and petroleum companies. The Senate Environment and Public Works Committee approved S. 2892, a five-year $7.5 billion reauthorization, but the Senate Finance Committee subsequently failed to act.[36]

Recognizing that CERCLA's taxing authority was set to expire in 1985, the House and Senate each passed their own Superfund reauthorization bills, but they were unable to reconcile their differences before Congress adjourned. The Senate bill again called for $7.5 billion over five years, to be financed by a broad business tax, while the House version again requested over $10 billion, financed principally by taxes on chemical and petroleum products. Realizing both that reauthorization was inevitable and that the program commanded broad public support, the Reagan administration had proposed its own far smaller $4.5 to $5.3 billion fund. EPA repeatedly claimed, with support from others favoring a smaller fund, that it could not efficiently spend more than $5.3 billion and that spending in excess of that amount would be wasteful.[37] EPA Administrator Lee Thomas said, "I don't think we can spend the $10.2 billion [proposed by the House] well. If we try to spend that much, the program will be a mess . . . We can't run this program faster than we're running it now."[38] Because the two chambers could not reach agreement, beginning in 1985 Superfund's taxing authority lapsed for just over a year while the program's efforts were significantly scaled back. EPA Assistant Administrator Winston Porter later acknowledged that the interruption "certainly slowed down a lot of the work, and we had to put a lot of projects on hold."[39] EPA Administrator Lee Thomas threatened to furlough workers if Congress failed to pass new legislation, adding that "we now face

a situation which threatens the very existence of the Superfund program,"[40] a program Thomas had earlier headed. Reflecting the frustration of the EPA staff, one regional EPA official recalled, "as soon as it
[Superfund] started to stabilize, something else went wrong."[41]

The House and Senate finally reached a compromise agreement in 1986
(H.R. 2005) authorizing significant changes in the existing law, which
President Reagan signed into law on 17 October (Public Law 99-499).[42]
The administration failed in its efforts to secure a smaller increase in the
fund, to $5.3 billion over five years, largely due to heightened congres-
sional mistrust of EPA's intentions. The Superfund Amendments and Reauthorization Act (SARA) created an $8.5 billion trust fund to be accu-
mulated over five years,[43] and set strict cleanup goals (through not
mandatory requirements, as the House wanted) for EPA: cleanup was to
have started at 275 sites within three years and, if that target was not
met, by another 175 RI/FSs within four years and a total of 650 within
five years; preliminary assessments were to be made at all identified sites
by 1988, and all sites inspected by 1989. Congress further directed EPA
to use permanent cleanup remedies where feasible and added an additional $500 million fund for addressing leaking underground storage
tanks (whose acronym "LUST" understandably was later changed to
"UST").[44] Environmental and grass-roots organizations won important
victories by adding to SARA a Title III "right-to-know" provision requiring industry to provide local residents with information about which
chemicals they use and dispose of, and a small grants program to fund
technical studies for local interest groups to interpret and possibly challenge EPA's proposed cleanup strategies.

Perhaps the greatest political battle over SARA involved not its aims—
everyone conceded that the program would be significantly expanded—
but rather how it was to be funded. The final outcome reflected the time-
honored political impulse to do no obvious direct harm to one's constituents. The $8.5 billion fund was to be generated from several sources:
$2.75 billion from a petroleum tax, $2.5 billion from a corporate minimum tax, $1.4 billion from a revised chemical feedstock tax, $1.25 billion
from general revenues, and $0.6 billion expected from cost recoveries
from liable parties and interest on unused portions of the fund. SARA's
tax base was broadened due to fears that a tax only on chemical products
would harm the international competitiveness of an industry where U.S.
companies historically have thrived. Oil-state senators were successful in
two ways: first, in eliminating a proposed waste-end tax, which (they
argued) would represent an uncertain funding source and encourage
"midnight dumping" (and which would have hit petroleum and chemical
interests hardest), and second, in imposing a higher tax on imported than

on domestic petroleum.[45] Lloyd Bentsen of Texas and others from oil-rich states were delighted to report that the tax did not harm domestic producers. However, the large oil companies, which import much of their oil, strongly opposed the tax scheme. The American Petroleum Institute termed the agreement "totally unjustified and unfair in its treatment of the petroleum industry," and the Treasury Department agreed by opposing what it viewed as an oil import fee.[46] The change was possible in large part because of the political power of the domestic wildcat drillers who were hard-hit by falling world oil prices, and who stood to benefit by the differential taxes on domestic and foreign oil.

A number of other changes were enacted under SARA as well. These included requiring health assessments at each site to be undertaken by the Agency for Toxic Substances and Disease Registry (ATSDR, part of the Department of Health and Human Services); requiring states or localities to pay 50 percent (up from 10 percent) of cleanup costs when the site is operated by a contractor for the state or locality; increasing penalties for violations of Superfund; expanding procedural coverage to facilities operated by the federal government (so-called federal facilities); affirming the use of strict, joint, and several liability; improving enforcement flexibility; and raising expenditure limits on emergency removal actions from $1 million to $2 million. SARA also significantly broadened the potential for public participation, requiring that the alternative remedial actions EPA considered, as well as proposed cleanup plans, be published with sufficient lead time for public comment. Section 117 requires EPA to respond to all significant public comments, particularly in the remedy selection phase, although many local communities still feel left out of cleanup decisions. It is important to remember that although clear goals have been established for Superfund cleanups, relatively few sites have been delisted despite EPA's original intention to provide "shovels first and lawyers later."

Stages of Superfund Cleanups

The steps in the cleanup process, from site identification to site remediation, are numerous and complex, due to a number of factors. These include the potential magnitude of the problem, the unproven technologies involved, the uncertainty in establishing "how clean is clean," the many agencies involved in the process, the size of the multibillion-dollar fund, and the intense lobbying efforts by interest groups. The basic features of the process are outlined here to provide a glimpse of the steps required for site remediation under Superfund; the stages of a Superfund site cleanup are summarized in figure 1.2.

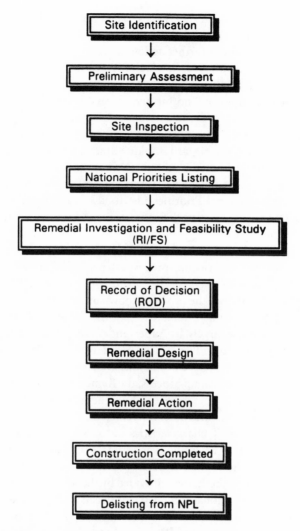

Figure 1.2   Stages of the Superfund site cleanup process.

The Superfund site selection process starts when potential sites are brought to EPA's attention, either through state and local officials, citizens, EPA's own identification procedures, and even hazardous waste handlers, who are required to notify authorities under RCRA. These sites are then placed in EPA's computerized inventory system, CERCLIS,[47] which contains approximately 35,000 sites. Starting in 1980 with an initial list of 8,000, sites have been added to CERCLIS at an average rate of 2,500 annually.[48] Once listed, a Preliminary Assessment is the first step in establishing site priorities. EPA tries to determine on the basis of past records what wastes were dumped at the site and how it was used. If a site is thought to warrant further action or is considered a high priority, a Site Inspection is conducted, in which EPA officials usually inspect the site. Sites designated as lower priority are either placed in a pending pool or designated as requiring "no further action." In about a third of the cases, no further action is deemed necessary as a result of these investigations.[49] If the site warrants additional study, the site's potential hazard is then evaluated using the Hazard Ranking System (HRS) to quantify the relative health hazard posed by the site.[50] Sites that exceed a designated HRS score—currently 28.5 on a 100-point scale—are then proposed publicly for the National Priorities List (NPL) in the *Federal Register*. Up to this point, only existing data are used to determine whether a site qualifies for the NPL.

Once a site qualifies for the final NPL (most do not)—a requirement for federal funding—the cleanup process can begin. Either the potentially responsible party (PRP) pays for the cleanup, in which case EPA and the state government oversee the process (known as an "enforcement lead") or, if the PRP is unwilling or unable to pay, the site may be designated a "fund lead" financed largely by Superfund.[51] The fund is also used to finance cleanups pending EPA's cost-recovery from recalcitrant PRPs; recovered expenses to date have been modest, however.

The next step in the cleanup process, the Remedial Investigation/Feasibility Study (RI/FS), surveys more carefully the extent and nature of site contamination and evaluates potential remedies. The RI assesses the geologic and hydrogeologic characteristics of the site as well as potential population exposure. At this point, an estimate is made of the risk posed by the Superfund site to the surrounding population. The FS evaluates the potential cleanup alternatives provided by the remedial investigation, after which the EPA regional administrator selects an appropriate remedy after detailed analyses of alternative strategies. A public Record of Decision (ROD) is then issued by EPA in the *Federal Register*, detailing the rationale for selecting a particular remedy. Once the ROD has been prepared, the next step is a Remedial Design outlining the engineering plans for conducting the remedial action. The Remedial Action is the actual site cleanup, to which the states must contribute 10 percent of the capital costs for privately owned sites; operation and maintenance costs are financed with state or PRP funds.[52] If EPA is satisfied with both the cleanup and the operations and maintenance stages, a site may then be removed from the NPL. In an effort to better communicate the progress of site cleanups, EPA administrator William Reilly added another NPL cleanup category, "construction completion," to include sites where the remedial work is completed but where final deletion from the NPL has not yet occurred.[53]

When a site is placed on the NPL, EPA can pursue several strategies. Basically, these boil down to either cleaning up the site, using federal Superfund monies, or forcing PRPs to remediate the site (for which SARA expressed a clear preference). In pursuing PRPs, EPA can take several approaches to gaining compliance. First, EPA can negotiate settlements with responsible parties, issuing a "consent decree," a legally binding agreement between EPA and PRPs specifying the cost-sharing arrangement involved with cleaning up the site. Section 122 directs the president (this power has been delegated to EPA) "whenever practicable and in the public interest" to enter into consent agreements. A second strategy is to issue an administrative order requiring PRPs to remediate the site. These "orders" can actually result in consent orders when PRPs negotiate with EPA over cleanup strategies. Administrative orders can be enforced in federal court by instituting penalties of up to $25,000 a day against recalcitrant PRPs; subsequent violations can cost PRPs up to $75,000 per day. Should the PRPs fail to comply with an administrative order, EPA can clean up the site itself and recover treble damages from the PRPs if they fail to provide just cause for the delay. SARA also added several new mechanisms that EPA can use to encourage settlements with PRPs. The first is a *de minimus* settlement for innocent landowners or for PRPs that contributed a small quantity of waste or waste with little or no toxic effect. Another is called "mixed funding," in which PRPs and the federal trust fund share costs to expedite the cleanup, while EPA subsequently pursues recalcitrant PRPs for their share of remedial costs; the presumption is that the government will sue those parties that did not settle for any expenses borne by the fund. EPA has been reluctant to use mixed funding, however, for fear of charges that it is giving special breaks to PRPs who ought to be liable for full cleanup expenses.

An important ingredient included in SARA to encourage settlements involves protection against countersuits by parties who do not settle. In the past, one PRP settling with EPA, for say 60 percent of cleanup costs, could later be sued by a nonsettling PRP if the latter claimed that the settling PRP did not contribute its full share of cleanup costs. Section 113(f) of SARA now allows PRPs who settle to be protected from added liability or claims of contribution, barring fraud or violation of other legal principles.[54] Further, because so many site cleanups are complicated by cost-allocation disputes among responsible parties, SARA added a discretionary process known as nonbinding preliminary allocations of responsibility, or NBARs. EPA holds informal hearings on questions of allocation, and PRPs (whose interest is minimizing their share of cleanup costs) present materials to make their case. The idea is to avoid the preremedial controversies that can hold up site cleanups for years.

Although virtually all site-specific decisions are made by the ten regional EPA offices, overall program strategies designed at EPA headquarters in Washington, D.C., have varied considerably over the program's history. In Superfund's early years, when EPA was headed by Anne Burford, the primary intention was to avoid "spending down" the fund. The belief at the time was that the fund was to be used as a last resort, and indeed little emphasis was placed on the cleanup program by officials who wanted to avoid the "son of Superfund." After William Ruckelshaus became administrator, the fund began to be used more vigorously, but by 1986 the program had been dormant for over a year for lack of appropriations. Expenditures were again kept to a minimum to avoid wholesale layoffs of Superfund personnel while awaiting program reauthorization. Lee Thomas's tenure saw a more vigorous enforcement process in conjunction with greater fund expenditures. Much of this was due to Congress's expressed desire in the 1986 reauthorization to leverage the fund as much as possible. President Bush appointed William Reilly as EPA administrator in 1989, and his first Superfund directive was a "90-day study" to review the Superfund program and to suggest program improvements. The result was an "enforcement first" approach to prompt greater regional activity. EPA has devoted much greater attention to speeding up the cleanup process by whatever means are available, particularly relying on unilateral enforcement orders, which EPA claims have stimulated additional remedial work and increased the share of cleanups performed by PRPs.[55]

Prior to Superfund, the most widely used and most cost-effective hazardous waste disposal technique was landfilling. Section 121(b) of SARA states the congressional preference (although not a requirement) that EPA, to the maximum extent practicable, use cleanup disposal techniques that "permanently and significantly" reduce on-site contaminant hazards. The intent was to avoid a "toxic merry-go-round" of hazardous waste disposal, in which wastes were carted from one Superfund site to a landfill destined to become a future Superfund site. In response to the tremendous demand for hazardous waste cleanups, far more remediation technologies are available to EPA than were before 1980. One EPA official commented that "we know a lot more about cleanup technologies now than we used to, and Superfund has a hell of a lot to do with that."[56] Technologies now available include chemical (neutralization), physical (stripping), biological (aerobic systems), and thermal (incineration) treatments, although the proven effectiveness of each varies considerably.[57] Many of the available technologies have been tried in laboratories but not at large-scale and complicated Superfund sites. EPA has established a Superfund Innovative Technology Evaluation (SITE) program to test new technologies on existing Superfund sites. Some have blamed EPA for not introducing new technologies faster, with one commentator complaining that "there is a real conservative mindset within EPA."[58] The hope, however, is that both problems can be solved simultaneously by the introduction of permanent, and possibly less expensive, technologies. Joel Hirschhorn, formerly of the Office of Technology Assessment (OTA), has said, "Sometimes people just automatically assume newer technologies will cost more when, in fact, often the opposite is the case. The purpose of innovation is not merely to create another solution, it is also to drive down the costs."[59]

In addition to the remedial process, EPA may remove hazardous substances that pose an imminent danger (of contamination, fire, or explosion) to the surrounding population. Known as "removal actions," these emergency activities may operate in tandem with, or as replacements for, the remedial action process described above. SARA raised the expenditure limits for removal actions from $1 million to $2 million each, although one site may require several removal actions over time. Naturally, emergency removal actions need not proceed through the lengthy evaluation and feasibility procedures required for remedial actions.

The current NPL comprises widely varying sites. According to an EPA survey published in November 1991, similar numbers of sites could be found in rural and suburban areas, with about 19 percent of NPL sites in urban locations.[60] Nearly half of the sites were larger than 20 acres, and the predominant land uses in the vicinity were residential, industrial, commercial, and agricultural. About half were privately owned industrial sites, and most were inactive at the time of the HRS score calculation. The industries most responsible for generating the waste at NPL sites include those manufacturing chemical and allied products, fabricated metal products, electronic and electrical equipment, electroplating, and lumber and wood products. Most sites (55 percent) were identified by state or local programs, followed by citizen complaints (15 percent); CERCLA notification accounted for only about five percent of site identifications. According to an EPA/Resources for the Future survey, about 52 percent of sites (369 of 708) were closed prior to 1981. At about 12 percent of sites (85), wastes are still being accepted. Of the 369 pre-1981 sites, owner/operators were responsible for 30 percent of the contaminated sites, and illegal disposal was present at 15 percent of sites.[61] Potentially responsible party settlements through the end of fiscal 1991 totaled $3.5 billion (to be spent over several years).[62]

State and Local Involvement

States and localities can play important roles in Superfund cleanups. Under CERCLA, EPA was required to "consult" with the state or other political subdivision regarding cleanup remedies; SARA, however, provided for an expanded state role. States can now impose their own cleanup standards on Superfund cleanups, even if they are more restrictive than federal requirements. However, state standards must be generally applicable and formally adopted, and cannot be so strict that they preclude any land-based hazardous waste disposal. As a further brake on states demanding overly stringent cleanup standards, states are required to pay for the incremental costs associated with attaining the more stringent standards. State pressures to "gold plate" cleanup efforts therefore are limited by the additional financial contribution required for fund-financed sites, particularly as states now wrestle with substantial budget deficits of their own. SARA also provides states with the added capacity to review and comment on many intermediate remedial stages, such as the RI/FS, remedy selection, and remedial design, as well as earlier settlement negotiations with PRPs.

Superfund requires states to provide matching cleanup funds, 10 percent for privately owned sites and 50 percent for state- or locally operated facilities (even those that were contracted out), and to pay for operation and maintenance costs.[63] In some instances, termed "state leads," states assume management responsibility for site remediation and in any event must provide facilities to dispose of the waste removed from the site. Under these "cooperative agreements," federal monies are transferred to the state, which then does everything from developing the remedial plan to letting contracts for site remediation. (These funds cannot be used for site discovery, however.) From fiscal 1981 through 1989, obligations to states under cooperative agreements have totaled more than $375 million.[64] If localities and other political subdivisions (counties, towns, and so forth[65]) take the lead in managing a site cleanup, either EPA signs a cooperative agreement directly with the state, which then joins with the locality to oversee the cleanup, or the state must sign a contract stipulating how the federal, state, and local governments will comply with the law.[66]

The point is that states cannot dodge responsibility for site cleanup by encouraging localities to manage the effort, which provides at least limited discipline on states to ensure proper local site management. In addition, EPA continues to monitor state performance in meeting its contractual obligations. EPA cannot delegate its enforcement authority to the states, although the relationship between federal and state agencies involved in enforcement actions is established informally. Between Superfund's start in 1980 and the end of fiscal 1989, state leads have completed 140 RI/FSs, 54 remedial designs, and 30 remedial actions. Beyond the NPL listing stage, federal fund-lead sites generally outnumber state-lead sites by at least two to one, although as of 1990 states had completed nearly twice the number of preliminary assessments.[67] In addition, states stand to forfeit significant federal funding unless they can properly dispose of all hazardous wastes projected to be generated internally over the next twenty years, to ensure that adequate capacity exists to dispose of treated wastes within the state.[68]

If the federal EPA takes the lead role in site remediation, termed a "fund lead," a state Superfund contract is issued, and federal contractors are employed, sometimes including the Army Corps of Engineers. In this case, the state plays a supporting role, but SARA still requires state involvement from preremedial through remedial activities. The National Contingency Plan (NCP),[69] the set of regulations with which Superfund cleanups must comply, requires that states become involved with listing and delisting NPL sites, negotiating with responsible parties, studying cleanup options, and implementing the selected remedy. The extensive state involvement in remedial actions does not apply to emergency removal actions, however, unless the cleanup actions will be delayed for six months or more (in which case they are no longer emergencies).[70]

Localities are frequently involved with identifying sites as well, although less so with site remediation. Local fire departments and other emergency services are sometimes the first authorities to discover and support emergency removal action cleanups. State and local officials also conduct community relations activities that encourage citizen participation in cleanup decisions in conjunction with EPA's own activities; indeed, an approved Community Relations Plan must be in place before remediation can occur.[71]

Many states have their own remedial hazardous waste cleanup programs. Not surprisingly, they are more modestly funded than the federal Superfund, working with multimillion-dollar rather than multibillion-dollar budgets. A 1989 EPA survey of state programs showed that total state "Superfund" balances totaled $415 million, an average of $8.3 million per state.[72] In addition, four states (New York, Michigan, New Jersey, and Massachusetts) had bond authorizations totaling $1.98 billion, with New York's representing over 60 percent of the total. There is significant

variation in state Superfund efforts that is not captured by averages, however. Although forty-eight states have cleanup funds, eighteen states have
balances below $1 million, while only eleven states have balances over
$10 million. New Jersey, with the most NPL sites of any state, also has
by far the largest state fund balance, in excess of $100 million across two
funds. Most states have been quite active in identifying sites; seven have
recorded over 1000 sites each, and another sixteen have identified 300
to 1000 sites in their state. (California leads the way by a large margin
with 25,000 identified hazardous waste sites.) Only five states do not
have a Superfund program.[73]

The number of sites identified by states threatens to dwarf the number
of federal NPL sites. One study reported that five to fifteen times as many
state sites (from 11,000 to 32,000 sites) will need to be remediated as
federal sites, using conservative assumptions. Depending on the type of
model used and the expected cost of cleanup, the report finds that nonfederal remedial cleanup costs are expected to be between $6 billion and
$64 billion.[74] Although a number of states have active and innovative
Superfund programs (such as Minnesota, New York, and New Jersey),
they are nominal in size compared with—and perhaps because of—the
colossal federal program. Indeed, in some cases it appears that states have
been far more reluctant to clean up sites than to identify them, perhaps
hoping that the federal government will ultimately finance their cleanup
instead. Daniel Greenbaum, formerly Massachusetts commissioner of
environmental protection, has said that "for every cleanup completed, a
dozen new sites are being added to the list."[75] EPA has expressed concern
about recalcitrant state programs, with one official stating that there are
states "unwilling to bite the political bullet" to establish sufficient state
funds, and adding that "we must not sanction states' inability or unwill-
ingness to dispose of wastes in the state."[76]

Federal Facilities

Approximately 10 percent of sites on the National Priorities List are federal facilities. Besides EPA, federal waste cleanup efforts have expanded
dramatically at other agencies as well. Estimates suggest that cleanup
needs at nuclear weapons production facilities operated by the Department of Energy could cost as much as $200 billion over thirty years for
122 sites.[77] Even individual weapons facilities contain massive contamination. At Washington's Hanford Reservation alone there are an estimated 1,100 radioactive and hazardous waste sites, not to mention the
highly radioactive used nuclear fuel and other contaminants that litter
the facility, part of which will be reduced to a "National Sacrifice

Zone."[78] The Energy Department has requested $5.3 billion for fiscal 1993 for all remedial cleanups, a 24 percent increase over 1992, and Hanford alone is estimated to cost in excess of $2 billion annually.[79] In addition, the Defense Department has requested $3.7 billion for fiscal 1993 to clean up its own sites at military bases, an increase of nearly $1 billion (35 percent) from fiscal 1992.[80] Ultimate cleanup cost estimates run much higher, however. A report by the National Toxic Campaign Fund called the military the nation's worst polluter (it is not alone in that judgment) and said that the cleanup cost could run from $20 billion to $200 billion since "most of the major military bases in the country are contaminated."[81] These problems plague many other federal agencies as well, from the Postal Service to the Central Intelligence Agency. The total "federal facilities" budget request from the president for fiscal 1993 totals nearly $9.5 billion, and expected future budgets continue upward at the same furious pace.[82]

The current and expected nationwide cleanup efforts have proven a bonanza for hazardous waste contractors at these federal facilities. The hazardous waste services industry reportedly grossed $10 billion in 1989 and is expected to double in size by the mid-1990s. One estimate put the congressional contributions by one political-action committee controlled by Waste Management, Inc. at $430,000 in 1987 and 1988.[83] At just one uranium processing plant in Fernald, Ohio, a cleanup contract of $5 billion is expected to be awarded.[84] A mass-mailing targeted to contractors leaves little doubt about the interest of some in prolonging hazardous waste cleanup programs. It begins: "Would you like to get a bigger share of the only growth area in defense spending? Defense waste cleanup! . . . Congress and the Bush Administration both want to pour big bucks into solutions—$4.4 billion in FY91 and more in 1992. Some companies see this as the start of a bonanza. . . . Cleanup of hazardous and radioactive wastes is where the action is."[85]

The growth of these cleanup programs has coincided with Superfund's expansion. Moreover, budget cuts at the Department of Energy (DOE), particularly in nuclear weapons production and research, and at the Department of Defense (DOD), have forced these agencies to look for other ways to preserve their budget levels and induced defense contractors to recast their expertise to include environmental restoration. As one said, "Everybody wants a piece of this cleanup business now. That's where the money is."[86] Waste cleanup programs appear to be an almost endless source of possible expenditures. Capitalizing on the success of Superfund at gaining substantial revenues, these other programs have quickly eclipsed Superfund's spending levels. A University of Tennessee study estimated that total hazardous waste remedial costs, including Superfund,

RCRA corrective actions, underground storage tanks, DOD, DOE, and other programs, will total between $480 billion and $1 trillion; less stringent requirements could lower the costs to between $370 and $690 million, while more stringent requirements could raise costs to over $1.6 trillion, excluding administrative and transactions costs.[87]

Critiques of Superfund Policy

With the possible exception of EPA officials, it is difficult to find anyone who approves of the way Superfund is running. Articles titled "Superfund: An Environmental Boondoggle," "Superfund: Still in the Dumps," "Superfund: A Program without Priorities," and many others litter magazines and journals. Critics range from environmental scientists and toxicologists to journalists, environmentalists, and even some vocal EPA officials.[88] While critics are many and diverse, they generally cluster in two categories: those criticizing the way Superfund is managed, and a smaller contingent questioning whether the program itself is worth the cost.

Management Critiques

Superfund's practices have come under a storm of criticism. But perhaps the most visible critics of Superfund management have been two government agencies that work directly for Congress: the General Accounting Office and the Office of Technology Assessment. In a long series of publications, often requested by specific legislators or committees interested in promoting Superfund, the GAO has roundly criticized the handling of Superfund in everything ranging from EPA's inability to determine the magnitude of the problem[89] to EPA's excessive use of contractors to implement the program.[90] The reports rarely question the intent of the statutes under which EPA must operate, instead focusing on EPA's weak record of implementation. Perhaps most alarming is GAO's finding that EPA has vastly underestimated the number of potential hazardous waste sites in the United States, and that EPA has failed to direct sufficient resources toward identifying all possible sites.

Other GAO reports have chastised EPA for a variety of Superfund management problems. These include EPA's failure to use administrative orders to compel site cleanups by responsible parties, problems with accounting systems that slowed the recovery of expended Superfund money, EPA's failure to adequately monitor contractor expenses and its overreliance on contractor services, EPA's inability to retain experienced staff (in part because they are lured away by better-paying waste management firms), EPA's failure to achieve uniform cleanup levels at the sites it does clean up, and many others. The more fundamental recommendations that GAO has made to Congress entail ways to compel better adherence to stated congressional objectives; congressional intent itself is rarely questioned.

The smaller Office of Technology Assessment has produced fewer but far longer and more comprehensive reports on Superfund. Like the GAO, the OTA focuses its evaluation of Superfund on EPA's failure to meet Superfund's statutory objectives. However, despite SARA's numerical requirements for site cleanups, OTA has been careful to distinguish the quality from the quantity of cleanups, and rightly contends that too often "bean counting" to meet congressional mandates replaces the permanent cleanup strategies preferred under SARA.[91] As such, OTA's statutory criticisms are subtle rather than confrontational, in keeping with the needs of its chief client, Congress. OTA has also been highly critical of many other facets of Superfund implementation: of EPA's decentralized management of Superfund; of its lack of technical sophistication to justify cleanup decisions; that Records of Decision (RODs) make false claims of permanence; that EPA is more responsive to PRPs than to community interests; that the cleanup process is excessively lengthy; that appropriate risks are not incorporated into EPA's analyses; that the technical quality of RODs varies substantially between EPA regional offices; and many others.[92] OTA has recommended that priorities for site cleanups be set based on current or future risks, establishing a more active federal site identification program to improve cleanup priorities and to understand the full scope of cleanup, establishing national minimum cleanup standards, changing the nature of "acceptable risk," redefining "permanent cleanup," and more than thirty other reforms.[93]

Not content to sit by idly while the GAO and OTA published their high-visibility studies, several congressional committees issued their own reports critical of EPA's performance. It comes as no surprise that these reports also fail to question legislative intent (since they are authored by strong Superfund supporters) and again focus on many of the same management "failures" recounted in GAO and OTA reports. One report, issued by Senator Lautenberg's subcommittee, states at the outset that it "is issued in the spirit of constructive criticism"[94] and goes on to admonish EPA because "the program continues to fail to meet expectations and in most cases actual statutorily mandated deadlines."[95] The report quite clearly blames many of Superfund's problems on EPA and adds that "were the law to be implemented as written the many problems documented here would not have occurred."[96] In addition, the report rebukes EPA's consideration of costs and cost-benefit analysis in reaching cleanup decisions, decries the delays and "red tape" for grants issued to citizens for technical advice, questions an excessive reliance on settlement rather than enforcement, criticizes the impermanence of cleanups, and cites a failure by states to comply with EPA's requirements, among other criticisms. The report does commend EPA, however, for progress in training, contracting reforms, and increased numbers of remedial activities.[97]

Even the Senate Budget Committee jumped on the bandwagon and issued a brief and critical report of EPA's implementation of Superfund. Although the report includes no new research or findings, it concludes that "the [Superfund] process has not worked"[98] and that the "results of this effort have been dismal."[99] The report also criticizes the Bush administration's 1991 budget request for an increase of $210 million for Superfund—a 12 percent supplement—as meager. Although the extra funding would start long-term cleanups at sixteen sites, the report acerbically notes that "in other terms, the Administration is requesting a 12 percent increase in Superfund in order to start long-term cleanups at 1.3 percent of the sites currently on the NPL."[100] (The report fails to mention that in recent years Congress has cut administration requests for additional Superfund funding. For example, the president's fiscal year 1992 budget request called for funding of $1.75 billion, although the final appropriation was cut to $1.62 billion, the first time in its history that Superfund had been level funded.[101] This congressional strategy may, however, be intended to prod EPA to make greater use of enforcement measures rather than the trust fund to finance cleanups.)

In addition to congressionally motivated critiques, environmental groups too have criticized Superfund, again targeting not the statute itself but rather EPA's poor management and foot-dragging. In two separate reports written less than two years apart, a team of environmental groups pooled their resources to evaluate all Superfund Records of Decision that EPA issued in the preceding year. The first report, published in June 1988, concluded that "Congress has provided the right train, but EPA has chosen the wrong track." It contends that only 8 percent of the treatment technologies chosen by EPA would remediate the site to the maximum extent practicable, yet adds that those same 8 percent constitute "proof that the Superfund program can be made to run well."[102] The report was harshly critical of EPA, calling EPA's effort the "Superfund shell game . . . [that] . . . has done little more than inspire the Agency's semantic creativity to rationalize remedies of the past."[103] The second report, issued after William Reilly was appointed EPA administrator, is far more optimistic and states that "there are several indications that the Superfund program is improving."[104] Like OTA, the report criticizes the decentralized nature of Superfund as a cause of inconsistent quality. Finally, the environmental groups' reports are critical of EPA's use of risk assessments, both because they are "based on suspect and unsubstantiated assumptions"[105] and because EPA is using the wrong risk targets.[106]

Program Critiques

Against this backdrop of reports critical of EPA's management of Superfund have come allegations that the entire program is ill-conceived. While many feel that sites like Love Canal justify federal intervention, Love Canal is viewed by others as a symbol of the problems with an excessive federal response. Some believe that Love Canal was blown far out of proportion by a news media "aroused . . . from its late summer torpor," which had, as one observer notes, "excellent photo opportunities [of] . . . mauve lawns, chartreuse basement walls, and irate residents."[107] Critics believe that Hooker Chemical Company, which originally discarded toxic wastes on the site, was an easy target, the perfect "corporate villain." They argue that the company was actually forced in 1953 to deed the site over to the local school board, which later sold the site to a residential developer, despite repeated warnings from Hooker. They claim further that "follow-up studies at Love Canal turned up no evidence of abnormal levels of morbidity or mortality." In short, some critics contend that the program is a "Superfraud."[108]

Many have been quick to publicly identify Congress as the chief culprit in creating the wasteful program. Economist Robert Crandall has stated that Superfund "is more a pork barrel than a serious environmental program."[109] Calling Superfund "a hazardous waste of taxpayer money," Fred Smith of Washington's Competitive Enterprise Institute contends that "the magnitude of health risks addressed by Superfund are small to nonexistent" and predicted that the $8.5 billion reauthorization would "unleash the largest pork barrel program in history, expend great sums to little result, and preempt more effective solutions to the problems posed by abandoned chemical dumps."[110] Smith further charges that "EPA finds itself selecting projects based on their political and public relations value" and claims that Superfund "reflect[s] an extremely successful effort to repackage a traditional pork barrel program as a human health and cancer prevention measure."[111] Others argue that "Superfund has become an expensive, wasteful pork barrel that has accomplished little cleanup," noting that "the passage of Superfund boosted the careers of a number of congressmen."[112] Former EPA administrator Anne Burford notes, in a book written well after she had left office, that in the early years of Superfund, "everyone in town soon knew three things: Superfund was the only game in town, the only new source of money; it was likely to be the only new source of money for the next four years; and it was enormously popular with the American public. So they all wanted their share of the pie. And, oh, what a big pie you have, Grandma!"[113]

In a 1988 article titled "Reforming Environmental Regulation: Three Modest Proposals," Paul Portney suggests an entirely immodest change to Superfund. Because he claims that the risks associated with Superfund sites pale in comparison to risks from other environmental hazards (he specifically mentions indoor radon), Portney argues that Superfund monies should not be restricted to cleaning up hazardous wastes sites, but rather, EPA should have the discretion to spend the money on those environmental problems that pose the greatest risks.[114] With the exception of Portney, none of these critics provides any evidence substantiating their allegations. Instead, they rely only on the theoretical likelihood that Superfund is a pork-barrel program. Subsequent chapters in this book show that some claims of Superfund pork fail to withstand scrutiny (chapter 6), although others are legitimate (chapters 7 and 8).

A final criticism leveled against Superfund involves its funding. Besides the expected lobbying by chemical and petroleum companies to reduce their share of taxes paid into Superfund, the insurance industry has joined the debate. In many cases responsible parties involved in Superfund clean-ups turn to their current or past insurer to recover damages. Insurance companies complain that Superfund's strict liability provisions create a program that is unfair (since businesses that legally dumped in the past are now being held accountable) and overly litigious. They claim that the costs involved are such that no one—neither the federal government nor industry—can be expected to bear the entire burden. Instead, they propose that a "National Environmental Trust Fund" replace Superfund's strict liability provisions when no regulations were violated at the time of the dumping. The fund would be financed by a fee on all commercial or industrial property-casualty insurance premiums paid in the United States, with an equivalent fee to be levied on those companies that self-insure.[115] (The last provision is particularly clever, since it would abolish the incentive created by the proposed fee for companies to self-insure instead of paying the trust fund fee, in which case insurance companies would lose out.) Insurance companies claim that the total amount generated by such a fund could reach $40 billion over the next decade, which they would collect and remit to EPA. They emphasize that they "are not proposing that Superfund be discarded, but rather that it be given a new and more effective way to finance its mission."[116]

Superfund's Overlooked Accomplishments

Superfund has been a bitter disappointment to many in Congress and elsewhere who expected EPA to quickly resolve the problem of hazardous waste sites. Congressional hearings on Superfund's reauthorization point to the testimony of a number of witnesses who charged that EPA had been stalling cleanup efforts, citing as evidence that EPA had remediated only six sites in four years. This one statistic received such widespread attention that it alone was thought to illuminate all that was wrong with Superfund, and critics continue to point to similar statistics as evidence of Superfund's utter failure.

The commonly cited statistic of six cleanups in four years, while factually accurate in 1985, is by itself grossly misleading and tells only a small part of Superfund's story. As of March 1989, by which time critics were complaining that EPA had cleaned up just forty-one sites, EPA's information system contained over 30,000 sites potentially requiring Superfund action, and EPA had conducted preliminary assessments at over 28,000 of them. Although at about 40 percent of sites no further action was planned, nearly 1200 were placed on the National Priorities List. Remedial investigations or feasibility studies were started at 845 sites, 300 sites were in the remedial design phase, and remedial actions were started at more than 200 sites. Moreover more than 1300 emergency removal actions had been performed, with 20 percent of those at NPL sites.[117] A former director of an EPA regional office, now in private industry, credits the removal action program for the fact that "no site today poses an immediate health threat to the public," and adds that "EPA and the states have done really well in terms of emergency response."[118] While this may be an exaggeration, significant progress had been made at many sites, despite the fact that final remediation was completed at fewer than 4 percent of the NPL sites.

The public perception of the slow pace of site cleanups follows in part from the average twelve-year period from the time EPA becomes aware of a site to final site cleanup,[119] as well as the lax EPA enforcement policy of the early 1980s. Critics' assertions in the mid-1980s that only six sites had been cleaned up ignored the many sites that were in various stages of the cleanup process. If this 12-year average cleanup time holds true for the future, then the ratio of remediated sites to NPL sites will appear increasingly favorable, not because of speedier cleanups but because the time lag between initial work and full remediation will have elapsed. The subsequent escalation in the number of sites cleaned up after SARA's passage may reflect more the end of a long gestation period for many sites than accelerated EPA procedures. In addition, the start-up costs for a program of Superfund's magnitude are considerable. While in the mid-1980s critics were charging that EPA had cleaned up only a handful of sites, EPA was quick to point to the substantial infrastructure development that was necessary to manage such a large and complex program, the development of new technologies for treating the waste, improved understanding of the health effects, better management procedures, as well as the many sites in the stages immediately preceding final remediation.[120] In addition, sites with contaminated groundwater may take thirty years to remediate effectively, so looking for results—defined as full site cleanup—after five years effectively denies EPA's ability to register any progress at such sites. One EPA official lamented, "No matter how hard they [EPA staff] work, they're never going to get the stuff cleaned up as quickly as the public wants"; he adds, "Now the response we get when we do succeed is, 'what took you so long?' "[121] Reflecting the frustration experienced by EPA officials who work with Superfund, Bruce Diamond, head of EPA's Superfund enforcement section, has said: "EPA seems to be tongue-tied when it comes time to telling people what's happening. When I say that there are 350 sites in long-term construction for permanent remedies, people are amazed. No one's ever heard that number. When I say . . . more than 2000 emergency actions have been taken over the last few years, practically no one has heard that. When I say we've got virtually $4 billion worth of work commitments out of responsible parties using the enforcement process, practically nobody's heard of that. They have heard of Joel Hirshhorn's criticisms [the primary author of the OTA studies], they have heard the complaining about the liability scheme, but they've never heard EPA's side of the story."[122] Another official said simply, "It's not as easy as anyone thought [to remediate sites]," and admitted, "We [EPA] have not been able to come up with good indicators [of success]."[123] While one official adds that, "we probably know enough now [in terms of technical capability] to do things more quickly,"[124] another identifies a critical political problem: "Superfund tried to promise too much too fast."[125] Another possible problem with excessive concern for the number of sites cleaned up is not a skewed perception of how well Superfund is meeting its goals, but improper methods used to remediate sites. An official with General Electric who favors the use of alternative technologies such as bioremediation in site cleanups believes, "As long as the EPA managers at toxic waste sites are rewarded for how many sites they clean up quickly, they are never going to select methods like bioremediation."[126]

Conclusions

For all of these reasons, many agree with the assessment that "Superfund became a super failure."[127] Superfund has been so widely criticized and is so politically potent that a term—"dump-stumping"—is used to characterize politicians visiting Superfund sites with the sole purpose of criticizing the program for the public relations value.[128] As a result, Superfund is both a political problem and a technical problem. A participant in Superfund negotiations notes that "as long as the program is perceived to be lousy, the only incentive the Democratic Congress has is to beat up on it, because it [has been] run by a Republican administration."[129] This, of course, has since changed, but the political obstacles to reform remain formidable.

Despite the fact that EPA has had to quickly address a large and complicated problem, nearly everyone has been harshly critical of Superfund's implementation, some with the funding mechanism, and a few with the program itself. Congressional critics, OTA, GAO, and environmental groups have all assailed EPA. For every positive indication that EPA is cleaning up more sites, these critics can point to the vast number of both identified and unidentified sites that they believe require prompt attention. If recent estimates that hundreds of thousands of sites exist hold true, it is safe to say that Superfund's critics will have no shortage of reasons to chastise EPA's progress for many years to come. Politically conservative critics, on the other hand, fault Congress for overreacting to an exaggerated incident at Love Canal and creating a pork-barrel program that is out of control. Both groups would do well to remember that Superfund's first several years were marked by opposition to Superfund at the agency's highest levels and that the program was effectively shut down when reauthorization was delayed until late 1986; a full-scale EPA effort was therefore not under way until 1987. EPA's progress appears more favorable when viewed in this context.

One problem is that the two groups of critics continue to talk past each other, since each has identified a different problem. Measures of Superfund's success too often focus on intermediate steps (such as the number of sites "cleaned up" or the quality of cleanups) and seldom if ever on more fundamental social concerns, such as the level of environmental and public health risk reduced. EPA could rapidly and permanently remediate a particular NPL site, but if the site posed relatively little risk to human health or the environment in the first place, the value of the cleanup is questionable. This focus on cleanup numbers and quality creates an incentive for EPA to remediate those sites where cleanup is relatively quick and permanent, rather than where the money will do the most good to improve public health and environmental quality. From EPA's perspective, there is no point in its tackling a particularly difficult site with groundwater contamination when it can clean up a small site permanently and get the same credit from Congress. By focusing concern on numbers of sites cleaned up and even the "quality," attention is diverted from the real purpose of the program. Much of the fault for this emphasis lies squarely with Congress. While explicit numerical site cleanup goals may have reflected Congress's intention to speed Superfund's implementation, they also create the incentive for EPA to clean up as many sites as possible and less incentive to prioritize site cleanup. After all, the longer EPA studies appropriate cleanup priorities, the less time it has to meet statutory deadlines. The requirement to clean up sites quickly also favors sites that have already been identified; when approving SARA, legislators could be relatively certain that a site in their district or state would be acted upon more quickly if it was already listed on the NPL.

Finally, EPA's public obligation is not just meeting the letter of the law. As Jerry Mashaw and David Harfst have noted, a regulatory agency's first priority is to be reasonable: "Any agency. . . . should always read between the lines of its statute an implicit qualification of the form: 'Don't forget that this statute does not exhaust our vision of the good life or the good society. Remember that we have other goals and other purposes that will sometimes conflict with the goals and purposes of this statute. If we forgot to mention all those potential conflicting purposes in your instructions, take note of them anyway. For heaven's sake, be reasonable.' "[130] EPA will surely continue to be dogged by Superfund's critics. For every Superfund dollar EPA spends, one side will claim that it could be better spent elsewhere (or not at all), another will claim that the money should have been raised in a different way, and still another will wonder why EPA is not spending more. Such is the nature of managing the new regulatory agency.[131] The true problems with Superfund lie less with "bean-counting" exercises concerning the number of sites cleaned up or facile measures of remedial "quality," and more with understanding the hazards such sites actually pose to public health and the environment. The failure to come to grips with Superfund's implicit goal of improving human health and the environment and the role that risk assessment and risk management can play in achieving that goal are taken up in chapters 2 and 3.

2 Assessing Risks

Members of the public are downright confused when it comes to assessing risks, and who can blame them? Assessing risks is a complicated matter, even in cases that appear to be quite simple. Simply deciding what is nutritionally best to eat has spawned a flurry of books, regular columns in major newspapers, and unresolved questions: How important is cutting cholesterol in reducing the risk of heart disease? Is margarine nutritionally better than butter? Should one avoid certain fruits and vegetables for fear of pesticide residues? How important is it to avoid irradiated food? While scientists have made inroads in addressing these basic questions, firm answers have yet to be found. Consumer confusion has led to fearing the unknown, with one commentator asking only half-jokingly, "What are Americans afraid of? Nothing much, really, except the food they eat, the water they drink, the air they breathe, the land they live on, and the energy they use."[1] Scientific uncertainty surrounds whether or not electromagnetic fields induce cancer. Similarly, even when risks are acknowledged to exist, the range of scientific estimates can be enormous. One researcher found that depending on which type of models were used for data on the risks of the pesticide ethylene dibromide (EDB), the probability of contracting cancer varied by a factor of one million.[2] At the recently closed Yankee Rowe nuclear power facility in Massachusetts, plant operators assessed the chances of a reactor failing to be 5 in 1 billion, while the Nuclear Regulatory Commission staff believed the chances ranged from 1 in 10,000 to 1 in 100,000.[3] While some warn of the hazards from radiation of living near a nuclear power plant, others contend that the risk of eating forty tablespoons of peanut butter is just as great as living within twenty miles of a nuclear power plant for 150 years or for five years at its site boundary and that bicycling for twenty miles is even riskier.[4] In the face of such scientific uncertainty and disagreement, how is it possible for the public to reach firm conclusions regarding risk?

Individuals face a variety of risks: increased exposure to ultraviolet rays from ozone depletion, driving, heart disease, crime, contracting AIDS, smoking, contaminated drinking water, polluted air, and so on almost without limit. Each of us responds differently to these risks: some individuals wear extra sunscreen, some buy safer cars, some exercise regularly, some avoid high-crime neighborhoods, some avoid unprotected sex, some quit smoking, some buy bottled water, and some place a premium on living where the air quality is highest. Reactions to these risks are widely accepted as individual decisions that for the most part do not affect the rest of us (although smoking is increasingly recognized as an exception).

The more vexing problem involves how, if at all, *society* should respond to risks from polluted air, pesticides, Superfund sites, lead paint, smoking, radon, and dozens of other environmental and public health problems. What are the expected health benefits of reducing radon in homes compared with limiting chlorofluorocarbon (CFC) production or removing asbestos from homes and schools? Are Superfund sites worth cleaning up and to what degree? In response to these and similar questions, the techniques of risk assessment (understanding which risks are present and their respective magnitudes) and risk management (deciding how to deal with risks) have been developed. While risk assessment and risk management by no means provide easy answers to these difficult public questions, they attempt to distill a large amount of complex information into a manageable form. Risk management—the process of deciding how society should respond to various risks—requires a knowledge of the environmental and health risks posed by various chemicals and pollutants. Such knowledge is acquired partly through the process of risk assessment. As the following overview shows, risk assessment is in many ways a crude and biased evaluation of these risks, but it remains, despite its many flaws, one of the best tools available for systematically comparing the relative risks of various environmental and public health hazards. It is best viewed only as a mechanism for providing and synthesizing relevant information, however, and should not be used uncritically for making public policy decisions.

Assessing Risks

Risk assessment is the systematic procedure of identifying and measuring the risks to human health and the environment posed by various activities, lifestyles, and substances. While it sounds straightforward, the process remains intensely controversial. Only over the past ten to fifteen years has it been even haltingly incorporated into decision making at regulatory agencies like the Food and Drug Administration, the Occupational Safety and Health Administration, and the Environmental Protection Agency. The controversy stems from several sources: the method of conducting risk assessments, the scientific uncertainties involved in performing them, and the policy results they sometimes are perceived to endorse. Although scientists generally conduct risk assessments, there is little scientific consensus concerning the appropriate procedures to use in any given situation, nor is there usually scientific agreement about the validity of the results.[5] A risk assessment requires finding the relationship between one risky activity and its environmental and health effects (independent of all other risk factors), the actual level of exposure, the number of people exposed, and the distribution of risk. In practice, each of these steps poses difficulties and requires strong assumptions that limit its scientific credibility and therefore public acceptance.

Animal Bioassays

One of the most difficult links to demonstrate is that between chemical exposure and its health impacts. This link is generally identified in one of two ways, an animal bioassay or an epidemiological study. A bioassay is an observed relationship between a controlled chemical dose ingested by animals (frequently mice or rats) and any associated health effects. Typically, at least two sets of animals—a control group and one or more test groups—ingest different concentrations of suspected carcinogens, mutagens, or teratogens. The animals must be kept under specially controlled living conditions, often for years, to isolate the effects being investigated. The animals are subsequently dissected to determine evidence of cancer, genetic change, or birth disorders. Scientists then try to establish links between (presumably) greater concentrations of chemical exposure and the higher incidence of disease. Although bioassays are the most widely used scientific technique to identify chemical carcinogenicity, despite multimillion-dollar costs, a host of problems limits the validity of the results.

The problems begin with an unusually high maximum tolerated dose (MTD) administered to animals to induce tumors, which may stunt growth, induce cancer, or create other illnesses because of its extreme toxicity (independent of the other effects under study). Moreover, extremely high doses may cause cells to divide rapidly, magnifying genetic errors and causing cancer.[6] These effects may not be present in animals ingesting lower doses. The use of MTDs is scientifically contentious, however, reflecting not only scientific disputes but ideological ones as well. A review committee headed by the director of the National Institute of Environmental Health Sciences concluded that "approximately two-thirds of the carcinogens would not be positive, i.e., not considered as carcinogens, if the MTD was not used."[7] While others disputed that the number should be closer to one-third, the overall concern was expressed by one researcher who concluded, "The problem is we don't know what the findings really mean."[8] A recent National Academy of Sciences report concluded with an unusual split recommendation: two-thirds of the panel recommended that the MTD be used in risk assessments, but the others believed that more moderate doses were appropriate. The project head concluded, "It's an ideological argument. But we just don't know which [approach] is right."[9] Consequently, MTDs are generally supported by environmentalists but opposed by industry representatives.

Statistically significant evidence[10] linking higher doses of the chemical with an increased probability of disease is only the start of the risk assessment, however. The next important and controversial steps in bioassays are two extrapolations: from animals to humans and from the necessarily high doses administered to animals (even if not MTDs) to the relatively low everyday exposure levels to which humans are subjected.[11] The problem is that high animal doses may not be valid indicators of low-dose responses in humans because the links between both the animal-human and the high dose-low dose relationships are tenuous.

The animal-to-human extrapolation is fraught with problems. Although animals are matched to humans for their physiological likeness as much as possible, the physiological relationships between chemicals and health effects in both animals and humans are frequently unknown. Moreover, animals metabolize substances differently than humans do. These differences can easily lead to errors in estimating actual risks to humans. In testing the effects of saccharin, for example, researchers noted that male rats were more likely to contract bladder tumors than females, and mice and monkeys were even less likely than female rats.[12] Further, the salt form in which saccharin was administered (as sodium saccharin or potassium saccharin) similarly affected the animals' responses.[13] Given these conflicts, which animal test is more likely to serve as an accurate indicator of the effects upon humans? A recognized cause and effect relationship in animals does not necessarily mirror that in humans, nor is the difference predictable (test animals are not x percent more or less likely to contract a particular disease than humans.) As a result, scientists cannot simply "correct" for the dose-response effect observed in animals and apply it to humans.

These problems are compounded by the fact that since test animals ordinarily live only about two years, their length of exposure to the chemical—although a similar proportion of their lives—is far less than a human lifetime of exposure. Further, test animals—generally rodents—

sometimes contract diseases from chemical exposure that humans do not, and vice versa. For example, while humans contract leukemia from breathing benzene, rats do not. On the other hand, humans may not develop nasal carcinomas from formaldehyde, while rats do.[14] Finally, extrapolating from animals to humans presents a unique dilemma: the physical dimension along which the extrapolation should be recorded is often arbitrary. For example, depending on whether the extrapolation from mice to humans was based on relative surface area or on body weight, one researcher calculated that a 1 mg dose found to be safe for a mouse could translate to a dose thought to be safe for humans ranging from 184 mg to 2500 mg daily.[15]

A second category of problems with animal bioassays involves determining the high-dose to low-dose relationship. Scientists can extrapolate from high animal doses to relatively low human exposures using *linear* or *nonlinear* dose-response curves. A linear extrapolation implies that the ill-effects of ingesting one additional part per million (ppm) of a chemical are equivalent whether one has already ingested a substantial quantity or not. This linearity assumption, which is most commonly used in federal agency risk assessments, has at least two effects. First, it denies the possibility of threshold effects, when an individual is only in danger after exposure exceeds a specific quantity. Second, since risks are assumed to be proportional to the dose, the linearity assumption implies that *any* effects found in animals will, however small, be found in humans as well. Nonlinear dose-response extrapolations, on the other hand, allow for the possibility of threshold effects and, as important politically as scientifically, for the possibility that some animal carcinogens (or mutagens or teratogens) will not affect humans. This extrapolation, if applied to public policy decisions, suggests that certain chemicals need not be regulated below specified threshold levels, since at low doses the negative health effects are minuscule or nonexistent. Whichever extrapolation method is used, a large disparity between animal doses and actual human exposures will make it more likely that the extrapolation method will produce the wrong results, thereby producing more scientific uncertainty and resultant public controversy over chemical regulation.[16]

There is no widely accepted method of extrapolation. Indeed, even within the class of carcinogenic chemicals, linear functions sometimes best fit the data for certain chemicals while nonlinear functions better fit the data for others. Besides the scientific controversy this produces, unscientific rationales for adopting one method over another have plenty of room to prevail. For example, because linear extrapolation often produces risk estimates that are several orders of magnitude greater than these predicted by nonlinear models,[17] a researcher wanting to show a correlation is more likely to find a human health impact using a linear extrapolation model than a nonlinear model.

How the bioassay is conducted can also affect its outcome, injecting greater uncertainty into risk assessment. Using relatively few test animals reduces the chance that subtle chemical effects will be uncovered, while testing larger numbers increases the likelihood. Some animals contract much higher rates of cancer than others, as is the case for formaldehyde doses in rats and mice (the former contract much higher rates of nasal tumors).[18] Thus, the results would be radically different, depending on whether researchers use the results of one animal test or the other. Consequently, a researcher (or policymaker) out to prove a chemical-health effect link could experiment with many highly sensitive animals, while another out to show that there is no effect could use fewer animals that are generally less susceptible to the suspected disease. Unfortunately, the problems plaguing bioassays are such that there is little scientific evidence to steer researchers in the right direction. Although the prospects are improving, those hoping for definitive bioassays in the near future will surely be disappointed.

Human Epidemiology

Because of these problems, some researchers have turned instead to human epidemiology to identify possible dose-response relationships between chemicals and the associated human health effects. By collecting data on human chemical exposures, scientists try to establish a link between those exposures and recorded human health effects. For example, if Los Angeles has higher recorded ozone concentrations than Chicago, and researchers observe that residents of Los Angeles also experience more (or more severe) respiratory problems *independent of other effects* (such as age, exposure to other relevant pollutants, and so forth), the additional ailments may be attributable to elevated ozone levels. By observing many individuals exposed to different ozone concentrations and experiencing different rates of respiratory illness, scientists can identify various points along the dose-response curve.

While this line of research frequently eliminates the problems of extrapolating from high animal dose-response relationships to low human ones,[19] since actual human exposures are nowhere near those of laboratory animals, epidemiological research suffers from other problems. First of all, epidemiology cannot be used to investigate newly introduced chemicals or those with long latency periods because it is an ex post facto appraisal that relies on observed exposures and outcomes. Another problem is identifying the size and type of chemical dose that individuals are actually exposed to (a problem that does not plague the laboratory-controlled bioassay). This requires accurate and abundant monitoring equipment (which frequently does not exist) to obtain continuous readings of chemical concentrations across many parts of the country. But for many ambient pollutants, the quality of monitoring equipment varies widely and there is insufficient coordination.[20] Therefore, epidemiological studies may be unable to link cause and effect simply because an individual's past history of pollution exposure cannot be accurately determined.

Epidemiological studies also suffer from the fundamental problem that many individuals are uniformly exposed to "background" levels of contamination (pesticides in food, air pollutants, and so on). In short, no one is unexposed. Consequently, there is only limited variation in exposure that can contribute to greater health risks. Epidemiological studies also require prodigious and detailed information about an exposed individual. For example, whether a worker who is exposed to x ppm of benzene on the job will contract cancer is a function not only of benzene exposure but whether, for instance, that worker smokes, is exposed to smoke at home, is exposed to indoor radon at home, and many other factors. Because group averages can obscure important individual characteristics, epidemiological research ideally uses data on individuals, although accurate information on individuals is difficult to come by. Surveys are often used to gather data on individuals, despite the problems in obtaining accurate information (people forget and embellish), and the confidentiality of medical records often precludes independent verification. Like bioassay results, the quality of the epidemiological results depends on the number of participants in the study, which is limited by the high cost of gathering data on individuals. In addition, because people are increasingly geographically mobile, an observed cancer may have been the result not of current chemical exposures but of exposures at a previous occupation or residence. Consequently, data should (but rarely do) include not only current exposure levels but also an entire personal history of exposure.

Another troubling problem with epidemiological research is that even if accurate individual exposure data are available, isolating the impact of the chemical in question can only be done statistically in an attempt to hold other relevant factors constant (smoking, alcohol consumption, job characteristics, exposure to other chemicals, and so on). This includes problems of proper functional form (linear or nonlinear models) and correctly measuring all relevant relationships (does the individual live in a house with an unventilated gas heater?) Finally, an extraordinarily large sample of individuals is necessary to determine statistical significance when dealing with actual human exposures to relatively low doses. Because of limited data availability and confounding factors, epidemiology requires highly elevated illness rates to confirm a suspected hazard; a negative result may not prove the absence of a hazard, only that it is too small to be detected by the study. Because epidemiological studies have difficulty distinguishing subtle health effects, one observer has claimed that "a good working definition of a catastrophe is an effect so large that even an epidemiological study can detect it."[21] Another admits that "epidemiology is a real crude tool for looking for associations."[22] In short, while epidemiological studies observe actual human health effects at common exposure levels, they suffer from a general inability to isolate with any confidence the impacts of a complex environment that bioassays can largely control in the laboratory. One researcher concludes that "The whole area of environmental epidemiology is a frustrating one."[23]

For all of the problems, some surprising evidence suggests that at least for broad indices of relative risk, epidemiological studies and bioassays sometimes produce similar estimates of risk. Michael Gough compared the results of two studies: EPA's *Unfinished Business* report that examined risks posed by thirty-one environmental problems, largely using bioassays for evidence that informed the opinions of "experts"; and an epidemiological study by Doll and Peto on the causes of cancer. Both studies support the conclusion that cancer risks from environmental pollutants are a relatively small proportion of all cancers: Doll and Peto estimated that approximately 2 percent of cancers were induced by environmental pollutants, while EPA's report found between 1 and 3 percent.[24] It should be noted, however, that the EPA study relied on the opinions of experts (see chapter 4), some of whom could have been influenced by the results of the earlier Doll and Peto study. Moreover, at the level of individual chemicals, the results of epidemiology and bioassays can vary widely, most commonly with bioassays suggesting carcinogenic risks and epidemiological studies finding fewer statistically significant relationships.

Exposures

Regardless of whether a bioassay or epidemiology is used, the dose-response results must be coupled with the number of people exposed, the type and frequency of exposure, and the particular sensitivities of certain groups. Determining who is exposed and how much can be relatively straightforward (workplace exposures) or highly complex (interstate transmission of airborne chemicals), depending on the media and the surroundings in which the chemical is transmitted. In many cases, it is not apparent whether the relevant "dose" for identifying health effects is an average daily exposure, the number of peak exposure levels, or cumulative doses. Researchers also need to decide whether benign and malignant tumors should be considered equivalent evidence of carcinogenicity.

Moreover, the type of exposure—whether the chemical is inhaled, swallowed, or absorbed through the skin—can affect its potency as well.

An individual's chemical sensitivity can vary with age, genetic characteristics, or lifestyle. For example, children are thought to be particularly susceptible to lead poisoning, and smokers appear to be more susceptible to asbestosis than nonsmokers. Unfortunately, many regulatory agencies, including EPA, assess risks with reference to a hypothetical "maximally exposed individual," one who lives 200 meters from the chemical plant (which sometimes puts the individual inside the factory's gates) and breathes outdoor air continuously for 70 years.[25] Naturally, this tends to overstate exposures in all but the most extreme cases. One commentator notes that EPA's exposure estimates produce "unrealistic scenarios like this one: the typical person is a 145-pound newborn with the appetite of a teenage boy, who works hard in the sun in front of his house 24 hours a day for 70 years, while an optimally bad breeze wafts toward him the maximum concentration of pollutant from the site."[26] Another commentator asks, only partly in jest, "Are humans to be regarded as behaving biochemically like huge, obese, inbred cancer-prone rodents?"[27]

The process of determining the number of people exposed and their levels of exposure can be at least as challenging as charting the dose-response function described above. Typically, exposure assessments are the result of estimates generated from air dispersion and other models. The leader of the OTA analysis on the effects of Agent Orange on Vietnam veterans, for example, stated that determining how many veterans were exposed and how much dioxin they were exposed to was "the most perplexing" part of the task.[28] And even when people are exposed to the same concentration of a known carcinogen, their rate of breathing, dietary patterns, and genetic factors all can affect the rate of absorption, and hence their likelihood of contracting the disease. Uncertainty in risk assessments does not end with dose-response functions; it pervades the entire process.

Popular Epidemiology

Popular epidemiology, in which local residents observe unusual correlations between health effects and proximity to potentially hazardous sources (such as elevated leukemia levels near Superfund sites), can be a useful tool for site discovery and evaluation.[29] Elevated disease levels may indeed indicate an environmental problem. However, this is no substitute for careful risk assessments and evaluations of whether the suspected sources actually caused the observed effects. Popular epidemiology can lead to "popular misconceptions" of two sorts. First, unusually high levels of cancer can exist in certain locations purely as a result of chance. Site-specific deviations in mortality or morbidity from national or statewide averages does not mean that pollution is the cause; it may be the result of random variation or such direct causes as a concentration of smokers, poor diet, genetic susceptibility, or exposure to carcinogenic substances (among many others). Variation is to be expected; indeed, it would be highly unusual for every town to mirror the national mortality and morbidity averages. Therefore, it is important to study the hunches formed through popular epidemiology systematically, using the latest risk assessment techniques, to determine if there is any credence to the claims.

On the other hand, the opposite effect can result, one that is surprisingly ignored by grass-roots environmentalists. As a result of chance, in other locations and in the absence of chemical pollutants, there would have been unusually low average cancer rates. In these areas, chemical pollutants may raise what would have been low rates of cancer to the national average. Popular epidemiology, however, would not suspect a linkage (even though one exists) because the observed cancer rate is not above average. The point is that observed cancer rates (and other indicators) by themselves tell only part of the story. While useful in directing preliminary investigations, popular epidemiology can lead to two potentially serious mistakes: one that suspects a health problem where none exists, and the other that ignores a serious health problem.

Are Risk Assessments Conservative?

A great deal has been made of how risk assessments are by design conservative. (In this context, "conservative" means to use assumptions in the risk assessment that in the end most likely overstate actual risks.) While these criticisms are appropriate as far as they go, they are in a broader sense incomplete and misleading. In short, critics are right that many errors of *commission* in risk assessments do tend to be conservative, but several errors of *omission* tend to understate actual environmental and public health risks.

How do researchers cope with the numerous uncertainties that compound themselves along each step of the risk assessment, and cumulatively produce wide ranges of potential risk? In certain respects, like engineers designing a bridge, scientists build into each estimate a conservative bias, to be "safe" in their final estimates of the chemical's impacts. Frequently, researchers estimate risk to only the most sensitive individuals, use the most conservative probabilities at each step, employ extrapolation models that most likely overstate human risks relative to animal risks, count both benign and malignant tumors equally, measure doses cumulatively over an entire lifetime, use dose-response models that deny threshold effects, extrapolate bioassay results using surface area rather than body weight, or some combination of these. Since virtually every risk assessment contains a plausible range of estimated probabilities and their consequences, using conservative estimates at each step can vastly overstate potential health risks. I outline several errors of commission below, which bias the results of risk assessments in a predictably conservative way.

Risk assessments are too often reported as a single point estimate, and the point estimate reported is usually an extreme one. Most commonly, it is extreme in the sense that there is only a 5 percent chance that the point estimate is too low, and therefore a 95 percent chance that the true risk is lower than the estimated value, given the model used. (This is a measure of statistical uncertainty, not an overall measure of uncertainty.) Figure 2.1 shows a hypothetical probability distribution of the risks of contracting cancer from a particular chemical exposure level; the horizontal axis shows the number of expected cancers, and the vertical axis indicates the probability of each outcome (the area under the curve therefore equals one). In this case, the expected value estimate is that four people out of 100,000 will contract cancer from a lifetime of chemical exposure. However, risk assessments (including those for Superfund sites) routinely report not the most likely estimate, but rather a 95th percentile upper-bound estimate, in this case nine cancer deaths. (The lower-bound estimate is almost always zero, since scientists cannot predict with certainty that there is an effect.) Although the expected value estimate is not necessarily likely to occur (in this example, the probability of four cancers actually occurring is below 50 percent), it is equally likely to understate as to overstate the true risk. With the reported risk, however, scientists are 95 percent sure that the upper-bound estimate overstates the true (albeit unknown) risk. Thus, when policymakers examine risk assessments to help form public policy, they are looking not at the most likely impacts but at nearly worst-case scenarios. EPA's 95th percentile risk estimate for dioxin is reportedly as much as 5,000 times higher than the expected value estimate, while for perchloroethylene (a dry-cleaning solvent) the difference jumps to 35,000 times.[30] While these may be extreme cases, they suggest wildly different estimates of risk based on technical assumptions rarely communicated to (or understood by) policymakers. The problem is not simply that 95 percent confidence intervals are used, but that the implications of this assumption are not communicated clearly to those making decisions.

To preserve a "margin of safety," estimating *all* risks conservatively may appear to be prudent risk management. Unfortunately, this fails to

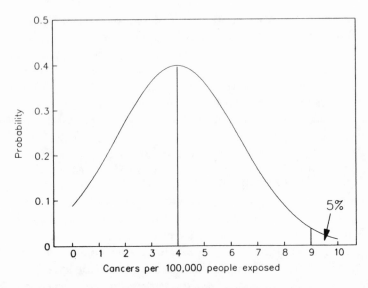

Figure 2.1   Expected value versus upper-bound risk estimates.

solve the problem. Figure 2.2 shows two hypothetical probability distributions for different chemicals, and their corresponding "expected value" and 95th percentile (upper-bound) risk estimates.[31] Panel A indicates that the upper-bound estimate is quite close to the expected value estimate, while in Panel B it is not. Because the levels of uncertainty vary from chemical to chemical, upper-bound estimates do not bear the same proportional relationship to expected value estimates, nor are they necessarily close. Expected value estimates therefore are not predictably related to upper-bound estimates. Conservatively estimating all risks still leads to overregulating some risks relative to others, albeit in an unpredictable manner. The magnitude of the error would then depend on the relative uncertainty of the risk assessment.

Were regulators to follow the results of risk assessments, 95th percentile estimates would mean excessively stringent standards for some chemicals and relatively lax requirements for others, compared with the expected value. The problem is exacerbated with asymmetric or multiple-peak probability distributions (or those without the familiar bell shape), where 50th percentile estimates are not even the most likely occurrences. Uniformly conservative risk estimates can produce results that would overregulate certain risks or activities and underregulate others. Ironically, conservative risk assessments may also stunt efforts to quantitatively evaluate noncancer health and environmental risks, since the sup-

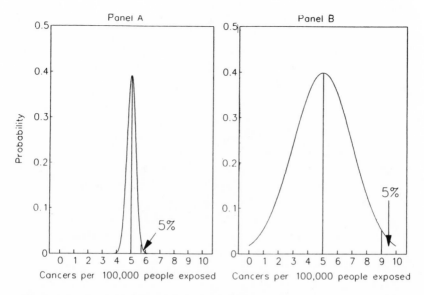

Figure 2.2 Uncertain relationship between expected value and upper-bound estimates.

position may be that conservative assumptions in estimating cancer risks already account for those factors, however crudely.

While many errors of commission are indeed conservative, several errors of *omission* suggest that risk assessments may underestimate actual risks. First, a bioassay demonstrating that there is no animal health effect does not necessarily imply that the chemical's effects are benign in humans. Political conservatives make much of "false positives," arguing that what is true in laboratory test animals may not be true in humans. Seldom, however, is it recognized that what appears safe in test animals may in fact be harmful to humans; just as some chemicals found to be harmful to animals appear to have little affect on humans, so too can chemicals benign in animals pose health risks to humans. These "false negatives" may be as important as false positives, where chemicals that perhaps should be regulated are not.

Second, important criticisms are aimed at how cancer risks are estimated, charging that in some respects risks are underestimated by examining each in isolation. Robert Paehlke argues that even low levels of exposure to carcinogens can be unsafe to humans because of bioaccumulation, the process by which toxic substances build in the food chain from "lower-order" to "higher-order" animals; natural resistance, whereby short-living, rapidly producing species can avoid the harmful effects of toxins that longer-living species like humans cannot; natural dispersion, in which traces of chemicals are longer-lived than had been expected, and therefore are subject to bioaccumulation; and biochemical interaction, the chemical interactions that can increase the toxicity of two chemicals whose risks are estimated independently.[32] These interactive chemical effects are generally assumed not to exist, not because of any particular bias, but due to a lack of information on synergistic effects.

Third, epidemiology is notoriously unable to uncover subtle chemical-health relationships, increasing the likelihood of false negatives (discussed above). Fourth, risk assessments too often examine only cancer risks, while risks to the environment, noncancer health risks, and economic risks are downplayed or ignored. While species loss and cancer risks, for example, cannot be aggregated and reduced to a single numerical risk estimate, this does not imply that risk assessments should focus only on those risks that are most easily quantified (usually cancer). Fifth, risk assessments sometimes focus on one exposure pathway (drinking water) while ignoring others (eating fish from contaminated streams). As a result, in sometimes significant ways risk assessments are biased to understate total environmental and health risks. The combined errors of commission and omission work together to magnify the uncertainty regarding the relationship between actual risks and those measured in the risk assessment, rendering interpretation of the results especially difficult.

Psychologist Paul Slovic notes that "higher-order impacts" of accidents, such as Three Mile Island (TMI), are neglected by risk assessments and can dwarf the impacts that are measured such as lives lost, illnesses, and reduced property values.[33] His argument implies that, far from being too conservative, risk assessments are deficient in their failure to include all social costs. In the case of TMI, where he argues "not a single person died, and few if any latent cancer fatalities are expected," Slovic asserts that the higher-order impacts include the costs of stricter nuclear power regulations, the devastation of the utility itself, expensive substitution away from nuclear power toward alternative energy sources (which can result in greater sulfur dioxide (SO_2) and carbon dioxide (CO_2) emissions), and possibly an added mistrust of other complex technologies. Slovic points to other examples such as the Challenger space shuttle accident, Union Carbide's methyl isocyanate leak in Bhopal, India, and hazardous waste incidents at Love Canal, New York, and Times Beach, Missouri.[34] However, while building these possible impacts into the final public decision may be altogether appropriate, it is questionable whether the proper role of scientists is to speculate what the public's reaction might be and modify their risk assessments accordingly, since so much of the analysis would be little more than a form of guesswork that risk assessors are unqualified to perform.

Besides the technical biases in risk assessments outlined above, the way they are communicated to decision makers can mislead as well. The presentation of risk assessments is a problem not with risk assessments per se, but with the oftentimes political demands for apparent precision where none exists. The bias in this instance is not to consistently overstate or understate risks, but to imply greater certainty than actually exists. There is too often an overriding search for a single numerical estimate of risk. Individuals want to know whether they should eat butter or margarine. Policymakers want to know which of two chemicals is riskier. Risk assessment is cheapened and sometimes downright misleading when a single number is used to characterize an environmental or public health risk. The more appropriate measure is a range of estimates that conveys the underlying scientific uncertainties. As a recent commentary rightly suggested, "The point is not to search for the one 'true' estimate of uncertainty but rather to convey the variation in such estimates."[35] Further, sensitivity analyses should clearly indicate the effects of varying important parameters (such as the means of extrapolation) on the final risk estimates. Ideally, policymakers should be presented with the entire risk probability distribution with a full disclosure of the uncertainties involved, but should at a minimum see the expected value, lower-bound, and upper-bound estimates, both to convey the level of uncertainty and to help them make more informed choices. No single-point estimate of risk (including the expected value) can convey the many uncertainties in assessing risks.

Expected-value risk estimates can be conveyed in a manner that is as misleading as conservative risk estimates. For example, it is said that drinking thirty 12-ounce cans of diet soda imposes the same risk as living near a nuclear power plant for fifty years,[36] or that a serving of peanut butter is eighteen times riskier than the Alar in a serving of apple juice. These estimates are comparisons of only two *points* on two different probability distributions, and therefore they fail to convey the true degree of uncertainty. Figure 2.3 shows how even though point estimates may show one risk to be substantially greater than another (in this case, twelve cancers compared with three), it is quite possible that the reverse is true since the probability distributions are overlapped. For example, despite the fact that point estimates show a serving of peanut butter to be eighteen times riskier than a serving of apple juice containing Alar, Adam Finkel of Resources for the Future has calculated that there is a one-third chance that the Alar is actually riskier than the peanut butter.[37]

There is nothing inherent in risk assessment that requires every impact

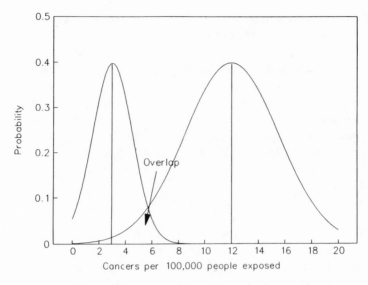

Figure 2.3   Expected value point estimates hide uncertainty of risks.

to be quantified. It is only the political demand for such apparent "precision," and the too frequent willingness of analysts to provide it, that leads to these simplifications. As one environmental scientist says of ignorance in Washington, D.C., regarding risk assessment, "people see an exponent and they say it's science."[38] Risk assessments should communicate both population and individual risks where they differ substantially. It may also be necessary to incorporate the informed judgments of outside scientists if the data are not conclusive.

Whether society wants to be conservative in its final policy decision is ultimately a political decision, not a technical one. Providing an "adequate margin of safety," which is the justification for many conservative technical assumptions, is a decision better left to policymakers and the public than to scientists. As much as possible, scientists' best judgments regarding the risks posed by certain chemicals, and how, if at all, governments should respond, should be separate decisions. This is not an impermeable layer, and risk assessment will inevitably and appropriately be driven by the concerns of risk management. Sheila Jasanoff writes that "the principles by which we organize the 'facts' of risks have to derive, at least in part, from the concerns of risk management."[39] Nevertheless, the current hodgepodge of conservative assumptions and nonconservative assumptions serves both to confuse regulators and to generate added public mistrust of an already embattled process. Overemphasizing the precision of risk assessment can lead policymakers to abdicate their responsibility to understand and incorporate into their decisionmaking the value judgments and attending uncertainties implicit in risk assessment. Jasanoff appropriately argues that "the answers have to come from risk management, for only the risk manager can say how conservatively we should draw up our policies for protecting public health and the environment."[40]

Implications of Biased Risk Assessments

The previous section illustrated how risk assessments are biased in ways that variously understate and overstate risks. The problems with understating chemical risks are apparent and well known: the failure to restrict the use or disposal of harmful substances. What is less understood and more subtle is the fact that overstating risks can be harmful to public health and the environment as well.

It is well known in engineering that conservative risk assumptions may not produce conservative structures because of the interdependence of materials in complex systems. Engineers can always increase the safety margin of airplane wings to ensure they will not fail, for example, but they do so at the cost of increasing the airplane's weight, which itself is dangerous.[41] A similar result holds for chemical risk assessments, although for somewhat different reasons. Banning a safe chemical has harmful consequences—albeit of a different type—just as failing to restrict or ban a hazardous chemical does. Cyclamates provide a case in point in which a chemical now widely acknowledged to be relatively safe was banned by the FDA in 1969. Not only did consumers pay higher prices for products with artificial sweeteners, but cyclamate substitutes, such as saccharin, were later banned for fear of even greater hazards (although Congress subsequently lifted the ban on saccharin). Dr. Richard Griesemer, deputy director of the National Institute of Environmental Health Sciences, has said, "Saccharin doesn't have much risk, and I don't think cyclamates have any risk at all."[42] Others have claimed that by banning EBD (an agricultural fumigant to attack small animals and molds) the additional risks were greater than that of the banned chemical because of the highly carcinogenic aflatoxin B contained in the mold, and diseases transmitted by vermin.[43]

If decision makers base policies on the results of risk assessments, then "conservative" assessments—and therefore policies—do not necessarily imply greater safety.[44] Some have argued that limiting the amount of synthetic pesticide residues permitted on fruits and vegetables will drive up their cost and thereby reduce the amount of cancer-preventing foods people consume.[45] Indeed, the battle over saccharin was fought on one side by groups who claimed that banning saccharin would actually *increase* risks because of the expected weight gain by people denied the low-calorie sweetener. Overreacting to relatively trivial risks causes problems that can be as substantial as failing to curtail the use of truly hazardous substances. Another example is the scare involving Alar (the commercial name for daminozide) on apples in 1989. Although scientists now generally agree that the risks posed by Alar were relatively small, and some contend that the observed animal carcinogenicity was an artifact of the genetic composition of the mouse strains used,[46] the wave of publicity generated by the Natural Resources Defense Council (NRDC) led to an EPA ban of the chemical. The result was that the Washington apple industry, which represents over half of total U.S. production, lost at least $125 million in sales in the six months following the publicity, and many family farmers lost their land to foreclosure. One farmer commented, "Pesticides, what we put in our food, deserve scrutiny. But we got hit with a knockout punch, and the result was that many innocent people went under."[47] Health costs, like the nutritional loss from children eating fewer apples, must be considered as well.

The greater the conservatism of risk estimates, the more likely society is to avoid using a dangerous chemical, but the greater the likelihood of banning harmless and beneficial ones as well.[48] Conservatism over some risks can lead to larger errors in others. For example, excess concern about the risks of vaccines could lead to a greater probability of spreading epidemics of preventable diseases in the future. The recent rise of inner-city measles is one such example.[49] Physicist H. W. Lewis cautions that a "deliberate error in a calculation, in a direction intended to be conservative, provides no guarantee that the result will be conservative. . . . A conservative assumption about anything is a deliberate falsity, and can therefore have any consequences, good or bad."[50]

Finally, conservative risk assessments are more frequently conducted for health-related risks and not, for example, for safety-related risks where more reliable historical and laboratory testing data are available (such as testing the risks of not wearing seat belts using crash-test dummies). As a result, relatively low-level health risks may appear to be more hazardous than more severe safety risks because of the built-in conservatism of the way the former type of risk is estimated. Whether or not the two are related, some research has shown a tendency to regulate health risks more stringently than safety risks.[51]

Lawrie Mott, a senior scientist at the NRDC, argues, "To the extent that risk assessment is flawed, the only morally acceptable course is to work even more aggressively to reduce and avoid exposure to carcinogens."[52] The problem is that risk assessments will always at some level be flawed. Does that mean policymakers should continue to ignore their findings, and any other relevant evidence, simply because the results are imperfect? The result would be important policy decisions made with even less information, an outcome that to a large extent may be determined by the strongest interest groups. David Doniger (also of NRDC) has said, "if you don't really know, if you have a wide range [of risk estimates], the only prudent thing to do in public health is to be safe rather than sorry."[53] The problem here is that if the "prudent thing" means to regulate or ban that substance, then the result may not be prudent at all. A blind allegiance to banning all products that have even a remote chance of being carcinogenic may make society worse off, because the result may be substitute products that are more hazardous, net job losses, and higher product prices. If society wants to be careful in regulating health and safety, both conservative and nonconservative biases can lead in the wrong direction, since overregulating can be as harmful as underregulating, and substitute products worse than the banned substances.

This argument does not imply that society should avoid conservatism in responding to the risks that chemicals pose to public health and the environment, or that it should never ban risky products and chemicals. The point is that the technical assumptions that variously overestimate and underestimate risk would be far better evaluated and discussed publicly rather than through hidden technical assumptions. Because these assumptions ultimately involve trading-off public health and safety with other social priorities, risk assessors should provide a range of plausible risk estimates. The problem is one of obfuscation: the public and regulators are too often unaware of the uncertainties involved in risk assessments, and analysts too often bury important assumptions in the technical details. A patina of certainty is applied to an inherently uncertain enterprise. Policymakers and the public, not risk assessors, have the right to be conservative. Deliberately false risk assessments depoliticize the question and substitute a technical fix. Decisions concerning the appropriate level of conservatism should be debated as matters of risk *management*, not buried in technical risk *assessments*. The desire of EPA and other agencies to protect human health is laudable and shared by most citizens, but there is no reason to do so by stipulating risk assessment guidelines that produce unpredictably conservative "scientific" evaluations.

Political Abuses of Risk Assessment

Risk assessment has been manipulated to political advantage, perhaps most obviously by the Reagan administration. As the above discussion indicates, there is plenty of room in risk assessments for nonscientific justification of the methods used. It was no secret that when the Reagan administration took office in 1981, environmental regulations that it considered to be antibusiness were a prime target. But because the administration recognized that it would face extreme difficulty in persuading Congress to go along with its ideas, it pursued an administrative course of action that included regulatory cost-benefit requirements embodied in Executive Order 12291, as well as more subtle changes in technical assumptions used in risk assessments. The latter were instrumental in setting guidelines for permissible concentrations of hundreds of chemicals and pollutants. The Reagan administration pursued an aggressive and controversial strategy to reverse scientific conclusions regarding risk assessments that were reached during the Carter administration, a strategy that one researcher termed "highly risk tolerant" and one that " clearly pointed regulatory and research agencies in a different direction."[54] These included greater acceptance of threshold effects and results from epidemiological studies, higher tolerable risks than permitted by the Carter administration, and other technical changes that could have profound policy implications. These were met with considerable controversy. One scientist criticized a memorandum outlining this strategy as "the sort of document that one would not expect an objective scientist to produce nor to be produced by a responsible public agency." Another called the events "the unraveling of a scientifically based federal policy."[55]

A more subtle potential political bias is that differences in risk assessments unfortunately can reflect the risk assessor's disciplinary training as well as technical assumptions. In the case of formaldehyde, toxicologists were judged to be more likely to accept the possibility of human risk than epidemiologists, not because of a reasoned conclusion from viewing all the evidence, but rather because each group discounted the other's study results.[56] Further, evidence suggests that whether scientists believe threshold doses exist for carcinogenic chemicals depends on their age, workplace, and political attitudes. Francis Lynn surveyed industry, academic, and government scientists on (among other things) their beliefs in cancer thresholds. He found that 80 percent of industry scientists believed that thresholds exist, compared with just 37 percent of government scientists. Moreover, younger academics were less likely to believe in thresholds than their older colleagues, and overall the belief in thresholds was found to be correlated with conservative political attitudes. Similarly, those who question animal bioassays were found more likely to be politically conservative.[57] While the study cannot be definitive in ascribing bias, since it is unclear whether thresholds do in fact exist (in other words, one group may not be biased but simply correct), these results point to the troubling likelihood that in the absence of scientific guidance, important and often-times hidden assumptions used in risk assessments may be the product of political beliefs and who signs the risk assessor's paycheck.

Assessing Superfund Site Risks

EPA risk assessments carried out at individual Superfund sites reflect many of the general problems with risk assessments discussed above: they are variously conservative and nonconservative.[58] There are several conservative procedures that EPA requires of its Superfund risk assessments. First, EPA relies on "slope factors" for toxicity assessments from the upper 95th percentile, meaning there is only a 5 percent chance that the actual risk is below the reported toxicity level. Second, linear dose-response functions are used to extrapolate from high to low doses, a conservative assumption because it implies that no threshold exists below which health effects are absent, and it generally overestimates risks. Third, EPA conducts separate risk assessments for each of the suspected carcinogenic substances present at the site. These individual risks are then added together to produce a measure of total site risk (for example, if one substance is found to have a risk of 1×10^{-5} and another 2×10^{-5}, the total risk would be 3×10^{-5}).[59] The problem is that since each is a 95th percentile estimate of the risk, adding the individual risks creates an artificially more conservative total risk estimate than each individual estimate.[60] This is a small concern if only a few substances are found at the site, but if dozens of carcinogens are present, which is not uncommon,[61] the cumulative impact can be significant.

EPA claims to use these conservative estimates of chemical concentration, contact rate, and exposure "in order to be protective."[62] EPA recognizes the biases and tries in other instances to correct for these cumulatively conservative risks. For exposure estimates, average body weight is used rather than the 5th percentile weight (which would make the effects of any dose that much more pronounced) to "reduce the number of upper-bound values that are multiplied together."[63] Thus, the result, which EPA terms a "reasonable maximum exposure" (RME), is a jumble of very conservative and average exposure estimates, which surely does not represent anything close to its best estimate of individual exposure. In addition, the total cancer risk exposure is the sum of the RMEs across each possible pathway exposure. Thus, even though no one individual may be exposed to air, surface water, and groundwater risks, RMEs from each pathway are summed to determine the composite site risk for any given chemical and then multiplied by the "exposed" population. When the aggregate RME is multiplied across hundreds or thousands of exposed individuals, only a few of whom are actually exposed to this degree, the result may be a gross overestimate of the site's total cancer risk. At one Superfund site, EPA found that the greatest risk was from arsenic exposure, which contaminated just one of 38 wells at the site. EPA then assessed the highest exposure rate for any one individual and applied it to the entire population (instead of only those people who drank water from the one contaminated well), therefore vastly overstating the total cancer risk.[64]

Interactive chemical effects may mean, however, that total site risks are most likely greater (although possibly less) than the summation of individual substance risks. Another factor, though not necessarily conservative, plagues EPA's risk estimates: since the carcinogenicity of certain substances is well documented (high doses of radon) and for others only suspected (dioxin), adding together the risks of all substances present at a Superfund site muddles the quality of the total site risk assessment. One commentator notes that "very little technical discretion has been delegated to the scientists" in making risk assessments at EPA.[65] The conservative estimates are due less to the fact that scientists believe that these estimates are the best possible than they are to the fact that they must follow specific agency guidelines. This allows decision makers to maintain control of risk assessments and to justify their policy decisions as the application of science to policy.[66]

All of the problems that plague risk assessments generally—and more—are to be found in Superfund site risk assessments. While relatively little is known of the risks posed by individual Superfund sites, what has been studied suggests that the environmental and public health threats vary considerably from site to site, and in many cases are relatively low. Evaluating Superfund site risks is particularly difficult, however, due to the wide variation in the type and amount of chemicals stored at the site, the hydrogeology of the surrounding land, the numerous exposure pathways (air, groundwater, surface water, biota), and the number and type of exposed individuals. Unlike other pollutants, there is no "average" Superfund site that represents the risks of all sites. Instead of characterizing the health effects of, say, airborne lead in order to formulate an appropriate regulatory policy, Superfund sites must be evaluated on a site-by-site basis because of the variety and varying quantities of hazardous materials present. One urban site may contain large quantities of PCBs and cadmium, while a rural site may hold small quantities of nickel, arsenic, benzene, and twenty-five other chemicals. The interactive chemical effects further complicate the risk assessment process.

As with most risk assessments, EPA's evaluation of Superfund site risks concentrates on cancer risks, to the relative exclusion of birth disorders, neurotoxicity, and other health effects; ecological risks are only haltingly integrated. A review of 15 Superfund risk assessments indicated four significant methodological problems.[67] First, inadequate data were available to measure important risks, and in many cases entire exposure pathways (especially air) were ignored completely. Second, the risk assessments concentrated on well-known chemicals, particularly carcinogens, and in many cases ignored other lesser-known chemicals for which toxicity factors have not yet been published. Third, arbitrary assumptions were used when data were unavailable to measure risks, assumptions that the author notes "are designed to be overly conservative rather than realistic."[68] Finally, the risks are poorly characterized, generally because less common chemicals are ignored, but also because of gaps in data, lack of attention to ecological risks, and so on. The result of these conservative and non-conservative assumptions produces estimates that bear an unpredictable relationship to actual Superfund site risks.

EPA conducts baseline risk assessments at Superfund sites to justify its selected plan of remedial action in the public Record of Decision (ROD). As noted above, these cancer risk estimates are generated using generally conservative assumptions (it is highly unlikely that the cancer risk is above the level EPA specifies), and therefore *cancer* risks are likely to be overstated. One study reviewed the risk assessments at fifty post-SARA RODs, for which quantitative risk assessments were performed at thirty-six sites.[69] The cancer risks posed by these sites, which is the excess individual cancer risk associated with a lifetime (70 years) of exposure to the carcinogenic materials present at those sites, ranged from 10^{-2} to 10^{-7} (or 0.01, one chance in a hundred, to 0.0000001, one chance in ten million) for most sites.[70] Two of the findings were particularly troubling. First, the authors were unable to identify any link between the decision to remediate the site and the health risk. (This conclusion is contrary to my findings in chapter 6, however.) Second, the risk reduction expected from the proposed remedial action was evaluated at only 12 percent (six) of the sites. These results suggest that the amount of expected risk reduction played little or no role in Superfund cleanup decisions. But since EPA appears to place greater emphasis on total site risk rather than the risk *reduction* potential of actual site remediation, the deck is stacked in favor of finding what appear to be cost-effective solutions; since EPA implicitly assumes that all risks are eliminated, the benefits of remediation are overstated and appear more favorable in relation to costs. The authors conclude that "current risk estimates fall within the range (10^{-4} to 10^{-7}) the EPA considers acceptable."[71]

There is no definitive study comparing Superfund site risks to those of other environmental problems. The paucity of data in assessing Superfund site risks has led to estimates whose scientific credibility falls somewhat short of conclusive evidence. The National Research Council of the National Academy of Sciences, in a study of the health effects of hazardous waste sites, concluded: "According to recent opinion polls, the American public believes that hazardous waste sites constitute a serious threat to public health. In contrast, many scientists and administrators in the field do not share this belief. On the basis of its best efforts to evaluate the published literature relevant to this subject, the committee [on environmental epidemiology] cannot confirm or refute either view . . . Critical information on the distribution of exposures and health effects associated with hazardous-waste sites is still lacking."[72]

It is true that existing evidence cannot definitively confirm or refute either view. But policymakers cannot discard what scientists have learned, however inconclusively, about the effects of hazardous waste sites. Knowledge in science evolves and is never conclusive. As Senator Moynihan maintains, "We cannot forget that knowledge need not be precise to be useful."[73] Even the best risk assessments will only be able to make probabilistic statements about potential risks: scientists will never be absolutely certain that a particular chemical causes a specific health impact. The best that policymakers can expect is increasing degrees of confidence in the results of risk assessments. It is essential, however, that EPA commit far greater resources to reducing the uncertainty of Superfund site risks. It is not simply that more studies are needed to make better decisions. Because of the relative information vacuum and the amount of money spent on Superfund, however, it is difficult to argue that improved information concerning Superfund site risks would not be well worth the cost if it better targets cleanup resources. But before better estimates are available—and their quality will vary from site to site—policymakers need to act now, based on current, albeit imperfect, information.

Conclusion

This chapter has tried to illustrate several points. First, risk assessments are crude instruments for assessing environmental and health threats, even from well-understood chemicals. Second, risk assessments are in different ways biased to overrepresent and underrepresent actual risks, the results of which lead to an unpredictable relationship between estimated and actual risks. Third, bioassays and epidemiologies have significant—and different—biases that generally cause bioassays to produce conservative estimates, while epidemiological studies often experience difficulty in independently linking observed risks to a specific cause. Instead of viewing the results of these two dominant forms of risk assessment as competitive, they can be better used as complementary ways to bound estimates of the risk in question. Because of their different biases, and assuming that both examine the same contaminant, in some cases it is reasonable to consider the results of an epidemiological study to be a crude lower-bound estimate of risk and a bioassay an upper-bound estimate. Finally, while risk assessments contain many flaws, if communicated honestly they do add to the public's knowledge of relative risks, and can therefore be useful to the management of risks (taken up in the next chapter). Risk assessments are not, however, "objective" or "rational" evaluations of risks based upon static and concrete methodologies. Risk assessments have a number of problems, and the procedure is necessarily subjective, from deciding which chemicals to study to finally characterizing the total risk quantitatively. In addition, risks include not only the threat of cancer but also noncancer health, economic, and ecological impacts. Aggregating these impacts is obviously more art than science. One researcher correctly notes that "risk assessment, like any artistic endeavor, requires the exercise of subjective judgment. It cannot be done by mechanically following the rules."[74]

Risk assessment will always be an imperfect tool in trying to improve risk management. Risk assessors must necessarily use value judgments in producing policy-relevant analyses, yet too often the underlying technical assumptions, however critical to policy applications, are of little interest to policymakers. Jonathan Lash notes that "risk assessors look at the narrowest of questions: What is the risk of cancer to a hypothetical population exposed to an assumed level of a specific substance?" Lash reminds us that "we still have to decide what values are important enough to us to protect us from risk, and how much risk is too much."[75] Every step along the way requires speculative assumptions and necessary shortcuts imposed by limitations in both data and science. To the extent that the science of risk assessment, however preliminary, can be separated from policy decisions, the technical quality as well as external trust in the results will be improved. This would require that policymakers tolerate the wide uncertainties inherent in any risk assessment and that the news media report the results of risk assessments less as facts than as tentative estimates.[76] Both decision makers and the public need to be informed that the labels "carcinogenic" and "toxic" are matters of degree, not simple yes-no scientific determinations.

Risk assessment is not currently up to the task of providing uniformly accurate evaluations of health and environmental risks. However, by combining the results of several risk assessments, particularly ones based on different methodologies, the degree of uncertainty can be significantly reduced. Policymakers should not demand excessive precision from any one risk assessment but rather should consider the weight of evidence available from many different assessments in reaching policy decisions. Both policymakers and risk assessors need to move beyond the perception that conveying uncertainty somehow undermines a study's integrity. Rather, uncertainty needs to be seen as ubiquitous and important information in its own right. Two authors appropriately conclude that "if scientific uncertainty is presented as an unavoidable outcome of risk assessment, it can generate confidence in the honesty of the process."[77]

Despite its problems, risk assessment is the best method currently available to systematically evaluate relative health and environmental risks (although other factors are relevant to risk management as well). Policies have been and always will be made with imperfect information. It is critical that decision makers are aware not only of the limitations of risk assessment but also of what it has to offer. Policymakers' unquenchable thirst for the "bottom line" may preclude the effective presentation of risk assessments, but it remains the obligation of risk assessors to present their findings honestly with a full disclosure of the assumptions used and the likely directions of their biases. Risk assessments should try to incorporate (qualitatively, if necessary) other environmental, aesthetic, and noncancer health impacts and identify those groups most likely to be harmed, and decision makers need to understand that the most appropriate product of a risk assessment is not a single number but a rather messy probability distribution coupled with descriptive evidence of other nonquantifiable risks to health and the environment. Without the honest appraisal of risk, an informed public discussion of priorities is impossible. While risk assessments obviously are no substitute for social values, values cannot be realized without considering the consequences of social actions. To this end, risk assessments can help.

3 Managing Risks

A waste hauler in the early 1970s spread oil over the unpaved roads of a number of small towns in eastern Missouri, including Times Beach, a town of just over 2,200 people about thirty miles southwest of St. Louis. While using oil to control dust was common practice, what was uncommon about this incident was that the contractor hired by local governments had contaminated the oil by mixing it with dioxin, at the time considered to be one of the most toxic compounds known. The use of dioxin went undiscovered until 1982, when the residents' alarm brought national attention from the press, EPA, and the Centers for Disease Control (CDC) in Atlanta. Some observers called the media reaction "the greatest torrent of 'time-bomb' journalism since Love Canal."[1] Based on then-current estimates of the human health risks from dioxin, the CDC recommended that the town be evacuated, and the EPA initially authorized over $30 million from Superfund to finance the relocation. Families and businesses were bought out and uprooted; the town disappeared in a matter of months. Times Beach, now fully abandoned and surrounded by a chain-link fence and security guards, is little more than an eyesore of 400 sagging buildings.[2] Dr. Houk of the CDC, who was central to the government's decision to buy out the entire town, said years later that in light of more recent evidence, "I would not be concerned about the levels of dioxin at Times Beach . . . the data we've accumulated in the last 10 or 12 years show we should not be that concerned."[3] The revision in the risk assessments of dioxin led Dr. Houk to conclude that if dioxin was a carcinogen, then "it is, in my view, a weak one that is associated only with high-dose exposures."[4] A director of environmental and occupational health at St. Louis University who studied former residents found "no significant chronic illness."[5]

While some may respond that it is "better to be safe than sorry," a considerable amount of fear and disruption was created for local residents, whose community was uprooted and scattered. Events of this sort produce potentially wasteful expenditures (the eventual expected cleanup costs now total more than $200 million), even viewed solely from the residents' perspectives. The risk assessments were communicated not as probabilities, but as certain results. Even Dr. Houk of the CDC now states, "We should have been more upfront with Times Beach people and told them, 'We're doing our best with the estimates of risk, but we may be wrong.' I think we never added, 'But we may be wrong.' "[6] Revisions in risk assessments can have human implications, as the former residents of Times Beach know all too well. How society interprets risk assessments and manages risks affects how public resources are used to protect and promote public health and environmental quality. Former EPA Administrator William Reilly has urged, "We need to develop a new system for taking action on the environment that isn't based on responding to the nightly news. What we have had in the United States is environmental agenda-setting by episodic panic."[7]

Risk management is the controversial and political process of deciding how society should respond (if at all) to risks like those at Times Beach. A fundamental first step in risk management is deciding what governments can actually do to reduce or eliminate certain risks. For example, governments cannot reasonably force people to eat low-fat foods or to stop smoking cigarettes or drinking alcohol, without violating what most would consider their personal freedoms. (Governments can, of course, encourage or discourage such behavior.) The public outrage over the National Highway Traffic Safety Administration's (NHTSA) mandatory ignition-interlock system in the early 1970s (where a buzzer sounded and the car would not start if the occupants' seat belts were unattached) provided ample warning to Congress that personal freedoms in the automobile were at least as important to Americans as requiring occupants to wear seat belts, even when saving a substantial number of lives was at stake. Programs to reduce risk can differ in technological possibility as well: governments cannot prevent earthquakes or hurricanes, although they can help to prepare for the consequences. Therefore, managing risk is fundamentally constrained both by the degree to which citizens feel that reducing risk impinges on personal liberties, and the technological capacity to alleviate certain risks in the first place.

Society already "manages" risks by deciding that certain problems are worthy of direct governmental action to reduce risks and others are not. Sometimes these decisions are made implicitly as a product of public policies. For example, if the federal government chooses—as it has in the past—not to require mandatory airbags in all automobiles, where the additional annual costs of an estimated $3.6 billion were at one time

deemed too high relative to preventing an estimated 17,000 annual auto-
mobile-related deaths, it is implicitly saying, for better or for worse, that
in this context, it is not worth spending $212,000 to prevent an additional
traffic fatality.[8] An example of an explicit risk management decision was
banning cyclamates—a suspected carcinogen—in 1970.

This chapter draws attention to two perspectives on risk management,
"rational" and "populist."[9] While distilling complex and subtle arguments about managing risks into the categories of "rational" and "populist" is surely simplistic, it is still a useful starting point for illustrating
these perspectives and their differences. The rational perspective argues
that technical means, including but not limited to risk assessments, can
be used to ascertain the best public policies. Disinterested experts' views
on relative risks are much more reliable than the views of the public and
should therefore guide public policy. The public's attention, it is argued,
is too often drawn to problems that pose relatively small environmental
and public health risks compared with others. As a result, vast public
resources are devoted to reducing some risks (hazardous wastes), but relatively little to more significant ones (indoor air pollution). The populist
perspective, on the other hand, argues that this choice is the public's to
make, for better or worse. The risks that the "experts" focus on are oftentimes different from and more narrow than those that ordinary individuals believe are important. Factors like the public's dread of the risk, its
distribution, and other factors allegedly ignored by the rationalists
should take precedence. These two views are almost diametrically opposed when it comes to evaluating Superfund risks. I argue that the failure
to consider relative environmental and human health risks, benefits, and
costs in forming public policy choices can steer policies in the wrong direction, sacrificing more public health and environmental quality than is
necessary. I conclude that the two apparently irreconcilable perspectives
on risk management—rational and populist—can in fact be reconciled
with respect to Superfund, so that both attention to costs and benefits
and "populist" concerns can be met.

The "Rational" View of Risk Management

An unfortunate consequence of scarcity is that committing all of society's
resources to achieving ever greater reductions in risk would lead to bank-
ruptcy well before eliminating even environmental risks, much less those
from smoking, sunbathing, overeating, driving, climbing ladders, swimming, and countless others. As a result, society is forced to confront the
sometimes unsavory choice of which risk-reducing programs will be
funded and which will not. The choices are rarely described in those

terms, however. Governments rarely weigh explicitly the relative benefits of, say, increasing Superfund funding against an equivalent expenditure in child nutrition or other programs. This does not make the trade-off disappear, however. Whether society faces them directly or not, regulatory and expenditure policies (or lack thereof) force these social choices anyway. The "rational" perspective on risk management distills these difficult social decisions into two related issues: How should society allocate its risk-reducing resources? and How much does society want to spend on programs that reduce risks (recognizing that other demands, such as education and health care, are also important priorities)?

Allocating Risk-reducing Resources

The rational perspective argues that whatever society is willing to spend on risk-reducing programs (both in private and public expenditures) should reduce as much risk as possible. To do otherwise would be to squander resources. This principle implies that no matter what investment society chooses to make, the maximum risk can be reduced only if the *marginal* cost of risk reduction is equivalent across all such programs. Take an example of two hypothetical programs whose sole benefit is to reduce future fatalities. Suppose that one costs an additional $200,000 for every expected future fatality prevented, and another costs $10 million; shifting resources from the latter program to the former would increase the number of lives saved. (For example, redirecting $10 million from the second program to the first would save 50 lives instead of one.) Any time discrepancies like this occur—where marginal costs of risk reduction vary from one program to the next—the greatest amount of risk is not being reduced with existing resources; therefore, this occurs only when marginal costs are equivalent. The rational perspective is not an argument for trading risk reduction or lives for dollars, but rather spending dollars with the single intention of saving the most lives or averting the most risk.

Rationalists point to evidence that suggests that large discrepancies in costs per life saved are commonplace in federal regulatory programs. One study found that an Occupational Safety and Health Administration (OSHA) regulation on formaldehyde cost $72 billion dollars for each future death avoided, while a NHTSA regulation requiring passive restraints cost just $300,000.[10] A subsequent update showed that costs per future life saved ranged from $100,000 for a ban on unvented space heaters to $5.7 trillion for EPA's hazardous waste listing for wood-preserving chemicals.[11] As a result, when studies indicate that the cost per statistical life saved (CPSLS) varies widely among federal agencies, the implication is that society is not saving as many lives as possible with its present resource commitment to these programs. Shifting resources from expensive programs to the less-costly would produce far greater benefits. (An important assumption here is utilitarian: that the distribution of risk is irrelevant, or at least of secondary importance. For example, a risk of 0.000001 (one in one million) that affects 1 million people is viewed as the equivalent of a relatively high risk of 0.001 that affects one thousand people. In both cases, one person is expected to die, even though one risk is diffuse and the other concentrated. In addition, risks to children and the elderly are treated equally, as are those that are voluntary and involuntary, those that affect current and future generations, and so on. Some of these objections have spurred alternative measures, such as "quality-adjusted life years," or QUALYS, which account for both the number of years of life remaining and some measure of their "quality.")

"Rational" risk managers argue that in addition to misallocating resources, the public is excessively concerned with artificial hazards compared with natural ones. Some researchers have calculated that Americans ingest at least 10,000 times as much weight in natural pesticides as artificial pesticide residues, although far greater attention is devoted to the latter.[12] Indeed, in an attempt to limit the use of pesticides, a strain of insect-resistant celery was developed that was found to contain carcinogenic *natural* pesticides that even produced rashes on workers handling it.[13] Some scientists have also estimated that the aflatoxins in raw mushrooms and a peanut butter sandwich are 200 and 75 times, respectively, more hazardous than EDB, the banned pesticide.[14] Ronald Hart, director of the National Center of Toxicological Research, concluded, "Just because something is natural doesn't make it good, and just because something is man-made doesn't make it bad."[15] While rational risk managers would not necessarily conclude that society should stop examining the implications of using artificial pesticides (particularly on those applying the pesticides) or that mushrooms and peanut butter should be banned, they believe that these and similar studies should serve to caution against an undue fear of *every* synthetic chemical relative to natural hazards.

Rationalists extend this line of argument to what many of them view as an excessive concern for environmentally induced cancers, compared with more significant contributors like diet and smoking. In perhaps the most comprehensive and careful study of the relative importance of various causes of cancer, Doll and Peto estimated that environmental pollution accounts for approximately 2 percent of all cancers, while tobacco and diet, the bulk of the problem, cause 30 and 35 percent, respectively. (These figures represent best estimates from a wide range of plausible risks. For pollution, the range of acceptable estimates is from less than 1 percent to 5 percent. Diet has the widest range, from 10 to 70 percent, while tobacco ranges from 25 to 40 percent.)[16] Other researchers conclude that "the widespread public perception that environmental pollution is a major cancer hazard is incorrect."[17] Michael Gough has calculated that even if EPA were to eliminate all cancer risks from environmental sources, annual cancer mortality would be reduced by 1,200 to 6,600 deaths annually, or only 0.25 to 1.3 percent of all cancer deaths.[18] Several scientists caution that "it is important not to divert society's attention away from the few really serious hazards, such as tobacco or saturated fat, by the pursuit of hundreds of minor or nonexistent hazards."[19]

How Much Should Society Spend on Risk Reduction Programs?

The rational perspective maintains that the maximum risk be averted with whatever resource commitment is deemed appropriate. This takes the argument only so far, however. An even more difficult policy question—both ethically and politically—is how much society should spend to prevent negative environmental and health effects. In other words, what resource commitment is appropriate? How much should Americans spend on programs that reduce the risk of death or injury, compared with programs that improve education, health, housing, and so on?

Specifying a particular cutoff point is where policy analysts run into ethical dilemmas. The distinction is approximately that between cost-effectiveness and cost-benefit analysis: while it may be ethically justified to specify a goal of saving as many lives as possible with a given resource commitment (cost-effectiveness), specifying how much society should spend to save an additional life (cost-benefit analysis) is implicitly placing a social value on preventing a future statistical death. This requires that the benefit—preventing an additional death—be quantified for comparison with the program's costs. Several approaches to this controversial issue are discussed below.

One early, and now mostly discredited, approach to deciding how much society should spend to save a future statistical (unidentified) life employs the concept of "discounted future earnings." The idea is that an individual's contribution to society is the market value of the goods and services that person produces; summing an individual's future lifetime earnings and discounting to the present produces a single value for a lifetime's contribution. For example, an individual earning $30,000 per year and expecting to work for another thirty years has discounted future earnings (at 6 percent annually) of nearly $413,000.[20] In other words, according to this view, society should be willing to contribute a maximum of $413,000 to prevent this person's untimely death. If an individual earns more (or less) than $30,000, the discount rate used is lower (or higher), or the expected working life is greater (or less) than thirty years, then the present value of this person's future earnings would be higher (or lower). Some have even argued that a more appropriate value is an individual's net contribution to society, so that one's future consumption would be subtracted from earnings to arrive at the maximum society should spend to save a life.

The problems with this approach are obvious. People who generally earn less income (minorities, women, retirees) are considered less valuable than others. More fundamentally, one's social contribution is thought to be reflected by earnings alone: billionaires are therefore judged to be more valuable than thousands of "ordinary" citizens, and Americans and others in industrialized and oil-rich countries would be considered to be generally more valuable than individuals from developing countries. Empirically, this approach produces relatively low estimates of the value of preventing a future death, usually below $1 million for average wage earners. Although courts continue to use this approach in awarding damages, policy analysts have turned to a second method.

The "willingness-to-pay" approach is predicated on the somewhat more appealing notion that governments should spend whatever individuals would to reduce risk to themselves. At first glance, this may appear to be a somewhat ridiculous point of departure: most would spend whatever they could get their hands on to prevent their own death or that of a loved one. Yet individual and public policy decisions rarely involve such obvious and weighty decisions. Instead, they more commonly involve small changes in the future statistical probability of injury or death to unknown people. Buying a safer car does not eliminate the chance of dying in an automobile accident, it only reduces it slightly. (Some have argued that automobile safety features can cause people to drive more recklessly, limiting or even eliminating any technological safety advantages.[21]) Individuals routinely engage in risky activities, presumably because they value the rewards more than the added risks (and in certain situations, such as rock-climbing, some may even value the risk itself). Frequently, otherwise identical jobs pay a wage premium to compensate workers facing greater risk, an implicit form of the "combat pay" found in the military. This wage premium, and the belief that it is voluntarily accepted, provides the basis for empirical estimates using the willingness-to-pay method. For example, suppose that skyscraper construction workers are paid $1,000 more annually than their counterparts at ground level, because they face an additional one chance in ten thousand that they will be killed on the job in any given year. If 10,000 such skyscraper workers were gathered, we could infer that as a group they are willing to accept a total of $10 million ($1,000/worker × 10,000 workers) in exchange for the statistically certain death of one of them.[22] The implication of the willingness-to-pay approach is that governments should spend no more than these individuals would to prevent their own premature death, or in this instance invest no more than $10 million worth of safeguards to eliminate the risk.

Recent studies suggest that implicit risk compensation in the United States is in the range of $2–9 million per person,[23] although the wage premium necessary to compensate for the risk in any given job is likely to vary with family income, risk preferences, the magnitude and type of risk, whether individuals are aware of the risk, and perhaps education, sex, marital status, and other individual characteristics. (Although risk-income trade-offs vary by these characteristics, presumably this approach would produce one value to be applied to all lifesaving programs. Therefore, lives of the wealthy would not be valued more highly than the poor, young wage earners more than retirees, and so on.) In other words, Americans together on the job act as if they are willing to accept several million dollars for the chance that one of them will die. Strictly applied, regulations or lifesaving programs that cost more than, say, $9 million per life saved, generally would not be adopted without compelling justification, while regulations or programs costing less than $2 million per future life saved would be implemented. Agency discretion would perhaps be allowed for cases in between.

A final approach to estimating what governments should spend on lifesaving or risk-reducing programs is related to Aaron Wildavsky's "richer is safer" hypothesis.[24] Stated briefly, Wildavsky argues that because richer societies are observed to have lower mortality rates than poorer ones, depriving a society of wealth (such as by imposing unnecessarily costly regulations) is to deprive it of safety. Because wealth produces safety, reducing wealth reduces safety. Ralph Keeney uses the results of several studies that document the relationship between income and risk in the United States to study the impact of potentially expensive regulations.[25] Because costly regulations often effectively reduce incomes by inducing lowered output, unemployment, and reduced wages, and because poorer individuals are subjected to greater risks of mortality, then even regulations that are intended to improve safety may actually reduce overall safety. For example, if a regulation that costs $100 million annually is expected to save two lives per year, Keeney asks whether the reduced wealth—which *perhaps* prohibits people from purchasing safer cars, better nutrition and health care, and other risk-reducing benefits— poses greater social risks. Using what he describes as "very preliminary" calculations, Keeney estimates that costs in excess of $3.14–$7.25 million induce one fatality, depending on how the regulation's costs are allocated (the more costs borne by lower-income individuals, the more induced fatalities) and how the link between income and mortality is measured.[26] In other words, Keeney argues that regulations imposing costs per life saved in excess of $7.25 million may actually diminish rather than enhance safety.[27] While Keeney himself does not place too much faith in these specific numbers, proponents argue that it should caution regulators that the consideration of costs is in the best interest of society's overall safety. Consequently, the issue framed in this form most obviously illustrates the moral and political difficulty of reaching public decisions that trade lives for lives, not lives for dollars.

Where programs offer benefits beyond preventing future deaths, such as reducing accidents and injuries, improving environmental conditions, and so forth, rational risk managers similarly call for weighing benefits and costs in allocating resources. Cost-benefit analysis is the best-known method, in which individuals' willingness to pay for a project or program (the benefits) and willingness to pay to avoid it (the costs) are compared. (Weighing benefits and costs need not restrict the decision to items that can be valued in dollars, however, such as the cost of installing a scrubber; it is necessary only that the pros and cons of a policy be compared systematically in reaching a decision.) Nevertheless, the important factor for comparison with the populist perspective is that the decision need not be reached with any public participation; only the policy analyst and decision maker need to be involved. This top-down approach to decision making, where risk management decisions are made by policy "elites," has come under criticism from those advocating popular involvement in risk management decisions.

The "Populist" View of Risk Management

Those who advocate managing risks rationally argue for better risk communication and better decision making at the federal level. Some believe that public perceptions are "grounded in ignorance and divorced from reality."[28] Because the public and experts often perceive risks differently, those advocating improved risk communication believe that if the public knew what the actual risks were, they would rank risks just as risk assessors do, or at least close to it. This assumes, of course, that the preferences of risk assessors and the public are identical—it is just that risk assessors know more about, and have better technical training to understand, relative risks. Many holding this view believe (at least implicitly) that the public is hopelessly driven by the "risk of the month" syndrome, in which newsworthy "horror stories" such as Love Canal, Alar, and cyclamates drive public policy episodically. Therefore, rationalists argue, improved decisions must come from government leaders whose job in part is to best protect the public from health and ecological risks.

This approach has been met with criticisms from those sharing a "populist" perspective on risk management. Risk populists argue that "if you scratch any economist you are likely to find an underlying belief that risk is a one-dimensional concept for which there are universal measures."[29] They contend that those who wish to rationally manage risks are missing a significant part of the picture. The public is not irrational or even significantly misinformed. Instead, the public's view of risk is far more expansive than that of risk assessors and includes factors that rational risk managers ignore: the public's dread of the risk, the distribution of the risk, whether the risk is involuntary or voluntarily accepted, whether it is widespread or concentrated in a few areas, and so on. Therefore, the public's assessment of risks should no more reflect that of risk experts than should an automobile's appeal to most buyers mirror an auto mechanic's evaluation; technicians have a narrow view of what the public sees as a much larger social decision. Where rational risk managers believe the public needs to be educated about the real risks posed by various sources, populists believe it is the risk managers who have something to learn from the public. Just as with the brief review of the rational perspective, there are numerous and subtle views on this subject, which I have reduced here to the "populist" perspective. Nevertheless, all agree that risk management covers more than just the environmental and health risks involved and that "rationality" is a much broader concept as well.

A study by the National Research Council (NRC) cautions that many people on all sides of risk debates have "unrealistic expectations about what can be accomplished by risk communication."[30] Others add that "given that there is an almost evangelical zeal for and belief in risk communication as a universal panacea, there are sure to be future disappointments."[31] Risk communication cannot be expected to reduce conflicts, the NRC study argues, because of the different values and preferences individuals hold, the resulting distribution of benefits and costs, and so forth. Just because individuals agree on the facts does not mean they agree on a proper course of action. Therefore, this first criticism of rational risk management contends that simply communicating risks to lay people will not resolve conflicts. The problem is that the conflicts are not technical but social and political, and rationality is conditioned by these various incommensurable beliefs and values.

Another criticism of the rational approach argues that lay people are not utilitarian in their approach to assessing risks but rather are more concerned with avoiding the worst-case outcome[32] (referred to as the "maximin" strategy, or trying to maximize the value of the minimum or worst outcome). The utilitarian perspective considers the probability of an event occurring and its consequences: multiplying the probability by the outcome, and summing over all possible probability-outcome combinations, yields the expected value result. For example, if there is a 25 percent chance of an accident that will cause 200 deaths and a 75 percent chance of no accident, then the expected number of deaths is 50 (or 0.25 × 200, plus 0.75 × zero). Low probabilities and small consequences therefore reduce the expected value outcome, and relative risks in those instances appear small compared with others. The maximin strategy does not concern itself with all possible outcomes, however, only the worst ones. For example, risk experts argue that although there is a chance of a core meltdown of a nuclear power plant, it is so small (compared to the probability of no accident) that the public should not be worried; the expected cost, after summing the probability-times-outcome possibilities, is negligible. The maximin strategy, on the other hand, is concerned not with the great likelihood of no accident, but with the worst-case scenario, in this case a core meltdown. The public may therefore fear nuclear power more than driving (even though the latter is a much larger risk from the rational utilitarian perspective) because a nuclear power accident has much greater social significance than a driving accident. While risk rationalists look at all possible outcomes and their likelihood of happening, the public may still fear nuclear power because of the potential for catastrophic consequences, no matter how small the chance.

Populists also argue that risk rationalists are inappropriately utilitarian when it comes to the distribution of risk. Instead of ignoring who is affected by different risks, as the utilitarian rationalist approach does (a life is a life, no matter whose it is), risk populists argue that who is affected is important in managing risks. Ethical beliefs may demand an equitable distribution of risk so that no one individual or group is particularly disadvantaged or that those imposing (and perhaps profiting from) risk must have the free and informed consent of those bearing the risk (presumably with some form of compensation).[33] While these considerations are not explicitly precluded by the rational approach, neither are they incorporated. Some have tried to build equity into cost-benefit comparisons explicitly, although they are a distinct minority.[34] (Chapter 5 deals explicitly with the relationship between equity and Superfund.)

Psychologists have tried to expand the rational framework by including other factors that may explain why the public views some risks as more worrisome than risk experts do, and vice versa. The public perceives risks differently from experts not only because of the dread of catastrophe but also because some risks are involuntary rather than voluntary, some are artificial rather than natural, some have never been experienced and are unfamiliar rather than familiar, some are regularly reported in the news media, and so on. They point out that "people seem to lack the intuitions and cognitive capacity for dealing with complex, probabilistic problems [and therefore] resort to rules of thumb that allow them to reduce such problems to simpler and more familiar terms."[35] Peter Sandman has argued that an "outrage factor" best explains why the public responds to some risks that experts believe to be minor.[36] The rational and quantitative estimation of risks therefore omits many characteristics that explain the difference in the public's and experts' perceptions of the same risks.

The final and perhaps most damning criticism is that rational risk managers discount the *procedures* by which risk management decisions are made. Specifically, risk populists argue that not only are the public's views of risk left out of rational risk management decisions, but the public itself is excluded from actual decision-making processes. The process by which rational risk management decisions are made leaves no room for public participation. Risk management and risk communication are viewed as top-down procedures, in which the public is "educated" about the real risks posed by various chemicals, technologies, and so on. However, as several populists argue, "Opening a public relations office will not create public trust."[37] The effective communication of risks is viewed instead by populists as bridging both rational and populist perspectives, not treating "the cultural model as an error to be corrected."[38] Risk populists argue that policymakers usually consider three options when confronted with a dissonance between what the public and experts judge to be the most important risk problems: (1) avoiding disclosure, (2) creating an authoritative panel or commission to convince the public, and (3) convincing the public that the risk experts are right.[39] In only the last case is there any communication, risk populists point out, and even then it is a top-down strategy. Risk populists believe instead that "decisions about the reallocation of social expenditures for human well-being should be made from the bottom up, not from the top down."[40]

Not only does the rational view exclude public participation, risk populists argue that "rationality and democracy are antagonistic to one another."[41] In fact, the technocratic dissemination of risks in quantitative terms may "actually exacerbate antagonisms between . . . the culture of experts [and] . . . popular culture" because it "reduces the possibility of a dialogue between the public and elites."[42] Risk populists instead favor a system that encourages mutual learning about the two perspectives. The rational perspective is intended to operate outside the sphere of public deliberation and debate and to deny the relevance of other considerations. On the other hand, they argue that "cultural [populist] reason does not deny the role of technical reason; it simply extends it."[43] One author concludes, "Determining when a risk evaluation is rational is as much the prerogative of the people as of the experts. Science need not co-opt democracy."[44]

A (Partial) Defense of "Rational" Risk Management: Why Costs and Benefits Matter

It is one thing for critics to protest *how* risk assessments are performed and how they are used in actual policy-making. Many of these are legitimate complaints.[45] But it is quite another to reject the notion that costs, benefits, and risks should be considered in reaching public decisions. Perhaps the most useful principle that can be drawn from so-called rational risk management is not that specific means of evaluating risks are the best ones (such as the willingness-to-pay measure behind cost-benefit analysis), but that a decision-making procedure—whether conducted by elites or by the lay public—that ignores costs and benefits can lead to risk management decisions that fail to achieve agreed-upon social goals (one goal may be to most reduce environmental and health risks). Although it will become clearer that I believe that the public must be more involved in (and sometimes make) risk management decisions, there are elements of the rational approach that should be integrated into any decision-making process. Moreover, as I argue later in the chapter, to the extent that the public is more meaningfully involved in risk management decisions, the evaluation of costs and benefits—including the use of risk assessment—will become a less politically charged and more central component of environmental risk management.

Quite apart from the political and technical constraints that limit what governments can do to reduce risks, the benefit of the risky activity or chemical is a balancing criterion that should inform risk management. By themselves, risks cannot dictate appropriate public responses, nor are they ignored by lay people. No one would decide whether or not to undertake a given activity armed only with risk information, for example that there is a one in one million chance of dying. Individuals respond quite differently depending on whether the activity entails driving 150 miles in a car, living for two days in New York City or Boston, living within five miles of a nuclear reactor for fifty years, living two months with a cigarette smoker, riding a bicycle for ten miles, paddling a canoe for six minutes, or drinking a half-liter of wine, each of which has been estimated to increase one's chance of dying in any year by one in a million.[46] Just as individuals consider both the benefits and the risks involved with any given activity, politicians and regulators too should consider the benefits forgone in curtailing public risks.

Even risky products and byproducts have (some) benefits. Asbestos was manufactured to be used as a strong and durable fire retardant, not to give workers asbestosis. Hazardous wastes are not produced for their own sake but are unfortunate byproducts of many manufacturing processes. Cars were not meant to injure and kill people, but this is one result of people wanting to be somewhere quickly, comfortably, and affordably. The point is that reducing or eliminating risks usually has some negative consequences, namely forgoing the benefits of the risky activity or chemical that is curtailed. It may still be worth it for society to reduce the risk, but that does not imply that its benefits be ignored.

Costs too should be an integral part of risk management for two reasons. First, if an identical social benefit (such as reduced air pollution) can be achieved in two ways, and one costs more than the other, resources are conserved by choosing the less expensive means. For example, if a reduction in SO_2 emissions can be had by either (inexpensively) switching to low-sulfur coal or (more expensively) installing scrubbers, then resources are saved—which can be used to address other social problems—by switching fuels. Therefore, viewed as a question of *cost effectiveness*, when the benefits are identical, cost should enter the picture if only to conserve resources that reduce air pollution to be able to devote them elsewhere.

Second, costs should be weighed for the simple reason that resources are scarce. In a world where needs or desires outstrip resources, committing resources to one problem necessarily denies them to another. If some future society is fortunate enough to produce an infinite amount of natural resources, clean air, technological advances, talent, kindness, energy, and so on, trade-offs would cease to exist and cost would be irrelevant in making social decisions: individual and group needs could draw from the inexhaustible pool of resources. However, today's society is constrained in its use of resources, and spending money on improved mass transit systems or cleaning up hazardous waste sites necessarily means that fewer resources are available to fulfill other social goals.

The concept of opportunity cost—understanding what society gives up by committing resources to a particular use—is fundamental to good risk management. The costs of reducing risks can vary widely, both across risk categories and within them. For example, kidney transplants are less expensive than heart transplants, and prenatal care for disadvantaged mothers is cheaper still in terms of preventing premature deaths and illnesses. Air pollution can be reduced by installing scrubbers, switching fuels, or relocating people to less densely populated areas, each at very different costs. Banning lead in paint and sharply reducing it in gasoline was socially beneficial both because lead is a serious health hazard and because relatively cheap substitutes were available. Another example is the reduction of chlorofluorocarbons (CFCs), required under the Montreal Protocol, where semiconductor circuit boards that were once cleaned using CFCs were found to be as effectively and less expensively cleaned using a solution of soapy water, and the energy savings from new appliances may exceed the additional costs of the CFC replacements, hydrogenated CFCs. Costs matter because other valuable things can be had from cost savings.

Some argue that where saving lives and the environment is concerned, cost should not even enter the risk management picture. Respondents to a CBS/*New York Times* poll, when asked whether they agree that "protecting the environment is so important that requirements and standards cannot be too high, and continuing environmental improvements must be made regardless of cost," routinely answered in the affirmative, rising from just over 40 percent in 1981 to over 70 percent by 1989.[47] (These figures decrease markedly, however, when abstract "costs" are stated in terms of jobs lost, reduced incomes, higher prices, and other more immediate and recognizable impacts.) Samuel S. Epstein and Ralph W. Moss concur, advocating "a sharp phase-out and ultimately a ban on the manufacture, use and disposal of carcinogenic chemicals," which they claim would "reverse the cancer epidemic now striking one in three and killing one in four Americans."[48] They add that "the Delaney law is crucial in protecting children from carcinogens in food."[49] (The Delaney clause to the Food, Drug, and Cosmetic Act requires banning any food additive that poses any cancer risk.) David Doniger of the Natural Resources Defense Council calls attempts to incorporate cost into cancer risk decisions "ethically and morally indefensible."[50]

First, distinguishing a carcinogen from a noncarcinogen is significantly more problematic than those advocating a ban on carcinogens would lead one to believe. Whether or not a chemical is a carcinogen is a probabilistic statement about whether or not a particular chemical ingested in a particular way over a particular period of time by a particular individual (or, more likely, mouse or rat) is likely to lead to some form of cancer, not a definitive yes-no determination. Certainly the confidence that a substance is carcinogenic varies widely, but nevertheless it is a statement of probability, not certitude. Therefore, deciding what should be banned and what should not would surely fall prey to nonscientific determinations of carcinogenicity.

More importantly, those who take the moral "high-ground" by suggesting that cost be ignored when discussing the potential to save lives would do well to recognize that the failure to do so jeopardizes the very lifesaving potential of those resources. To believe that cost has no role is to deny scarcity and the opportunity cost of resources, which includes the ability to prevent deaths or improve the environment in other ways. If resources are devoted to replacing every chemical that is suspected to be carcinogenic with more costly alternatives, those additional expenditures cannot be used to prevent deaths from automobile accidents and other causes, to provide better education and infrastructure, reduce poverty, and meet other important social needs. Far from being morally upright, ignoring costs can actually *reduce* safety and health and the general welfare, which surely can be viewed as immoral in its own right. Balancing costs and benefits is important because the costs of increasing safety and the benefits of the activity may eclipse the benefits of reducing the risk.

Why do some environmental advocates oppose considering costs in reaching environmental and public health decisions? First, critics may believe that the opportunity cost of using resources to, say, clean up hazardous waste sites is not to serve some other legitimate social goal (such as addressing other environmental problems) but rather to squander them on inappropriate programs. For instance, some would argue that if given the choice between spending money on Superfund or the Strategic Defense Initiative (or "Star Wars"), tobacco subsidies, and grazing subsidies, Superfund is the clear winner. Philip Shabecoff, the longtime environmental reporter of the *New York Times*, makes this case clearly:

> Take, for example, Weidenbaum's [former chair of the Council
> of Economic Advisers in the Reagan administration] contention
> that society had to choose between additional tailpipe emissions
> limitations that could save twenty lives and ambulances that
> could save 500,000 lives from heart attacks. Even if his numbers
> are right . . . why would we have to make that particular choice?
> Why not choose between reducing auto pollution and reducing
> expenditures of weapons systems such as the B-2 bomber? Or
> between spending on pollution and spending on subsidies for
> tobacco or low taxes on alcohol, which significantly increase the
> incidence of heart disease and cancer and cost society many bil-
> lions in medical bills and lost productivity of workers?[51]

The idea that resources *could* be used to address other important health or environmental problems does not dictate that they *will*. It is therefore a false choice that proponents of "rational" risk management espouse.

These alternative ways to spend resources foster a healthy debate. Pitting many environmental or regulatory programs against the net benefits of prenatal care is sure to make the former pale in comparison, just as, for many, comparing the same programs with tobacco subsidies make them appear quite attractive. This argument is simply a form of cost-effectiveness analysis: putting resources where the broadly defined payoff is greatest. This debate is one that promotes the fulfillment of public priorities and forces citizens to consider which resource commitments are most important. But the fact that other questions are relevant too does not obviate the importance of asking whether environmental resources are doing the most good.

Second, with some justification environmentalists and so-called consumer advocates have argued that industry inflates the cost estimates of everything from installing passive restraints in automobiles to reducing and eliminating CFC production. Shabecoff argues that "cost-benefit analysis, properly employed, certainly could be a more rational way of allocating resources," but that "one serious flaw . . . is that the costs are easy to calculate and easily inflated, but the benefits are inevitably difficult or impossible to quantify."[52] As a result, the estimates of opportunity cost can be vastly exaggerated and do not truly reflect the much more modest resource costs necessary to address the problems at hand, yet benefits are routinely understated.

This criticism is similar to that of risk assessment: many believe that risk assessment is potentially a useful tool in deciding how to manage risks, recognizing that it is only one factor, but that risk assessments are too often manipulated to reflect not the wishes of environmentalists but those of industry. In some instances these are apt criticisms, but they are not against risk assessment and cost-benefit analysis per se but rather how the analyses are performed. This suggests that while reasonable people can disagree about how a cost-benefit analysis (CBA) is executed, it is possible for risk management and CBA to inform public debate in a less adversarial atmosphere than many current public debates.

Third, critics may believe that excessive waste exists in federal programs and that opportunity costs are really false trade-offs. It is not necessary, in this view, to trade off Superfund cleanups with pesticide controls, for example, because new initiatives can always be financed by eliminating wasteful government spending. One problem with this argument is that there is a finite amount of government waste. No matter how much one thinks there is, it is limited; at some point—when all the "waste" is eliminated—trade-offs will again be necessary. In addition, one person's waste is another's livelihood. Some consider timber subsidies to be wasteful, but entire towns in the Pacific northwest depend on the timber industry for economic survival. The same could be said of some water resource projects, farm subsidies, mass-transit subsidies, Amtrak, and a host of other distributive programs that some have argued are wasteful federal expenditures. Therefore, widely agreed upon definitions of waste may be elusive. Finally, some have argued that wastes associated with pork-barrel politics actually have important benefits that ultimately facilitate coalition-building in Congress.[53]

Lawrie Mott of the NRDC has said, "We should strive to solve all, not just some, environmental problems. To admit that we can do anything less, as comparative risk assessment necessarily does, indicates our ultimate failure to protect public health and the environment."[54] But what our failure to "solve" all environmental problems reveals instead is twofold. First, it reveals that resources are scarce, and we cannot address, much less solve, every social problem. Second, it reflects the social commitment to other concerns as well, such as AIDS, health care, education, housing, and crime. This does not indicate that the public is unconcerned about environmental protection and public health in the absolute sense. Instead, it shows that relative to other social concerns, society may not believe that public health and the quality of the environment deserve all of its resources and energy. Addressing each problem demands resources, which necessarily denies them to some other use. Advocates of comparative risk assessment do not create these conflicts. They are instead the product of scarce resources in the face of almost unlimited social needs. To ignore costs is to deceive ourselves into believing that risk reduction can be had without other social implications.

A final criticism of evaluating costs and benefits to reach policy decisions pertains to the use of discount rates to devalue future benefits. Because many government programs exact costs now in exchange for future benefits (such as building schools, roads, and dams; funding vaccine programs and national defense; and cleaning up Superfund sites and lead paint in threatened homes), cost-benefit analysts ask what the *present value* of future benefits is to compare them with the present value of costs. But since many environmental and health benefits extend far into the future, the effect of discounting, critics argue, is to trivialize future benefits by converting them into present-value terms. For example, at a discount rate of 5 percent, benefits of "x" fifty years hence translate to $0.09x$, or a 91 percent reduction in present value terms. (The present value decreases exponentially with time; the same benefit of x in one hundred years has a present value of $0.008x$, or more than a 99 percent reduction; a benefit of $1 million one hundred years hence is thus valued at only $8,000 in present value terms.)

The discount rate appears to reflect, however, the manner in which individuals prefer benefits today rather than in the future (and costs in the future rather than today.) Ask yourself: would you give up $100 today in exchange for $100 (plus an inflation adjustment) in five years? Just as markets reveal that savers need to be compensated by more than the rate of inflation to part with their money, individuals view public programs the same way. A study by Resources for the Future asked 2,600 individuals their attitudes about hypothetical programs that save lives immediately compared to those that save lives in 5, 10, 25, 50, or 100 years.[55] The results were striking. Not only did people discount programs that saved lives in the future, but they did so heavily. For example, 38 percent of respondents preferred a program that saved one hundred lives today over one that saved four thousand lives in twenty-five years, and overall a program that saved one life today was judged as worthy as a program that saved eleven lives in fifty years. The researchers also compared respondents' discount rates for money versus lifesaving programs and found that discount rates were similar and fell as the time horizon lengthened. (Discount rates were around 17 percent for a five-year horizon, and less than 4 percent for a hundred-year horizon. Moreover, individuals with high (or low) discount rates for money had high (or low) discount rates for lifesaving programs; people appear to be consistently patient or impatient.) This suggests that future benefits are not as valuable to individuals as present benefits, yet the relatively low discount rate over a hundred-year time horizon also suggests that people are not entirely selfish either, since all but the most optimistic are unlikely to believe that they will personally reap any of the benefits. Moreover, this evaluation is in a nonmarket setting, suggesting that individual discounting has nothing to do with money or markets. Therefore, critics of using discount rates need to make the case that social decisions should depart systematically from the preferences of individuals.

Is Considering Benefits and Costs "Valuing Life"?

Some claim that putting a limit on what governments can do to prevent future fatalities "ignore[s] an essential meaning of life as we commonly understand it—that each life is unique and irreplaceable."[56] These authors paraphrase an OSHA regulatory analyst as believing that "it is wrong for society to say that it will trade lives for dollars in any circumstances, wrong because of the set of meanings we attach to human lives."[57] In essence, one point argued by critics is that advocates of a balancing or trade-off approach are "valuing life" by reducing social decisions to dollars and cents.

The decision to limit expenditures on programs that could save future lives is not, however, a decision between a pile of cash and someone's life. It is a decision about how best to use scarce government resources. The "dollars" the OSHA analyst refers to are simply a metric used to denote the alternative possibilities that the resources could provide. Is it any different to describe the trade-offs as one between, on the one hand, lives saved using air bags in automobiles and $x billion and, on the other hand,

lives saved using air bags versus lives saved by spending $x billion clean-
ing up Superfund sites? The dollar comparison is simply a placeholder of
alternative opportunities, not a crass "dollars for lives" comparison.

Steven Kelman has argued that to specify a limit that society will spend
to prevent a future statistical death is to cheapen the value of life.[58] In a
sense, Kelman is right that we may cheapen that which is explicitly valued. Yet unfortunately society is left with the choice of either doing so
implicitly or explicitly. The choices society must confront over whether
to improve health and the environment in one way or another, recognizing that not every goal can be adequately addressed, is not a product of
scheming policy analysts; it is the product of scarce resources and multiple social problems that need to be acted upon. Thus, confronted with a
situation where *something* must be done (i.e., resources will be allocated
in one way or another), Kelman's ethical claim to avoid valuation is
diminished.

We kid ourselves by asserting that government policies should treat life
as priceless, for applied to public policy this implies spending whatever
resources it takes to prevent future deaths. Not only is it technically
impossible to prevent all future (even premature) deaths, but we would
recognize that at some point other social priorities (such as promoting
the *quality* of life) should take precedence. While we can individually
regard life as irreplaceable and priceless, appropriate limits are necessary
unless we deny the value of everything else those resources could provide.
This does nothing to degrade or devalue life, it only recognizes that there
are limits to what societies can do to prevent future untimely deaths. Does
our failure to set highway speed limits at five miles per hour—which
would dramatically reduce highway fatalities—suggest that our society
has made the wrong decision by valuing time and convenience more than
life?

Even discussing the notion that at some point governments can no
longer fund programs that prevent future statistical deaths is such an
anathema to current public discussion that debating what that value
should be is almost a purely academic exercise. It should do no harm to
our sense of morality to recognize that governments cannot prevent every
untimely death. And only the most zealous of economic purists would
argue that a precise cutoff "value of life" is appropriate. Government
officials naturally should consider not only benefits, costs, and risks, but
also equity (across income groups, geographic regions, and generations),
administrative feasibility, and the role of public participation in reaching
those decisions. The important point here is not that analysts should
spend a great deal of time quibbling about the appropriate "value of life,"
but rather that agencies, like individuals, should act as though cost mat-

ters and that many trade-offs are ultimately unavoidable. Consequently, while the ethical case against valuing life explicitly is a strong one, considering that these social decisions must be made anyway, is it better to hide them behind implicit expenditure and regulatory decisions, or to be explicit about appropriate resource commitments to such programs?

Whether that limit is best determined by how individuals act in market situations is another matter. Critics of economic valuations contend that individuals qua citizens behave—and should behave—differently from individuals qua consumers, and therefore governments should respond differently from the way individuals do under market conditions. In one of the better critiques of economic approaches to environmental policy, Mark Sagoff writes that individuals may vote for public transportation even though they love their cars, that others may donate money to wilderness areas they will never visit and to causes that provide them no gain (such as opposing capital punishment), and will engage in other private decisions that seem to be at odds with their public preferences.[59] Pursuing this logic, governments should not follow economists by observing individual behavior in private markets to determine appropriate public decisions. In the case of "valuing life," then, governments should not apply individual risk-benefit trade-offs to public decisions involving life-saving programs.

Few would argue that market outcomes have any external validity, to represent wisdom or common deliberation.[60] But the belief that costs and benefits should be compared has nothing to do with markets, other than that market prices *can* (but do not have to) be used to assign monetary values to costs and benefits. The relative values or "shadow prices" on goods and services produced through market exchanges is but one way to value resources. Because individuals act as though they value their own lives at about $3–9 million apiece does not mean that governments should do likewise. Part of the reason for governments is to allow us to express public preferences as citizens that we are unable or unwilling to express as consumers. This does not eliminate the need to make trade-offs in policy decisions, however. Indeed, one of the reasons for environmental, health, and safety regulation in the first place is free market inefficiency in the presence of public goods, externalities, and informational asymmetries.

To determine appropriate public values, Sagoff prefers to search for political rather than market outcomes. He rejects the results of the market process and instead accepts the results of a (presumably democratic) political process as the affirmation of American values. Sagoff argues that "the *goals* of social regulation are based in public values and are found in *legislation*" [emphasis added].[61] There remain at least two problems, however. First, because legislators are sometimes inclined to promote symbolic legislation,[62] some legislative goals are bound to conflict. Full employment (as legislated in the Full Employment Act of 1946) can conflict with pursuing stringent worker safety and environmental standards: since the costs to businesses are higher with worker safety and environmental legislation, they will be able to hire fewer workers. All are laudable social goals, but when put into practice there are inevitably trade-offs that must be, and either implicitly or explicitly are, made.

The second problem is that legislative specifics often reveal a meaner political world than legislative intention allows. To say, as Sagoff does, that "these statutes [ending legal racial discrimination, improving public safety and health, controlling pollution, and enhancing the quality of life] represented a considered moral judgment about our responsibilities to one another, to future generations, and to the environment"[63] is to ignore the influence of special interests in shaping the specifics of the legislation. Did Congress also reflect our considered collective moral judgment in protecting eastern coal miners in passing the Clean Air Act at a cost of billions of dollars, or did it instead represent the legislative influence of senators from eastern coal mining states?[64] Did the more stringent controls on new pollution sources reflect a moral judgment, or did it instead represent northeast and midwest senators ganging up on their southwestern colleagues in order to protect their aging industrial bases?[65] While most citizens endorse the broad intent of these statutes, the specifics tell another story of political manipulation, logrolling, and legislative self-interest, in short anything but a hopeful expression of the American character. Congress passes some good laws (the Voting Rights Act) and some bad ones (tobacco subsidies), just as free markets are generally considered to be good at producing and allocating some goods (paper clips) and lousy at others (pollution control). Only informed and intelligent public deliberation, and not the simple results of free markets or enacted legislation, will reveal anything like the collective social character.

Few proponents of the use of risk management or cost-benefit analysis argue that society should act solely on these results. The consideration of risks, costs, and benefits is more appropriately viewed as an input to the decision process. Cost-benefit or risk analysis is a tool, which does not necessarily co-opt democratic deliberation and replace it with the viewpoints of elites. Risk management does not imply that all policy implications should be simplified, quantified, and put into dollar terms, cramming incommensurables like public health, wetlands protection, and endangered species into a single number. Critics sometimes refer to a cost-benefit "test,"[66] as if it is a necessary threshold or hurdle to be cleared before public action is taken. The intent of cost-benefit analysis is not to say yes or no to a particular decision, but rather to inform public debate with a detailed consideration of the benefits and costs of action or inaction.

Similarly, this line of argument does *not* imply that society should avoid going to great lengths to retrieve hostages or rescue trapped coal miners or others in similar situations. In these cases, most would consider it patently offensive to even discuss costs, and appropriately so. The reason is less that human life is involved—for it is in many environmental, health, and safety decisions—than that we would be morally offended by anything less. (It could also be viewed as a manifestation of self-interest: "If I'm ever in that situation, I would want the same public response.") Moreover, many feel a greater obligation to prevent identifiable deaths than abstract future deaths. In the case of environmental, health, and safety policy, however, society sometimes ignores important and preventable risks and sometimes devotes considerable resources to trivial ones. Of course, it is fully society's right to do so. My point is that the consequences of such actions pit *ethical* arguments defending the right to breath clean air or work under safe conditions against an equally compelling claim that society should maximize risk reduction with any given resource commitment.

To believe that the costs and benefits of government actions should be compared before reaching policy decisions does not necessitate a belief in free markets or a predisposition to business interests. The underlying belief that *some* cutoff should be used to determine resource allocation is independent of one's preference for or aversion to markets. At the heart of a "balancing" approach is the simple call for the recognition of opportunity costs—what society gives up by banning a chemical, legislating zero-risk (such as the Delaney clause), building a shopping mall on former farmland, or polluting the air. The method does not urge that land and oceans be further polluted so oil is a little less expensive, that coal be stripmined to reduce electricity prices, that old-growth forests be decimated to fractionally reduce housing costs or improve the trade balance, or that shopping malls replace farms because they improve access to stores. Instead, balancing simply encourages an explicit comparison of advantages and disadvantages, including the financial, aesthetic, cultural, and distributive consequences, in short whatever people care about. If a town wants to preserve open space rather than build a new housing development, it is not the role of the policy analyst to pronounce it wrong. It is, however, the analyst's role to detail all the consequences of doing so, such as lost property tax revenues (which might be used to upgrade emergency medical services or improve schools), greater economic activity for local merchants, and other costs against the benefits of the beauty of the open space, the preservation of a long-standing local way of life, the income earned by the farmers, and so forth. The approach does not in any way discredit the value of public deliberation, seek to replace public values with private ones, or promote consumerism over the role of the citizen. It instead seeks to *inform* public debate, recognizing that it is just one facet of the decision, so that citizens know the consequences of their, and their representatives', actions. Observers are right when they say, "To substitute this [cost-benefit] way of thinking for an informed public discussion is to abdicate political responsibility."[67] I am not suggesting anything like substitution, only that the public debate be fully informed of the consequences of public actions.

Political Uses of Risk Management and Cost-Benefit Analysis

Risk management and cost-benefit analysis have suffered in the public's eye because much of their implementation coincided with, and in some ways aided, the Reagan administration's foot-dragging on environmental and other social regulatory issues. One observer has noted that in the Reagan administration, "Setting priorities was a euphemism for cutting."[68] One example of how cost-benefit analysis (CBA) has been used for political purposes is revealed in a section of the cost-benefit analysis manual issued by the Department of Transportation in 1984.[69] It recommends the following guidelines in conducting a CBA:

> For example, regarding the question of cost magnitude, over a 10-year period Alternative A may indicate benefits of $8 billion, though costing $2 billion, while Alternative B may indicate benefits of $1.5 billion, though costing $500 million. The net benefit of A is $6 billion and its benefit-cost ratio 4:1; while the net benefit of B is $1 billion and its benefit cost ration [sic] 3:1. Although A is more beneficial than B by both criteria, the decisionmaker must also weigh whether the nation or the industry can afford $2 billion in additional costs to achieve this objective, *regardless of how meritorious it is*[70] [emphasis added].

This is a rather blatant attempt by some in the Reagan administration to magnify the cost to industry beyond a consideration of the policy's social benefits. The more appropriate question is whether society can afford to forgo the sizable net benefits of alternative A in exchange for catering to industry interests by preferring alternative B.

No one disputes that CBA can be and is misused for political gain; this is just one obvious example. There are many examples of CBA systematically overestimating certain benefits at the expense of environmental and other "intangible" costs. One is the Army Corps of Engineers' historic use of discount rates that were unusually low, in the range of 2 to 3 percent, to estimate the present value of flood control benefits. Not only did the future value of flood control benefits appear larger than they would using more realistic (higher) discount rates, but environmental damage was, if even considered, relegated to footnotes and not formally considered in the final benefit/cost ratio that the corps uses to support its budget justifications. Other examples abound where industry exaggerates the costs of regulation. But there is nothing inherent in the conduct of cost-benefit analysis that leads in the direction of preferring industry interests over others. It is understandable that some have come to distrust such analyses for the way they have been abused in the past, but it makes no more sense to discard cost-benefit and risk analyses because they are sometimes misused than it does to ban baseball bats and automobiles because they too are misused. The analysis needs to be improved. Like risk assessment, cost-benefit analysis is more art than science, but it can still be improved by eliminating obvious biases like those described in the previous chapter.

Steven Kelman conducted a revealing survey of the attitudes of environmentalists, industry environmental lobbyists, and congressional staffers toward the use of economic incentives (specifically pollution taxes or charges) in environmental policy.[71] Among his findings were, first, that relatively few respondents cited the efficiency argument (that pollution reduction could be had at least cost) supporting pollution charges. Second, and most important here, Kelman finds that "proponents of charges were endorsing, in a general ideological way, 'the market' and excoriating government and bureaucrats; opponents of charges were uneasy about or hostile to 'the market' and more convinced of the necessity for the government, bureaucrats and all."[72] This pattern of proindustry interests supporting anything that sounds like "market" incentives and environmentalists opposing it—no matter how little each understands the concept—reflects the political difficulty of promoting the use of some form of a balancing approach. Because these methods are equated with free markets, opponents see CBA and risk management as promoting industry interests, when in fact these methods can be used to value whatever individuals believe is important, including environmental, aesthetic, and other values. Because CBA is based on the concept of "willingness to pay" (which is actually a combination of one's preferences and one's ability to pay), a wealthier person can reveal personal preferences more forcefully in the market than a poorer person with identical preferences. Supporters argue, in its defense, that a properly conducted CBA includes every person's values, unlike the political process where some groups' interests are underrepresented, such as those of the poor.

The view that costs and benefits are important components in making environmental and public health decisions has been incorrectly linked with political conservatives and industry interests, largely through the publicity received by the Reagan administration's attempts to use these tools for obvious political ends. Although it has been misused due to both ignorance and political calculation, the consideration of costs and benefits does not inherently favor policies that tilt in a particular direction. In some cases CBAs will endorse policies that are probusiness, and others that are proenvironment. Indeed, cost-benefit analysis was critical in EPA's decision to dramatically reduce the amount of allowable lead in gasoline.[73] In addition, CBA and risk assessment are increasingly being used to bolster the arguments of environmental groups such as the Environmental Defense Fund, the Wilderness Society, and the National Wildlife Federation. (As noted earlier, others, notably the NRDC, strongly criticize the use of CBA and risk assessment, however.) Moreover, advocates of the use of CBA are not limited to political conservatives. Cass Sunstein, to cite one example, writes in the *American Prospect*, "We need to know which risks are most severe, and we need to address these risks . . . . Cost effectiveness and cost-benefit analysis aren't just for conservatives. These should be part of the new [Clinton] Administration's credo."[74] One need not be politically conservative or antienvironment to advocate a consideration of costs and benefits in reaching risk management decisions.

Reconciling the Rational and Populist Views of Risk Management

With the possible exception of the risks from nuclear power, the public and risk experts are perhaps nowhere further from agreement than over the value of cleaning up Superfund sites. As the next chapter shows, the public views hazardous waste sites as the most serious environmental problem. Most risk experts, however, believe the environmental and health risks of most sites are relatively low. Risk populists argue that the public is the best judge: because the public demands Superfund cleanups, it is the responsibility of democratic institutions like the EPA to respond to those wishes. Rational risk managers, on the other hand, argue that Superfund's resources are excessive compared to the level of risk removed. These arguments over risk management are not primarily about the "facts" of relative environmental and health risks (such as whether radon poses a greater health threat than Superfund sites), although these too are uncertain and disputed, but are more fundamentally about defining "risks" and what action (if any) governments should take. Rationalists define risks technically: the observable ecological and health impacts of various substances. Risk populists instead view risks more fluidly, as whatever people believe them to be. It goes without saying that neither approach is uniquely objective or "rational," and neither is sufficient to guide public policy because of the significant omissions of each.

Rational risk managers ignore several components of managing Superfund site risks, including that they are involuntary, artificially created, concentrated in certain communities, of unknown character and consequence, and possibly unfairly distributed as well. The policy recommendations of risk populists, on the other hand, ignore the available evidence suggesting that the environmental and public health risks that Superfund addresses are generally quite small. Populists effectively call for EPA to abdicate any leadership role, and simply cede to the wishes of individuals. Not only is this financially impossible, since the fund is not large enough to permanently remediate every site identified, but it reduces democratic representatives to mere delegates of popular will. Individuals sometimes are uninformed about environmental and health risks (just as risk assessors and other "experts" are sometimes uninformed about other types of risks), and a naive devotion to interest-group politics can produce results that are anything but democratic.[75]

More importantly, both perspectives ignore the institutional arrangements that produce conflicts between rationalists and populists in the first place. The variety of institutional arrangements for different policy issues reduces any risk policy solutions to ad hoc choices. In certain policy debates, such as those over nuclear power, the obstacles separating the views of rationalists and populists appear to be insurmountable. With Superfund, however, these perspectives can to some extent be reconciled, although two points need to be understood. First, there is nothing irrational about the public's perception of Superfund site risks, particularly viewed in the context of the large federal government subsidies that make site cleanups appear from the local perspective to be less costly than they actually are. Second, given the best available information, the public's perception of the relative *health and environmental risks* from Superfund sites probably is wrong, although other factors may be judged to be more important in managing risks. Populist and rationalist perspectives cannot be reconciled by improving risk communication, or "educating" the public about which risks are really important. Instead, to be effective, risk communication will first require iterative communication between the public and risk assessors. In addition, risk communication—and therefore risk management—will have to be promoted in a political context in which risk assessments are viewed as honest (and fallible) evaluations of environmental and human health risks.

Risk assessments are currently viewed with skepticism by participants in policy debates in large part because of their implied policy responses. Risk assessments too often come from interest groups advocating a particular policy change, or from EPA recommendations, in the case of Superfund, that a less expensive cleanup is sufficient to address all important risks. As a National Research Council report on risk communication concluded, "Those most strongly motivated to communicate about risk are often also those with the strongest interest in the decision."[76] Risk assessments are judged by their origins: a risk assessment suggesting that a Superfund site posed only a small environmental and health risk would be viewed with much greater skepticism if it came from the Chemical Manufacturers Association than from Greenpeace, just as many would have greater confidence in an assessment indicating large site risks it if originated with the CMA. Under the circumstances in which many communities with Superfund sites find themselves—with an unknown but possibly dangerous collection of chemicals nearby that they want permanently removed—it is no wonder that risk assessments should be viewed with skepticism: they are part of the rationale for why full site remediation is judged to be unnecessary by powerful political institutions.

In addition to the dissonance between the intention of local communities and the objectives of rational risk managers, communities with Superfund sites shoulder little of the direct financial responsibility for cleaning up the sites. It is, as I argue in the final chapter, entirely appropriate that responsible parties and the federal government finance site cleanups. The problem is that from the perspective of the local community, there is no opportunity cost for a permanent, "gold-plated" cleanup. Why spare any expense if someone else is footing the bill? To reiterate my position above, this is not simply a trade-off between money and health threats, but between health threats of Superfund sites compared with other hazardous waste sites as well as other environmental contaminants; saving money on remediating one Superfund site can free those resources to address other more serious sites or environmental hazards. This is no fault of the local communities involved; it is perfectly understandable—even "rational"—to expect and demand permanent cleanups, given the institutional arrangements surrounding Superfund. Under these conditions, it would be foolish to expect that risk assessments would be viewed as helpful, since the only "help" they could provide would be to explain why some risks are not as large as the communities believe. No matter how large the risks, communities understandably want the wastes permanently removed or treated.

Making risk management decisions more meaningful for Superfund (and all other environmental and health problems) will entail changing the institutional arrangements that create or at least foster the conflict already present between risk rationalists and populists, communities and EPA, responsible parties, and so on. As several authors appropriately concluded about risk management, "The problem is not public ignorance or irrationality but the adversarial nature of the social, institutional, legal, and political systems of risk management in the United States."[77] I do not pretend to have an institutional solution for reconciling disparate views over how most kinds of risks should be managed. However, I agree with Susan Hadden's assessment that "although in one sense the role of government is limited to providing the information, a more realistic description of this kind of ['right to know' legislation] recognizes that government must also create or support institutions for participation and decisionmaking that will help citizens make use of their new information."[78]

Superfund is a program that can accommodate both rational and populist perspectives through institutional redesign. In the recommendations of chapter 9, I suggest that because Superfund site risks are geographically isolated (not necessarily small-scale, but not global either), a substantial portion of the current Superfund should be allocated to allow local communities or states to make risk management decisions themselves. However, these communities or states would be permitted to allocate Superfund resources to other remedial environmental problems if they so chose. This would allow individual citizens to make important risk trade-off decisions and would permit risk assessments to enter the decision-making process with less political advocacy than now takes place. The ideally iterative and informational role of risk assessment would flourish far better under new institutional arrangements than with top-down risk management advocated by others. If given greater control, individuals will (I think) use risk assessments to inform decision making to a far greater extent than at present. Risk assessments would be used to compare the risks at one Superfund site with those at another, a Superfund site versus a radon remediation program, and so on, and would therefore be judged to be far more pertinent to the decision at hand than they are in the adversarial setting in which risk assessments are debated.

The road to greater public acceptance and improved role in risk decisions (and therefore better decisions) starts with allowing the public greater local control over risk decisions where appropriate (such as where significant environmental spillovers or externalities are not present). The public needs to be involved in risk management decisions, yet the public must accept the responsibility of wrong decisions as well. In the case of Superfund, if the public believes that cleaning up a Superfund site is more important than removing lead paint from public or private buildings, when all indications are that lead is the greater threat, then that community will suffer the consequences. The more positive implication is that the community will see directly the gains from risk management decisions that tackle what it believes to be the most important risks. Moreover, the state or community will see the importance of considering cost directly: spending money to "gold-plate" a Superfund cleanup makes less money available for other environmental and public health priorities. Only under new institutional arrangements can risk management follow former EPA Administrator William Reilly's vision for EPA: "Guided by the best information we can find on the relative risks of various environmental problems, we *are* thinking carefully about where our limited discretionary resources can most effectively be spent."[79] Battles pitting the public against large, technically armed political institutions will not promote the proper management of risks. Instead, where possible, the public needs to be involved meaningfully to make risk management more effective and more democratic.

2 Efficiency, Equity, and Distributive Politics

4 Is Superfund an Effective Use of Environmental Resources?

Regardless of one's views on the merits of the "rational" or "populist" perspectives on risk management, it is important to understand the consequences of managing risks in a particular way. Whether one defines "risk" narrowly to include only identifiable human health impacts or more broadly to include the public's dread of the risk, whether it is artificial or natural, and so forth, the object is to best reduce risks with available resources, which will always be finite. How do Superfund site risks compare with other environmental and health risks? In broad comparison with other identified and controllable risks, Superfund sites probably present relatively small environmental and public health threats. (I say "probably" because the conclusions remain tentative.) Even when the comparison is limited to other *remedial* environmental and health problems—here restricted to radon, lead, and asbestos—the environmental and public health risks from Superfund sites appear to be modest. A Superfund specialist concludes that "90 percent of mainstream . . . scientists do not regard chemical hazardous wastes as a major long-term environmental health threat, certainly not of the magnitude of some other problems . . . This [difference with public opinion] forms a fundamental public policy problem."[1] In addition, several problems in allocating resources *within* the program suggest that resources now channeled to Superfund are not reducing environmental and public health risks as much as they might. While this does not immediately lead to the conclusion that Superfund monies ought to be rechanneled to other problems, it does raise concerns both about whether Superfund expenditures are appropriate (compared with other problems) and whether current resources devoted to Superfund are being best spent.

Comparing Superfund Sites with Other Environmental Risks

The U.S. Environmental Protection Agency has evaluated the relative risks of a wide range of environmental problems, including Superfund sites, to establish a framework for priority-setting practices within the agency. The first report, *Unfinished Business*, published in 1987, examined the impact of thirty-one environmental problem areas, generally corresponding to existing programs or statutes, including industrial water pollution, oil spills, indoor air pollution, nuclear power plant accidents, toxic air pollutants, and Superfund and RCRA sites. Risks were evaluated across four risk categories: cancer risk, noncancer health risk, ecological risk, and welfare effects.[2] No weights were assigned to any risk category, nor were risks aggregated across categories (such as adding cancer and ecological risks). Over the course of nine months, the group of seventy-five experts and managers, drawn from all EPA programs, examined studies and documented evidence of the risks posed by various environmental problems. The evaluation was not a formal risk assessment of the type described in chapter 2, however. There was no independent research, and substantial gaps in the scientific literature were filled with the experts' own evaluations and informed judgments. The report concludes, however, that "the participants feel relatively confident in their final relative rankings."[3]

Unfinished Business concludes that EPA's priorities do not correspond to the experts' evaluations of risks. Experts identified high risks where EPA effort was low in controlling indoor radon, other indoor air pollution, stratospheric ozone depletion, and global warming. The report points to several cases where EPA expends great effort, but where its panel of experts held that risks are moderate or low. These include Superfund and RCRA sites, underground storage tanks, and municipal nonhazardous waste sites. EPA's priorities were found to more closely mirror the public's perception of risks than the beliefs of experts.

Superfund sites specifically were ranked eighth (out of twenty-nine) in terms of cancer risk, relatively low risk in noncancer health risks, medium in ecological risks (fifth out of six groupings), and medium in welfare effects. While the group admitted to considerable uncertainty in rendering the final rankings, the moderate-to-high estimated cancer risk was based on an extrapolation from thirty-five sites to their estimate of twenty-five thousand sites in the United States, over twenty times as many sites as currently on the National Priorities List, and more than twice as many as OTA estimates may ultimately need to be cleaned up. As such, the total cancer risk may be substantially overstated due to inflated exposure estimates, although they correctly point out that at some sites "individual risk can be relatively high."[4] The study concludes that "total [Superfund] health impacts do not appear to match public concerns," although it adds that "the importance of this problem, especially as it relates to public concerns, may not be fully reflected in the risk categories studied in this project."[5] Using one example, an EPA official (not connected with the *Unfinished Business* study) said, "I don't think that there is anyone in the scientific community that will argue that these risks are greater than for different types of air pollution."[6]

This path-breaking study was followed by similar studies conducted by regional EPA offices, which reached similar conclusions. A follow-up national study, commissioned by the newly arrived EPA Administrator, William Reilly, was published by EPA's semi-independent Science Advisory Board (SAB) in 1990.[7] Increasingly, the agency was coming to believe that environmental priorities were being shaped excessively by, as one EPA official said, "what the last phone call from Capitol Hill or the last public opinion poll had to say."[8] Importantly, while *Unfinished Business* was conducted mostly using in-house EPA employees, the SAB study team was comprised mostly of prominent social and natural scientists, thus lending the report greater scientific credibility. The process was not without controversy, however. The subcommittee studying health effects refused to rank problems because of the lack of data and because of studies that used inconsistent assumptions; instead the group listed eleven problems they believed would rank high using any criteria. Perhaps most importantly, however, the group sanctioned the use of comparative risk assessment in setting environmental priorities.[9]

The SAB's report, *Reducing Risk*, began with a critique of the methodology and conclusions of *Unfinished Business (UB)*, yet continued to emphasize the importance of comparing relative risks in order to direct future environmental policy. *Reducing Risk* questioned some of *UB*'s economic assumptions, the accuracy of human health risk data, and the 31 categories *UB* investigated. Instead of continuing *UB*'s taxonomy of environmental problems, which the SAB study said lacked "a consistent basis for comparison" and failed to include problems like habitat loss and declining genetic diversity, *Reducing Risk* examined risks to "ecology and welfare" and "human health."[10] However, instead of ranking the risks of all environmental problems, the Ecology and Welfare Subcommittee grouped problems into high, medium, and low categories, while the Human Health Subcommittee only identified problems for which existing data suggested that the risk may be high.[11] High-risk problems in ecology and welfare include habitat alteration and destruction, loss of biological diversity, stratospheric ozone depletion, and global climate change, while high human health risks include ambient air pollutants, worker chemical exposure, indoor pollutants, and drinking water pollutants (largely from problems in plumbing, such as lead pipes or solder).[12] Although Superfund sites were not ranked specifically, groundwater pollution—a chief concern of residents near such sites—was ranked a low-risk problem by the Ecology and Welfare Subcommittee. Like *Unfinished Business*, the 1990 report recommends that environmental protection efforts be based on reducing risk. Unlike *UB*, however, *Reducing Risk* appropriately cautions EPA to focus as much attention on reducing ecological risks as it does on reducing human health risks and recommends that the agency emphasize pollution reduction rather than expensive cleanups to reduce risk.[13] This emphasis on prevention rather than remediation was shared by EPA Administrator William Reilly, although publicly he was careful to avoid any criticism of Superfund or other remedial programs.[14] It is also shared by some environmentalists. John H. Adams, executive director of the Natural Resources Defense Council, has said, "Nothing scores better on the cost-benefit scale than prevention, and nothing protects health and ecology so completely."[15] Neither report was expected to change EPA policy in the short term. The intention of *Unfinished Business* and *Reducing Risk* was in large part, in the words of an EPA official, "an educational role that, frankly, we are just beginning to play."[16]

The conclusions of both studies suggest that Superfund site risks are small compared with other environmental problems. In addition, the wealthy nations of the world (including the United States) drew up a set of environmental priorities for financing cleanups in central and eastern Europe, which reached conclusions similar to those of *Unfinished Business* and *Reducing Risk*. Called the Environmental Action Plan, the report rates air pollution as the most serious health hazard, including lead, sulfur, and particulates; drinking water is second, and the third priority is addressing irreversible natural damages. Remedial measures such as cleaning up hazardous waste sites and rivers, decontaminating military sites, and so forth were given no priority with the limited funds available.[17]

Superfund Site Risks

The results of *Unfinished Business* and *Reducing Risk* are borne out by what data are available on individual Superfund site risks and the number of people exposed. Population exposures at a range of Superfund sites have been estimated in two studies. A follow-up study by EPA's region 1 (Boston), *Unfinished Business in New England*, sampled 13 regional sites and found that the median number of people exposed to the chemicals at each site was 250 (the maximum was 1500), with site-specific individual risk estimates—based on maximum-likelihood, not conservative, assessments—ranging from 1.3×10^{-2} (0.013) to 1.3×10^{-6}. A second study by the Agency for Toxic Substances and Disease Registry (ATSDR, in the U.S. Department of Health and Human Services) found that 4.1 million people lived within a one-mile radius of the 725 sites they examined, an average of 5,655 per site.[18]

Combining the available risk data with exposure data and costs of site remediation produces an admittedly rough estimate of the cost per statistical life saved (CPSLS) at Superfund sites. Since risk and exposure estimates vary substantially from site to site, I use the reported upper and lower bounds of each to calculate the CPSLS. For high-risk sites, where risks (using the *UB in New England* study) are in the neighborhood of 0.013, with between 250 and 5655 people exposed, the expected number of people contracting cancer over their lifetimes is between 3.25 and 73.52. If remedial efforts cost on average $25 million per site, then the CPSLS is between $340,000 and $7.7 million, generally well within what individuals reveal themselves to be willing to pay to avoid a future statistical death and consistent with other regulatory costs. For low-risk sites, however, where individual site risks can drop below 1.3×10^{-6} (arguably, some risks approach zero), the number of people expected to contract cancer over their lifetimes is between 0.00735 and 0.000325, translating to a CPSLS of between $3.4 billion and $76.9 billion. *UB in New England* found that the median risk of contracting cancer was 1.3×10^{-5}, which represents a CPSLS of $340 million to $7.7 billion, less cost-effective than virtually any regulation, environmental or otherwise, issued in the United States. The implication of these risk estimates is that remediation of some Superfund sites is reasonably cost effective, while cleaning up low-risk/low-exposure sites is an extremely expensive way to prevent future cancers.[19] One former EPA official concluded that with Superfund cleanups, "we are aiming cannons at gnats."[20]

These are only approximations of the risks posed by Superfund sites, but a number of conservative assumptions were used. First, the estimates assume that site remediation is permanent and removes all risk from the site, contrary to the results of several studies that have criticized EPA's cleanup decisions as impermanent and insufficient to reduce risks (see chapter 1). Second, I assume that people would contract cancer immediately rather than far into the future (as is more likely). Since most individuals exposed will not contract cancer until much later in life, some will die from other causes in the interim, and studies have shown that individuals substantially discount future deaths.[21] Moreover, future medical technologies may render cancer and other diseases less life-threatening than today. For these reasons, it is quite likely that the CPSLS will exceed the numbers calculated above.

Two assumptions point in the opposite direction, however. First, I assume that cancer risks are the only risks, when presumably noncancer health and ecological risks are sometimes present as well. However, EPA's studies have indicated that these generally are smaller concerns at most Superfund sites (although ecological risks are significant at some). Furthermore, other possible benefits of remediating Superfund sites have not been counted, possibly including improved visibility, removal of an eyesore, nonuse benefits to people not directly exposed to Superfund site risks, and the deterrence of future illegal dumping. Other costs, however, such as cleanup workers' exposure to the harmful chemicals, the danger of transporting the hazardous wastes, and the risks posed by those chemicals where they are finally dumped (if not safely treated on-site), similarly are not included. (At some sites, such as the large Vertac site in Arkansas, environmentalists believe that some treatment techniques—particularly incineration—are more dangerous than storing the wastes.[22]) In addition, the assumed exposures are only for current residents. If the site is not cleaned up, other individuals may move to the area and be exposed to the site's hazards. On the other hand, local residents may move from the area to avoid the hazard, thereby reducing current and future exposure.

Although the net effect of these complicating factors is unknown for any particular site, the CPSLS numbers calculated above are probably understated. Even if these estimates are wrong by an order of magnitude in underestimating the risks, it is extremely difficult to project a scenario in which the cleanup of some Superfund NPL sites is cost-effective. The *UB in New England* report found that even after accounting for all 1570 identified regional sites, only 59 of which were on the NPL, the estimated risk for all New England sites was just four cancers over a seventy-year period. I do not intend to minimize the pain and suffering for those expected four people in New England who contract cancer, nor their families and friends, from exposure to Superfund sites. To differing degrees, virtually all Superfund sites pose *some* risk—sometimes large but frequently small—to surrounding populations. Nevertheless, while the data are far from conclusive, the results indicate that other environmental and public health problems pose far greater risks than many Superfund sites. Consequently, channeling excessive resources to remediating Superfund sites may mean that other more important public health and environmental problems are denied attention. The resources required to eliminate those four cancers could instead be deployed to eliminate far greater cancer threats in other programs. As one environmental engineer concludes, "Does it make sense to spend millions of dollars cleaning up a site that only has a tenth of an ounce of contamination? . . . All we're doing in most cases is throwing money at a problem without improving public health or the environment."[23] A former EPA official told me, "You have to hope that over time the weight of professional opinion will start bringing people around . . . and at some point, newspaper reporters will be embarrassed about writing scare stories about Superfund sites."[24]

As a means of comparison, table 4.1 shows the number of exposures at any given Superfund site necessary to justify cost-effective cleanups for different levels of risk. For example, if the individual site risk is calculated to be 10^{-4}, then at least 25,000 people must be exposed to that level of risk to make a $25 million cleanup cost-effective (where the cost per statistical life saved is $10 million, at the upper extreme of most studies). The table illustrates two points. First, individual risk information is insufficient to make policy decisions; if enough people are exposed to relatively low risks, remediation is cost-effective. In addition, for individual site risks below 5×10^{-4}, it is unlikely that there are sufficient exposures to justify a $25 million remedial action. While a strong argument can be made that some individuals should not be subjected to high site risks (such as fifty people exposed to a 0.05 risk), a compelling argument can be made to provide compensation (up to $500,000 per person in this case) and restrict access to the area rather than remediating the site. For sites where fifty to one hundred people are actually exposed to site risks, many may prefer compensation of $250,000 to $500,000 per person to relocate rather than remediating the site, particularly when individuals doubt that all risks will be eliminated by a Superfund site clean up.[25] Indeed, one environmentalist I interviewed suggested approvingly that buying out property owners is not as costly as remediation in many instances. Moreover, Hugh Kaufman of EPA has said that when a Superfund site is near a populous area, "the best thing we can do is evacuate people if they want, then put up a fence and a flag that says stay away."[26] Where remedial efforts are not cost-effective (when the costs per person affected are even higher), the latter argument becomes that much more compelling.

Comparing Superfund Sites with Other Local Remedial Environmental and Health Risks

To place Superfund site risks in better perspective, it is useful to compare hazardous waste site risks with those of other environmental or public health problems whose effects are *local* and require *remedial* action. Like Superfund sites, radon, lead, and asbestos are environmental hazards whose cleanup would require local, site-specific remedial action, whose cleanup benefits are concentrated at that site, and which potentially affect millions of Americans. Not only are the environmental and health risks

Table 4.1   Combinations of Risk and Exposures Necessary for Cost-Effective Cleanups

Individual Site Risk	Minimum Number of Necessary Exposures
5×10^{-1} (0.5)	5
1×10^{-1} (0.1)	25
5×10^{-2} (0.05)	50
1×10^{-2} (0.01)	250
5×10^{-3} (0.005)	500
1×10^{-3} (0.001)	2,500
5×10^{-4} (0.0005)	5,000
1×10^{-4} (0.0001)	25,000
5×10^{-5} (0.00005)	50,000
1×10^{-5} (0.00001)	250,000
5×10^{-6} (0.000005)	500,000
1×10^{-6} (0.000001) (one chance in one million)	2,500,000
5×10^{-7} (0.0000005)	5,000,000
1×10^{-7} (0.0000001)	25,000,000
5×10^{-8} (0.00000005)	50,000,000
1×10^{-8} (0.00000001)	250,000,000

Note: "Cost-effective" is defined as a cost per statistical life saved of $10 million or below; a present value cleanup cost of $25 million is assumed.

from these problems most likely greater than those from many Superfund sites, but the federal policy response to these other three environmental hazards has been dramatically different as well. As in all cases, the results of risk assessments reported below are subject to substantial uncertainties; point estimates should be interpreted in that context.

Radon

Radon is a naturally occurring inert gas derived from uranium in the earth's crust. Although radon's half-life is less than four days, because it is inert it is quickly inhaled and exhaled with little damage to the lungs. The problem is that the radon decays and produces progeny—such as lead or polonium—which are not inert. Because progeny can stick to the lung's lining, they can cause serious lung damage through their own decay.[27] Radon is virtually inescapable, although outdoor air contains on average only about 0.25 picocuries per liter (pCi/l).[28] The health problems associated with radon, however, concern not background concentrations in outdoor air—for which little can be done—but indoor air. EPA's *Unfinished Business* and subsequent studies conclude that indoor radon is one of the most serious public health risks, tied for first place in cancer risk (with worker exposure to chemicals) and ranked fourth out of thirty-one overall. EPA originally estimated that upwards of 21,000 lung cancers annually were attributable to radon, although it has subsequently lowered its estimate to 16,000 (compared with a total of approximately 130,000 deaths in the United States from lung cancer annually).[29] Still, compared with other environmental risks, radon is probably a prolific killer.

The problem of radon is not uniform across the United States, however. Outdoor concentrations can vary by more than an order of magnitude (Alaska and Hawaii contain on average 0.03 pCi/l, while parts of Colorado contain 0.76 pCi/l), and indoor concentrations vary by more than three orders of magnitude. The reasons for the greater variability of indoor radon are both that structures trap radon to different degrees and that the rate of soil entry varies as well.[30] Radon becomes trapped in cellars and other poorly ventilated parts of the house, enabling it to decay into the harmful progeny. Radon can enter the home through private wells (municipal wells are rarely a problem, since the radon dissipates into the air before it enters the home), through cracks in cinder blocks or a concrete, dirt, or stone foundation, and sometimes from building materials such as large stone or brick fireplaces.[31] As a result, indoor radon concentrations in one building may vary significantly from those in other buildings in the same neighborhood. In addition, concentrations vary throughout the day (early morning is the highest), by the level of the house (basements have the highest concentrations), and other factors.[32] Improvements in home energy efficiency, such as new insulation and ventilation techniques, have reduced the amount of air exchange and thus increased potential indoor radon concentrations. The EPA recommends that action be taken if measured levels exceed 4 pCi/l, with increasing urgency at levels exceeding 200 pCi/l, the highest observed concentrations in homes.[33] Average indoor concentrations have been estimated at about 1.5 pCi/l, and EPA estimates that an annual exposure to 4 pCi/l of radon is comparable in risk to two hundred chest x-rays per year.[34]

EPA's radon risk estimates have been subject to controversy, owing mostly to the fact that no convincing epidemiological study has documented the dose-response function. The evidence linking radon with lung cancer relies on data collected on uranium miners of the Colorado Plateau exposed to high concentrations of radon, but also to nitrous oxides and mineral dusts. Moreover, many were smokers, and the evidence suggests that smokers are most affected.[35] Thus, separating the independent effects of radon and extrapolating from high to low doses (using linearity assumptions) has confounded scientists' efforts to document risks. One critic of what he considers EPA's overemphasis on radon programs concludes, "EPA has no solid evidence that low levels of radon cause lung cancer, especially in nonsmokers."[36] EPA representatives have countered these criticisms by stating "The radon policy of EPA . . . reflects scientific consensus developed through review of the extensive epidemiologic data on thousands of underground miners exposed to a broad range of radon concentrations," and "there is strong evidence that radon causes lung cancer in humans."[37] Putting the issue in broader perspective, however, Jonathan Samet, professor of Medicine at the University of New Mexico, has stated, "The scientific basis for concern [with radon] is more certain than for most environmental pollutants, the magnitude of the risk is large, and indoor radon can be measured and mitigated."[38]

Unlike Superfund sites, the public does not appear to consider radon to be an important public health or environmental threat. Radon in homes and other buildings was rated next to last in twenty-nine categories of environmental problems in a 1990 public opinion poll; only 17 percent of respondents considered it "very serious," down four percentage points from a similar poll two years earlier.[39] (Other indoor air pollutants fared little better, with only 22 percent of respondents rating chemical cleaners, tobacco smoke, aerosol sprays, asbestos, and so on as very serious problems.[40]) Even in states where the radon problem is particularly severe, such as New Jersey, residents have been slow to react to the warnings issued by public officials. A state study estimated that at least 320 New Jerseyans contract lung cancer annually from radon exposure, compared with 31 from both active and inactive hazardous waste sites, 10 from drinking water contaminants, and 184 from pesticide residues. But only 10 percent of New Jersey residents have had their homes tested for radon, even though the tests cost as little as $10, and free tests are available from the state to confirm unusually high radon levels. In stark contrast to hazardous waste sites, one state representative commented, "The reaction from the public has been one of overwhelming apathy and skepticism."[41]

The cost of identifying and partially remediating radon contamination has been estimated at $20 billion over thirty years, with an estimated twenty-five hundred cases of cancer averted annually.[42] This translates into an average expected cost per future life saved of $267,000, below that of many federal regulations, far lower than the average Superfund site cleanup, and comparable in cost-effectiveness to remediating only the most hazardous Superfund sites. Costs to meet the goal of the Toxic Substances Control Act's (TSCA, Public Law 100-551) 1988 amendment to make indoor air "as free of radon as the ambient air outside of buildings," however, are estimated to be between $700 billion and $1.12 trillion. This has been estimated to reduce annual radon lung cancer deaths by 11,000 cases per year, at an average cost per statistical life saved of $3 million (still reasonable, compared with other environmental regulations or remedial efforts, although it is difficult to conceive of a public effort to reduce indoor air pollution at anywhere near that cost).[43] It is important to note that, just as with Superfund, cost-effectiveness varies dramatically from site to site, as does the cost of remediation. Targeting radon policies to areas with the highest known concentrations, some of which reach levels one hundred times the national average, could dramatically improve the cost-effectiveness of any federal radon program.

Federal radon policy to date has been largely aimed at informing the public about the risks of radon and recommending precautionary and corrective actions for residences. Title IV of Superfund's 1986 reauthorization requires EPA to establish a radon and indoor air quality program, and the 1988 amendments to TSCA not only established the indoor radon goal mentioned above, but authorized technical and financial assistance to states to develop testing and mitigation programs, train personnel, and distribute public information, and required EPA to study radon levels in schools and federal buildings. A House report did recommend establishing construction standards for builders to control radon in new buildings,[44] but significant opposition from builders and the real estate industry hastened its defeat in conference. EPA has been accused of conducting an "alarmist—and often misleading or inaccurate—public information effort"[45] to reduce exposure to radon, but never was a federally financed cleanup program like Superfund seriously contemplated by Congress, ostensibly because of delicate privacy issues of federal intervention into homeowners' affairs.

The federal EPA insists that because radon is a local problem, solutions should rest with state and local governments so as to be tailored to local conditions, even though for Superfund—itself largely dealing with local problems—the federal response has been markedly different.[46] It has been argued that because of privacy, the EPA cannot require homeowners to remediate their own radon problems (although EPA has proposed regulating the allowable radon levels in tap water under the Safe Drinking Water Act,[47] and has issued proposed voluntary guidelines for builders to follow in constructing new houses).[48] While true on its face, there would be no violation of privacy by instituting cost-effective subsidies or grants to homeowners to test their houses (targeted to houses or areas known to contain high radon concentrations, say those above 20 pCi/l) and perhaps to finance remediation where radon levels are high and the resident's ability to pay is insufficient. There are at least two possible alternative explanations for why radon has received so little federal funding compared with Superfund, both of which have little to do with the public health effects or the local nature of the problem. First, radon is odorless and invisible, lacking the visual (and therefore television news-worthy) impact of oozing hazardous waste drums. Second, there is no easily identifiable constituency to blame for the presence of naturally oc-curring radon, unlike the chemical and petroleum industries that contrib-uted directly to hazardous waste sites.

Lead

Like radon, lead is a geographically concentrated health hazard that poses significant risks, especially in children. Dr. James Mason, assistant secretary for health at the Centers for Disease Control (CDC), has called lead poisoning "the most common and societally devastating environ-mental disease of young children in the United States,"[49] and "the number one environmental poison for children."[50] Highly elevated blood lead lev-els (greater than 80 micrograms per deciliter (μg/dl) can cause convul-sions, coma, and death in children.[51] While low blood lead levels (10–15 μg/dl) in children do not cause noticeable symptoms, they can signifi-cantly impair intellectual and neurobehavioral development.[52] Based on several recent studies, the CDC has concluded that there is strong evi-dence that low lead levels (10 μg/dl) in children have a negative effect on the development of I.Q., hearing, the nervous system, and physical stature.[53] The results in children are often learning, developmental, and sometimes behavioral problems.[54] Children appear to be at greater risk than adults for several reasons: their developing neurological systems are more susceptible; they have more day-to-day contact with soil and are also more likely to eat paint chips; their bodies absorb a higher propor-tion of lead relative to body weight; and they tend to have poorer nutri-tion, which increases lead absorption levels.[55] There is also concern for adults. EPA classifies lead as a class B2 human carcinogen (some evidence of tumors in animals at very high exposure levels; no evidence in hu-mans). There is evidence that it increases blood pressure in adult men, and pregnant women can transfer lead to the fetus.[56]

Many factors contribute to the problem of elevated blood lead levels: lead-based paint, lead in dust and soil, airborne lead,[57] lead-contami-nated drinking water, and lead in food.[58] Of these, there are two primary ways in which lead-based paint contributes to elevated blood lead levels in children. The most common exposure route for children is lead in house dust and soil, which enters children's systems through normal hand-to-mouth contact.[59] Not all the lead in soil and dust is a result of lead-based paint, however. For example, a great deal of lead in soil is thought to be the result of emissions of lead used in gasoline, up to five million metric tons.[60] There is also some evidence to suggest that lead-contaminated outdoor soil contributes to the problem of lead in house dust.[61] A less common form of exposure for children is eating lead-based paint (by either eating chips that have fallen on the ground or gnawing on painted objects).[62] The childhood disease "pica," a tendency to eat nonedible objects, is thought to be the most frequent cause of children eating paint, which itself produces highly elevated levels of lead in the blood of children.

The problems of lead-based paint are widely distributed, potentially affecting millions of households with children, but the problem of lead poisoning has been shown to be distributed disproportionately among racial minorities.[63] Adjusting for nonmetropolitan areas, the CDC estimated that three to four million children nationwide have blood lead levels in excess of 15 μg/dl.[64] EPA Administrator William K. Reilly estimated in 1991 that 15 percent of U.S. children have levels above 10 μg/dl.[65] It is estimated that there were eighty thousand cases of severe lead poisoning (blood lead levels above 40 μg/dl) among children in 1980.[66] One study estimated that up to 560,000 children in California between ages 1 and 6 were in danger of significant health effects from lead exposure—including neurological and behavioral impairment—and the federal government further estimates that there are 400,000 cases annually of newborns with toxic lead levels.[67]

The CDC argues that a successful effort to eliminate childhood lead poisoning must address and remove the primary sources of lead in the environment of children. Since lead-based paint is considered to be "the most common source of high-dose lead poisoning" and is also thought to be a large contributor to the overall elevation of lead blood levels in children, the CDC argues that complete abatement of lead-based paint should be "a high priority."[68] Several methods exist to reduce lead-based paint hazards in homes. Traditional abatement methods have typically consisted of scraping away peeling paint at a level up to four or five feet (the height a child can reach). While this is less expensive, it is thought to be an ineffective way to deal with the problem, since it may create more lead dust, and there is some evidence that it has little effect in lowering blood lead levels in children.[69] Other abatement methods may prove more effective. Paint can be removed (through scraping or chemical means) and replaced; it can be covered with acrylic-type coatings (encapsulation); and in some cases paint on walls can be enclosed underneath some sort of covering (enclosure). The long-term durability and effectiveness of encapsulation is unknown (there has not been sufficient time to study its long-term effectiveness), although it is considered to be an effective short-term abatement method.[70] But because each is a relatively new technique, the overall effect of these abatement methods on blood lead levels is unknown. Both HUD and EPA have undertaken studies of different abatement methods and their relative effectiveness.[71]

There is evidence that proper abatement can be beneficial, however. Dr. Mason of the CDC argues that "childhood lead poisoning is entirely preventable."[72] Moreover, a recent study suggests that the effects of even moderate lead poisoning are partly reversible (measured by improved test scores) if blood lead levels are reduced.[73] If care is taken to avoid high levels of lead dust in the process, abatement (sometimes coupled with one-time medical care) can significantly lower blood lead levels in children living in treated homes.[74] The costs of these abatement methods can vary considerably. For abatement of low-priority homes (where paint is intact and dust levels are low), removal and replacement costs an average of $7,700; encapsulation costs an average of $5,500. Abatement is more expensive in high-priority homes (those with peeling paint, high levels of dust, and so on): removal and replacement costs on average $11,900; the average cost of encapsulation is $8,900.[75] But these average costs overstate the economic costs because they do not allow for varying levels of paint. In fact, most (54 percent) homes with lead-based paint could be treated by either encapsulation or removal for less than $2,500 per home.[76] Of the high-priority homes, 24 percent (encapsulation) to 26 percent (removal) could be treated for less than $2,500. Another 20 to 23 percent could be treated for between $2,500 and $5,000, while between 9.2 percent and 15 percent of homes will require more than $25,000.[77] Added costs include those for testing for lead paint in homes, which can average $375 per unit.[78] However, demographic data can be used to target high-risk areas before actual testing or remediation begins.[79] Approximate estimates of the annual cost of testing and treating all older homes are $36 billion for encapsulation and $50 billion for removal. Treating only priority units would cost approximately $22 to $28 billion; confining action to those homes with small children, the cost is expected to range from $8 to $10 billion.[80]

The CDC conducted a cost-benefit analysis comparing the costs of treating all pre-1950 lead-painted homes with the benefits of decreased medical and education costs and increased lifetime earnings. Although the study notes that the benefit calculations most likely understate actual benefits, abating the problem in each home produces discounted net benefits of $2,098 (benefits are $4,323, with costs of $2,225). The aggregate discounted *net* benefits of treating 23 million homes total $28 billion over twenty years (benefits are estimated at $61.7 billion, with costs of $33.7 billion).[81] Residential remedial costs are estimated to be about $10,000 per unit, totaling $19 billion for the estimated 1.9 million residences with hazardous lead levels occupied by low-income owners. Nevertheless, even if the estimated 188,000 children exposed to 25 μg/dl or more (where immediate medical treatment is urged) are the only beneficiaries of the cleanup (although millions of other children are exposed to between 10 and 25 μg/dl), the cost per case averted is only about $100,000.

Federal action to date has been significant, particularly in reducing airborne lead and the lead content in residential paints. Lead in paint was phased out in the 1950s, and in 1978 the Consumer Product Safety Commission banned the sale of lead-based paint and its use in residences. Lead in gasoline is being phased out as well. But little has been done about residences of children who are likely to be exposed to high lead levels. The Bush administration, while acknowledging that two to three million American children may be at risk from lead poisoning, only lowered the concentration (to 10 μg/dl) of lead considered to be hazardous and recommended that every child under age six be screened.[82] Even this, however, has come under criticism from some who allege that the data do not support such a standard.[83] Although it has been billed the "number one environmental hazard to children"[84] with well-documented health effects—which the CDC terms "so overwhelming and compelling"[85]—the Bush administration committed only $50 million to a remedial "demonstration" project.[86] The Bush administration held that it saw "no reason for the Federal Government to legislate or regulate" lead cleanups.[87] The administration's strategy focused on public information, research into the extent of the problem, encouraging development of better abatement technologies, support for local testing programs to identify high-risk children, and cash grants and loans to states and localities for testing and abatement. These grants are not specifically earmarked for lead, but they can be used in that manner if states and individuals wish, therefore potentially diminishing their impact on lead poisoning. Compared with Superfund sites, lead paint removal has received minimal federal attention despite the severity of the health threats involved.

Asbestos

Asbestos, another localized environmental hazard that affects communities across the nation, has a somewhat longer recorded history than either radon or hazardous wastes. Asbestos is actually six mineral fibers, not one. Some of the same characteristics that make asbestos attractive as a building material, such as its flexibility, durability, and tensile strength, also unfortunately enhance its ability to remain in the human body. More than fifty years ago, scientists recognized that workers exposed to asbestos had scarred lung tissues (asbestosis) and that asbestos inhalation could be fatal. Subsequent research, again primarily on workers, showed that lung and other cancers as well as mesothelioma resulted from prolonged exposure to asbestos. Over 90 percent of asbestos in the United States is chrysotile, however, which is considered far less dangerous than amphiboles.

While there is little scientific resistance to the notion that airborne asbestos is hazardous and should be controlled—OSHA imposed workplace asbestos standards in 1971, and EPA issued standards in 1989, eventually leading to a phased-in ban on the use of asbestos in the United States by 1997—considerable controversy remains over what to do about the millions of tons of *installed* asbestos. Asbestos has been used to insulate walls and pipes for soundproofing, for fireproofing fireplaces and walls, in strengthening compounds, and in floor and ceiling tiles, in what EPA has estimated to be 733,000 buildings in the United States, as well as in automobile brake linings and appliances. The principal scientific and policy argument is over whether in-place asbestos is better left undisturbed, contained on the premises, or removed. Removal can cause asbestos fibers to disperse, posing greater exposure risks, particularly if done haphazardly by cleanup crews.[88] One problem is that homeowners, for fear of plummeting housing values, have frequently chosen removal over containment, even though the hazards may be greater. And a $3 billion per year asbestos removal industry has evolved, further fueling the incentive for removal over containment.[89]

Estimates suggest that past asbestos exposure results in about four thousand fatalities annually.[90] A trust fund was established, largely financed by the Johns-Manville Corporation, one of the largest asbestos manufacturers, to compensate past victims of exposure. Thousands of victims have filed for billions of dollars in claims against asbestos manufacturers, and the result has been a litigious nightmare. It is estimated that attorneys' fees for asbestos cases have used up about two-thirds of the resources provided by the fund.[91] The federal government has contributed little in the way of victim compensation, relying on the original "polluter" for financing. Nevertheless, many victims will be only modestly compensated, if at all, after lawyers' fees and the claims of others have been settled, despite serious and ultimately fatal illnesses.

Accurate assessments of the current exposure to asbestos are unavailable, as is the dose-response relationship. There is no well-established threshold for safe exposure to asbestos, although EPA has gone to some length to dispel the "one fiber can kill you" theory.[92] Asbestos remains in outdoor air (for example, from the wear of automobile clutch and brake linings), although the bulk of concern is for the far greater concentrations in indoor air, particularly in schools. Congress passed the Asbestos Hazard Emergency Response Act (AHERA, Public Law 99-519) in

1986, amending TSCA. Much of the act requires EPA to issue various regulations—mostly regarding schools—and to study liability insurance and the health risks associated with asbestos. In addition, AHERA established a trust fund to finance assistance to local school districts in identifying and abating asbestos problems. EPA found that between 35,000 and 45,000 schools (out of 110,000) contain friable asbestos materials. However, the trust fund is minuscule, at least relative to the problem, which has been projected ultimately to cost $51 billion to rectify.[93] The president's fiscal year 1992 budget request, for example, called for only $24 million to be available for appropriations, most of which comes from asbestos loan repayments and unappropriated previous fund balances.[94]

Federal actions to date, as mentioned above, served to sharply reduce the use of asbestos in the United States (although it is still used in many other countries). Proposed OSHA requirements, for example, would lower the permissible levels of asbestos from 12 fibers per cubic centimeter of air to 0.1 fibers in 1990.[95]

Nevertheless, exposure to already installed asbestos remains a potentially serious problem. EPA's *Unfinished Business in New England* study found that the individual cancer risk from ambient urban exposure to asbestos was about 10^{-5}, whereas for rural areas the risk was 10^{-7}. Nonoccupational exposures were found to run risks as high as 10^{-4}. But because the number of people exposed is so high, the study found that while only five people in New England were likely to contract cancer annually as a result of ambient asbestos exposure, nonoccupational exposures are likely to cause another 177 cancers in New England alone.[96] Metropolitan areas in New England were estimated to contain 10.2 million persons, and nonmetropolitan regions 2.4 million in 1985. Extrapolating to the over 225 million people in the United States at the time, the number of expected annual cancers jumps to over 3,000 annually. Occupational exposures can be expected to add significantly to these numbers, not to mention cancers caused by earlier exposure. If the ultimate cost of remedying asbestos exposure is about $51 billion, then over thirty years the cost per statistical life saved, discounted at 5 percent annually, is about $1.3 million. Asbestos could probably be contained in place for much less than $51 billion, however, and the evidence indicates that the risks of on-site containment would be far lower than those of removal anyway. Concern purely for public health would dictate that far more attention be paid to inventorying and inspecting in-place asbestos, not only in schools but also in private buildings and residences, and that asbestos found intact should be contained in place rather than removed.[97] A summary report concludes that "uncontrolled disturbance of ACM [asbestos-containing materials] should be avoided wherever possible."[98] Therefore, it appears that a significant remedial effort, beyond monitoring and containment, may not be worth pursuing when asbestos can be contained in place. Indeed, the study contrasted the relative risks of asbestos exposure (4–6 excess cancers per million people exposed), indoor radon (5,000–20,000 cases) and environmental tobacco smoke (2,000–5,000 cases), the latter two posing far more serious health threats.

Cost-effectiveness and Superfund

The environmental and health risks from most Superfund sites are relatively small compared with other environmental problems and even the three remedial and local problems covered above. In addition, there are substantial inefficiencies in how Superfund monies are allocated in addressing risks. At least two risk management problems arise in how Superfund monies are used to address site cleanups. The first involves how sites come to be placed on the National Priorities List for federal cleanup. The second is related to the level to which each site is remediated, or the question of "how clean is clean?" In both instances, Superfund fails to allocate resources to best protect human health and the environment.

Which Sites Should Be Remediated?[99]

The primary vehicle for quickly assessing the hazards posed by potential Superfund sites is the Hazard Ranking System (HRS), developed for EPA by an independent contractor, the MITRE Corporation. The system in use in 1989 generated an overall HRS score based on the results of three hazardous waste migration routes, or pathways: groundwater, surface water, and air. (A new HRS scoring method, issued in December 1990, adds a fourth, "soil" exposure pathway, among other changes, although it applies only to NPL sites added after 1990.[100]) Only those sites scoring over 28.5 on a 100-point scale are eligible for listing on the NPL.[101] The HRS is not a full-blown risk assessment (which is not undertaken until the RI/FS stage), but rather a simple tool to determine whether or not a site should be added to the NPL. Thus, it is not intended to direct EPA's efforts beyond filtering out those sites hazardous enough to warrant future federal action. The choice of 28.5 as the cutoff score was an arbitrary one, meant simply to ensure that the initial congressionally mandated minimum of four hundred sites would be included on the initial NPL.[102] This particular choice of cutoff is particularly important, however, since it defines whether or not future sites will qualify for the NPL. The average HRS study was expected in 1989 to cost nearly $150,000,[103] although an EPA field analysis of the cost of each revised HRS ranged from $100,000 to $311,000, with a slightly higher average of $176,000.[104]

A number of problems threaten the ability of HRS scores to accurately evaluate site risks. Scoring sheets with detailed instructions allow workers to enter site-specific data on such characteristics as the number of people potentially exposed via each pathway, the levels of toxicity, the quantity and type of hazardous waste, and so forth. The data, some of which necessarily are qualitative (such as the soundness of containers holding the hazardous materials), are not entered directly, however, but through a coding system. For example, in the groundwater pathway calculation a 1 is entered if the affected population is between 1 and 100, increasing nonlinearly to 4 if it numbers from 3,001 to 10,000, up to a maximum of 5 for over 10,000 people affected. As a result, a similar score of 5 would be entered no matter if Little Falls, N.J., or Los Angeles fell within the population distance limit.[105] In other cases, ordinal data are converted into cardinal relationships. An observed release in any of the three pathway calculations merits a score of 45, while "no release" scores 0. Simplifications such as these are used throughout the HRS calculations. While the complex coding system may improve the consistency of the HRS scores calculated by the many different individuals scoring sites, it obscures the relationship between the site's potential hazard to the public and the final HRS score.

Based on the scores developed for each independent pathway, a final HRS score (for pre-1990 sites) is calculated using the formula

$$HRS = [(GW^2 + SW^2 + A^2)/3]^{1/2},$$

where HRS = combined score,

   GW = groundwater pathway score (0–100),

   SW = surface water pathway score (0–100), and

   A = air pathway score (0–100).

Since each pathway score can range only from 0 to 100, the formula constrains the total HRS score to the same range. Thus, regardless of how onerous the consequences of any one exposure pathway to the resident population, it cannot score over 100 points (in other words, it cannot contribute in the extreme more than 57.74 points to the final HRS score). Moreover, each pathway's contribution to the final score varies with the level of the other pathway scores. For example, consider adding an air pathway score of 20 under two circumstances. If both the other pathway scores are 0, the HRS increases from 0 to 11.55. But if both other scores are 100, the HRS increases by only 0.81 (from 81.65 to 82.46). Illustrated another way, extreme scores in one pathway produce higher HRS totals than do moderate scores in all three pathways. For instance, a score of 90 in the air pathway, with GW = SW = 0, produces an HRS score of 51.96, while scores of 30 in each of the three pathways yield an HRS total of just 30. Thus, potentially significant pathway risks may add little to

final HRS scores, despite their added severity, or relatively minor pathway risks may qualify a site for inclusion on the NPL. The formula therefore amplifies the impact of the dominant pathway while discounting secondary and tertiary scores. As a result, sites with one extreme pathway
score will receive higher scores than those with a multiplicity of problems.
Despite these problems, generally speaking a site that scores 80 is thought
to pose a greater risk than one that scores 50, although the difference
between sites scoring 55 and 60 is less certain.[106] Sites that score close to
28.5 are double-checked to ensure accuracy, and the error rate has been
estimated to run as high as 20 percent.[107] Nevertheless, because the formula is intended only to determine whether a site qualifies for the NPL,
one especially hazardous pathway can produce a sufficiently high total
HRS score. Although the required 28.5 total HRS cutoff score represents
one way to categorize sites as more hazardous or less hazardous, only a
tenuous relationship exists between the score and the site's hazard potential, and the cutoff in no manner represents a benefit-cost test of the value
of spending federal money to clean up the site.

Beyond the technical problems with the HRS, there are more serious
policy implications to this process of creating a National Priorities List.
Two types of problems exist: sites for which cost-effective remediation
is possible which are not included on the NPL (false negatives) and NPL
sites that are not cost-effective to remediate (false positives). Since the
HRS scores are not risk-based, it is likely that even if the system were
able to rank all sites appropriately in terms of risk, the cutoff score of
28.5 would fail to distinguish the most important sites to remediate from
lower-priority sites. The Office of Technology Assessment has estimated
that as many as 2,000 or more out of the 17,000 sites rejected for the NPL
may be false negatives due to errors, even ones as simple as arithmetic
mistakes.[108] More fundamentally, the crucial elements of marginal costs
and marginal cleanup benefits are completely disregarded by the HRS.
The NPL is therefore composed not of sites that are cost-effective to remediate but of those sites that are considered by the quite crude HRS to be
the most hazardous. How large are these errors likely to be? From the
results earlier in this chapter, it appears that for at least some NPL sites,
remediation costs far outweigh the public health and environmental benefits. Far less certain, however, is the number of sites excluded from the
NPL that could, at least in part, be remediated cost-effectively. One researcher critically concludes, "The NPL has become the program,"[109]
while an industry representative adds, "It is doubtful that the NPL includes all the worst sites."[110] The combination of the arbitrary HRS cutoff
score, some relatively inexpensive methods to at least limit exposures (if
not to fully remediate the site), and the thousands of possible sites not on

the NPL, all suggest that many sites can in some manner be treated cost-effectively.

How Clean is Clean Enough?

Superfund cleanup levels can range anywhere from restricting access with a fence to removing all traces of contamination from air, soil, surface water, and groundwater. Restoring Superfund sites to a pristine level, indeed cleaner than the surrounding area, is beyond what even Congress envisioned under CERCLA. One commentator has stated, "if the [more stringent Superfund water cleanup standard] won out as the cleanup target, people would be moving to Superfund sites because that's where the cleanest water in America would be!"[111] Because resources are limited (even those now allocated to remediate Superfund sites), knowing when to stop correcting one site to better reclaim another is critical to reducing as much environmental and health risk as possible. Consequently, it is worthwhile to consider how clean is clean enough.

The question of appropriate cleanup levels depends critically on the future use of the site. It makes little sense to impose the same site cleanup standards on a future airport or industrial site as on a future playground. Even Jim Florio, a congressional architect of Superfund, has said, "It doesn't make any sense to clean up a rail yard in downtown Newark so it can be a drinking water reservoir."[112] One key to Superfund's cleanup levels should be generating the maximum risk reduction per dollar spent. This seemingly sensible approach leads to a very different process than that currently undertaken by EPA, however. While EPA cannot foresee exactly how the land will be used in the future, it is a reasonable bet in some cases that, for example, land now surrounded by interstate highways or industrial parks will not be a future school or residential area. EPA does not own the sites it remediates, but it can factor into its cleanup decisions whether people are likely to be exposed to any remaining contaminants on the land. Where future site uses are uncertain, probabilistic estimates of future exposures can be substituted for definitive projections. Moreover, a site with class A chemicals, which are considered to be human carcinogens, should be treated before a site with equivalent expected risks from class B (probable human carcinogens) or class C chemicals (possible human carcinogens) because of the relative certainty of the hazards involved.[113]

Even if a site currently poses a substantial risk to nearby residents and even if fully treating all potentially hazardous materials to return the site to a pristine level is cost-effective, this does not imply that Superfund's limited resources spent in this manner will most reduce the environmental and public health threats. Instead, the relevant question that should be asked (but is not) is whether the extra benefits of site cleanup, broadly defined, exceed the additional costs. For example, suppose a Superfund site currently imposes risks of 10^{-2} (0.01, or one in one hundred) to 2,000 people exposed to the contaminants, and that the cost of full remediation is $25 million, yielding a cost-effective CPSLS of $1.25 million. This implies only that full cleanup would be cost-effective *relative to no action*. Suppose, however, that 95 percent of the health effects can be eliminated for $5 million. Does it make sense to spend the remaining $20 million on 5 percent of the problem? In this case probably not. The extra $20 million could better reduce environmental and health risks by remediating 95 percent of the risks at four other sites rather than expensively purging the last contaminants from one site. Therefore, the relevant question is not whether full cleanup is cost-effective relative to doing nothing, but whether each successive step of the cleanup is cost-effective. EPA officials have estimated that at least half of Superfund expenditures have been to comply with what are termed "dirt-eating rules," or requirements that specify such stringent cleanup levels that one could (if so inclined) safely eat the dirt. This argument rests on the same principles stated in chapter 3 and reiterated above, namely that *one* goal of Superfund should be to use scarce resources in ways that most improve public health and the environment.

On the other hand, finding that a total cleanup at any given site is too expensive relative to the environmental and health benefits does not imply that no action is warranted or that the site should not be included on a priority list. Modest remedial efforts could well be justified on the same cost-effectiveness grounds outlined above: modest risks could be reduced at even more modest costs. Indeed, much of Superfund's success lies with the removal action program, which has removed more than 2,600 immediate threats to health and the environment since 1980 and has reduced substantial risks at many sites at relatively little cost. Thomas Grumbly of Clean Sites believes that EPA's removal program "has probably eliminated most of the *immediate* health risks posed by abandoned hazardous waste sites," and adds, "To date, little credit has been given to EPA for the risk reduction these removal actions achieve."[114] Indeed, much of the public's outrage over leaking drums filled with hazardous waste has been eliminated, leaving Superfund sites that usually appear benign on the surface, despite serious threats that in some cases may remain unseen.

Some have argued that even for those Superfund sites that do not impose significant (or even any) environmental or health threats, property values will decline once a site has been discovered. Therefore, it is argued that economic benefits of site cleanups exist even in the absence of documented environmental and health risks. One study found that at the OII

Landfill in Los Angeles, property values for the surrounding 4,100 homes dropped about $40 million before the site was closed and $20 million even after closure.[115] The authors suggest that even though risk beliefs in many cases overestimated the site's "true" health risks (as measured by toxicological and epidemiological studies), the increase in property values resulting from the site cleanup should be counted as a benefit in any cost-benefit analysis. While this may be true in some instances, the problem with including these "benefits" is that they bear no relationship to actual improvements in health or environmental quality. Suppose, for example, that EPA were to convincingly dupe a community into believing that their site has been fully remediated (at little or no actual cost except, perhaps, to remove some barrels emitting noxious odors), and consequently property values rise from their previously depressed levels. Should the property value increase be counted as a benefit of the "cleanup"? Illusory benefits of this sort are no more actual cleanup benefits than are property value declines based on mistaken estimates of environmental or health risks.

Others argue that "how clean is clean?" is not really an issue at all. Robert Brandon of the Citizens/Labor Energy Coalition has said, "There's a lot of talk about how clean is clean and debate over technicalities. That is just setting up a straw man. To tell somebody who lost a child or had some serious health problems that it's okay if this stuff leaks a little bit into his drinking water and [EPA] can't be responsible for totally stopping it—that's not acceptable."[116] The issue is not a matter of "technicalities," however, but rather of determining how to best use scarce resources. To turn the example around, what do we tell the several hundred additional people who may die annually from exposure to lead or radon because the resources that could have removed peeling paint or properly ventilated a residence were instead used for a Superfund cleanup expected to prevent one cancer fatality over the next seventy years? While this is not necessarily the opportunity cost of Superfund spending, and everyone can pick their favorite government program to supplement instead, the opportunity cost argument is anything but a "straw man."

In summary, several problems exist in allocating Superfund's resources. First, some sites on the NPL pose relatively minor risks and should not be remediated to the levels specified in the statute. Second, some sites are not on the NPL and therefore receive no federal monies (except for possible emergency removal actions), even though at least some remedial action would be cost-effective. Finally, there is no general principle to allow EPA to determine "how clean is clean." Some cleanups are "gold-plated," while other sites, where at a minimum access should be restricted, are ignored by the federal government because they do not attain a sufficiently high HRS score to qualify for the NPL. Instead of stopping when marginal cleanup benefits no longer exceed cleanup costs, EPA spends an excessive amount of money at a few NPL sites and too little on some non-NPL sites.

Conclusion

Even this brief review of relative risks suggests that Superfund gains a disproportionate share of funding compared with the observed environmental and health risks of hazardous waste sites. Although the health and ecological risks are relatively low, Congress has chosen to pour money into cleaning up abandoned waste sites, even though radon and lead, which receive only a tiny fraction of Superfund's expenditures, appear to be far more serious threats to public health. These results do not imply that Superfund monies should be immediately rechanneled to these programs. However, even restricting our examination to other *remedial* environmental and public health threats that are *local* in nature, these results do suggest that other risks are most likely far greater than those from Superfund sites. And this ignores improvements in highway design, prenatal care, and a variety of other policies that could reduce far greater risks for the same cost.

Superfund's defenders correctly state that "the conclusion that such sites pose no real hazard and that we should be more worried about indoor radon . . . is unproved."[117] Regrettably little is known about Superfund site risks, and it is even possible, given the scientific uncertainties, that some Superfund sites are *more* risky than radon contamination or other environmental problems discussed above. Nevertheless, while unproven, the overwhelming conclusion from the scientific community and federal regulators has been that ozone depletion, habitat destruction, wetlands preservation, biodiversity, and others are more important environmental issues. While Superfund supporters can correctly point to the absence of scientific data showing that site risks are small, they are similarly unable to demonstrate significant health risks at many NPL sites and therefore to defend multibillion-dollar remedial expenditures *based on public health or environmental threats*. While it is unreasonable to think that dollars would be shifted from Superfund to other important social programs, chapter 9 suggests a new institutional design in which Superfund resources could—if the public wishes—be shifted to deal with radon, asbestos, lead, and other local and remedial cleanup efforts.

While many individuals support the continuation and even expansion of Superfund, I know of no one who buttresses the argument with reference to the public health or environmental benefits of site cleanups.

Rather, the arguments are based on other factors such as fairness, "making the polluter pay," a public demand for action, and so forth. These may all be justifiable reasons, but we should not delude ourselves into either believing that the environmental and public health risks from Superfund sites are fully understood or that they are known to be large. It is possible that they are large, but the best evidence we have now suggests just the opposite. Risk populists have argued that other factors should inform the decision: the degree to which the risk is voluntary, the age of the person, and the quality of life after one is "saved" (such as by a liver transplant), whether the risk is isolated or widespread, whether or not the public clamors for action, and whether the individuals to be "saved" are identified in advance or not. Perhaps this is so. My point is simply that policymakers should have some pretty good reasons for deviating from a policy of averting as much environmental and public health risk as possible.

The examples of lead and radon underscore the importance of deliberating about opportunity costs. Former EPA Administrator William Reilly has argued, "It seems only prudent to ask if society's resources are being used in ways that will contribute most efficiently over the long haul to the health and well-being of our citizens and our environment. And we will be unable to give a positive answer to that question as long as we continue to spend the bulk of our environmental resources on cleanup, while neglecting front-end investments in pollution prevention and environmental planning."[118] The point is not so much that no risk is reduced by remediating Superfund sites, but rather that with the amount of money now spent on litigation and site cleanups, it is likely that far more future cancers and illnesses could be prevented by shifting the money into other public health and environmental programs. For example, the federal government announced its largest antismoking campaign program ever, which it estimated would cost $135 million across seventeen states yet was expected to prevent 1.2 million smoking-related deaths, or about $113 per death prevented.[119] Even if the estimates overstate the number of reduced deaths by a factor of 1000, the costs per life saved are probably still lower than those of all but the most hazardous Superfund sites. Moreover, there are other social goals besides public health that may be worthy of public attention, such as higher quality education, health care, and housing, which lie outside the environmental field. The appropriate allocation of scarce resources, then, should consider not only environmental alternatives but other social goals as well. Armed with the best available evidence, one is hard-pressed to justify Superfund expenditures, based on environmental and public health benefits relative to other social programs.

Nevertheless, although *on average* Superfund sites probably do not pose significant risks, some individual sites do. The problem with Superfund is not that the program exists at all, for some sites appropriately deserve public attention, but rather that in terms of reducing environmental and health risks, its resources are misallocated. Sites with low risks are placed on the NPL alongside sites that pose serious potential health and environmental threats, while cost-effective strategies are most likely available for many non-NPL sites as well. This stems from the apparent reluctance to compare the marginal cleanup benefits with marginal cleanup costs. Moreover, there is no appropriate stopping point in remediating Superfund sites. The "how clean is clean" issue has become "it is never clean enough." This is not to say that sites not currently deemed sufficiently risky should be forgotten, because low-risk sites can become high-risk sites over time. As a result, it is critical that risk analyses take into account the potential for significant future risk as well as present risks, and that sites be regularly monitored.

A recent newspaper article posed the following question: "Two drugs for treating people with heart attacks are equally effective in saving lives, according to two important studies. One drug costs $2,200 a dose, and the other $76 to $300. Which should be used?"[120] The choice seems to be easy. However, just as in the United States many doctors prescribe the more costly drug, environmental and safety policy frequently imposes very different costs per life saved. In the case of doctors, some have attributed the use of the more expensive drug to the aggressive marketing tactics of its manufacturer. In the case of Superfund, the question is more puzzling: Why are so many resources devoted to a relatively small environmental and health problem, and why is the program so persistent even with huge budget deficits and in the face of other health and safety risks not being fully addressed? In the next chapter, I evaluate the degree to which Superfund has upheld another fundamental public policy goal, equity. The results, alas, are not encouraging.

5 Environmental Equity and Superfund

The concerns of distributive environmental equity form an important criticism of "rational" risk management. Risk populists argue that the most vulnerable members of society are usually those subjected to the greatest risks; they argue that proponents of "acceptable risk" are in fact advocating that those who must "accept" the risks are too often the poor and racial minorities. Modest overall Superfund site risks are unimportant if poorer areas are disproportionately subjected to site hazards; low "average" risks may obscure the fact that the poor or racial minorities are particularly exposed. Not only must the magnitude of the risk (broadly defined) be factored into public policy decisions, but who is bearing the risk must be considered as well. Are those forced to accept involuntary risks the most unprotected in society, or are they the wealthier members of society who both can move and are less likely to face other risks (such as those from poor nutrition, poor health care, and crime)?

Underlying this perspective is the growing realization that not all Americans are equally affected by pollution. Newspaper articles frequently have reported links between environmental quality and race and class,[1] and a fall 1991 conference of African-American, Hispanic, native American, and Asian-American groups was organized around the theme of what has been termed "environmental racism."[2] National Public Radio, the *MacNeil-Lehrer News Hour,* and other news programs have devoted segments to the subject.[3] Responding to mounting external pressures, EPA issued the widely publicized 1992 report *Environmental Equity,* which reviewed the literature on environmental equity and suggested modest policy proposals for EPA.[4] Environmental equity is increasingly important to understanding and analyzing environmental policy.

Despite mounting public attention and concern, surprisingly little research has examined systematically the relationship between different types of environmental quality and the demographic and socioeconomic characteristics of affected populations. There is little question, however, that owners of landfills, heavy metals processing plants, and other polluting facilities find it easier to locate these facilities where jobs are scarce and incomes low. For example, the decision of Recontek to try to locate its heavy metals recycling facility in Orange, Massachusetts, was clearly related to the town's high unemployment rate and generally depressed economic outlook. In addition, a depressed West Virginia town approved an enormous landfill facility whose developer promised jobs and improved local services in exchange, only to have its decision overturned by the state.[5] While many can point to instances where poorer sections of cities and towns are also the most industrialized and presumably the most polluted, little systematic research has been undertaken to determine whether or not national trends reveal a similar pattern. One study documented the greater willingness of firms looking to expand their hazardous waste facilities to locate them where political resistance and other costs are lower.[6] A statistical analysis commissioned by the United Church of Christ (UCC) documented "a striking relationship between the location of commercial hazardous waste facilities [both RCRA and Superfund sites] and race," and found that "the issue of race is an important factor in describing the problem of uncontrolled toxic waste sites."[7] The report argued that because hazardous waste sites disproportionately affect racial minorities, "the cleanup of uncontrolled toxic waste sites in Black and Hispanic communities in the United States should be given the highest possible priority."[8] Robert Bullard, relying partly on evidence from a General Accounting Office study,[9] charged that the patterns reveal intentional racism in facility siting.[10] A study by Clean Sites, Inc. found that although relatively few Superfund sites are located in rural poor counties, they often threaten to contaminate the groundwater on which most of these residents depend.[11] A study by Gould found that both the rich and the poor suffer from toxic waste exposure, noting that "affluence no longer suffices in the evaluation of a safe place to live."[12] A study of mine found that both race (percentage of nonwhites in a county) and class (a composite variable of wealth, income, and formal education) are positively related to the levels of many pollutants.[13]

With regard to Superfund, some contend that the relatively small environmental and health benefits of cleaning up many sites (see chapter 4) are beside the point, since equity is the most important principle behind Superfund. "Superfund is, in part, about fairness," argues Senator Durenberger, a strong Superfund supporter, "it is not just about public health."[14] Superfund is justified on both procedural and distributional grounds of equity. The "polluter-pays" feature is the chief defense of Superfund's procedural fairness, since it is argued that those who generated the pollution are—at least ideally—made to pay for its cleanup. Superfund is defended on distributional grounds as well. It is argued that because, like other forms of pollution, Superfund risks disproportionately affect the poor and racial minorities, governments have an obligation to remediate sites for those who cannot afford to escape the risks.

The concept of equity is especially difficult to analyze because it is judged so differently from various perspectives.[15] Because of the diverse conceptions of what "equity" means, it is necessary to evaluate the equity of any program from several procedural and distributional perspectives. While many have criticized Superfund for its managerial inefficiencies, virtually no systematic attention has been devoted to the questions of who pays for and who benefits from Superfund cleanups.[16] This chapter analyzes the equity implications of Superfund in terms of both procedure and distribution. In the following sections, I evaluate equity in terms of Superfund liability provisions and financing (who pays?) and the distribution of Superfund sites (who benefits?). The president's fiscal 1993 budget request called for an annual increase of well over $100 million in Superfund's budget authority, to $1.75 billion, amidst proposed cuts in thousands of other federal projects and programs.[17] Why has such a massive and apparently inefficient federal program existed for more than a decade when stringent budgetary pressures have all but halted new domestic spending? The findings below suggest that while there are some equity advantages to Superfund, in many respects the program is both procedurally and distributionally inequitable.

Superfund Liability: Does the Polluter Really Pay?

Perhaps the most fundamental motivation behind Superfund is procedural equity: those who have been harmed by waste site hazards—physically, psychologically, or financially—should be compensated, and those who improperly dumped contaminants should pay for any damages. During the floor debate over CERCLA's passage in 1980, legislators frequently referred to the injustice of their constituents being faced with abandoned hazardous waste dumps. Former Senator Stafford of Vermont declared that the problem was "an issue of justice, because we are dealing with human lives that are devastated by the impacts of these chemicals; children born with permanent defects, adults stricken with crippling diseases, entire communities with their supplies of drinking water contaminated beyond use."[18] A strong sense also emerged from the debate that past polluters should be required to pay for the cleanup of these waste dumps. Representative Railsback of Illinois said, in but one example, "I feel industries which contributed to the problem should bear most of the responsibility for cleanup costs."[19] But to equitably assign responsibility, it is necessary first to identify the beneficiaries of past improper or illegal dumping. In other words, who are the polluters that should be made to pay?

The "polluter-pays" principle is potentially an effective and procedurally equitable policy instrument in regulating *prospective* pollution. By forcing polluters to pay the external costs imposed on others, using taxes or some other means, private decisions can be made to reflect social values. If appropriate emissions penalties are established, an electric utility, for example, will factor into its decision making not only the costs of purchasing coal, hiring workers, and so on, but also the environmental damage that results from emitting sulfur dioxide and other air pollutants. If the level of the tax or regulation is set properly, the utility would limit its sulfur dioxide and other emissions to the point where the marginal costs of pollution reduction equal the marginal benefits.[20] The polluter-pays principle also provides incentives to shift from polluting to nonpolluting technologies, since nonpolluters would enjoy comparative cost advantages. Therefore, the appropriate level of pollution reduction can be had by charging directly those responsible for polluting.

The principle applied to prospective polluters also recognizes that those responsible for pollution include not just industrial enterprises, but consumers who, given the choice, buy the products that in the absence of regulations are less expensive (and which also produce more pollution). It is well known that regulatory compliance costs imposed on polluters are in part passed on to consumers of those products in the form of higher prices. For example, passive restraints in automobiles, such as air bags, raise the price of new cars. In addition, regulatory costs would be passed on in part to workers in heavily polluting industries who may lose income or even their jobs (although some or all of the job loss could be made up by employment growth in less polluting industries). Consequently, those sharing the cost of environmental improvement include not just corporate owners (who suffer diminished profits) but consumers and workers alike. This also appears to be procedurally equitable, since those responsible for the pollution—from those who create it to those who buy the products—end up paying the costs. Because of the political payoffs, some politicians are fond of fostering the perception that only industry foots the bill for pollution regulations. The symbolic political advantages to making the "polluter" pay in part explains the focus of many regulations on the polluting *industry,* although forcing polluting industries to pay ensures that costs will be far more widely diffused.

Abandoned hazardous waste sites represent a different pollution problem, however, because Superfund addresses *past* behavior, not prospective behavior (although indirectly Superfund has the latter effect as well, as discussed below). Costs are far easier to assign to prospective polluters (steel producers, automobile manufacturers, or current hazardous waste producers), in part because there are fewer of them, and because costs will be diffused widely through market mechanisms without administrative intervention. Identifying past beneficiaries of improper waste dumping and recovering their portion of the ill-gained benefits, however, is enormously difficult, to which the litigious atmosphere surrounding Superfund testifies. Who benefited in the past from what is now considered to be improper hazardous waste dumping? On the corporate side, former shareholders and rent-seeking managers of corporations enjoyed the fruits of higher corporate profits. In addition, past consumers enjoyed lower product prices because the full social costs of hazardous waste disposal were not imposed on waste producers (and were therefore not shifted in part to consumers in the form of higher prices).

To take the most straightforward example, when a single party is found to have contaminated a waste site and to have done so illegally, then forcing that party to finance reparations appears to satisfy the polluter-pays principle. After all, the firm that once polluted is now forced to pay. It should first be noted that only a small portion of NPL sites fall into this category. According to a survey conducted by EPA and Resources for the Future, 89 of 903 sites (about 10 percent) were caused by illegal operations, and of those 89 sites, 35 (39 percent) were related to actions of the owner-operator.[21] Therefore, at only 35 of 903 NPL sites, or less than 4 percent, were owner-operators responsible for illegal waste disposal.

But even in this extreme case there is reason to question whether the polluter really does pay. Some of the cleanup costs will be borne by *current* shareholders and workers, some will be shifted to *current* consumers through higher product prices—and lower output and wages, and fewer jobs—if the company is financially viable, or the company could be forced out of business. (At one extreme, if a firm facing high cleanup costs is the only one liable in a perfectly competitive industry, then it may be unable to pass along cost increases to its consumers for fear of losing its market share. Less competitive industries or those where cleanup costs are borne by most firms, possess a greater ability to pass costs on to consumers.) In short, those who will actually pay for the cleanup—current shareholders, consumers, and workers—may not be the same ones who benefited from the improper dumping of decades past. At one extreme, an EPA official recalls a site at which the difference between past polluters and those who would now finance cleanups is glaring, since "the disposal [of an arsenic compound] started in 1865."[22]

Both because the consumers of current products are likely to be different from those who benefited in the past and because the owners (shareholders) of corporate entities are likely to be different as well, making past beneficiaries pay for present cleanup costs is virtually impossible. As a result, almost any retroactive liability scheme violates the standard of equity called for by the polluter-pays principle. Costs are not for the most part borne by the historical polluters, those who actually benefited from improper hazardous waste disposal. In this sense, Superfund is fundamentally different from forcing polluters to pay for prospective pollution.

Further complicating matters is the possibility that individuals and companies may have dumped wastes *legally* in the past, using then-accepted practices, unaware that more stringent regulations would take effect. In addition, potentially responsible parties (PRPs) may genuinely have been unaware of the potential hazards of the many wastes whose health effects remain speculative and inconclusive to this day. The procedural fairness of requiring individuals or companies to pay for wastes dumped legally and properly decades before they were even considered to be hazardous is questionable.[23] A striking example is provided by a high-ranking regional EPA official and former employee of the Vermont Department of Water Resources, who in his capacity in the Superfund program received an unexpected telephone call one day from a PRP contesting its liability for cleaning up a Vermont Superfund site: "The responsible party said 'tell your boss we don't think we're responsible for this [waste cleanup], and show him this letter.' What it was was a letter [dated in 1952] written by me in the Vermont Department of Water Resources to this company that said, 'we've considered what to do with your sludge, and we think you ought to put it into the landfill because that will keep it out of the water and not cause a problem.' And here it is 30 years later and I'm suing them for doing exactly what they did that was in accordance with my letter. We didn't know this was going to cause a problem, and didn't even suspect it."[24]

Superfund suffers from a fundamental problem in assigning liability: it attempts to finance present-day cleanups caused by past damage where responsible parties are sometimes either unable to afford restitution, cannot be identified, or are long since out of business. In many cases it is difficult to determine the content and quality of what was dumped decades ago. As a result, CERCLA has been interpreted by the courts to carry a powerful weapon—strict, joint, and several liability—to stimulate significant compliance, settlement, and cost recovery. The potential effect is to force even a minor polluter at a Superfund site to pay for the full cleanup costs if other responsible parties cannot be prosecuted, regardless of the number of other polluters. Besides being potentially unfair to small polluters, high cleanup costs provide an incentive for PRPs to delay cleanup through litigation, a process in which many Superfund remedial efforts are now mired. And because EPA concentrates its efforts on making deep-pockets polluters liable for cleanup costs, these companies can best afford the costly litigation that delays site remediation. Since site cleanup costs are so high, now averaging over $25 million and sometimes exceeding $100 million, there is substantial incentive for PRPs to devote considerable legal resources to reducing cleanup costs or prolonging the legal process. One regional EPA official laments, "We had one or two attorneys in the region [to conduct Superfund actions]; now we have 35."[25] Another adds that the liability rules slow site remediation: "the fact that this is not a public works program does slow the program up."[26]

The process is further hampered by the difficulty of coordinating negotiations with dozens of PRPs at many sites, each of whom must agree on a remedial plan and a cost allocation scheme. Even when EPA seeks settlements or cost recoveries from one or a few deep-pocket PRPs, these parties frequently turn around and sue other PRPs to recover their contributions to the waste site. Some of the same legal procedures that allow the federal government to extract significant concessions from PRPs enable the responsible parties in turn to sue smaller waste contributors. Thus, although *federal* legal expenditures may be reduced by concentrating on larger PRPs, they are often replaced with private litigation costs through secondary lawsuits and disputes between insurers and the insured. Federal litigation expenditures therefore represent only a fraction of all transactions costs. It is clear that one of the principal reasons why strict, joint, and several liability is so favored by EPA—even though its officials have acknowledged that it is potentially unfair[27]—is because it helps shift the transactions costs of organizing onto PRPs. This was shown in the testimony of two EPA officials in a Senate hearing in 1985. Henry Habicht testified that he believed forcing one party contributing 1 percent of the waste to finance 100 percent of the cleanup costs to be unfair. At the same hearing, EPA was trying to justify retaining strict, joint, and several liability, which could, strictly applied, result in such an action. Another EPA official, Gene Lucero, stepped in to address the potentially embarrassing situation of why EPA was supporting a position that it believed was unfair. In justifying strict, joint, and several liability, Lucero argued that its principal advantage was that "it changes who bears the burden of the transaction costs" from the federal government to PRPs. Lucero previously argued that "it [eliminating strict, joint, and several liability] would be seriously disruptive, especially in those larger cases, if we didn't have the kind of coalescing mechanism that joint and several liability forces."[28] Of course, the "coalescing mechanism" Lucero refers to is the panic an identified waste contributor faces when it recognizes it could be held liable for the entire cleanup cost.

Municipalities have also been dragged into many Superfund lawsuits, not chiefly by EPA's actions but rather from secondary lawsuits from PRPs. There is a great deal of concern about municipalities, school districts, and small businesses being potentially liable for their contributions to hazardous waste sites that can amount to tens of millions of dollars. Municipalities are particularly vulnerable because virtually every landfill is a potential Superfund site (even though most garbage is not hazardous), and insurance to cover costs is prohibitively expensive. For example, Alhambra, California, with an annual budget of $55 million, could be liable for a $20 million cleanup. James Florio, one of the principal authors of Superfund, has argued that Congress had no intention of forcing small businesses and municipalities to pay: "The very clear intent of the law is that corporate polluters are to be made responsible for cleaning up toxic wastes. Congress never contemplated that solid municipal waste was toxic and municipalities would be responsible for cleanups."[29]

But citizens do finance cleanups, whether indirectly through higher prices or reduced dividends or directly through municipal taxes. The outrage caused by the possibility that municipalities could be liable for Superfund claims partly represents an inability to recognize this. Congress wants PRPs to be responsible for cleaning up Superfund sites, but only if the PRPs are large corporations. Only by forcing corporate PRPs to finance cleanups can a symbolic political victory be claimed. Once it is recognized that municipalities—and even individuals—can be held liable for Superfund cleanups, the unavoidable conclusion is that many of *us* are part of the problem as well. Moreover, the ability of PRPs to publicize Superfund's inequity and influence subsequent policy changes by suing municipalities may actually encourage them to do so.

A painful reminder of the magnitude of transactions costs is that at some sites the costs of litigation threaten to exceed cleanup costs. At one site the government reportedly sought cleanup costs of $6 million, while private parties' legal fees for the pretrial portion of the case totaled between $5 million and $11 million.[30] A study by Putnam, Hayes, and Bartlett estimates total Superfund transactions costs at between 24 and 44 percent of direct cleanup costs.[31] While probably an exaggeration, this suggests that if the Superfund program grows to the size (over $500 billion) that some have estimated, transactions costs easily could reach tens of billions of dollars. A recent study by RAND found that 88 percent of the Superfund-related claims paid by the insurance companies surveyed were transactions costs, although for large PRPs and single-PRP sites the costs were lower.[32] This is a high price to pay for the dubious procedural equity of identifying the alleged "polluter." It should come as no surprise that CERCLA has been called "a welfare and relief act for lawyers."[33] Senator Domenici reportedly said that lawyers had been "salivating" over the prospects of Superfund's liability provisions.

There is little question, however, that Superfund's stringent liability provisions have heightened corporate awareness of the importance of the proper current disposal of hazardous wastes. Fortune 500 and other deep-pocket corporations dread the prospect of their current hazardous wastes winding up in a future Superfund site and therefore exercise sometimes extraordinary control over its final destination. Environmental audits are now commonplace in major land transactions, since the new owners (including lenders) could be held liable for cleanup costs even if the costs are no fault of their own. One recent newsletter advertising its ability to inform prospective buyers asks, "Will your real estate deal turn out to be a toxic time bomb?"[34] Many view this increased awareness as one of the chief advantages of the Superfund program. Bill Roberts, legislative director for the Environmental Defense Fund, contends that because of Superfund, "businesses now scrutinize their waste management activities. They spend millions of dollars to carefully manage their wastes and, more importantly, to change their production practices to reduce the waste they generate in the first place. They clean up old contamination on their property to make their businesses more attractive to potential purchasers and more dependable to financial institutions looking for reliable collateral . . . And all of this goes on without a single EPA employee in sight."[35] A regional EPA official argues, "Anyone in their [sic] right mind who handles hazardous wastes and hazardous substances is going to handle them properly . . . RCRA helps. RCRA says how you should handle wastes properly, and if you don't, I've got penalties of $25,000 per day. But what really gets your attention is not the $25,000 per day penalty, it's the fact that you might end up inadvertently creating a $50 million Superfund cleanup."[36] But others suggest that Superfund's strict, joint, and several liability leads to inefficient overcontrol and monitoring and that the availability of environmental liability insurance has been limited as a result.[37] Furthermore, it is important to ask whether *implicitly* regulating current hazardous waste disposal under Superfund is the appropriate vehicle, when directly regulating hazardous waste disposal may better address the problem. Some counter that the regulatory advantages can only be gained by a strict liability scheme like Superfund's: "The fact that [Superfund] is so outrageous is why it has gotten companies' attention."[38]

The notion that the polluter pays for site cleanups therefore appears to serve symbolic goals more than actually punishing past wrongdoing. Even in the most clear-cut case, where a single, financially viable firm knowingly and illegally dumped hazardous materials in the past and has been forced to finance the remedial efforts, some of the cleanup costs may be passed on to *current* consumers of these products, in the form of higher prices. Moreover, punishing firms for past behavior fails to reward those who have improved their environmental records. Therefore, regardless of who pays directly for Superfund site cleanups, those costs ultimately extend well beyond a single firm. While no one would argue that it is fair that parties not responsible for Superfund sites bear some of the cleanup costs, it is difficult to identify who is responsible, and nonresponsible parties will bear some of the costs *anyway*. This is not a fault of the legislation, but rather the necessary result of trying to apportion current liability using the polluter-pays principle for inappropriate past behavior.

Financing the Trust Fund

When CERCLA was passed overwhelmingly in 1980, the $1.6 billion five-year fund was financed principally by taxing petroleum products and forty-two chemicals, thereby targeting industries historically responsible for the bulk of hazardous waste production. Some have argued that "it makes the makers of toxics pay."[39] By 1986, however, many argued that the burden of the tax should be distributed more widely. Congress wanted a vastly expanded fund, and many feared for the international competitiveness of the chemical industry if Superfund taxes were to be raised significantly. The result—a political compromise after a ferocious battle between interested parties—was a combination of revenue sources totaling $8.5 billion over five years: $2.75 billion from a revised tax on petroleum products, $2.5 billion from a 0.12 percent tax on minimum corporate income over $2 million, $1.4 billion from a revised chemical feedstock tax, $1.25 billion from general revenues, and $0.6 billion from cost recoveries from liable parties and interest on unused portions of the fund. Most cost recoveries constitute only a small portion of Superfund's budget, however. For example, in fiscal year 1990, EPA fines and recoveries totaled just over $105 million, less than the $150 million earned by the *interest* on the unexpended trust funds.[40] Most of the cleanups are funded by PRPs, however. Therefore, most fund disbursements represent net federal expenditures, albeit "off-budget" expenditures. While the previous section focused on cases where responsible parties finance site cleanups, I now turn to whether the fund itself is so financed that it either promotes vertical equity or forces polluters to pay.

One element to be considered is the possible effect of Superfund financing on regional redistribution. One study found that a state's contributions to the Superfund excise tax are unrelated to the number of hazardous waste sites in the state, the cleanup expenditures obligated to the state, and the state's ability to pay.[41] The authors conclude that "Superfund tax and expenditure provisions result in disproportionate penalties for some regions of the country and disproportionate benefits for other regions."[42] While this may be true, it should also be recognized that millions of Americans benefited from the products that generated hazardous wastes. Consequently, while Superfund may have the redistributive effects these authors identify, it could reasonably be argued that this simply rectifies the past inequity of some municipalities bearing a disproportionate burden of the wastes generated by others.

More fundamentally, both the original and the amended versions of Superfund financing necessarily fail to help assign appropriate blame. Superfund's original funding scheme placed much of the burden on producers of petroleum products and chemical feedstocks. While it may be true that these *industries* are responsible for most hazardous waste production, it is not necessarily the case that placing a burden upon these industries will also burden the same *individuals* who benefited from environmentally flawed past disposal practices. The same principles that apply to liability apply to financing Superfund: costs are spread far beyond individual companies, and punishing companies today does not necessarily redress wrongs committed by other corporate owners. It should also be remembered that not all Superfund sites originated with large corporations. For example, the Superfund site in Rye Brook, New York, was contaminated when a chemist now 79 years old carelessly handled mercury for use in dental fillings, in a laboratory in his garage (unbeknownst to his neighbors).[43] Moreover, chemicals and allied products, which account for most hazardous waste production, are not only sold as retail products, they are mostly sold as inputs to other industrial processes.[44] Thus, any past price reductions gained at the expense of improper dumping would have been passed on to millions of consumers. Furthermore, current corporate shareholders may have had no part in enjoying ill-gained excess profits of the past, and the products taxed beginning in 1981 may be entirely different from those that were made more profitable by improper dumping in the past.

Finally, the taxes impose costs indiscriminately and unfairly. Past polluters and environmentally responsible industries are penalized alike, since the tax does not distinguish between responsible and irresponsible hazardous waste dumpers. And while the tax penalizes those industries that use large amounts of the taxed chemical and petroleum products, it does not distinguish between companies that produce a great deal of hazardous waste and those that produce little. Unless there is a direct relationship between feedstock use and hazardous waste externalities, the tax provides no incentives to reduce wastes. Indeed, those who do reduce wastes put themselves at a competitive disadvantage by incurring additional costs. Unfortunately, a significant trade-off exists between waste-end taxes that would internalize the costs of hazardous waste dumping, yet would provide a smaller and less certain revenue stream, and the existing feedstock taxes that provide large and predictable revenues, yet with none of the equity and efficiency advantages of the waste-end tax.

The funding sources earmarked in the 1986 legislation, notably the corporate minimum tax and general revenues, obviously fail the polluter-pays principle. According to a recent report, the corporate environmental tax provided approximately 30 percent of total Superfund trust fund revenues in fiscal 1990; over 50 percent was generated from the manufacturing sector; 17.4 percent from finance, insurance, and real estate; 16.3 percent from transportation and public utilities; and the remainder from various industrial sectors.[45] Although a careful tax-incidence analysis has yet to be performed for Superfund taxes, it is clear that virtually all sectors and all products are affected by the tax, both directly and indirectly. But since the polluter-pays goal cannot practically be attained for *past* damages, the issue turns on the vertical equity of the other funding sources. Since the feedstock taxes are in part passed on to consumers in the form of higher prices, lower-income consumers will be disproportionately affected. To the extent that corporate profits are reduced, stockholders will suffer. While some of these stockholders are wealthy investors, others are individuals of moderate means who invest indirectly through, for example, pension plans and mutual funds. The most vertically equitable source of funds is general revenue, where the tax burden is probably slightly progressive. However, increasing Superfund's reliance on general revenues would substantially reduce its political appeal, since the program would then have to compete for funding with other domestic priorities. Superfund has been shielded from such trade-offs by appealing to a polluter-pays principle dubiously applied, which fails to withstand scrutiny both in many liability cases and for Superfund financing. Ironically, efforts to improve the vertical equity—and probably the efficiency—of Superfund financing by increasing its reliance on general revenues would jeopardize its political viability.

Regulating prospective pollution can be made procedurally fair, and it has the potential to appropriately and effectively control pollution. But because Superfund requires current efforts to remediate past environmental degradation, liability and financing will necessarily be procedurally unfair. Restricting Superfund financing to those cases in which responsible parties are identified and can afford restitution would produce a much smaller fund than proponents want. But even here, recovering benefits that accrued to past owners and consumers from improper waste disposal is virtually impossible. Conversely, expanding the revenue base to rely more on broad-based taxes would mean that some polluters would not be held responsible for past illegal discharges. In either case, the belief that the polluter actually pays is highly questionable.

In short, the polluter-pays principle underlying Superfund has been oversold, in terms of both the liability scheme and the financing of the federal trust fund. Both corporations and consumers bear some of the responsibility for past hazardous waste production and disposal. This principle is well recognized when regulations force companies to pay for reducing pollution, although it is never advertised to the public that it too is bearing a substantial amount of the pollution control costs in the form of higher product prices. In the case of Superfund, consumers are bearing some of the burden of the excise taxes used to fund some cleanups, and they bear a burden even in the cases where PRPs finance cleanups. The problem is that those who benefited in the past from improper dumping are only weakly related, if at all, to those who now are forced to finance Superfund cleanups. Unfortunately, there is no simple way to recapture the ill-gained benefits from those who improperly dumped hazardous wastes in years past, because it is virtually impossible to find all the polluters and compel restitution. In passing CERCLA, Congress was more interested in avoiding significant federal contributions to the fund through general revenues than in achieving equity or efficiency in Superfund financing. As a result, the question of procedural equity was forsaken.

Who Benefits from Superfund Site Cleanups?

The question of who benefits from Superfund site cleanups is an important one, in large part because it addresses the issue of distributional equity. Many risks, some have argued, "harm those who already bear many of society's adverse impacts."[46] Therefore, two questions must be addressed in the debate over the distributional equity of Superfund: What individuals are most affected by current Superfund site risks? and, Who stands to benefit from their remediation? Even if environmental and health risks are acknowledged to be relatively small, Superfund cleanups may be justified by an appeal to equity. Because those who are affected by site risks may be the least advantaged members of society, forcing them to shoulder additional hazards imposed by others would be fundamentally unfair. The most vulnerable members of society should not be forced to bear the additional risks.

Because the character of the population affected by Superfund site risks varies from site to site, broad generalizations can be misleading. Nevertheless, some initial observations are revealing. Research indicates that nearby property value declines are most pronounced when the waste site is added to the NPL, a decidedly newsworthy event.[47] In addition, it appears that the magnitude of property value declines is unrelated to site risk, at least as measured by EPA's HRS scores, and that the property value declines may disappear once the site is officially remediated.[48] Since Superfund cleanups will raise area property values, these gains will accrue chiefly to landowners. Where housing markets are competitive some of the increased land values will translate into higher rents, to the benefit of landlords and the detriment of generally lower-income renters. Naturally, nearby residents will gain from the possibly improved environmental and health conditions as well.

But are those who stand to benefit from site cleanups the same people who have suffered financially, physically, and psychologically from their proximity to the sites? A fundamental problem, again related to current remediation of past pollution, is that the financial benefits of a Superfund cleanup will accrue to *current* landowners, who may or may not have owned the land since the site was discovered to be contaminated. If current property holders purchased their land at a discount after a Superfund site was discovered, site remediation will provide them with windfall profits. On the other hand, property owners who sold the land upon learning of its potential hazard will have suffered an unrecoverable loss. Consequently, only benefits accruing to longtime (non-PRP) landowners through site cleanups should be regarded as justly compensatory. In addition to property owners who will gain from increased land values, waste cleanup firms stand to reap substantial profits as well. The national waste cleanup business is one of a few projected growth industries of the 1990s. Indeed, over seventy cleanup firms have recognized the potential value of their industry by establishing a national lobbying organization—the Hazardous Waste Treatment Council—to advance their interests. Finally, lawyers stand to gain handsomely from the legal fees involved in settling Superfund cases, representing a significant portion of the transactions costs noted above.

Geographic Distribution of Superfund Sites

Little attention has been devoted to the question of who lives near Superfund sites, and therefore who stands to gain from their cleanup. Psychometric research has shown that various risk characteristics, including familiarity, control, and *equity,* help to explain public acceptance of that risk independent of its magnitude.[49] The apparent perception that Superfund sites are inequitably distributed—for example, by wealth or race—may help to explain the seemingly lopsided public concern over hazardous waste sites compared with other environmental risks, and therefore public demands for remedial action. In addition, Theodore Lowi observes that those policymakers advocating risk assessment and management strategies are generally not the people confronting those risks. He notes that "those [in the Reagan administration] who spoke loudest against risk-alleviating policies were among society's most risk-insulated persons."[50] The idea that less privileged members of society cannot afford to move away from heavily polluted areas, buy safer cars, and rid their older homes of lead-based paint—that "acceptable risks" are only for those who *must* accept them—is unfair under many (although not all) definitions of equity.

To assess the equity of the distribution of Superfund sites, and therefore who stands to gain from remedial cleanups, I collected data on the socioeconomic characteristics of each county in the United States, and on the number of proposed and final NPL sites in each county as of 1 January 1989.[51] It should first be noted that there is no single "correct" level of geographic resolution that is appropriate for analyzing the socioeconomic characteristics of the individuals surrounding all sites. The appropriate level of geographic resolution would be the one that includes the population affected by each site, but this varies dramatically from site to site. At one extreme, some sites, like the Newmark Superfund site in San Bernardino, California, have contaminated acquifers from which hundreds of thousands of people get their drinking water.[52] At other sites, like one in Rye Brook, New York, mercury contamination affected only nine residential properties.[53] Moreover, it is not always clear which people are affected at certain sites because the scope of the problem is poorly understood. The virtue of using counties as the unit of observation is that they provide substantial variation nationally and also sufficient size spatially to include most of the environmental and health effects of Superfund sites; use of finer geographic resolution (such as ZIP codes) would better identify the unique characteristics of the immediate neighborhood but might omit site impacts that extend beyond those boundaries; larger areas (such as states) have the opposite problem. While the county as a unit of analysis may exceed the scope of the affected populations at some sites, it also reduces the likelihood of including sites that border, say, neighboring ZIP codes, and it is more likely to include those communities affected by some groundwater contamination.

The issue at hand is whether the number of Superfund sites in a county is correlated with its socioeconomic characteristics, and specifically, whether Superfund site risks disproportionately affect the poor or racial minorities. Ideally, the analysis would investigate the entire universe of sites considered for the NPL and explain why some sites are on the list and others not. Unfortunately, there is no well-defined universe of potential sites, as sites are continually being added to EPA's inventory, and potentially many thousands of sites could become NPL sites. Nevertheless, from those sites EPA intends to remediate (those on the NPL), one can derive the likely distribution of program benefits, regardless of how the NPL sites were selected in the first place.

The number of NPL sites in any given area can be considered a function of the following characteristics: the amount of hazardous waste likely to have been generated in the area, residents' demands to have a site placed on the NPL, and the region's social and economic composition. Explanatory variables employed here include the quantity of hazardous waste generated in each state in 1985 and the percentage of each county's economy composed of manufacturing. (All variables are measured at the county level unless otherwise specified.) The degree of potential political mobilization is measured as the percentage of residents who are college educated, the percentage of housing units that are owner-occupied, and the percentage of new housing units built from 1970 to 1980. Higher values of the first two variables are expected to contribute positively to political mobilization, as would lower values of the third variable. Socioeconomic characteristics (as measures of distributive equity) include the median housing value and the percentage of county residents living below the poverty level, unemployed, and nonwhite. The county's population density is used as a control variable to identify urban/rural differences. Sample statistics for each of these variables are presented in table A.5.1 of the Appendix.

Estimation results are shown in table 5.1 for both "unweighted" and "weighted" data.[54] The problem with the unweighted or raw county data is that since counties vary substantially in population, the per-county variation in pollution may differ from per-person impacts. Ignoring a county's population is to ignore the number of people actually exposed to Superfund sites, and it puts small counties (in terms of population) on equal footing with large ones. Therefore, weighted estimates are included as well, which effectively count counties with large populations proportionately more heavily than counties with small populations. The unweighted results can be interpreted as representing variation by county, while weighted results represent the more meaningful per-person variation.

Table 5.1   Distribution of NPL Sites by County: Unweighted and Weighted Tobit Estimation Results (dependent variable = number of final NPL sites per county)

Independent Variable	Unweighted Coefficient (t-statistic)	Weighted[a] Coefficient (t-statistic)
Intercept	0.11(0.07)	5.12(2.98)***
Quantity hazardous waste	−0.00(1.17)	0.00(1.60)
Manufacturing (%)	0.05(7.23)***	0.04(4.72)***
College educated (%)	0.07(2.72)***	−0.01(0.37)
Owner-occupied housing (%)	−0.07(4.18)***	−0.09(5.14)***
New housing units, 1970–80 (%)	−0.02(3.72)***	−0.04(7.67)***
Median housing value (/10,000)	0.55(5.15)***	0.95(12.7)***
Below poverty level (%)	−0.18(6.97)***	−0.30(8.18)***
Unemployed (%)	0.05(1.58)	−0.05(1.11)
Nonwhite (%)	0.02(2.09)**	0.05(4.57)***
Population density (/10,000)	−0.58(1.09)	−3.45(8.30)***
Observations (N)	3138	3138
Log likelihood	−2202.39	−5992.58
Chi-square (10)	475.53	980.01
Prob > chi-square	0.0000	0.0000

[a]Weighted by county population.
***Significant at 99% level; **95% level; *90% level (two-tailed test).

As expected, a greater manufacturing presence is strongly associated with more county NPL sites, in both the weighted and unweighted estimates. (The fact that the amount of hazardous waste generated is not correlated with the number of NPL sites in the county may be because it is from statewide, not countywide, data.) Other coefficients reflect mixed results, however. A higher percentage of college-educated county residents is correlated with more NPL sites (unweighted only), and a higher level of owner-occupancy (a proxy for potential political activism) is associated with fewer NPL sites (in both estimates). However, more new housing is strongly associated in both cases with fewer NPL sites. These unexpected results on political mobilization may be due to the dual incentives facing a politically active community. First, while it may be more likely to recognize a site as hazardous, have it placed on the NPL, and finally have it cleaned up, the incentive also exists for communities to bypass the cumbersome and time-consuming federal NPL procedure altogether and negotiate directly with the responsible parties or seek remedial action from the state. Moreover, because property values decline when the site is listed on the NPL, some towns may hesitate to lobby for inclusion. These empirical results attest to the fact that there is no clear theoretical explanation for how politically motivated communities will act in response to an identified abandoned hazardous waste site.

On the other hand, the results are quite clear in terms of an area's economic characteristics: poorer counties do not contain more Superfund sites than others. To the contrary, the results indicate that more economically advantaged counties (in terms of both wealth and the absence of poverty) are likely to have *more* Superfund sites. The county's median housing value is strongly and positively correlated with the number of NPL sites, using both weighted and unweighted data. Similarly, higher poverty levels are strongly associated with fewer NPL sites in both cases. Higher unemployment rates are not statistically associated with the number of NPL sites in either case. However, a disturbing finding is that counties with higher percentages of nonwhites have more NPL sites than others, holding other factors constant. (This corroborates the findings of the UCC study, which included all hazardous waste sites.) Therefore, while wealth is related to more Superfund sites, and poverty to fewer, nonwhites stand to benefit disproportionately from site cleanups, holding these other factors constant.

Finally, population density is negatively related to the number of sites in the weighted regression, suggesting that urban counties have fewer sites, holding the other factors discussed above constant. To ensure that urban/rural differences were not truly underlying the results, since urban counties generally are more prosperous than their rural counterparts, the model was estimated with only urban counties included. The results were similar to those above, although race and the manufacturing base were no longer significant explanatory variables. However, with any specification of "urban" employed, the median housing value was consistently a highly significant explanatory variable. Thus, holding other factors constant, it appears that NPL sites tend to be located mostly in established communities with a strong manufacturing base, and the evidence suggests that counties occupied by the wealthy, well-educated, and nonwhite stand to benefit disproportionately from cleaning up Superfund sites.

Statistical analyses are fundamentally summaries of relevant data, and because the results in table 5.1 are "average" coefficients representing the broad tendencies of more than 3100 counties nationwide, other significant causal relationships within subsets of the data may be overlooked. Many NPL sites may be located in counties overrepresented by disadvantaged (for example, poor and unemployed) groups, even though the overall picture does not reflect this conclusion. Instead of examining all U.S. counties, I next examine subsets of counties that contain high propor-

Table 5.2   Average Number of NPL Sites per County

Poverty above 15.78 percent (N = 1292)	0.106* NPL sites
Unemployment above 8.7 percent (N = 1274)	0.230* NPL sites
Nonwhite population above 11.89 percent (N = 1195)	0.332 NPL sites
Median housing value above $35,296 (N = 1254)	0.738* NPL sites

*Statistically different from the average of 0.37 sites per county at the 99+ percent confidence level.

tions of individuals living under the poverty level, the unemployed, non-whites, and people living in lower-valued housing. This is analyzed in two ways: (1) whether counties that are disproportionately represented by racial minorities, the unemployed, and so forth have significantly more than the average of 0.37 Superfund sites per county, and (2) whether counties that contain many NPL sites are composed largely of these same groups.[55]

High levels of county poverty, unemployment, and ethnicity and median housing values are first defined as exceeding the national average for counties: 15.78 percent (poverty), 8.7 percent (unemployment), 11.89 percent (nonwhite), and $35,296 (median housing value). Examining only those counties that exceed the national average in each category, the analysis reveals the average number of NPL sites per county (table 5.2).

Using each of the first three measures, the number of NPL sites in counties highly represented by the poor, the unemployed, and nonwhites is *below* the national average, and in the first two cases significantly so. (The number of NPL sites where the percentages of the poor and racial minorities are below the average necessarily exceeds the national average.) Further, significantly more NPL sites are located where median housing values are *higher* than the national average for counties. Examining only the 43 counties where the population of nonwhites exceeds 50 percent, the average number of NPL sites is 0.326, again slightly below the national average, although (as above) the difference is not statistically significant. Therefore, these results indicate that NPL sites are located predominantly in more affluent counties and generally irrespective of race.

Another way to view the distribution of sites is to examine the characteristics of counties with large numbers of NPL sites, or what could be considered Superfund "hot spots." Thirteen counties contain ten or more NPL sites. In these counties, the average poverty and unemployment rates are far below average (8.29 and 5.48 percent, respectively), and the median housing value is well above average ($59,623). (Each of these differences is significant at the 99+ percent confidence level.) Only the nonwhite percentage (12.14) is slightly higher than average, though not significantly so. Similar results obtain for analysis of only counties with at least five NPL sites ($N = 53$) and when the number of sites per square mile is examined.[56] These results again support the conclusions reached above, that large numbers of NPL sites exist in overall wealthier counties with lower levels of poverty and unemployment.

Some might argue that irrespective of the number of sites, the most hazardous sites are located in poorer or ethnic areas. To test this hypothesis, the Hazard Ranking System scores for each of the final NPL sites were collected. Although HRS scores are not formal risk assessments, they represent a first pass at risk estimates, and they have been conducted for all NPL sites, unlike the risk assessments undertaken at the RI/FS stage. (Recall that it is necessary to score above 28.5 to be considered for the NPL.) The worst sites, in this case the 35 sites that scored above 60 on the 100-point HRS scale, were examined for the racial and economic characteristics of the counties in which they are located. For each measure, the surrounding population tends to have lower poverty rates, lower unemployment rates, lower percentages of nonwhites, and higher median housing values, all in contrast to allegations that these sites disproportionately affect the poor and minorities.[57]

Finally, it is possible that the multivariate Tobit analysis in table 5.1 obscures simple—and more readily observed—relationships between Superfund sites and measures of ethnicity and class. In other words, is there a simple correlation between the number of NPL sites and *either* race, poverty, unemployment, or median housing value? Simple bivariate Tobit estimates were calculated to determine the independent relationships between the number of county NPL sites and poverty or unemployment rates, median housing values, and percentage of nonwhites in the county (plus a constant term). Estimated separately, the results indicate strong relationships between more NPL sites and *low* poverty and unemployment, higher housing values, and (surprisingly) lower percentages of nonwhites.[58] Thus, the multivariate estimates appear to be reasonably consistent with these indicators of distributional equity, with the exception of nonwhites, and again imply that there are more Superfund sites in wealthy counties and fewer in counties overrepresented by individuals unemployed or living in poverty.

These results indicate that wealth and poverty are indeed strongly associated with the location of Superfund sites, but not in the direction some allege and not because of a naive correlation, based on observed bivariate relationships. Furthermore, it is possible that the presence of hazardous waste sites depressed the area housing values used in this study and that wealthier families migrated away from these areas. If migration is an important contributor, we would expect a tendency for poorer neighborhoods to be near Superfund sites, not the reverse. To the degree that the presence of waste sites was capitalized into housing prices (the data are from 1980, before the program existed but after the discovery of Love Canal and other waste sites), these results indicate that, if anything, Superfund sites are located in even wealthier areas than identified in this analysis.

In What Ways Can Superfund Be Considered Equitable?

Despite the many ways discussed above that Superfund is anything but fair, there are several respects in which Superfund can be viewed more charitably in terms of fairness. The first is that Superfund seeks to prohibit some individuals from being exposed to higher risks than others. Therefore, although aspects of the program's implementation may be procedurally unfair, at least it seeks to avoid concentrating risks on the minority of individuals exposed to Superfund site risks. Even if overall site risks are small, subjecting some individuals to large site risks is unfair, and Superfund attempts to redress that inequity. A second sense in which Superfund can be considered equitable is that uniform cleanup standards mean that actions taken at every site will (at least theoretically) meet similar goals. Therefore, because sites are in this respect treated equally, the program is fair because the policy outcome is equal protection from risks. Third, the program at least *attempts* to make those responsible for dumping wastes finance cleanups, and arguably, in some cases it succeeds. Moreover, even if largely unsuccessful, it forces current waste producers to exercise greater care over the disposal of hazardous materials. Fourth, the Superfund program addresses risks that have been imposed involuntarily on individuals living near sites. Because the informed consent of those individuals living near Superfund sites was never obtained, Superfund can be considered fair in the sense that it is redressing a past inequity.

The final way in which Superfund could be considered equitable is indirect: because Superfund addresses the concerns of grass-roots constituencies and largely ushered in grass-roots environmentalism, it has enhanced citizen involvement not only in hazardous wastes but in environmental equity and other political arenas as well. Who cares, it may be argued, whether the program is succeeding in meeting its goals equitably? It has provided substantial indirect benefits by empowering individuals who previously had little influence over politics or policy and therefore has set the stage for greater political equity in other programs.

Conclusion

If Kevin Phillips is right in arguing that the politics of the 1990s will be based increasingly on income and class differences,[59] then the geographic distribution of pollutants may in part affect the future pattern of environmental policy generally and Superfund policy specifically. Along some dimension the distribution of Superfund risks is necessarily inequitable: some people are more exposed than others. The issue turns on whether the distribution of sites discriminates against certain groups. The preceding analysis indicates that from several different perspectives, Superfund is anything but fair, in terms of either process or outcome. While the program attempts to redress past wrongs, it does not—and indeed cannot—fairly assign sufficiently compensating liability, nor does it equitably raise tax revenues or redistribute federal cleanup resources to the disadvantaged. Indeed, the polluter-pays principle on which Superfund is built, in many ways fails to meet its objectives. Superfund sites are not predominantly located in poorer counties, although nonwhite counties may be disproportionately affected. Rather, the evidence indicates that Superfund sites are more often located in wealthier areas of the country and those with lower rates of poverty. While Superfund is defended by grass-roots proponents as a populist reaction to the excesses of big business, the net effect of cleaning up abandoned hazardous waste sites is most likely to redistribute resources regressively from consumers and taxpayers chiefly to wealthier communities.

Perhaps most importantly, the arguments supporting the fairness of Superfund in the previous section can all be sustained, even with a significantly reformed Superfund program. Because many elements of Superfund are inequitable and because the transactions costs at Superfund sites are so high, I recommend significant reforms in chapter 9, which improve the involvement of grass-roots interests (who are in many instances minor players in Superfund cleanup decisions) and permit sites and other environmental hazards that local communities believe are most important to be addressed. In addition, because the incentives provided by a strong Superfund program compel responsible handling of current hazardous wastes, I propose in the last chapter to distinguish between those sites that were abandoned before the Superfund law was passed in late 1980 and those sites closed since. In the former case, where sites were abandoned before Superfund became law, public financing of site remediation will dramatically reduce the transactions costs required to deter-mine who dumped what and where and will eliminate the inequity of forcing some companies to finance entire cleanups when their disposal practices were legal—and in some instances even sanctioned by govern-ment authorities. The reforms outlined in chapter 9 attempt to preserve and enhance the few equity advantages that Superfund currently enjoys and to eliminate the many inequities that currently limit the program's appeal.

6 How EPA Allocates Superfund's Resources

One concern for both environmentalists and members of industry is how EPA reaches decisions in allocating Superfund resources. Understanding what strategies EPA pursues—as revealed by the decisions it makes rather than by its public rhetoric—helps in understanding how the program actually works; but more importantly, it can help to guide policy reforms. For example, discovering that congressional committees exert influence (through EPA) over which sites get cleaned up first and how would indicate the futility of directing policy reforms to improve decision making solely at EPA. If instead it is discovered that EPA tries to spread its cleanup resources around the country to maximize political support for the program, then reforms targeted at statutory changes may be off target. As it turns out, there is no evidence of the former influence and some evidence of the latter. But before tackling the specifics of how EPA allocates Superfund's resources, I examine the issue within the broader framework of agency decision making.

How do government agencies reach policy decisions? Scholarly research supports several different theories. Bureaucratic behavior is seen variously as the product of agency or congressional self-interest, concern for some notion of the public interest, distributive equity, or influence by "fair-share" budgeting. Chapters 4 and 5 argued that Superfund is neither effective in reducing environmental and public health risks, nor can it in many ways be considered equitable. A significant amount of scholarly research supports the position that certain programs lacking the advantages of both efficiency and equity are motivated by a legislative self-interest to distribute resources to districts represented by powerful legislators through log-rolling, commonly known as pork-barrel politics. (The omnibus Army Corps of Engineers' river and harbor projects bill is perhaps the most publicized example.[1]) A number of analysts charge that

Superfund too is a pork-barrel program designed to help members of Congress secure reelection. This chapter examines how Superfund's considerable resources have been allocated in the 1980s across hundreds of NPL sites. Are Superfund's resources channeled to reduce the most risk? Do they instead provide distributive equity? Are the resources spread evenly around EPA regions and the country to ensure fair-share budgeting? Or are key legislators using the program to further their own interests by cleaning up waste sites in their districts at the expense of the public's broader interests?

There are clearly instances of individual legislators successfully intervening on behalf of their constituents. Public accounts of the influence of individual legislators on behalf of their constituents over Superfund cleanup policies surfaced in the 1989 New Jersey gubernatorial campaign. In the first televised gubernatorial debate, the Republican candidate, Jim Courter, claimed that he had helped ensure that a toxic waste site in his district was the first in New Jersey to be cleaned up under Superfund. James Florio, his Democratic opponent, responded "Give me a break! The people in his district had to call me to get some action on the dump site." As local officials tell it, Courter arranged for local representatives to meet with EPA officials, which ostensibly led to the agency agreeing to finance the cleanup.[2] The site, Krystowaty Farm in Hillsborough, was ranked 103d on the Superfund priority list, and was the highest ranked site in Courter's district. Nevertheless, 15 sites in New Jersey had higher HRS scores, seven of which had not started cleanup. In addition, the projected present value cleanup cost for Krystowaty Farms ($3.62 million) was considerably lower than that for the higher-ranking New Jersey sites for which RODs had been issued. Therefore, even such blatant congressional intervention on behalf of their constituents may be more widely justified by the site's relatively high HRS score and relatively low cost of cleanup.

This chapter seeks to determine empirically overall patterns of Superfund expenditures and cleanup priorities, not simply to recount anecdotal evidence suggesting pork. The following sections describe EPA's statutory obligations in making Superfund cleanup decisions and the various bureaucratic and legislative incentives that theoretically may be expected to guide actual Superfund spending. Following this, EPA's Superfund site cleanup decisions are analyzed statistically to determine which motivations actually condition EPA's actions. The findings indicate that risk-reducing motives are far more compelling explanations for the pattern of Superfund expenditures and cleanup priorities than traditional allocative pork-barrel politics or other alleged agency behavior.

Superfund's Statutory Requirements

Congress was intentionally vague in specifying under CERCLA exactly which sites should be cleaned up, how each should be cleaned up, and to what degree. The result is a considerable delegation of executive authority to EPA. When EPA failed to meet Congress's high expectations for Superfund in the early 1980s, the 1986 reauthorization specified which criteria should inform EPA's decision, although it provided little guidance on how to trade off and balance these criteria. Section 121 of CERCLA (as amended by SARA) on cleanup standards requires the president[3] to select long-term remedies that protect human health and the environment and are cost-effective, and it specifies that any remedial actions must meet federal or state legal requirements. In addition, the ATSDR is required to perform health assessments for every site proposed or already included on the NPL.

Apart from its statutory obligations, the EPA must follow the National Contingency Plan (NCP) in implementing Superfund, a set of regulations Congress requested of EPA under Section 105 of CERCLA.[4] Published in March 1990, the NCP lists nine criteria (some of which restate the statutory requirements mentioned above) to gauge the overall acceptability of cleanup alternatives:

Threshold criteria

(1) Protection of human health and the environment
(2) Compliance with applicable or relevant and appropriate regulations (ARARs)

Primary balancing criteria

(3) Long-term effectiveness
(4) Reduction of toxicity, mobility, or volume through treatment
(5) Short-term effectiveness
(6) Implementability
(7) Cost

Modifying criteria

(8) State acceptance
(9) Community acceptance

While these criteria are intended to guide remedial decisions, their ambiguity presents difficulty in practice. The first two criteria, protection of human health and the environment and compliance with applicable or relevant and appropriate requirements (ARARs), are termed "threshold criteria," which must be met to select a remedy.[5] However, it is not entirely clear what "protection" of human health and the environment really means: zero risk? no additional risk? acceptable additional risk? ARARs are only applicable when state requirements are stricter than federal (where promulgated) and where the state identifies the requirements promptly. Included as part of the Remedial Investigation and Feasibility Study, ARARs can be waived under certain circumstances, such as when states inconsistently apply their standards or when complying with the ARAR will impose greater risks than noncompliance.[6]

The next five criteria, termed "primary balancing criteria," include long-term effectiveness and permanence; reduction of toxicity, mobility, or volume through treatment; short-term effectiveness; implementability; and cost. With regard to the use of the cost criterion, the NCP is somewhat vague: it states only that "overall effectiveness is then compared to cost to ensure that the remedy is cost-effective. A remedy shall be cost-effective if its costs are proportional to its overall effectiveness."[7] This is clearly not a call for cost-benefit analysis (it is not apparent what "proportional" means here), but nevertheless the NCP quite plainly recognizes the need for balancing among the seven nonthreshold criteria. The NCP is clearer than the statutory designation of the importance of cost, however, and it is apparent that cost-effectiveness is the intention. The practical effect is that EPA should choose the least expensive alternative when confronted with several cleanup remedies providing equivalent benefits. However, the NCP also states with respect to the cost criterion that "costs that are grossly excessive compared to the overall effectiveness of alternatives may be considered as one of several factors used to eliminate alternatives." Thus, a crude cost-benefit comparison is apparently at times permissible, but this is a far cry from requiring, or even allowing, cost-benefit studies of each possible remedy. The legislative history of CERCLA similarly blurs congressional intent on the cost-benefit question.[8]

The final two criteria, both state and community acceptance, are what EPA calls "modifying criteria."[9] The NCP stipulates that in order to protect humans from carcinogenic risk, "acceptable exposure levels are generally concentration levels that represent an excess upper bound lifetime cancer risk to an individual of between 10^{-4} and 10^{-6}," unless federal or state ARARs are more protective.[10] These requirements apply to both government and private-party cleanups. In the case of drinking water, which is a common concern at Superfund sites, the requirements become a bit more complicated. The Safe Drinking Water Act stipulates what are called Maximum Contaminant Level Goals (MCLGs) that must be achieved by any Superfund cleanup. However, if the MCLGs require zero risk or if EPA considers them not relevant to the cleanup, then a less stringent Maximum Contaminant Level (MCL) may be substituted. Because the relevancy of the cleanup standard is frequently EPA's decision and the more stringent MCLGs have not always been used as guidelines, environmental groups have criticized EPA's selection of cleanup risk targets as insufficiently protective of human health.[11]

In most instances, the nine NCP criteria are impossible to meet jointly, and conflicts naturally arise. For example, cost and community acceptance, cost and permanence, and short-term and long-term effectiveness can all conflict in selecting cleanup remedies. While the NCP outlines the necessary criteria to consider when selecting a site remedy, taken as a whole it is both vague and of little assistance to EPA in weighing the importance of each criterion. Many have been critical of the process. Thomas Grumbly of Clean Sites, Inc. notes that instead of deciding in advance the appropriate level of protection and the likely future use of the site, EPA first evaluates every alternative cleanup method. He concludes that the "current remedy selection process works backwards."[12] A former EPA official notes caustically, "the process is totally screwed up."[13]

In order to justify its remedy selection, EPA relies upon risk assessments conducted as part of the Remedial Investigation and Feasibility Study, later used as justification of its Record of Decision (ROD). However, the practical use of the risk assessment has been questioned in a study by Carolyn Doty and Curtis Travis of the Oak Ridge National Laboratory's Office of Risk Analysis.[14] Their survey of fifty RODs found that remedial decisions were not based on the level of risk *reduction*, since risk reduction was calculated for only 12 percent (6) of the sites evaluated. In addition, actual human exposure was found at only 22 percent of the sites, all of which were cleaned up. Finally, they report that "cost appeared to be the most significant factor in the selection of remedial alternatives."[15] They conclude that, "Equal attention and resources are generally given to all sites, regardless of risk."[16] In short, the study suggests that the role of risk assessment in Superfund cleanup decisions has been modest at best, although the results should be understood in the context of a relatively small sample of sites and the lack of any formal statistical analysis to isolate independent contributing factors. A more sophisticated study of 110 Superfund cleanup decisions, by researchers at Resources for the Future and the University of Maryland, showed that cost-effectiveness and permanence were important contributors to EPA's site-specific decision making.[17]

Bureaucratic Incentives under Superfund

How do agencies decide how to allocate funds? One explanation is "fair-share" budgeting, in which different geographic regions or sections of the agency receive their fair-share of agency resources. Another is that "pork-barrel politics," or some form of congressional control, actually conditions agency responses. A final explanation is that some form of distributive equity—where disadvantaged regions disproportionately benefit from the largess of the federal government—best explains how agencies allocate resources. Each hypothesis is applied directly to Superfund below.

EPA's Budgetary Allocations and Fair-Share Budgeting

The EPA distributes Superfund monies to its ten regions to finance the various stages of site investigations and remedial actions. Because the regions make virtually all site-specific cleanup decisions, the way that money is allocated is central to understanding Superfund's priorities. Basically, the process involves what EPA terms a "modified Delphi" technique.[18] Based on interviews with EPA officials, the process contains the following steps. First, EPA headquarters in Washington draws up budget plans for the year, based on three spending categories: study, design, and construction. Using these preliminary figures, the EPA Superfund branch chief in Washington and representatives from each of the ten EPA regions (generally regional branch chiefs) meet to decide how much funding each region will receive. Each region approaches the meeting with a prioritized list of sites on which they would like to see action taken, and the merits of each site action are debated. The final product is a list of nationwide sites ostensibly ranked according to risk. Starting from the top of the list (the riskiest sites), EPA headquarters allocates funding sequentially until the year's appropriations are exhausted, in effect establishing a cutoff point for funding.

The fact that significant input is drawn from EPA's ten regions suggests that a form of "fair-share" budgeting is possible.[19] The idea is that regardless of the merits of each region's request for funding, there will be a tendency to distribute resources so that no one region's budget is either cut or enhanced significantly from the previous year's budget. Each region is therefore expected, under this theory, to receive its "fair share" of additional resources, irrespective of merit. This is especially likely in the case of Superfund, since each region is equally represented (one person per region) at these meetings despite wide variation in the number of NPL sites in each.[20] Naturally, some regions will receive greater funding than others, based purely on merit (such as the number of sites and the relative hazard posed by each). But the fair-share concept predicts that the tendency will remain to distribute resources more evenly among regions than merit would allow. Indeed, empirical evidence presented later in the chapter shows that the fair-share factor has had at least a modest impact on Superfund expenditure and cleanup patterns.

Distributive Equity

Economist Robert Inman has shown that the pattern of the distribution of federal aid to states and localities is not well explained by traditional public finance rationales for federal aid—the presence of national public goods, interjurisdictional spillovers, and within-community allocative inefficiency—but rather by across-state equity and especially distributive politics. With regard to equity, Inman states that "federal aid is almost always inversely related to the level of state income," and he notes the "observed equity bias to federal aid."[21] Therefore, Superfund sites may be allocated in such a way as to target greater expenditures to poorer sections of the country, motivated by concerns for distributive equity.

The Nature of Pork-Barrel Politics

A number of researchers purportedly have shown that self-interested legislators can tilt geographically based policy outcomes in their favor.[22] In these studies, legislators are assumed to be rational "utility maximizers" seeking only reelection. To be reelected, legislators "look out for their own" by supporting projects that bring net benefits to their districts, even if these projects are inefficient from a national perspective. As a result, local beneficiaries have an incentive to reelect such legislators, since the locality bears only a small fraction of the costs while reaping a lion's share of the benefits.[23]

The empirical studies that allegedly demonstrate pork-barrel politics generally proceed like this: programs are analyzed where geographic benefits are distributed either directly by Congress or by an executive agency. The studies then try to find a statistical relationship between the relevant oversight or appropriations committees in Congress and the geographic distribution of projects. The usual conclusion (at least that of the studies that wind up in academic journals) is that since committee membership is associated with project distribution (for example, transportation committee members may receive more transportation projects in their districts than nonmembers), pork-barrel politics dominates the process. This relationship is alleged to hold true even if the agency directly allocates program benefits instead of Congress, because agencies are still thought to be beholden to indirect congressional influence.[24]

There is, however, ample room for skepticism that pork-barrel politics is the appropriate conclusion to draw. A primary problem is that a correlation between project funding and committee membership fails to identify the direction of causality: Does committee membership influence the agency's project selection process—the classic pork-barrel—or does the district's need for the project drive committee assignments (or both)? In other words, the committee-project correlation could be the result of a legitimate procedure. Legislators could be serving on the relevant committees simply because reasonable people would agree that their constituents should receive those projects. A project with reelection benefits to a legislator does not preclude efficiency, equity, or some other public interest justification. An observed correlation between committee membership and project funding could be the result not of the inherent political influence of these positions, but rather an indication of those regions most deserving of certain federal projects.[25] At the very least, some consistent measure of a project's social value is necessary to separate the possible public interest component of the program's resource distribution from political influence. An employment discrimination analogy is appropriate: Just as one cannot fairly claim that an employer is discriminating based on gender in its hiring without controlling for the legitimate qualifications of the applicants (such as their aptitude or quality of references), neither can one say that a political decision process is characterized by pork without an unbiased measure of the project's merit.[26] This is the heart of the issue of whether Congress chooses projects based on legislative self-interest or its perception of the national interest.[27]

Indeed, there is descriptive evidence that legislators actively pursue goals other than reelection.[28] There is not, however, any evidence establishing if, or how, legislators trade off public interest and political objectives. Political scientist John Ferejohn has investigated systematically the presence of pork-barrel politics in rivers and harbors legislation at the Army Corps of Engineers.[29] Although he found a relationship between Corps project selection and congressional committee membership, the causal connection remains unclear.[30] The pork may have been allocated efficiently, based on legislators' public interest objectives, or may have been distributed inefficiently and inequitably, based purely on political influence. Other authors[31] have included a measure of "regional demand" in their models to try to isolate the choice process from agenda-setting. Although their significant contributions are thought to represent the current state of the art,[32] what is still missing from the analysis is an answer to the question of whether the project is in the larger public's interest. Specifically, the models developed by Arnold and many others[33] cannot test for distributive politics in the manner suggested above because project merit is ignored.[34] In short, these empirical studies have promoted the development of a systematic analysis of federal programs, but they do not reveal whether the policy mix itself is inefficient or inequitable due to self-interested legislative influence.[35] The models employed simply test whether the distributive politics model better predicts observed behavior than no model at all. Indeed, it would be startling if legislators did not represent their constituents' interests!

For the purposes of this analysis, it is important to distinguish between two types of pork-barrel or distributive politics. The first is what I call *allocative pork,* in which legislators direct site-specific federal resources to their districts in a manner that violates the public interest. For example, there is evidence that powerful congressional subcommittee members were able to direct greater numbers of inefficient Army Corps water resource projects to their districts than nonmembers.[36] The second, *programmatic pork,* occurs when legislators expand a program to include more regions of the country than merit would allow in order to generate sufficient political support.[37] Perhaps the best example is the Model Cities program, which was expanded well beyond its originally modest scale in order to attract enough congressional support (by establishing a sufficient number of experiments in different congressional districts).[38] Below I investigate claims of allocative pork, or site-specific influence over Superfund expenditures and priorities that legislators may have in directing federal resources to their districts. Chapter 7 examines programmatic pork in greater detail.

According to the distributive politics model, the allocation of Superfund resources reflects not broader public goals, but rather the particular geographic distribution of congressional power on which EPA must depend for support. One of the best ways for legislators to improve their chances of reelection is to provide services to their districts by responding to constituent requests and channeling federal dollars to the district. Because Congress can direct bureaucratic behavior through oversight, appointments, and budget control, agencies that depend on congressional approval (such as EPA) can be expected to respond to the requests of key legislators in order to enlarge their agency's budget and scope of authority.[39] Allegations that Superfund is a pork-barrel program spring from a variety of sources. Economist Bruce Yandle, among many others, has voiced concern that Superfund is "an attractive politician's pork barrel."[40] Even former EPA administrator Anne Burford has said: "An aspect of the Superfund Act that always kind of tickled me was that it says, though not quite so bluntly, 'By the way, while you're at it, try to find a Superfund site in every Congressional district.' Congress knew it had all the earmarks of a classic pork-barrel opportunity. And . . . it has not failed to live up to that opportunity."[41] Superfund's critics can make a strong case for the *theoretical* likelihood that Superfund is ripe for distributive politics. After all, the program confers local benefits while spreading cleanup costs nationally; a site could turn up in virtually any congressional district; it provides legislators with the opportunity to publicly castigate corporate polluters; the program is highly visible to the public and the media; it is well funded; and one can never tell how clean is clean, meaning that virtually limitless federal money can be spent cleaning up a local site. However, despite a strong theoretical basis for expecting Superfund pork, the allegations have been decidedly lacking in supporting empirical evidence. The debate lacks a discussion of how Superfund monies are being spent and how priorities are actually established. EPA has spent billions of dollars evaluating and cleaning up inactive hazardous waste sites. How does EPA actually allocate the funds? What criteria are used to make these decisions? After reviewing the institutional incentives that EPA and Congress bring to Superfund, I evaluate statistically the determinants of EPA's spending and resource allocation priorities.

Agency Incentives

The EPA is charged with allocating Superfund monies, although Congress has set no explicit guidelines for determining funding priorities or the pace of cleanup. The legislation similarly is vague regarding the type of cleanup required at any one site. Superfund does promote certain bureaucratic objectives, however. Indeed, Superfund's advantages to both EPA and Congress are difficult to overlook. Superfund is a major source of the agency's funding, which represents power through sheer budget size and staffing capabilities. Superfund expenditures are growing in proportion to EPA's total budget (see figure 1.1 in the first chapter), a trend made particularly pronounced by reductions to localities in the sewer construction grant program over the last decade. Much of the increase in absolute dollars can be traced to Superfund's increase in excise tax receipts, which rose from $244 million in fiscal year 1982 to over $1 billion by 1989.[42] Not only does Superfund represent a large portion of EPA's total budget, but the primary funding source—a tax on petroleum and chemical feedstocks—is removed from the vagaries of the federal budget process. Superfund's financing therefore serves to prevent zero-sum legislative battles: cleaning up a Superfund site does not reduce directly monies for other popular programs. Finally, Superfund also allows EPA to expand its domain by becoming involved in public health and cancer-fighting issues.[43]

Legislative Incentives

Superfund represents a two-edged sword for legislators. Abandoned hazardous waste sites, unlike flood control projects and military bases, are not facilities that legislators covet in their districts. Legislators surely do not welcome the publicity of having their local landfill designated as one of the nation's worst and placed on the National Priorities List, even if the site's creation was no fault of their own. While in the early 1980s states were actively promoting their sites for the NPL, states are now far more reluctant to do so, and in some cases consider their past actions to have been a mistake.[44] In some instances, states have even tried to keep sites off the NPL for fear of the site cleanup becoming bogged down in the federal cleanup procedures.[45] In addition, companies and communities may not want the negative publicity brought about by a Superfund site to affect sales or property values. Finally, a locality may fear that the local business will go bankrupt if forced to remediate the site, taking local jobs along with it.

Once a site has been discovered or placed on the NPL, however, legislators have an opportunity (some would say an obligation) to provide well-publicized federal support for their constituents. By pressuring EPA to clean up a particularly onerous Superfund site in their district, legislators can demonstrate their influence in Washington and claim credit for waste site cleanups. As a result, a legislator's incentives take an abrupt change of course once a site has been placed on the NPL. While the legislator is not apt to discover or publicize a waste site, nor to welcome the attending publicity, there is an incentive to claim credit once the site is discovered for any cleanup or federal expenditures in the district. Given public opinion towards hazardous waste sites, there is also a considerable political payoff despite the lengthy remedial process.

The type of distributive politics expected under Superfund is somewhat different than that expected for traditional pork-barrel programs, however. For one thing, the district does not stand to reap an economic windfall if its site is selected for cleanup. The chief beneficiaries are not local workers, but the large national contractors chosen to clean up the waste sites. Nonetheless, indirect benefits of added spending in the district are likely to assist the region; for example, cleaning up a waste site is likely to raise previously depressed property values.[46] Moreover, even while the site languishes on the NPL with little cleanup action forthcoming, legislators can blame EPA, not themselves, for holding up the effort. After all, nearly every legislator can claim credit for voting for the final CERCLA legislation and SARA amendments, which together provide billions of dollars for waste cleanup efforts, presumably absolving them of any further responsibility. Although the incentive—to provide for their constituents—is similar, the legislator's impetus for action is to rid the district of hazardous waste sites rather than to provide direct economic benefits.[47] These incentives have moved many to indict Superfund as a wasteful pork-barrel program. One commentator has said, "Although its defenders try to represent the Superfund reauthorization as a decisive action by Congress to address a matter of urgent national importance, the legislation is in fact one of the worst examples of budget-busting pork-barrel politics in recent history."[48]

Site-specific congressional influence over the Superfund cleanup process can reveal itself in several ways. First, given the vast pool of hazardous waste sites, legislators may try to secure larger numbers of NPL sites for their districts, thereby increasing the chances for federal funding. Legislators can increase the probability of a federal cleanup by exerting influence over the initial placement of sites on the NPL, so they can be eligible for federal funding. Second, once a site has been proposed for the NPL, legislators may press EPA for faster promotion of the site to the final NPL, a necessary requirement for sites to receive federal cleanup funding. Third, legislators may try to generate larger federal Superfund expenditures in their districts either to demonstrate their influence in Washington to their constituencies, or to provide at least indirect economic benefits to their constituents. In addition, legislators may try to "gold-plate" cleanup efforts by convincing EPA that a more expensive remedy is required. For example, they may pressure EPA to remove or treat all affected wastes and groundwater, rather than restricting entry to the site or providing alternative water supplies. Fourth, legislators may try to increase the pace of EPA's cleanup efforts. They can improve their own reelection chances by convincing EPA to clean up their district's Superfund site more quickly. Finally, an influential legislator may be able to take advantage of the less formal emergency removal procedures to secure a federally funded removal action for the district, again to claim credit for helping the district and demonstrating influence in Washington.

Unfortunately, the first hypothesis—that legislators deliberately increase the number of NPL sites in their district in order to claim credit for federal cleanups—is virtually impossible to test systematically. The reason is that the pool of sites from which the NPL sites are drawn is unknown (estimates range from 30,000 to over 400,000 possible waste sites); and, because most sites are not even in EPA's site inventory system, preliminary HRS scores have not been calculated. Nevertheless, it is possible to estimate the impact with the minimal information available, by regressing the number of NPL sites in each state against key congressional committee assignments and other factors. The number of NPL sites in each state is intended to measure whether certain committee assignments, or the state's production of hazardous waste, are associated with large numbers of final NPL sites in each state. A statistical analysis relating the effects of political and manufacturing variables on the number of NPL sites per state illuminates important correlations.[49] First, two specific and strong relationships exist between the number of final NPL sites per state and key subcommittee assignments. A House or Senate authorizing subcommittee chair is associated with a significant increase of about sixteen sites in the state. Aside from authorizing subcommittee chairs, however, none of the other subcommittee positions is associated with large numbers of sites on the final NPL. Second, a state's hazardous waste production is positively related to the number of sites in the state. This is not surprising since we would expect that states producing high volumes of hazardous wastes would have more Superfund sites. It is important to emphasize, though, that this analysis does not determine the direction of legislative influence, in other words whether the large number of NPL sites in the state attracted legislators to the Superfund subcommittees, or whether subcommittee chairs were able to secure more sites for their states. The remaining hypotheses are examined below.

Testing What Influences Superfund Priorities

This section employs an integrated model of public interest and distributive politics to determine whether the overall pace of cleanup efforts and funding of Superfund sites in the 1980s was dictated by either of several factors: self-interested congressional influence, public-interest motives (including distributive equity), or maintaining EPA's regional parity by fair-share budgeting. An important consideration is whether political influence remains after accounting for the social merits of site remediation. The typical distributive politics model would contend that the speed with which Superfund sites are cleaned up and the level of funding for each are based on congressional committee influence and, in the better studies, state and local demand. This model adds the possibility that EPA makes decisions based on public-interest motives including site cleanup benefits and equity.

Including a measure of a site's public benefit (in this case, the Hazard Ranking System (HRS) scores) serves two important purposes in estimating the potential influence of congressional subcommittee positions. First, the public benefit of cleaning up a particular site isolates whether the site is worthy of consideration independent of political objectives. As a result, the degree to which EPA chooses sites in the "public interest" (recognizing that a multiplicity of interests exists) and which serve key congressional districts at the expense of the general public, can be distinguished. Second, the HRS scores allow the self-selection bias inherent in models of legislative influence to be attenuated. Most models do not specify whether committees influence agency behavior or whether district needs propel committee membership. Including the HRS score, an albeit imperfect measure of the health benefits to the district of cleaning up a site, enables legislative influence on agency behavior to be distinguished from the district's need for federal aid.[50] Because the HRS formula is explicit and the documents for compiling the pathway scores are sufficiently routinized, there is little potential for site-specific congressional manipulation. Formalized HRS scores have both limited the ability of EPA to respond to certain sites that may expose the public to particularly onerous consequences (to the extent that HRS scores may fail to reflect health impacts) and attenuated the possibility of legislative or agency manipulation of HRS scores to justify federal expenditures in a particular district (as has been found, for example, in cost-benefit analyses conducted by the Army Corps of Engineers).[51] The HRS scores are intended to serve, however, as a rough approximation of the overall level of risk to the exposed population, the only such measure available for all NPL sites.

Data

Data are drawn from various EPA sources, and include cross-sectional site-specific characteristics from the Superfund site inventory system (CERCLIS) as well as socioeconomic data at the congressional district and state levels, compiled from 1980 U.S. Census sources. The data include one observation for each of 799 sites on the final National Priorities List as of 31 December 1988, from a total of 1177 on the entire NPL.[52] The dependent variables used in the analysis were selected to address the four testable hypotheses outlined above. The first is the length of time between a site being designated "proposed" and "final" on the NPL, which may be a function of either a legislator's particular influence or site-specific characteristics. Two variables measure EPA's past and expected future financial commitment to each site: total expenditures on each site through 1988 and the discounted present value of EPA's planned future obligations for each site. The third dependent variable is the pace of site cleanup, which again may be a function of either legislative influence or the public health hazard posed by the site. This is measured using a composite variable combining three site cleanup stages: whether a site has started the RI/FS process, whether the ROD has been signed, and whether remedial action has started. The final outcome is whether or not a removal action has occurred at each site, which again may be influenced by the site's potential health hazard or by legislative clout. Together, these policy outcomes should yield some insight into whether distributive politics or public interest concerns most influence EPA's decision-making process.

Independent or explanatory variables include evidence of public benefit (the three HRS pathway scores),[53] congressional committee influence (the four relevant House and Senate subcommittees),[54] and equity (per capita district income, percentage of county residents below the poverty level, the county's median housing value, the percentage of residents who are nonwhite, and the percentage who have attended four or more years of college). Three variables are included as measures of the state and local "demand" for site cleanup.[55] The first, whether the state designated the site as its highest priority, reflects state demand for cleanup, while the second and third, the percentage of long-term residents in the county and the percentage of housing that is owner-occupied, are intended to capture the likely degree of local political cohesion and therefore support for the cleanup.[56] In order to test the fair-share budgeting hypothesis mentioned above, a variable indicating the number of final NPL sites in each EPA region is included as well. If the fair-share hypothesis is true, one would expect that a site located in a region with many sites would, considering the merits of each site (their HRS scores), receive less funding than an equivalent site in a region with few sites. A variety of control variables are included as well, such as the year the site was added to the final NPL, whether federal Superfund monies are the chief funding source, and whether the site is federally owned. Variable definitions and sample statistics are presented in tables A.6.1 and A.6.2, respectively, of the Appendix.

Higher values for each of the dependent variables indicate faster progression to cleanup, higher levels of federal funding, and more removal actions. As such, the distributive politics model would predict positive coefficients representing the influence of each of the congressional subcommittees. The model also would predict that the "public interest" variables representing equity and public benefit would have no influence over Superfund site decisions since they are not expected to affect self-interested legislators. Naturally, the public interest model predicts that the site's relative health hazard and various equity measures strongly influence EPA decisions over Superfund priorities and that congressional committee assignments reflect not undue influence but rather the state and local demand for cleanup (which is assumed to drive committee assignments). Local demand, as represented by each state's priority site designation and a high concentration of long-term residents (who can be expected to exert greater political pressures than transient neighbors), can be expected to contribute positively to the pace of cleanup, level of funding, and so forth. Federal funding for site cleanup can be expected to generate strong congressional support and should also increase the amount spent for remedial action. The agency fair-share hypothesis predicts that larger numbers of sites in an EPA region would slow cleanup efforts at any one site in favor of maintaining greater regional parity than merit would permit. Finally, the earlier a site is designated final on the NPL, *ceteris paribus*, the more federal funding it should have received and the greater the likelihood that it would have passed the various stages necessary for cleanup.

Results

Table 6.1 presents multiple regression, ordered probit, and logit results, corresponding to the four hypothesized policy outcomes described above. The first outcome is the length of time a site is designated as "proposed" on the NPL. Are certain legislators, by dint of their committee assignments, able to reduce the length of time before a site becomes eligible for federal cleanup funding? The multiple regression results in the first column of numbers in table 6.1 reveal two unexpected findings. Higher HRS scores (for all three pathways) and state-designated priority, both of which could be expected to promote rapid site progression to cleanup, significantly lengthened the time period between proposed and final NPL status.[57] In addition, federal sites and sites finalized in later years were found to be positively related with the length of time a site was proposed. As the distributive politics model predicts, two subcommittees (Senate authorizing and House appropriations) are associated with reducing the length of time a site is proposed. As expected, the proxy for local cohesiveness, the percentage of long-term residents in the district, also hastened significantly a site's passage from proposed to final status. The higher the value of local housing, however, the slower the progress to final NPL status.

The surprising findings with respect to HRS scores and priority sites may be explained by the fact that nearly one-half of the sites (388 out of 788) were finalized in 1983, most of which were on the proposed list for only 9 months. The rapid initial selection of sites produced some unusual results. By reestimating the equation with only those sites finalized after 1983, the results indicate that the HRS scores are no longer significant determinants of length of time proposed, nor are priority sites.[58] The congressional influence exhibited approximately the same pattern. Federal sites and sites finalized in later years also remained strongly associated with a longer length of time proposed. However, the coefficients for median housing values and owner-occupied housing were both positive and significant, indicating that sites in these areas made slower progress

Table 6.1 Site Progression to Final NPL Status, Expenditures and Obligations, Cleanup Pace, and Removal Actions

			Dependent Variable		
Independent Variable	Pace to Final NPL (t-stat)	Expenditures ($000) (t-stat)	Planned Obligations ($000) (t-stat)	Cleanup Pace (t-stat)	Removal Actions (t-stat)
Intercept	−10.82(10.0)***	14030(2.42)**	−73540(0.94)	19.65(7.15)***	−0.19(0.03)
HRS score (air)	0.00(3.45)***	25(5.42)***	178(2.90)***	0.01(4.25)***	0.02(4.95)***
HRS score (surface water)	0.00(3.30)***	21(4.08)***	187(2.70)***	0.01(3.37)***	0.01(1.75)*
HRS score (groundwater)	0.00(3.90)***	7(1.56)	122(2.13)**	0.00(2.07)**	0.01(1.41)
State priority?	0.61(7.44)***	1261(2.84)***	6369(1.07)	0.03(0.14)	0.47(1.11)
Fund lead?	−0.06(1.90)*	1174(6.69)***	7467(3.16)***	0.59(7.12)***	1.20(6.67)***
Federal site?	0.93(10.6)***	−35(0.07)	−9204(1.46)	−0.84(3.60)***	−1.98(1.89)*
Year final on NPL	0.14(12.2)***	−139(2.19)**	1019(1.19)	−0.22(7.36)***	0.01(0.16)
Senate appropriations subcommittee	−0.01(0.94)	−44(0.54)	−863(0.79)	−0.00(0.03)	−0.18(2.01)**

Senate authorizing subcommittee	−0.08(2.77)***	−71(0.48)	−2015(1.01)	−0.01(0.18)	0.06(0.41)
House appropriations subcommittee	−0.12(2.16)**	−290(1.01)	−1559(0.40)	−0.18(1.31)	0.09(0.33)
House authorizing subcommittee	0.04(1.21)	−55(0.29)	−824(0.33)	0.06(0.67)	−0.05(0.25)
Below poverty level (%)	0.01(1.47)	−64(2.09)**	−114(0.28)	0.00(0.12)	−0.08(2.38)**
Unemployed (%)	−0.01(1.73)*	7(0.21)	−265(0.57)	0.01(0.51)	0.00(0.05)
Median housing value ($000)	0.00(2.15)**	0(0.66)	0(3.60)***	0.00(0.71)	−0.00(3.30)***
Nonwhite (%)	−0.00(0.86)	4(0.33)	10(0.07)	0.01(0.92)	0.03(2.17)**
Owner-occupied housing (%)	0.00(0.91)	−21(1.54)	−277(1.51)	0.01(0.97)	−0.01(0.79)
College educated (%)	−0.00(1.13)	−43(1.84)*	−1079(3.41)***	0.00(0.19)	0.02(0.64)
County residents since 1975 (%)	−0.01(2.22)**	2(0.15)	32(0.14)	−0.01(0.65)	0.00(0.10)
Sites in EPA region (N)	−0.00(1.26)	−3(1.96)**	−1(0.06)	−0.00(3.20)***	−0.00(2.26)**
Observations (N)	788	788	788	788	788
R^2	0.414	0.188	0.067	—	—
Log likelihood	—	—	—	−854.48	−395.12
Likelihood ratio statistic	—	—	—	0.463	0.277

***Significant at 99% level; **95% level; *90% level (two-tailed test).

to final NPL status. These findings indicate a relatively strong relationship between two congressional subcommittees, as well as the influence of more established communities, in diminishing the length of time a site is on the proposed NPL. In addition, the results suggest that the later a site is proposed for the NPL, the longer it will take to reach final status. Final NPL status does not, however, guarantee federal expenditures or cleanup efforts. A more important step for testing the distributive politics and public interest models is analyzing the pattern of EPA's expenditures and planned future obligations.

Columns 2 and 3 of table 6.1 show the results of two multiple regression analyses, the first employing total federal expenditures on each site (as of 1 January 1989) as the dependent variable, the second using the present value of EPA's planned future obligations. The same set of independent variables is included. As the results indicate, the independent HRS pathway scores are associated with consistently higher expenditures as well as planned federal obligations. The air and surface water HRS score coefficients are consistently larger and more significant than the groundwater coefficients.[59] The results provide strong evidence that even after accounting for the site's hazard potential, the federal fund lead is associated with significantly higher expenditures, as are sites designated by states to be their highest priority. The equity coefficients reflect mixed priorities: high poverty levels and low housing prices are associated with fewer expenditures and planned obligations, respectively, but so are highly educated communities. Finally, the fair-share hypothesis is supported by the pattern of total expenditures (more sites in the region slightly decreases each site's expenditures), yet there is no significant impact on future obligations. Most prominent, however, is the lack of any significant congressional subcommittee influence over either past expenditures or planned obligations.[60] At least in terms of subcommittee influence over total expenditures or obligations, there appears to be little evidence of allocative pork-barrel politics.

One may expect, however, that if, as indicated above, subcommittee members have not systematically been able to pressure EPA to intervene on their behalf by increasing expenditures for certain sites, they may have been able to "gold-plate" the cleanup effort once EPA has decided to proceed with remediation. We would therefore expect that of the set of sites for which the type of cleanup has been determined (where RODs have been signed), those in well-represented congressional districts would be targeted to receive higher federal expenditures. This hypothesis was tested by regressing the total estimated present value of expected cleanup expenditures listed in the ROD on the same set of independent variables included in table 6.1. The findings[61] indicate a strong relationship between the HRS pathway scores and the planned cleanup expenditures.[62] Somewhat surprisingly, the federal fund lead was not associated with significantly higher estimated cleanup costs, although both it and the state's priority designation coefficients are positive. In addition, the variable representing the number of members on the House Subcommittee on Transportation, Tourism, and Hazardous Materials from the site's district was significantly and positively related to increased planned expenditures. Therefore, some evidence points to possible "gold-plating" of cleanup efforts on the part of at least one congressional subcommittee.

The third legislative incentive outlined above is committee influence over the stages each site must pass through before cleanup procedures are initiated. In this analysis, three measures of the speed of cleanup are employed. Three progressive stages that a Superfund NPL site must pass through before final cleanup include an initial Remedial Investigation and Feasibility Study (RI/FS) that analyzes the consequences of alternative strategies, the Record of Decision (ROD) that outlines and defends EPA's choice of a cleanup remedy, and the actual cleanup, or "remedial action." Accordingly, the dependent variable is coded 0 if none of these cleanup stages has been reached, 1 if the RI/FS has been started, 2 if the ROD has been signed, and 3 if a remedial action has begun. Therefore, higher numbers represent further progress toward final remediation. The pace of site cleanups is modeled as a function of the site's potential health hazard, possible state and congressional political influence, the racial and economic characteristics of the region, and the ability of district residents to mobilize and hasten the remedial effort.

Ordered probit estimates for the measure of site cleanup progress are shown in the fourth column of numbers in table 6.1.[63] The most important indicators of whether a site has reached a particular cleanup stage are the HRS scores (higher hazard scores are associated with a greater probability of reaching any given stage of the cleanup process), a federal fund lead, a federally owned site, and the year of the final designation on the NPL.[64] Political representation was for the most part insignificant in determining cleanup pace. There is, however, virtually no relationship between a site reaching a particular cleanup stage and the county's socioeconomic characteristics. In contrast to the results in chapter 5, where socioeconomic characteristics were found to be significant indicators of Superfund site locations, the pace of federal cleanup efforts bears no relationship to a county's racial and economic composition. There is, however, significant support for the fair-share hypothesis: the greater the number of sites in the region, the less likely is a site to advance to another cleanup stage.

The most surprising result to come from these analyses is the absence of legislative influence over a variety of critical stages in the Superfund cleanup process. The relevant congressional subcommittees had little or no revealed impact on expenditures (past and planned) or in reaching various stages of cleanup. One possible explanation is that congressional influence may spill over into other districts, and therefore a legislator's impact may not be captured by examining only the pace of cleanup in a single district. However, separate estimates, using the number of representatives on the appropriate subcommittees from each site's *state* rather than the district, turned up no such evidence of subcommittee influence.[65]

Another possible explanation for the apparent lack of congressional committee influence is that the Superfund process is so constrained by administrative guidelines, through efforts to encourage local public participation and many other standard (and time-consuming) operating procedures, that legislators cannot exercise much direct control over EPA's spending or cleanup priorities.[66] However, EPA's emergency removal decisions are by design less routinized and would represent one area in which Superfund priorities could be guided by key legislators without upsetting EPA's standard operating procedures. Legislators presumably could claim a significant amount of credit by engineering emergency removal actions in their district. Data were gathered indicating whether or not each site on the NPL had received an emergency removal action. The final column of table 6.1 shows the results of the logit analysis on the same set of independent variables used above. Despite the absence of rigid standards for emergency removals, there is no indication that these congressional subcommittees influenced their pattern of application. The variables most likely to influence the probability of receiving a removal action were higher HRS scores (though less significantly than for previous analyses) and a federal fund-lead designation. Oddly enough, Senate Appropriations subcommittee membership is associated with a reduced likelihood to having had a removal action. And again, the implications for equity are unclear. While lower housing values and a larger proportion of racial minorities are associated with a greater likelihood of an emergency removal action, so are lower poverty levels.

Conclusions

Several conclusions about the allocation of Superfund's resources can be drawn from this analysis. First, the most consistently dominant finding is that the most hazardous sites—measured by the admittedly crude HRS scores—are cleaned up faster than others. (However, in the absence of cost information, it is not clear that resources are best allocated by targeting the most hazardous sites. One relevant consideration is a comparison of marginal risks abated with marginal costs.) In addition, sites that have been on the NPL for a longer period of time, nonfederal sites, federal fund-lead sites, and state priority sites all have generally received greater attention from EPA. Finally, although the variables reflecting equity were sometimes significant indicators of EPA's priorities, they were inconsistent in direction. For example, counties with higher median housing values are linked to an increased length of time between proposed and final NPL status and are less likely to have removal actions, yet they were associated with larger planned cleanup obligations. Thus, the important and predictable direction of the equity coefficients was mixed.

As important as those factors that influenced EPA's decisions are those that did not. Most importantly, congressional committee influence had no effect over the distribution of resources or the pace of cleanups. Thus, the *allocative* pork discussed above appears not to influence Superfund decision making, as many have charged. However, this does not preclude the possibility of *programmatic* pork. Indeed, even this analysis leads us to suspect that programmatic pork may be at work through each state's priority designation. The fact that state priority sites reach final NPL status faster than others and more money is spent on them, indicates that Superfund's resources are being distributed widely, although not apparently to benefit any specific committee members. Thus, the incentive built into CERCLA's original language to include at least one site per state on the NPL (that site in many cases being designated as the state's priority) has served its intended purpose: to distribute cleanup resources to states that might not otherwise receive them.

The evidence suggests that the common mechanism of distributive politics, the inefficient influence of particular committee members, does not appear to be pervasive once a site has been designated as final on the NPL. It appears that with the available evidence of the benefits of cleaning up each site (HRS scores), EPA's site-specific decisions have been made more with the potential site hazards in mind than with the influence of key legislators.[67] It is not as though legislators are uninterested in site-specific cleanup decisions, but rather that their interest appears to be more informational than confrontational. In the words of a high-ranking regional EPA official, "Inquiries from congressmen are not lobbying, but for their information so they can respond to their constituents."[68] If the Superfund program is an ineffective way to reduce environmental and health risks, then the findings in this chapter would imply a more deeply rooted pork-barrel program that perhaps, much like the Model Cities program, was expanded in order to survive. Regardless of Superfund's inefficiency, these findings suggest that EPA is not catering to specific congressional committee requests and is devoting efforts to cleaning up first those sites that pose the most significant threats to the environment and human health.

These results also suggest that the model of distributive politics needs to be reconsidered with respect to Superfund. Either the model is wrong (legislators are not able to influence agencies to commit federal funds for inefficient cleanup efforts in their districts) or, more likely, the specification of the political payoff for legislators is incomplete. One explanation is that the governing committees or subcommittees may no longer exercise significant control over agency actions: other (and perhaps much larger) legislative coalitions may influence agency policy. Another misspecification may be that the payoff for individual committee members extends beyond conventional district or state boundaries. For instance, legislators may try to build reputations outside their districts, based upon a single issue (such as the environment). We would then observe such legislators supporting not only Superfund sites in their own districts, but the entire program itself. These legislators may be self-serving not by trying to satisfy only immediate constituents, but by expanding their constituencies through broader program appeals. For example, James Florio substantially enhanced his reputation as an environmentalist and champion of an important state issue by becoming a principal figure in promoting Superfund legislation. Even though estimates show that he did not influence EPA to direct additional resources to New Jersey's first district,[69] he expanded his constituency to the entire state—and was subsequently elected governor—by appealing to an issue of great concern to many New Jersey voters.

There is little question that some sites are in need of federal assistance to facilitate their cleanup and that the (nonpolitical) benefits of such assistance would outweigh the costs. If a resource allocation problem with Superfund exists, it appears to be not that specific committees are controlling EPA's site-specific Superfund decisions, but that the program is sufficiently entrenched so that most districts now can benefit from increased funding. Although committee-based allocative pork does not seem to dominate EPA's cleanup policies, an analysis of *programmatic* pork is fundamental to understanding Superfund policy. This is taken up in the next chapter.

7 Why Have Legislators Voted to Expand Superfund?

Incentives for undue political influence or corruption exist any time a federal program distributes money. The issue is whether, given the properties that make Superfund particularly attractive to self-interested legislators, broad empirical evidence supports the allegation of pork-barrel politics.[1] The results of the previous chapter indicated that if distributive politics is defined as committee-based influence beyond public interest motives, then the past site-specific allocation of Superfund expenditures and cleanup priorities reflects the far greater influence of the site's hazard potential than congressional influence. However, this illuminates only part of the picture. Pork-barrel politics can derive either from committee-based influence *or* from self-interested legislators voting to expand programs from which their constituents stand to gain a disproportionate share of the benefits in relation to costs. Naturally, this also benefits legislators themselves by increasing their chances for reelection through credit-claiming. In this fashion, the intention to expand Superfund could have derived from the desire to attract enough legislators to sustain a congressional coalition. Although the previous chapter showed that Congress does not dominate site-specific decisions, the question of programmatic pork remains.

To support the contention that Superfund is a pork-barrel program, it is necessary to show *either* that individual subcommittees are effective in channeling Superfund money to their constituents or that legislators from districts that stand to benefit from program expansion are voting for Superfund in greater numbers than those from districts that stand to gain little. The presence of either condition would support the distributive politics model; the denial of both would cast doubt that Superfund is driven by pork-barrel intentions. This chapter seeks to determine whether Superfund exists in its present form because self-interested legislators have voted for their own districts' interests or because legislators have voted according to their environmental and economic beliefs.

Congressional Self-Interest and Distributive Politics

Theoretical research supports the contention that legislators find it in their self-interest to distribute concentrated benefits but spread costs widely.[2] The alleged link between congressional self-interest and policy decisions derives from a substantial, albeit somewhat inconclusive, empirical literature.[3] Two methodologies exist for separating self-interest from the larger public interest in voting studies: specifying the public interest directly through the particular issue being studied (is voting for or against the proposal in the public interest?) or separating legislative self-interest from a legislator's independent ideology in voting for a particular piece of legislation.

Using the first method, one study on congressional campaign expenditure ceilings alleges that legislators' self-interest dominates public interest motives in voting (although both self- and public interests are statistically significant explanatory variables).[4] However, the author's view of what constitutes the public interest rests solely on his judgment of whether a particular stand on the issue itself is in the public interest. The public is better served, he contends, if legislators vote against restricting campaign expenditures, using as his justification that "economists would generally agree that limitations on advertising, whether for goods or for candidates, are unlikely to serve the public interest."[5]

Although this line of research is potentially fruitful, to the degree that the public interest component of any vote can be identified, this approach has problems that limit its widespread applicability to other policy issues. First, it is treacherous for any researcher to put a personal imprimatur on the public interest merits of one policy proposal over another, even one with wide acceptance among both political scientists and economists.[6] For example, while many agree that limitations on campaign spending favor incumbents, this does not imply that limitations necessarily work against the public interest without a more refined definition of the public interest. It is not necessarily true that more campaign spending conveys more *meaningful* communication between candidates and voters. Indeed, it is possible that limitations on spending could sufficiently change the type of communication (from thirty-second television advertisements to less costly but more detailed position papers, for instance) and that, as a result, more meaningful information would reach the electorate, thus enhancing the public debate. Furthermore, spending limitations may redirect legislators' priorities away from the virtually incessant demands of fund-raising and, perhaps, toward more legislating, serving constituents, and other more worthy pursuits. The point is that definitive statements that a certain position on an issue enhances the public interest must be met with some measure of skepticism. Rarely are policy issues so straightforward. And even with those issues where there is widespread agreement (such as opposition to protectionist measures), it is not clear that legislators should not represent the interests of their constituents even if the policy is harmful to the nation as a whole. There may be perfectly good public-interest reasons for favoring campaign finance restrictions (which, for example, Common Cause supports) which would explain a legislator's voting position just as well as self-interest in retaining a seat.

A second problem in this line of research is its inability to recognize the existence of legislative log-rolling.[7] Just as legislators trade votes to gain support for their pet programs or projects, legislators may also trade a vote opposing one "publicly interested" program in order to support another more important public-interest position. As a result, opposing a bill that appears to promote the public interest may be motivated not by a desire to subvert good policy, but rather to promote an even better policy. The researcher examining the votes on the former bill would, however, naively conclude that the public interest was ill-served. Thus, vote-trading can seriously complicate any single-issue voting analysis without verification of the assumption that it either does not exist or is insignificant.[8,9] To the extent that clearly public-interest versus self-interest votes cannot be isolated, these efforts to separate self- and public interests have only limited applicability.

Joseph Kalt and Mark Zupan take another more common and widely applicable approach by separating legislators' interests from their ideologies.[10] By decomposing Senate votes on coal strip-mining into a Senator's desire to satisfy local interests (an example in this case is coal-consuming electric utilities) versus a personal environmental and economic ideology, they find evidence that a strong ideological component to congressional voting remains, even after going to great lengths to account for interests representing themselves through measures of ideology. To its advantage, this line of research does not necessitate *ex post facto* judgments regarding the social value of a specific voting position, but it does require specifying explicitly the distinctions between a legislator's interest and ideology. A study by Kau and Rubin similarly finds support for the strong influence of ideology on congressional voting patterns.[11]

In contrast, several studies support the role of congressional self-interest in environmental affairs; interests, not ideology, were found to determine voting outcomes.[12] In short, a considerable amount of evidence suggests that even in environmental matters, where one may expect a large role for ideology, legislators' voting decisions frequently are guided more by their own narrowly defined interests in reelection than by their independent environmental ideologies. This chapter shows, however, that even for an environmental program with both symbolic environmental and public works aspects to it, representatives' ideological positions have greater explanatory power than the region's economic interests they are so often alleged to serve. Nevertheless, there is some evidence of programmatic pork in Superfund voting behavior as well.

Integrated Model of Congressional Self-Interest and Ideology

As the previous chapter indicated, even though legislators are unlikely to publicize hazardous waste dumps in their districts, and in some cases may even work to prevent a site from being listed on the NPL, they are likely to press for cleanup *once the site has been discovered and brought to the public's attention*. They can then claim credit for bringing federal resources to bear on a local problem, ensuring their constituents that their clout in Washington can be exercised again in the future, if they are reelected. This incentive can reveal itself in one of two ways. First, legislators can pressure EPA to clean up their district's site(s) before others, even though the merits for doing so may be dubious. Second, perhaps failing to convince EPA that their districts require special attention, legislators may take the longer view and vote for Superfund program expansion with the hope that a large proportion of future cleanup monies will flow to their districts. Thus, legislators can promote their own self-interest either by specific subcommittee influence (investigated in chapter 6) or by voting for program expansion, which I address here. Under the latter scenario, legislators vote to expand Superfund not because they view it as in the public's best interest, but rather because they believe future net benefits will accrue disproportionately to their districts, improving their chances of securing reelection.

To investigate this claim, a vote to expand Superfund is viewed as a function of both local economic and environmental interests and a legislator's ideology, including legislative self-interests (such as petroleum, chemical, and environmental interests), the legislator's ideology (derived from environmental and liberal ratings by interest groups), the local public demand for Superfund cleanups (the number of NPL sites in the state or district), and other attributes expected to affect Superfund voting (such as regional socioeconomic characteristics). This model is used to examine a Superfund program that has (1) a strong public works component, which according to the legislative self-interest hypothesis would indicate a strong role for local interests; (2) an expensive taxation component, which would suggest a significant effort on the part of petroleum and chemical interests to oppose Superfund expansion; and (3) a strong environmental component, which would imply a strong lobbying effort by environmental interest groups. From an ideological perspective, a legislator's liberal and environmental reputation on other votes besides Superfund, as well as party affiliation, should be expected to play a strong role in voting decisions. Superfund is particularly unusual in its combination of public works, targeted taxation, and environmental components, which uniquely allows interests and ideology to play multiple roles and permits their relative influences to be tested against one another systematically.

Measuring "Ideology"

Legislators' ideologies are represented by their liberal economic and environmental ratings by interest groups and by the party they choose to join. Various interest groups compile the votes of legislators on issues important to them and produce a score, usually on a 0–100 scale, rating the degree to which each legislator supported a particular position in the preceding year (such as an environmentalist or a foreign policy conservative). The results are intended to publicize which legislators frequently support a particular "ideology" and lets them know that their voting record is being watched by people who can affect outcomes. Legislators who are liberal on economic issues and those who rate highly according to environmental indices, for example, can be expected to vote for Superfund expansion. In addition, holding liberal and environmental ratings constant, Democrats can be expected to vote for Superfund expansion more than Republicans because of their acknowledged relative preference for federal government solutions to public policy problems.

The problem in empirical work, as has been shown by several researchers,[13] is that an interest group's measure of "ideology" represents more than ideology alone. Indeed, a legislator's interest-group rating (such as the League of Conservation Voters ratings on environmental issues) may reveal as much about legislators' interests as it does independent ideology. Peltzman has shown that the separate effects of these "ideology" measures are significantly compromised by the introduction of independent variables reflecting the constituencies' socioeconomic characteristics.[14] In other words, legislators may not consistently vote for environmental issues because of their ideological preferences, but rather because their constituents demand that they vote that way. These legislators are presumably interested not in environmentalism per se, but only in reelection. If Peltzman is right that interest group measures of "ideology" reflect in part constituency characteristics, then it is possible theoretically to isolate that part of ideology exclusive of constituents' interests.

The basic idea is to separate that portion of interest-group voting ratings that represents constituent interests from other factors, which are assumed to represent ideology. Following the methods of Kalt and Zupan,[15] two measures of "ideology"—the legislator's ratings on environmental and economic indices—are isolated by first purging them of the influence of their constituents' observable socioeconomic characteristics. The theoretical underpinning of the technique is the median voter model, in which deviations between a legislator's voting record and constituents' interests are assumed to reflect ideology.[16] This is performed by regressing each interest-group measure of ideology on a number of independent variables reflecting the socioeconomic characteristics of the region served by each legislator. The differences between actual scores and those predicted by constituent interests are assumed to reflect the legislator's "pure" ideology. The dependent variables are the League of Conservation Voters' average environmental ratings over the three years preceding the vote in question (to ensure that the vote in question is not part of the "ideology" measure) and the National Journal's composite liberal scores on economic issues in that year. The independent variables include a dummy variable for the legislator's party (1, Democrat; 0, otherwise), per capita income, percentage of residents unemployed, percentage who completed four or more years of college, the median value of housing, the percentage of residents who had lived in the same county for the five years preceding 1980 (from 1980 Census data), the share of state gross domestic product (GDP) comprised of manufacturing, population density, percentage of the population living in an urban area, percentage white, and whether the state is in the South or West. With the exception of the manufacturing share (and obviously for the South and West variables), which are statewide, all other variables are at the district level for House members and the state level when evaluating senators' ideology ratings.

The results indicate that socioeconomic variables explain between 60 and 78 percent of the variation in economic and environmental interest group ratings for both representatives and senators. (Table A.7.1 of the Appendix shows the regression results for 1985.) The independent variables explain more of the variation in liberal economic ideology scores than the environmental scores (explaining more than 75 percent of the variation in economic ideology), but even environmental ideology scores are significantly represented (over 60 percent of the variation is explained by the independent variables). In addition, Senate voting ratings are better explained than House scores, perhaps partly owing to the use of state-wide data for manufacturing. The percentage of the variation in liberal and environmental ratings predicted by these socioeconomic measures for other years shows a similar magnitude and pattern.[17] It should be stressed that although several individual parameter estimates are significant at the 99+ percent level of statistical confidence, this effort is not intended to model the socioeconomic determinants of ideology scores. The intent instead is to isolate "pure" ideology by explaining as much of the constituents' interests as possible, without any special regard for individual parameter estimates.[18] For each year and for each legislator, "pure" economic and environmental ideology scores were calculated as the difference between actual group ratings and those predicted by the district's socioeconomic characteristics.

Voting Data

The dependent variables in this study include important House and Senate Superfund roll-call votes between 1981 and 1988 that were sufficiently close to produce meaningful distinctions between the characteristics of the legislators and their districts.[19] The votes involve the degree to which Superfund is to be expanded; five votes took place in the Senate, three in the House. The first Senate vote (the Symms amendment to S. 51, Superfund Reauthorization, in 1985) was to reduce the amount of spending authorized for fiscal years 1986–90 from $7.5 to $5.7 billion. It was rejected, 15–79; a vote of "No" is considered to be one supporting Superfund expansion. The second vote, also in 1985, was on the Senate's version of H.R. 2005, which would have reauthorized Superfund spending at $7.5 billion over five years. The bill passed, 86–13, and a vote of "Yes" is considered to be one supporting Superfund expansion. The third Senate vote was on the Domenici motion to table the Lautenberg amendment to increase fiscal year 1987 budget authority by $350 million, $41 million of which would have restored funding for Superfund to the level contained in S. 51, the Senate-passed version of the reauthorization. The motion was agreed to, 54–44 (thus killing the Lautenberg amendment), on 30 April 1986. Therefore, a vote of "No" is considered to be one supporting Superfund expansion. The fourth vote involved whether or not Senator Bradley would be allowed to offer his amendment, for a $6 billion Superfund extension, to the Continuing Resolution (whether the amendment was "germane"). The House had already voted for a five-year, $10 billion Superfund extension, but the Reagan administration opposed the Bradley amendment. Bradley's position was supported by many environmental groups, but was ruled nongermane, 38–59, on 2

October 1984. A vote of "Yes" is one supporting Superfund's extension and expansion. The final Senate vote occurred in 1982, after the Budget Committee had frozen EPA's funding for Superfund at fiscal year 1982 levels. The Moynihan amendment would have added $60 million to the First Budget Resolution (Senate Continuing Resolution 92) for Superfund. The amendment was rejected, 41–53, although subsequently $20 million was drawn from other EPA programs and added to Superfund. A vote of "Yes" is considered to be one supporting Superfund expansion.

Important House Superfund votes included one for the adoption of a rule (H. Res. 570) for House floor consideration of renewing and expanding Superfund in 1984. The rule was adopted, 218–199; a vote of "Yes" is considered to be one supporting Superfund expansion. The second House vote is the Conable amendment to H.R. 5640, which would have ended the petroleum and chemical industry tax to finance Superfund after one year, instead of continuing throughout the full five-year extension. The 1984 amendment was rejected, 142–205, despite support from the Reagan administration. Although the Superfund extension passed in the House, it died in the Senate (see the Bradley amendment, Senate vote 4, above). A vote of "No" is considered to be one supporting continued Superfund expansion, since a "Yes" vote would have sharply curtailed the chief source of Superfund revenues. The final House vote analyzed is the 1985 Downey amendment to H.R. 2817 (Superfund Reauthorization), which was to strike the broad-based tax and to provide $10 billion over five years from chemical feedstock and petroleum taxes, hazardous waste disposal taxes, and general revenues. The amendment was adopted, 220–206. A "Yes" vote is considered to be one supporting Superfund expansion.

The independent variables (described in greater detail in table A.7.2 of the Appendix) include both the interests that legislators are expected to serve through the Superfund program and the ideological beliefs that others have alleged to be important in explaining congressional voting behavior. Congressional interests include the relative contribution of the chemical and petroleum industries to the state's total economic output, and the tons of hazardous waste deposited in each state. The number of Superfund NPL sites in each state or district represents the local demand to promote Superfund expansion, with more sites contributing to greater local demand for cleanup.[20] Representatives from states with significant chemical or petroleum industries are expected to oppose Superfund expansion, since a substantial portion of the tax revenues originate from these industries through excise taxes. Similarly, hazardous waste producers (to the extent they differ from chemical and petroleum companies) would try to prohibit Superfund expansion for fear that more sites will be discovered and that they will be forced to finance additional cleanups or at least engage in costly litigation. Thus, the quantity of hazardous waste in each state can be expected to be negatively correlated with votes to expand Superfund. However, a large number of existing Superfund sites in the state (independent of industry interests) should motivate legislators to vote for program expansion in the hope that a large share of the funding will accrue to their constituents. The House voting analysis also includes a variable representing the number of final NPL sites in the state (in addition to those in each district) to account for the possibility that state delegations vote as a block or that legislators may be trying to expand their appeal for a run at state-wide office.[21] Finally, legislators may be serving environmental interests by voting to appease such groups in their state. Thus, the portion of the state's voting population that belongs to one of the six largest environmental groups (at that time, they were the Environmental Defense Fund, Friends of the Earth, National Audubon Society, National Wildlife Federation, Sierra Club, and the Wilderness Society) should be positively correlated to votes for Superfund expansion, in keeping with the congressional self-interest hypothesis.[22]

Residual "pure" economic and environmental ideology measures, derived above, and party affiliation variables are included to represent the legislator's ideology. Control variables include the district's or state's population density (to control for urban/rural differences) and whether the legislator is from the South or the West (to account for regional variation). (Sample statistics for both dependent and independent variables are presented in table A.7.3 of the Appendix.) A logit model is estimated separately for each vote, to examine vote-specific differences in the influence of legislative ideology and self-interest, and the results of a pooled model are presented as well.[23] As the following sections indicate, for each vote, ideology measures taken together were strong indicators of congressional voting patterns. Significantly, the effects of special interests were far stronger when ideology ratings were purged of constituents' characteristics. In other words, Peltzman's contention that ideology scores are comprised in part of constituent interests is verified, even though "pure" ideology still accounts significantly for congressional Superfund voting behavior.

Superfund Voting Estimation Results

The statistical results for the Senate are presented in summary form in table 7.1, and for the House in table 7.2. For ease of interpretation, each vote (dependent variable) has been recoded so that the legislative initia-

Table 7.1 Logit Results for Senate Voting (absolute value of t-statistics in parentheses)

Variable	Vote 1	Vote 2	Vote 3	Vote 4	Vote 5	Pooled
Intercept	−1.29(0.75)	0.75(0.32)	−5.22(2.70)***	−5.72(2.97)***	−5.45(2.32)**	−1.72(3.48)***
Final sites (N)	0.02(0.21)	0.26(1.49)	0.09(2.14)**	0.05(1.71)*	0.06(1.73)*	0.03(2.77)***
Chemical share	44.49(0.73)	23.59(0.35)	−15.66(0.56)	20.20(0.66)	33.49(0.88)	—
Petroleum share	27.63(0.42)	243.89(1.19)	9.89(0.13)	−107.47(1.36)	−23.58(0.36)	3.42(0.34)
Hazardous waste (×10⁻⁵)	−4.88(0.63)	−38.98(1.86)*	10.38(1.74)*	−9.48(1.74)*	−5.67(1.11)	−2.70(1.84)*
Environmental interests	393.15(1.99)**	912.07(1.82)*	326.88(2.12)**	301.52(2.09)**	202.87(1.19)	147.62(3.37)***
Economic ideology	0.01(0.19)	0.35(1.56)	0.07(1.80)*	0.06(1.65)	0.07(2.55)**	0.03(2.81)***
Environmental ideology	0.19(2.36)**	0.34(1.90)*	0.12(3.23)***	0.07(2.22)**	0.11(2.53)**	0.06(5.44)***
Democrat?	3.37(2.05)**	7.40(1.70)*	3.32(3.39)***	4.58(4.26)***	5.63(4.26)***	2.19(7.79)***
Pop. density (×10⁻⁵)	2719.62(0.87)	−308.47(0.34)	401.15(2.02)**	385.04(1.94)*	124.82(0.67)	184.08(2.36)**
Southern state?	−2.18(1.09)	1.16(0.45)	−5.45(3.00)***	1.00(0.79)	−0.79(0.52)	−0.39(0.97)
Western state?	−5.04(2.10)**	−8.30(1.87)*	−1.62(1.24)	−4.01(1.92)*	−0.84(0.63)	−1.25(3.22)***
Observations (N)	94	99	98	97	93	481
Percentage correct	92.6	96.0	90.8	86.6	90.3	79.0
LR statistic	0.789	0.869	0.639	0.617	0.665	0.357
LR test (chi-square)	102.79	119.21	86.84	82.96	85.70	238.36

*** Significant at 99% level; **95% level; *90% level (two-tailed test).

tive to expand (or not to diminish) Superfund is denoted by 1, and otherwise, 0. Thus, positive coefficients for each variable indicate support for Superfund expansion, while negative coefficients reflect opposition.[24]

In the analysis of Senate votes (table 7.1), the number of final sites in the state is positively related to voting for Superfund expansion, as the modified pork-barrel model predicts; in only one case (vote 3) is it strongly significant, however. In addition, the petroleum and chemical interests appear to have no significant impact on Senate Superfund voting, and the state's hazardous waste production is only weakly significant (though as expected generally negative) across the five votes. The most significant interest in Senate voting is the environmental lobby, which is significantly and positively related to Superfund expansion votes in three of five cases at the 95 percent level, with another at the 90 percent level. Thus, it appears that the interests supporting Superfund expansion were far more influential in affecting Senate Superfund voting than those favoring curtailment.

The most striking feature of the Senate voting analysis is the importance of ideology. In every case, strong economic and environmental ideologies favored Superfund expansion, many times significantly. A Senator's environmental ideology is stronger in explaining Superfund voting behavior than economic ideology, and in every case it is significant above the 90 percent level of confidence (and in four of five votes over 95 percent). As expected, Democrats, even holding the other factors—notably ideology—constant, regularly supported the legislative efforts to expand Superfund, with four of the five votes significant at the 95+ percent level of confidence, and all over 90 percent. The control variables indicate a slightly greater tendency for Senators representing more urban states to vote for Superfund expansion, and for southerners and westerners to vote against expansion. Only three of the fifteen control-variable coefficients are statistically significant at the 95 percent level, however.

On the House side, the results of which are shown in table 7.2, the influence of industry interests is more pronounced in votes 1 and 3 than in any of the Senate votes. Only for vote 1 did the number of Superfund sites both in the representative's state and district have a significant, and as expected positive, influence over expanding Superfund.[25] (However, bivariate logit estimates show that when the vote is regressed only against the number of sites in the state, plus a constant term, the number of NPL sites is strongly related to a greater probability of voting for Superfund expansion in all three cases.)[26] A state's hazardous waste production is, as expected, also associated with opposition to Superfund expansion, and is significantly so for votes 1 and 3. The revealed power of the large environmental groups appears to have evaporated in the House voting (after

Table 7.2 Logit Results for House Voting (absolute value of t-statistics in parentheses)

Variable	Vote 1	Vote 2	Vote 3	Pooled
Intercept	−7.19(4.42)***	−3.33(2.63)***	−0.07(0.10)	−1.73(3.75)***
Final sites in state (N)	0.06(4.52)***	0.01(1.15)	0.01(0.87)	0.01(2.95)***
Final sites in district (N)	0.19(1.70)*	0.00(0.00)	−0.02(0.40)	0.00(0.00)
Chemical share	−13.23(0.71)	−18.11(0.91)	−17.84(1.47)	−10.17(1.33)
Petroleum share	−33.72(1.14)	16.01(0.50)	−170.38(4.26)***	−37.72(2.60)***
Hazardous waste ($\times 10^{-5}$)	−4.44(2.42)**	−0.42(0.27)	−3.01(2.30)**	−1.80(2.55)**
Environmental interests	−127.10(1.01)	157.15(1.17)$_\lambda$	143.36(1.70)*	75.00(1.53)
Economic ideology	0.04(2.30)**	0.06(3.41)***	−0.00(0.13)	0.01(2.05)**
Environmental ideology	0.05(2.92)***	0.09(5.34)***	0.04(4.15)***	0.04(6.46)***
Democrat?	8.78(7.51)***	4.63(8.31)***	0.93(3.59)***	2.80(15.7)***
Pop. density ($\times 10^{-5}$)	5.27(1.85)*	37.01(2.32)**	7.00(1.75)*	4.91(2.16)**
Southern state?	1.04(1.43)	−0.81(1.44)	−0.98(2.60)***	−0.46(1.92)*
Western state?	−0.98(1.22)	−0.56(0.63)	−0.32(0.72)	−0.34(1.16)
Observations (N)	412	342	419	1173
Percentage correct	91.7	88.3	75.7	77.66
LR statistic	0.668	0.602	0.294	0.340
LR test (chi-square)	381.29	285.20	170.58	553.04

***Significant at 99% level; **95% level; *90% level (two-tailed test).

accounting for ideology) and is only weakly related to Superfund expansion in vote 3. For vote 3, the petroleum, hazardous waste, and (more weakly) chemical interests revealed their effective opposition to an amendment for a $10 billion cleanup program that would be financed (at least directly) through increased taxes on their products.[27] Thus, it appears that industry interests influenced House Superfund voting when the stakes were large enough. The significant ideological coefficients are in the expected direction, again with a representative's environmental ideology dominating the influence both in magnitude and significance (significant in each case at the 99+ percent level of confidence). Similarly, a representative's liberal economic ideology is a strong indicator of voting for Superfund expansion, with the exception of vote 3. Finally, Democrats supported Superfund expansion significantly in each vote, and as in the Senate, a legislator's party choice was frequently the most significant indicator of all. In addition, representatives from southern and western states generally opposed Superfund expansion, with the exception of southerners in vote 1; in only one case is the relationship significant, however. And as in the Senate, higher population density is related to greater legislative support for Superfund. For the House, this may represent the fact that a greater proportion of urban constituents are likely to be exposed to any particular Superfund site than their rural counterparts.

The results discussed so far have proceeded by analyzing each vote separately, but the influence of the various interests and ideologies for all the votes combined is revealing as well. A model in which the House and Senate votes were pooled is estimated to determine patterns of influence over the several votes from each chamber.[28] The results are shown in the last columns of tables 7.1 and 7.2. In the Senate version, the significant interests include the number of final NPL sites in the state and the portion of the voting population that belongs to one of the large national environmental groups. Both are significant at the 99+ percent level, while hazardous waste production is negatively (though weakly) related to votes for Superfund expansion. In evidence again is the strong influence of both economic and environmental ideology, as well as a powerful Democratic preference for enlarging Superfund. As for the control variables, a state's population density is positively related, and western states negatively related, to Senate votes for expanding Superfund.

On the House side, the number of final sites in the state (though not the district) is a significant explanatory variable. The influence of the number of sites in the state, but not the district, may be due to either (1) a representative trying to appeal to a wider constituency in the hopes of a run at a Senate seat or the governorship, or (2) the perception that if the neighboring districts contain one or more Superfund sites, in the future the legislator's may as well. In addition, petroleum and hazardous waste interests are, as expected, negatively related to votes to expand Superfund, although environmental interests were not significantly related to expansion. Ideology continues to play a significant role in House Superfund voting behavior, with the significance of the environmental ideology particularly pronounced. And as in the Senate, Democrats and the district's population density are strongly related to voting to enlarge Superfund.

A more systematic test of the relative influence of interests and ideology is conducted using a series of J-tests.[29] The model is first estimated with all independent variables included *except* interests (which number five in the Senate and six in the House). Next, the model is estimated with all independent variables except the ideological components (two or three, depending on whether the "party" variable is included, in both the Senate and House models) but also including the predicted probabilities from the first—ideology only—analysis. A simple *t*-statistic determines

Table 7.3 J-Test Results Comparing Interest and Ideology Hypotheses (absolute value of *t*-statistics in parentheses)

	H: Ideology (w/party) = 0	H: Ideology (w/o party) = 0	H: Interests = 0
Senate votes			
Vote 1	Reject (3.20)***	Reject (2.95)***	Cannot reject (1.38)
Vote 2	Reject (2.46)**	Reject (2.55)**	Reject (2.24)**
Vote 3	Reject (4.28)***	Reject (3.81)***	Reject (3.14)***
Vote 4	Reject (4.59)***	Reject (2.97)***	Reject (2.78)***
Vote 5	Reject (5.23)***	Reject (3.73)***	Cannot reject (1.28)
Pooled votes	Reject (9.53)***	Reject (7.08)***	Reject (4.22)***
House votes			
Vote 1	Reject (8.60)***	Reject (4.87)***	Reject (4.95)***
Vote 2	Reject (9.73)***	Reject (7.36)***	Cannot reject (0.55)
Vote 3	Reject (5.81)***	Reject (4.77)***	Reject (6.79)***
Pooled votes	Reject (16.8)***	Reject (9.20)***	Reject (6.49)***

Note: Results indicate whether or not the hypotheses that "interests" or "ideology" are significantly different from zero in explaining voting behavior for each Senate and House vote. For example, a "reject" in the "interests" column signifies that the hypothesis that interests do not matter is rejected, while "cannot reject" means that we cannot statistically reject the hypothesis that interests are irrelevant. The column representing "Ideology (w/party)" indicates that the dummy variable "Democrat?" is included as an ideology; the second column counts ideology as simply the "pure" economic and ideology measures, excluding the party dummy.
***Significant at 99% level; **95% level; *90% level.

whether the ideology model (the predicted probabilities) adds explanatory power to the interest model (whether it differs significantly from zero). If so, the hypothesis that ideology is irrelevant in this particular vote can be rejected. The process is then repeated in the opposite manner (by first excluding the variables representing ideology) to test the relative importance of interests. The results of these tests are shown in table 7.3.

Plainly, for every vote the hypothesis that ideology is irrelevant to congressional Superfund voting decisions can be confidently rejected. Indeed, even when the strong party variable is excluded from the measure of ideology, the importance of the environment and economic ideologies remains strongly significant. The results for interests, in keeping with earlier observations about the individual coefficients in the preceding discussion, are more mixed, although generally interests too are significant. On the Senate side, neither votes 1 nor 5 indicate that interests, taken as a whole, matter significantly to voting decisions. In the House votes, however, interests are significant in two of the three cases.[30] Results of J-tests on the pooled votes show similar patterns. For the Senate, hypotheses that either ideology or interest are irrelevant are convincingly rejected ($t = 7.08$ and $t = 4.22$, respectively), as they are in the House ($t = 9.20$ and 6.49, respectively). In each case, the level of confidence is higher for rejecting the irrelevance of ideology, suggesting that the two measures of ideology are at least as strong as the five or six measures of interests in explaining Superfund voting behavior.

Is Superfund a Pork-Barrel Program?

The results point to the strong influence of ideology over individual congressional voting decisions and to the more moderate influence of the various interests that could be expected to influence Superfund. These results indicate that "programmatic pork" does at times influence both House and Senate voting, since legislators with larger numbers of Superfund sites in their districts sometimes are more likely to vote to expand the program. The results also confirm the influence of ideology, even in congressional voting on a program ripe with pork-barrel potential. It appears that although Senator Lautenberg, former Representative Florio (both of New Jersey), and others from states with large numbers of Superfund sites have pushed for years for an expanded federal role in cleaning up hazardous waste sites, there is only modest evidence that congressional voting decisions have been influenced consistently either by the number of sites in the legislator's district or state or by strong industry and environmental interests. (Although the pooled analysis shows that the number of NPL sites in the state is a strong predictor of congressional

Superfund support, only two of the eight individual votes significantly reveal this pattern of influence.) The most significant variables, both interests and ideologies, indicate support for Superfund expansion, while in only one instance (vote 3) is an interest strongly related to opposing Superfund. Instead, legislators' individual liberal and environmental ideologies, environmental interests (in the Senate), and party affiliations are the dominant forces in explaining Superfund voting decisions.

The symbolic appeal of Superfund as an environmental program that (at least indirectly) targets big business for financing appears to eclipse the attractions offered by various interests. Taken together with the results of the previous chapter, which indicated little congressional committee influence over the allocations of Superfund expenditures or cleanup priorities, evidence suggests that despite the properties that lead many to charge that Superfund is a pork-barrel program, these two manifestations of pork do not dominate site-specific or congressional voting decisions (although clearly there is greater evidence of programmatic pork). As a result, its existence as a relatively inefficient, and in many respects inequitable, environmental program must be traced largely to political foundations other than these types of pork-barrel politics.

3 Explaining and Reforming Superfund

8 The Political Rationality of Superfund

Nearly everyone agrees that Superfund has been a failure, but few agree which aspects of the program are most problematic. Affected individuals and communities feel left out of the cleanup process and subject to seemingly endless delays in removing and treating hazardous wastes. Environmentalists think EPA takes far too long to remediate sites, that cleanup standards are too lax and inconsistent from site to site, and that the fund is too small to meet cleanup needs. Chemical and petroleum companies believe they are unfairly singled out in funding the program through excise taxes on their products, in addition to being major PRPs financing cleanups themselves.[1] Other PRPs complain of a liability scheme that they believe is fundamentally unfair. Municipalities feel they are too often dragged unfairly through a legal process that they had little to do with in the first place, and they argue that it was not part of Congress's intent in passing CERCLA that they become partially liable for cleanup costs. Insurance companies feel ensnared in a web of litigation and potential liability that limits their ability to underwrite insurance and ultimately may threaten their financial viability. Legislators want EPA to speed the cleanup of NPL sites, yet they feel pressure from insurance companies and PRPs to change the liability provisions, from oil and chemical interests to reduce their share of the excise taxes, from the business community in general to reduce or eliminate the environmental and corporate minimum tax, from the scientific community to study the true health effects before proceeding too quickly, and from their constituents to do something about the local Superfund site. For its own part, EPA has dramatically improved its performance in carrying out CERCLA since the early 1980s, yet it remains in a seemingly "no-win" situation: Superfund cleanups are neither rapid enough, nor thorough enough, nor fair enough to all parties, nor scientifically based, nor responsive to each community's needs.

These criticisms of Superfund derive from the panoply of objectives each group expects from Superfund. Environmental groups want permanent cleanups at many sites. Industry groups want fairly apportioned liability and assurances that their future liability will be limited once existing claims are paid. Local interest groups typically want rapid cleanups that treat the waste rather than carting it away,[2] and Congress and EPA want to respond to all concerns. Consequently, no one agrees what the problems are, much less the solutions. No side publicly recognizes that Superfund cannot possibly fulfill everyone's expectations, even with the copious resources afforded EPA. In short, no one appears to be happy with Superfund, and given their expectations, no one can be.

The past seven chapters have pointed to a number of Superfund's policy problems, but they have also shown that a number of alleged problems are not really problems at all. First, broadly speaking, the best available evidence suggests that most Superfund sites do not pose substantial environmental and health risks, although some sites do. Second, there is no evidence that the location of Superfund sites discriminates against the poor and racial minorities; if anything, chapter 5 showed that Superfund NPL sites are located in wealthier areas of the country, which are the best equipped politically to have their sites placed on the NPL. Indeed, the political constituency served by Superfund may explain partly why the political support for the program remains so powerful, particularly since most of the sites have not yet been remediated. Third, Superfund is not a program dominated by traditional *allocative* pork-barrel politics. While there certainly are instances of legislators pushing EPA for favored treatment, the overall results in chapter 6 suggest that powerful subcommittee members and chairs do not exert disproportionate influence over the pace of cleanups, the levels of past and planned expenditures, or removal actions. Finally, Superfund is not presently plagued by the political scandals and mismanagement of the early 1980s. The EPA has made great strides in accommodating congressional intentions and improving the program, a point acknowledged by several congressional Superfund supporters themselves.[3]

By showing that many alleged problems are not problems at all, the preceding analysis of Superfund points to issues that reforms need *not* address. The search for appropriate Superfund reforms necessitates not only identifying the underlying problems the program faces, but first understanding how and why they developed. The fundamental problems with Superfund are that the magnitude of the problem is still unknown, that the program is in several respects both inefficient and inequitable, that the public is alienated from the process and does not trust the perspectives that EPA and risk experts bring to the issue, and finally that the program continues to experience substantial political and public-relations problems.[4] These problems have been explored at some length in the preceding chapters, but I have not focused on *why* Superfund policies have evolved the way they have. The evolution, I argue below, is not simply the result of ineffective or inefficient government management or some form of bureaucratic irrationality, but in many cases, it is the product of a political rationality whose consequences often work to the detriment of the public's better interests. The remainder of the chapter explains how Superfund's most fundamental problems have evolved and discusses the implications of those problems for program reform.

Explaining Superfund's Problems

Magnitude of the Problem Remains Unknown

The 1980 Superfund congressional debates speak of a long list of hazardous waste sites, from Jackson Township, New Jersey, to Lathrop, California, and the public health threats and economic devastation created by each. The health effects at these sites were even more uncertain in 1980 than they are today. Nevertheless, these and thousands of other waste sites were lumped together and described as the largest public health and environmental threat of the decade. Representative Maguire of New Jersey, the state that even then was acknowledged to have one of the greatest problems, was particularly emphatic: "I do not think there is anything Americans are more fearful about than the possibility that their families or their children or their children's children will be exposed to cancer, nerve disorders, birth defects, from substances that may not have been dealt with as carefully as they ought to have been, substances that may be found in drinking water, in consumer products, in play areas where children may amuse themselves. A kind of silent, unseeable threat which is all the more fearful because it cannot be adequately measured or understood."[5]

Comments like these were not limited to legislators from states with relatively large hazardous waste site problems. Senators Chafee of Rhode Island, Culver of Iowa, and even Dole of Kansas echoed a similar tone in the floor debates.[6] There was apparently no limit to the dangers caused by exposure to hazardous wastes. Senator Stafford of Vermont invoked the name of the most prominent government public health official to underscore the severity of the issue: "The Surgeon General of the United States considers toxic chemicals to pose the major threat to health in the United States for the decade of the 1980s."[7] (This, of course, is difficult to believe in the face of the health threats from diet and smoking.) He adds that many call it "the most serious health and environmental challenge of the decade," and calls the proposed Superfund bill "the major preventative health bill to come before the Congress in 4 years."[8]

All of this was said amidst a remarkable level of ignorance regarding the ultimate scale of the problem. A handful of members, mainly conservatives who perhaps wanted to avoid a large federal remedial program in any event, brought their concerns about hasty decision making to the floor debate. Representative Stockman of Michigan cautioned that "we have not defined the problem. We have heard all the wild statements and discussions, and there is a great numbers game going on as this escalates . . . Some members waived around [a list of 7,000 waste sites nationwide] to indicate that there is a considerable threat in every corner of the country facing us. The point is that well over 90 percent of those pose no threat whatever, after investigations have been carried out to find out the exact nature of the problem."[9] Although Stockman was far from alone in trying to derail what he recognized as a substantial looming federal presence in cleaning up hazardous waste sites, the voices of concern and outrage ultimately prevailed. Politically, there is little mystery why. Anecdotal evidence was virtually everywhere, linking presumed exposure to hazardous wastes with all sorts of public health problems. "Popular epidemiology" and constituents' outrage were all the evidence legislators required.

Anecdotal evidence of human health effects from exposure to hazardous wastes emanated from many sources. Discussing Love Canal, Representative LaFalce of New York recalled, "I went into the basements of the people who lived on either side of the site on 97th and 99th Streets. I knew from what I saw and I knew from what I smelled that we had a serious problem there that was probably affecting the health of the people living in the nearby area."[10] Senator Mitchell of Maine recounted the remarks of Love Canal resident Ann Hillis: "[Chemical companies] have produced children with extra fingers, extra toes, double rows of teeth, cleft palate, enlarged hearts, vision and hearing impairment and retardation."[11] On the Senate floor, Senator Mitchell also told of a little girl in Missouri, named "Andrea": "She liked to play on a farm in Moscow Mills, Mo. One day a truck drove up and sprayed the barn floor with what the driver said was salvaged motor oil, to keep the dust from blowing around. Three days later, the birds began to die. Andrea was later hospitalized with bladder disease, inflamed kidneys, nausea, and headaches. She had actually been exposed to the deadly chemical dioxin. This was one company's way of disposing of contaminated wastes."[12]

Although the Senate subcommittee knew that the Environmental Protection Agency had completed no direct study of the health effects of hazardous waste sites,[13] Senator Culver, among many others, spoke of "the numerous examples of the damage caused" as if it were common knowledge and scientifically derived.[14] Prompted by Senator Stafford's questions regarding health effects, however, the EPA noted, "To date EPA has not conducted any direct research on the health effects of hazardous waste."[15] Assistant EPA Administrator Jorling later acknowledged that "there is a great need to document the effects of hazardous wastes on human populations," and that "animal experiments are very helpful, but there is no substitute for human data."[16] Because of the mounting pressure to do something amidst little knowledge of the health effects, one environmental lobbyist subsequently noted that the idea of a Superfund became a "solution in search of a problem."[17]

A few members of Congress were willing to publicly acknowledge how little they knew about the problem. Senator Riegle of Michigan admitted, "One of the most frustrating aspects of this issue is our lack of knowledge. We simply do not know the size of the problem, nor the total costs of the cleanup efforts."[18] A few others, including Senators Domenici, Bentsen, and Baker, recognized the difficulty in linking exposure to hazardous wastes with human health impacts: "The difficulty in pinpointing the cause of a disease or exposure to a single chemical is well-documented. For example, in the case of cancer, a multitude of factors could play a role in the contraction of the disease. Those factors include genetics, personal habits (such as smoking and diet), occupational exposures and environmental exposures."[19] They also noted that Love Canal's illnesses were not traced to specific causes, despite all of the studies conducted. Still others cautioned against chemical phobia. Representative Martin of North Carolina said, "As we move to clean up these hazardous dumpsites that have festered about the country as an offshoot from this industry, let us be very careful that we do not engage in trying generally to create a phobia and a general fear among the public about this industry and about the important chemical products which are of such great value to us."[20]

The perceived problem was also something of an embarrassment for both the Congress and EPA: despite significant environmental legislation in the 1970s, the "horror stories" appeared to show how little RCRA had done to address the problem. Senator Alan Simpson of Wyoming noted the irony: "Finally—and most significantly—I find that this bill is a damning admission that the last decade of sweeping environmental legislation which has been processed by this Committee and the Congress has failed to provide the level and degree of environmental quality and safety to public health that was intended to be secured—or that the American people believed had been adopted."[21] Representative Brown of California acknowledged, "Our significant mistake in 1976 [the year RCRA was enacted] was to underestimate the national scope of this problem, and the extent of hazardous wastes already dumped throughout our land."[22] Partly as a result, EPA's competence to manage Superfund was called into question in 1980, due to its performance in other environmental areas. Representative Dannemeyer of California suggested, "We are by no means sure that EPA is the best Agency to play the lead role in hazardous waste cleanup . . . Giving EPA money and authority is not synonymous with getting quick results."[23]

But despite scant systematic knowledge of the scope of the problem (beyond the copious anecdotal evidence) and hesitancy on the part of some regarding EPA's ability to implement such a program, Congress overwhelmingly passed the $1.6 billion cleanup fund. Earlier bills had called for much larger appropriations, but the election of President Reagan in November pressured Democrats to scale back their proposals. Senate bill 1480, as reported to the full Senate, called for a $4.1 billion fund, although after President Reagan was elected, the fund size was cut to $2.7 billion and finally to $1.6 billion, and the victim's compensation provision was deleted. That the prospect of an incoming conservative Republican administration did not doom the Superfund effort entirely in 1980 is testimony to the political appeal for both Republicans and Democrats of a hazardous waste cleanup program seen as vital by their constituents.

Some have argued that the magnitude of the hazardous waste problem became apparent to Congress in the intervening years between the original CERCLA legislation in 1980 and the 1986 reauthorization, SARA. Citizens, state and local agencies, and others were busy locating abandoned hazardous waste sites across the country, it is argued, whose numbers appeared to surprise many legislators by the mid-1980s.[24] But this view is difficult to reconcile with the fact that in 1979 EPA had issued a study producing what it termed a "ballpark" estimate that approximately 1,200–2,000 abandoned hazardous waste sites required cleanup, with an average cleanup cost of $25.9 million each.[25] In light of the uncertainty at the time, both figures are remarkably close to today's estimates of the scope of the problem. Indeed, approximately 1,200 sites are now on the NPL, and EPA estimates that ultimately 2,000 sites will require remediation. Average site cleanup costs are now thought to run $25–30 million. On June 20, 1979 (before CERCLA's passage), Thomas Jorling testified that between 30,000 and 50,000 sites contained hazardous wastes and that 1,200 to 2,000 were potentially serious. Emergency measures costs were expected to be $3.6 to $6.1 billion, while ultimate cleanup costs were estimated at $26.2 to $44.1 billion (not including property damage compensation, victims compensation, and so on).[26]

Why did Congress not wait for a more sober assessment of the actual scope and scale of the problem before proceeding with significant legislation? The first reason is that legislators were being bombarded by their constituents to simply do something. Senator Chafee of Rhode Island expressed the attitude of most members, who were hardly in the mood to appoint a commission to study the problem: "Some say we are rushing headlong into this issue without thinking, that we need more time in order to be rational about the problem. I challenge those who feel that way to come to my State of Rhode Island. I challenge them to meet with my constituents who fear that their drinking water is poisoned, their health endangered, and their resources contaminated. Will these citizens and millions of others like them find it reasonable to wait another few years for help? I doubt it, and I do not blame them."[27] Legislators could scarcely have told their constituents that Congress would study the problem and get back to them in a couple of years with a more responsible program. Congress was forced to act by grass-roots pressures.

The second reason is that the Democratically controlled Congress recognized that its best hope of passing significant legislation was in jeopardy when Ronald Reagan was elected president. Earlier in the year, when it appeared that President Carter would be reelected, Superfund's passage in 1980 was doubtful. The Senate had held onto the House-approved bill for months and appeared to be in no hurry to act. It was only after the November elections that Congress scrambled to enact legislation. The bill that passed the Senate significantly revised the House version of the bill, yet because time was running out, the House was confronted with the option of passing the Senate bill or having no program at all. Senators Stafford and Randolph sent a letter to Representative Florio saying that any amendments to the Senate bill would doom the entire program. Florio and the rest of the House were outraged. Representative Harsha wondered aloud whether the House was "a coequal branch of the legislature or 'patsys' next to the Senate."[28] Many members wanted to add amendments, but Florio responded, "Some Members have come to me and said we should amend this, add things on, send it back to the Senate and let them take the heat, let them do something and be responsible for the bill dying if it dies. I am not prepared to play chicken with this issue because that is a game where there is only one loser and it is not the House, it is not the Senate, it is the American people."[29] Representative Gibbons of Florida added, "Certainly if this bill goes back [to the Senate], it will never see the light of day."[30] The threat of Superfund's demise with a Senate filibuster carried the day with House members, who finally approved the Senate's version, even though it had deleted several measures important to House members, especially victims' compensation and oil-spill liability coverage.[31]

The National Research Council and others have recently criticized EPA for not assessing the magnitude of the environmental and public health threats from Superfund sites more carefully.[32] Two reasons that EPA has not done so are apparent. First, in the early 1980s local and state organizations, including citizens, were identifying thousands of sites, so EPA efforts appeared unnecessary or duplicitous. In addition, EPA was struggling to get the program up and running, and site identification—already undertaken by others—was simply not a high priority compared with emergency removals, identifying cleanup technologies, assessing health and environmental risks at hundreds of sites, establishing the initial National Priorities List, and others. Moreover, CERCLA was viewed as an emergency response action aimed at quickly remediating significant problems at selected sites (although it subsequently ran aground when confronted with the massively complex cleanup program). As a result, it did not make sense at the time to develop a comprehensive assessment of all possible sites when the program was perceived to have different and more immediate goals.

Second, by the time SARA was passed in 1986, Congress was explicit in requiring EPA to clean up existing sites, not find new ones. In short, there were no organizational incentives to find new sites. After all, in light of the political beating EPA took over cleaning up only six sites by 1985, finding new sites would make EPA appear even less competent, since the ratio of remediated sites to all identified sites would appear to be even smaller. A recent study by the National Research Council concluded that the Superfund "process as a whole is directed at remediation rather than at the assessment of public health risks,"[33] which is not surprising, given EPA's explicit instructions to remediate sites on the existing NPL. Finally, the conventional measure of "delay" that has been used to assess EPA's progress, the length of time between site identification and deletion from the NPL, provides incentives for EPA not to discover new sites, since this only serves to prolong the "delay." In short, EPA has not concentrated its energies on identifying new sites because it already has over thirty thousand sites in its inventory, and it has focused on remediating NPL sites largely because that is what Congress wants it to do. The numerical cleanup goals specified under SARA only strengthened that conviction. As one EPA official put it, "our plate is full."[34]

Superfund Program Inefficiencies

One of the most significant problems with Superfund remains inefficiency. First, the environmental and health risks from Superfund sites are most likely relatively small, even compared with other remedial public health problems like lead and radon, not to mention those of smoking, poor diet, and other far more serious threats to public health (see chapter 4). It bears repeating that far too little is known about Superfund site risks, and indeed those of other environmental threats as well, but the best evidence available clearly suggests that although some Superfund sites pose significant risks, many sites do not pose significant public health and environmental problems. One reason for Superfund's excessive scope is that it was deliberately expanded to achieve a winning coalition in Congress to assure passage. (This is discussed in some detail later in the chapter.)

The second inefficiency in the program is that a significant portion of program expenditures are not channeled to remedial efforts or emergency removal actions, but rather to "transactions costs": fees for lawyers, consultants, and others involved in allocating responsibility and cost-sharing for remedial efforts. One environmental consultant complained that "the interpretation of our test results was always that more studies need to be done because the consulting engineers get paid for more studies, not for cleanup . . . I couldn't believe how ridiculous the process was . . ."[35] Because of the nature of transactions costs—which are in many instances borne by private parties—adequate data to gauge their magnitude are unavailable. Nevertheless, recent estimates suggest that transactions costs may be drawing significant resources away from actual site cleanups. The most thorough study to date, published by RAND, uses data drawn from a small sample (four) of insurance companies, who in many cases ultimately foot the bill, to estimate transactions costs. If these companies are representative of the industry as a whole, the study concluded that insurance companies spent $470 million in Superfund-related claims in 1989. Of that, $410 million, or on average 88 percent, was devoted to transactions costs, split almost evenly between coverage disputes and policyholder defense. Transactions costs are not random, however. Not surprisingly, they are higher when multiple PRPs are involved than with a single responsible party,[36] and the report states that transactions costs have fallen over time. As a result, the ratio of actual cleanup expenditures to total expenditures is expected to rise as more sites are remediated. In contrast, over 80 percent of expenditures by major PRPs represent actual cleanup costs, with only 20 percent devoted to transactions costs.[37]

The 1986 reauthorization significantly escalated cleanup costs—some have suggested cleanup costs could easily have tripled—mostly because "permanent" cleanup levels were required. Transactions costs can be expected to rise minimally in proportion to total costs: as corporate liability becomes more expensive, it becomes that much more worthwhile to litigate rather than remediate. Finally, the problem of transactions costs is exacerbated by three factors: insurance companies have every incentive to litigate, since they can keep the premium payments and any interest that accrues during the litigation; the knowledge that most cases are resolved by compromise;[38] and, supporters have argued, because insurance companies are in most cases genuinely not liable for cleanup costs.[39]

A third inefficiency in Superfund involves cleanup prioritization, where several problems are apparent. First, the National Priorities List, which is supposed to be the list of the nation's worst hazardous waste sites, bears little relationship to actual site risk and, more important, is arbitrary in size. The development of Superfund policy can also be traced to a seemingly insignificant congressional requirement in 1980. After passing CERCLA, Congress had little sense of how large the potential cleanup problem would become. Nevertheless, it required EPA to establish an NPL of at least 400 sites, which at the time appeared sufficient to address the problem (and, it has been noted, to potentially deliver a site to each congressional district). Because relatively few sites had been identified at the time, EPA determined that an HRS cutoff score of 28.5 would separate approximately 400 NPL sites from the remaining identified sites. As the number of identified sites subsequently grew, however, so did the NPL, since many of the newly discovered sites scored above 28.5 on the HRS. As a result, the NPL now contains over 1,200 sites, and is expected to grow to over 2,000; eligibility for the NPL therefore bears little relationship to those sites that can be cost-effectively remediated.

The importance of the virtually arbitrary 28.5 cutoff score can scarcely be overstated. Had more sites been identified at the time or had Congress required fewer sites on the initial NPL, eligibility for inclusion on the NPL would be much more stringent, and fewer sites would now be designated as "requiring" federal cleanup. On the other hand, had Congress required an NPL of more than 400 sites, the HRS hurdle would be significantly lower, and the eventual size of the NPL that much larger. Moreover, early tests of the revised HRS scoring system have shown that the new scores are typically much higher than they would have been under the old system.[40] As a result, the number of sites that qualify for the NPL may increase not because the newer sites are riskier, but rather because they have been scored under a different scheme. The ballooning NPL can only increase public (and therefore congressional) appeals for greater Superfund resources, and it obscures the importance of cleaning up the worst sites first, since hundreds of sites are at least formally on equal footing.[41] The point is that much of Superfund's expansion was due not to intentional congressional or EPA efforts—to the contrary, EPA has been criticized for devoting too little attention to site identification[42]— but rather to the seemingly arbitrary establishment of a benchmark cutoff score that dilutes site cleanup prioritization and bears little relationship to cost-effectiveness. The size of the NPL is as a result open-ended and potentially overwhelming, especially if anywhere near the hundreds of thousands of potential sites estimated to exist by the General Accounting Office come to be placed on the NPL.

A second problem involving site prioritization is EPA's seemingly sensible policy of remediating first the worst Superfund sites. Don Clay, then EPA assistant administrator in charge of Superfund, has said, "We have a strong commitment to do the worst sites first, and the worst parts of each site first."[43] While remediating the worst NPL sites first may be politically rational, since those sites may have generated the greatest public demand for cleanup, this strategy is not necessarily consistent with eliminating the greatest public health and environmental risk with the resources available. The reason is that the policy does not consider the cost of remediation and the level of risk *reduction*. Clay reiterates this intention in the same published interview: "Reducing risk is our priority, not just getting sites off the NPL."[44] The problem is that EPA's policy of addressing the worst sites first can run counter to its efforts to reduce the most risk. To achieve the greatest environmental and public health benefits, the relevant objective would be to maximize the risks reduced per dollar spent. If the worst sites are also extremely expensive to fully remediate, then shifting some of those dollars to less risky sites where costs are far lower could reduce larger cumulative risks (over a greater number of sites) with the same resource commitment. If reducing risk is indeed EPA's priority, it should instead concentrate its efforts not necessarily on the worst sites first, but rather on those sites where the ratio of risk averted per dollar spent is highest. This is not, of course, a well-defined calculation, but it would represent an important change in emphasis if Congress and EPA intend to maximize the public health and environmental benefits of the program.

A third problem of site prioritization is a result of the failure of Congress to resolve the "how clean is clean?" issue. The need to define a sufficient cleanup level stems from the general problem of addressing almost limitless risks with limited available resources. In a world of unlimited resources or few social needs, the "how clean is clean" issue is trivial: permanently remediate every identified site. As discussed at some length in chapter 3, spending excessive resources at some sites necessarily denies cleanup resources to other sites or other environmental and public health problems. The consequence of the goal of permanent cleanup when resources are limited is excessive remediation at a few sites and the neglect of others. One environmental attorney has commented, "The incentives are definitely in the wrong place . . . There is absolutely no incentive right now for somebody to be creative and save money on a cleanup."[45] Resources remediating some sites may better be used to protect health and the environment at another site.

Finally, EPA generally has focused too much attention on "input" indicators of success and too little on the program's health and environmental "outputs," a form of organizational "goal displacement."[46] By this, I mean that EPA has been driven to achieving numerical cleanup goals as specified under SARA, and as a consequence has not acted to most reduce risks. While presumably the intention of meeting numerical cleanup goals is to most reduce the environmental and public health risk, the two can work at cross-purposes. The agency could achieve its statutory requirements by remediating the least hazardous or the least complex sites first, neither of which would serve to eliminate the greatest risks. Undue attention to input goals that are inconsistent with the agency's goal of most reducing risk is counterproductive. Moreover, as the agency begins work at more and more sites, the relatively stable number of NPL sites means that input indicators of progress will necessarily decline over time (since the number of NPL sites at which construction can start will diminish). This has led to the situation where EPA has started work at many sites although fully developed plans have yet to be implemented. One commentator noted, "EPA has a strategy for getting a lot of balls in the air, but not for getting them down."[47] These consequences are not the product of "bean counting" at EPA, but rather congressional insistence upon quotas for the number of sites reaching particular cleanup stages, the number of sites deleted from the NPL, and so on. (It should also be noted, however, that the congressional reaction itself was largely a consequence of EPA's mismanagement of Superfund in the early 1980s.) Consequently, inefficiencies both in the scale of the program and the process of site-specific cleanups have been the result of factors serving political objectives.

Inequities in Financing and Assigning Liability

In many respects Superfund appears to be addressing a hazardous waste problem that is involuntarily and unequally distributed across the country. Recalling a local Buffalo television interview, Lois Gibbs, a chief activist at Love Canal, conveys the frustrations of many who live near Superfund sites: "The man who did the interview drove us crazy. He kept saying, 'Why don't you move out? If it's so bad, why don't you just all get up and go? If you worry so much about your health, why don't you move?' He couldn't get it through his head that we didn't move out because we couldn't afford to."[48] The combination of a site suddenly recognized as potentially dangerous and the financial inability of nearby residents to move away (which is exacerbated by the sometimes precipitous decline of property values immediately following site identification and placement on the NPL) appears plainly to be unfair and to justify some corrective measures. But despite the many instances of individuals being unable to move away from a waste site, chapter 5 indicated that Superfund sites were located disproportionately in counties that had higher median housing values and lower levels of poverty (but were also, according to some measures, disproportionately nonwhite). The median housing value in counties with Superfund sites is $44,225, compared with a national county average of $35,296. As a result, the argument that Superfund is compensating poor communities *in general* is specious.

Aside from the fact that financially better-off communities stand to benefit disproportionately from remediating the existing NPL sites, the issues of how to clean up and who should pay naturally arise as well. As discussed at some length in chapter 5, the strict, joint, and several liability scheme has important regulatory impacts (in compelling present polluters to better control the amount and destination of their wastes), yet it also appears to be inequitable both in terms of procedure and outcome.

The supposed equity of making the polluter pay for past damages through the financing of current cleanups is the cornerstone of the Superfund program. Without it, the program would be significantly smaller both because general revenues would most likely be significantly smaller than current trust fund receipts and because the public would recognize that they too are really paying for the cleanups. The polluter-pays principle addressed two important political concerns that endure today. First, it limits the federal financial commitment to the program. Initially the fund was believed to be self-replenishing; the idea was that in those instances where the fund had to be used to quickly remediate a site, cost recoveries would sustain the fund. (It has become apparent that this was a miserable failure, since cost recoveries represent only a small portion of federal Superfund expenditures.) The second political advantage of the polluter-pays principle was to isolate certain industries as the political culprits, at whom Congress and the general public could point fingers of blame. No matter that most citizens consumed these products, paid little attention to dumping of hazardous wastes at either the federal or local level before 1976, and benefited from the lower product prices that resulted from casual dumping. While these points surely do not justify the improper handling of hazardous wastes, and those violating statutory and common laws should be prosecuted fully, it should serve to blur the line between those who caused the waste and those who claim innocence.

Legislators apparently believed they could get away with arguing that the polluter pays for fund financing as well. Representative Brown of California, in whose district lies the infamous Stringfellow site, argued that the proposed tax would impose the full costs of the product on the market: "Industry points out correctly that the cost will be passed on to the consumer; this simply means that the true cost of a product in its broad sense will include the hidden costs which were previously omitted."[49] This is a perfectly good argument as applied to current disposal practices: those who buy products whose byproducts are hazardous should pay for the full social costs involved. The problem with Superfund is that the damage is already done. A tax on hazardous waste *production*—which the current Superfund tax clearly is not—would do little or nothing to assign appropriate blame for past improper dumping. If it is considered appropriate to pass on hazardous waste costs to current consumers, which includes millions of Americans, why is it not permissible to finance the cleanup fund from general tax revenues, which would probably be a more progressive form of financing?

Evidence from the floor debates over both CERCLA and SARA indicates that members of Congress were not ignorant of the degree to which cleanup costs were ultimately passed on to consumers. Legislators were fully aware that businesses pass on costs to those consuming their products, yet they apparently preferred these *hidden* costs to consumers over direct federal funding. In response, Representative Gramm of Texas argued,

> In all the debate which has occurred here and which occurred in the committee, we continually have references made to making industry pay. Is anybody here so naive as to believe that an industry fee which is imposed across the board is not going to be passed 100 percent on to the American consumer? Let us not fool ourselves. This is a tax, not a fee, and the same person is going to pay this tax who pays every tax, and that person is the American consumer . . . I assert if we look at who is paying and who will suffer the unemployment, we will find it is exactly the people we always hear spoken on behalf of here on the House floor—working Americans, poor people who are going to pay. Rather than dealing with this in an above-board straightforward but politically unpopular method, and that is by using general revenue funds to deal with the problem, rather than imposing a fee which in no way is related to who is guilty, I think that violates all our legal precepts, and it is an idea that I abhor.[50]

Representative Santini of Nevada argued that Superfund should be financed using general revenues: "The proponents of H.R. 7020 also argue that industry fees are necessary because of the difficulty of persuading appropriations committees to support large governmental expenditures. It seems to me that if the problem is as great as described there should be no difficulty in obtaining adequate Federal funding.

Clearly if this legislation is of such high priority the appropriations should be available. I am concerned that as fiscal constraints become tighter, superfund will serve as a precedent for funding new governmental programs out of the pockets of industry, and ultimately, the consumer . . . Then we can proudly point to our 'balanced' budget. The taxpayer would not have the burdens but the consumer will."[51] Even Senator Bentsen of Texas, a strong supporter of Superfund (yet also representing an important oil state), argued that "the consumer always ends up paying for it [the fee] anyway so the economic impact overall probably remains the same."[52] In short, members of Congress were well aware that Superfund costs would ultimately be borne by consumers, yet the size of the cleanup fund they envisioned could come only from industry in the face of substantial budget deficits. There was simply little room for appropriations out of general revenues, although hidden taxes were apparently politically acceptable.

As a means of justifying shared federal and industry funding, members also argued that society had benefited from chemicals. Representative Staggers of West Virginia acknowledges that industry has been "negligent and even reckless in disposing of their wastes" but also that "we as a society have benefited by the scientific and technological advances that have occurred in these high-growth industries; and that to a degree the problem is societal in nature and calls for a commitment from the Federal Government as well as from the industrial sector."[53] Legislators wrestled with a trade-off: the first option was a hazardous waste-end tax that would have provided incentives to limit the production of hazardous waste, but that would have produced a small and unstable revenue stream; the second option was a broad-based tax that embodied no waste-reduction incentives yet generated substantial revenues. As it turned out, large tax revenues easily defeated appropriate incentives.

Most importantly, the use of a dedicated tax shielded Superfund revenues from alternative environmental or other programs, serving to stabilize the future of the program. The purpose of using trust funds in the past, in the words of Representative Ullman of Oregon, "is to give some assurance to the particular industry that the money taken from them will be used for the intended purposes." The political quid pro quo, particularly in the case of Superfund, is that, in Ullman's words, "In return for the guarantee offered by the trust fund mechanism, we have found industries are less opposed to the new taxes."[54] The trust fund was therefore established both to insulate Superfund monies from other possible uses and to ensure industry that its contributions would serve particular purposes for which they could claim credit or, at least, limit additional future taxes.

Perhaps most unusual about the debate over CERCLA was that legislators were well aware that the size of the proposed fund was insufficient to address a problem of this scope. Representative Moffett of Connecticut is but one example: "I know there is a lot of money involved in this bill. Some of my colleagues are very concerned about that. I think we all are, but the fact is 10 years from now when we really begin to see the magnitude of this, unfortunately there are going to be so many people come back and say that was chicken feed compared to what the problem really needs. I hate to say that, but I think many Members on both sides know this is a fact. It is chicken feed compared to what is really going to be needed to address this problem. It could be $50 billion by all estimates . . ."[55] Representative Volkmer of Missouri added, "Even a $1.2 billion fund will cover only the tip of the iceberg as far as complete cleanup of all waste sites is concerned."[56] Representative Dannemeyer of California noted, "We do not know how many sites there are, much less how best to clean them up . . . We are just guessing—as the competing versions of the bill illustrate—on the amount of money that will be needed."[57] The legislators were implicitly acknowledging that cleanup costs would be mostly borne by the fund, and apparently they believed that PRPs probably would not contribute significantly. These statements suggest that the committee never felt that Superfund would be self-replenishing, for if it was expected to be, the initial size would be nearly irrelevant, since it would be a revolving loan fund with no expected budgetary impact (save for administrative expenses).

The size of the fund that Congress established had almost nothing to do with the magnitude of the expected cleanup expenses, however. It was motivated instead by the ability and willingness of industry to pay. EPA estimated that a $400 million fee system would raise the pump price of gasoline less than 7/100ths of one cent, while chemical prices were expected to rise by less than 1 percent; petrochemical feedstock prices would rise by less than 2 percent, and organic chemical prices by 0.6 percent. EPA concluded optimistically that the fee would result in no "production shifts, employment losses or plant closing."[58] This is also revealed in the Senate Environment and Public Works Committee Report, which first stated, "The evidence before the Committee clearly illustrates that the demand for moneys for Government response far exceed the amounts authorized in this bill." The report goes on to justify an even larger appropriation than finally passed: "Thus the $4.085 billion six-year fund derived from fees and appropriations is less reflective of demand than it is of a balance managed and used in the time period allotted and *that amount which economic analyses show to not stress the well-being of affected industries*"[59] [emphasis added]. Congress had three requirements that could be met only by taxing industry: the perception of "polluter pays," a sufficiently large fund, and a path of political least resistance. This came at the expense of increased costs to consumers through taxes that were largely hidden but appeared to be financed by polluters. This turned out to be a successful political trade-off: costs were hidden from consumers, who would ultimately bear a significant portion of the tax, yet legislators were able to tell their constituents that those responsible for creating Superfund sites were being compelled to pay for their remediation. What has never been conveyed is that virtually all Americans are paying for Superfund cleanups, and probably regressively through higher product prices on (mostly) chemical and petroleum products.

Why did Congress choose to create an inequitable program? The principle reason is that early on the problem was defined as a national problem caused by big business, and big business would be forced to pay. The fundamental distinction between the polluter-pays principle applied to past and future pollution, that behavior can be appropriately modified in the future but not the past, was ignored. Instead of focusing efforts on cleaning up Superfund sites, Congress chose first to place blame, not a surprising reaction given the volatile nature of the public's reaction to "toxic time bombs" discovered in their neighborhoods. Virtually all of Superfund's financing and liability problems flow from this fundamental mistake. By making it appear that one set of industries was to blame, the entire liability and taxation schemes were simple extensions of political expediency. Congress went to great lengths—and ultimately inequitable ones—to make it appear that industry would finance most of the cleanup.

The second reason for the funding and liability scheme is that Congress was determined to keep federal contributions to a minimum. While federal budget deficits in the late 1970s appear by today's standards to be enviably small, they were then at historic levels that constrained new spending. Even though the original fund drew 87 percent of its revenues from the chemical and petroleum industries, there were still substantial pressures to limit its size, a pressure compounded by Ronald Reagan's November 1980 election victory. Moreover, the emphasis on limited federal expenditures amidst public cries to do something about the abandoned waste sites dotting the country led directly to a liability scheme that ostensibly makes the polluter pay. That firms could be held liable retroactively, even where their contributions were minimal, and that consumers would ultimately bear a substantial cost were at the time small matters compared with the effort to accomplish rapid cleanups with as small a federal contribution as possible.

Only the strictest liability scheme could motivate PRPs to finance the bulk of the problems, a fact not lost on responsible parties, especially large corporations. One commentator close to the negotiations observes that EPA's "enforcement first" strategy—rather than first financing cleanups through the trust fund and recovering costs later—has "angered the responsible party community by what they regard as a return to soaking the 'deep pockets.'"[60] Moreover, the liability scheme served two purposes: first, to make the polluters pay, and second, to directly attack no particular political constituency, since those firms would be hesitant to reveal themselves publicly, and because they straddled dozens of industry groups, from manufacturing to mining to municipalities. The liability designs therefore served the political imperative to do no direct harm to any one well-organized constituency. The intent of the liability scheme was not to achieve fairness or efficiency, but rather to shift costs from the federal government to corporations. The liability provisions neither deter future illegal dumping nor provide corrective justice. Instead, they provided a way to make industry pay for cleanups. Because Congress obviously intended to limit the federal government's contribution to Superfund cleanups through general tax revenues and because of the symbolic value of "making industry pay," there will be a great deal of political opposition to any change in financing.[61]

The third inequity, that the program's cleanup resources are likely to benefit wealthier communities, is due to the likelihood that better-organized communities with better political connections are better able to have their sites placed on the National Priorities List to receive federal funding. There is no direct evidence to this effect, mostly because there is no set of potential Superfund sites upon which to observe structural differences between those that reached the NPL and those that did not. However, it is not implausible to believe that communities with greater political influence were more able to attract the attention of state and federal officials to have their sites considered for the NPL. As a result, the NPL probably does not represent a random set of the worst sites in the country, but rather overrepresents sites in communities with political influence. While EPA apparently has not channeled resources to Superfund sites based on the racial or economic composition of the surrounding communities, the fact that sites are disproportionately located in wealthier areas means that most of the cleanup efforts benefit those residents. If Superfund is at all a class issue, it appears to be less a matter of the poor being victimized and more that better-off constituents have dominated its implementation. However, one can argue that the poor are being victimized by Superfund in two ways. First, they are forced to pay higher product prices on goods subjected to Superfund excise taxes. Second, there may be more sites in poorer areas, but those communities may be unable to organize in such a way as to convince state or federal authorities that their sites deserve to be on the NPL.

Finally, it cannot be ignored that the significant Superfund transactions costs represent a large and growing source of revenues to many law and consulting firms. Lawyers collectively have a significant interest in retaining the litigious atmosphere surrounding Superfund cleanups. Dell Perlman, assistant general counsel for the Chemical Manufacturers Association, recounted his experiences with a preliminary hearing on a hazardous waste site: "EPA had to hold it in the gym, because so many people turned out. . . I looked around the stands, and I realized they were full of lawyers, all billing their time at around $200 per hour. Extrapolate those kinds of costs over the next ten years, and you come up with quite a figure."[62] It has been said that "there are more than 20,000 U.S. attorneys now specializing in environmental litigation and issues, up from fewer than 2,000 when the Superfund was created in 1980."[63] Naturally, not all of this increase is due to Superfund, but a significant portion of it may be. The adversarial nature of Superfund cleanups, which at some sites produce transactions costs that exceed cleanup costs, benefits a substantial, politically powerful, and growing constituency. One former EPA official concludes, "You have to place a lot of criticism on lawyers [who] made the program pretty irrational."[64] The influence of construction firms and consultants involved in the remedial actions represents an effective lobby for Superfund as well.

Public Mistrust and Public Relations Problems Have Damaged Superfund

One of the most serious problems with Superfund is its adversarial nature. This is evidenced not only in the enormous transactions costs involved in negotiating settlements and cost shares but also the frustration with the program that many communities, municipal governments, banks, PRPs, environmental groups, insurance companies, and others share. The adversarial process pervades Superfund policy in everything from getting EPA to recognize the waste site to identifying responsible parties to apportioning cost-shares to determining the appropriate remedial action. The existence of Superfund site risks can be divisive within the community as well. Within some communities, one group believes that the site is a significant risk and therefore agitates for action and publicity. Others, however, believe the risks to be trivial and are concerned that property values will decline markedly as a result of the publicity.[65] Superfund creates adversaries not only among competing interest groups but within affected communities as well.

Although adversarial environmental policy, which some have termed "environmental brinksmanship," is not unique to Superfund and indeed has a long history in U.S. environmental regulation,[66] it has profound consequences for running the program. EPA is viewed with suspicion by the public, both for its failure to remediate a significant number of sites as well as for its apparent preference for policy driven by risk management, which is perceived to deprive the community of immediately treating or removing the wastes. Lois Gibbs's views illustrate how the perspective of risk experts is unlikely to persuade the general public: "Would you let me shoot into a crowd of one hundred thousand people and kill one of them? No? Well, how come Dow Chemical can do it? It's okay for the corporations to do it, but the little guy with a gun goes to jail . . . What they throw at me is that I'm a single-issue person. Yeah, I am a single-issue person. I look at the issue of people being poisoned and it makes me mad and I wonder why it doesn't make everybody mad. It's a moral issue and that's why we won't go away. This is a movement for justice and, if people have their morals and ethics intact, regardless of what issue they face, they'll be okay."[67] The risk assessments prepared by EPA (or, more accurately, EPA contractors) for particular sites are viewed by some as beside the point. Because Superfund sites depreciate property values as well as pose potential environmental and public health threats, informing communities that the health threats are relatively small addresses only part of the problem. Moreover, EPA is sometimes seen as trying to find excuses to limit its responsibility or at least limit the extent of the remedial action to preserve the cleanup trust fund. Therefore, risk assessments do not represent important contributions to the policy debate within the community because they are coming from an opposing party in an adversarial process and oftentimes are communicated in a confusing or condescending manner.

In order to furnish communities with their own technical expertise, SARA required EPA to provide Technical Assistance Grants so communities could hire scientists and others to present a different view of the site's hazards. The mistrust of the "experts" stems from the fact that the public sees the experts representing a policy agenda. Indeed, research indicates that the views of "risk experts" are shaped as much by their occupation as by strict adherence to scientific principles.[68] The public is more likely to be convinced by an expert's opinion if that person or group is not associated with a particular policy preference or professional bias. From the community's perspective, EPA is as a result viewed as an "outsider" rather than as a cooperative agency seeking to address an important policy problem. Many communities believe that EPA does not provide timely, relevant, and comprehensible information concerning the site and that they are too often talked at rather than listened to.[69] Therefore, EPA's risk assessments will remain unconvincing, no matter how expertly they are conducted, because of the policy agenda they are believed to promote.

The public's mistrust of EPA was perhaps best evidenced when residents of Love Canal held two EPA officials hostage. While the two men ultimately were unharmed, at least one of them apparently was terrified of what the angry mob would do. As Lois Gibbs, a principal spokesperson for Love Canal residents, recounted the story, she noted that while one of the hostages appeared relaxed, "the other man was not as calm. He looked white. He sat there as if he were waiting for something horrible to happen to him."[70] The incident involving EPA officials and the public is not an isolated event. Don Clay, former assistant EPA administrator, has said, "I've been out on sites and almost been taken hostage." He adds, "You have to remember, people can be very emotional on this subject. You may not find people getting very excited about ozone depletion, but if they live next to a Superfund site, you'll know it."[71] Shortly after the kidnapping at Love Canal, a high-ranking regional EPA official recalls "running a public [Superfund] meeting, and having one of our people pass me a note saying, 'I have been tipped off that you may be kidnapped, and should call the FBI.'"[72] Despite these problems, EPA officials publicly acknowledge that "it's very important that citizens who live near the sites be part of the [decision-making] process."[73] Nevertheless, EPA has been criticized for too little meaningful public participation. An environmental attorney argues that "We don't bring the community into the process early enough to avoid the problems that can occur when they feel left out. Part of the reason for the EPA's reluctance to be innovative is that they feel burned by the community uproar that can result from such efforts."[74]

Many of the reasons for mistrust of EPA by both local communities and many in Congress derives from EPA's own actions in the early 1980s, when Superfund was managed so as to prevent a "son of Superfund." It is difficult to overestimate the impact the Burford-Lavelle years at EPA had on the progress (or degeneration) of Superfund. The CERCLA legislation was the product of a joint administration and congressional effort, while SARA, coming in the wake of the EPA scandals, instead originated almost entirely in Congress. This difference reflects the degree of mistrust between Congress and the administration over Superfund's implementation, ultimately leading to the congressionally imposed site-cleanup timetables, improved public participation, more money, and a variety of other changes intended to both bolster support for and expand the program.

In addition, following CERCLA's passage in 1980, expectations were high for a quick cleanup of relatively few waste sites. When a site is placed on the NPL, a great deal of publicity is generated, and the expectation is raised—as well as the political stakes—that the site will be cleaned up. In addition to past EPA abuses, there are also technical limits to the speed of cleanup; pumping and treating groundwater contamination, for example, can take decades in some cases. Further, the public feels alienated from the process when small landowners and municipalities are designated PRPs in secondary lawsuits. (Even though EPA policy has been not to sue municipalities for damages, PRPs can and do.) Many municipalities, already squeezed by fiscal pressures, cannot afford the costly litigation, much less the cleanup costs, involved with Superfund remedies.

To be sure, EPA is partly to blame for the public-relations disaster that Superfund has become. As both a product of ignorance and an effort to pass cleanup legislation in the late 1970s, EPA failed to convey to Congress the technical difficulty of quickly remediating abandoned waste sites that contained dozens of unknown chemicals with unknown health effects emerging through several migration pathways. The expectations that CERCLA could quickly address the problem were as a result badly overstated, not just because of EPA's actions, but also because Congress did not want to confront the enormity of the problem. By the mid-1980s, it was nearly indisputable to say that Superfund's slow progress was due to the politicization of the program. However, by the early 1990s, amidst calls that the program still was moving too slowly, the politicization charge held less currency. Instead, it became evident that the cleanup process was genuinely lengthy, in part because of a combination of congressional requirements: speedy cleanups, cleanups that meet stringent requirements, ones that stipulate that PRPs must pay, and so on. These incompatible goals, spelled out under SARA, significantly slowed EPA's progress.

While some of the frustration with the program arises from the slow pace of cleanups, the high transactions costs, the lack of communication, and so forth, much is also due to EPA's inability to communicate to the public and Congress both Superfund's complexity and successes. EPA has been unable or unwilling to publicize Superfund's successes with Congress. As one EPA official told me, "EPA is inept at tooting its own horn, utterly inept."[75] Many agencies are all too willing to notify members of Congress when they plan actions in the legislator's home district. The Department of Energy, for example, notifies federal legislators when even an investigation of a DOE facility is planned in the member's district or state. No such indication comes from EPA, even when a remedial action is to take place, not to mention site investigations and other active EPA participation.[76] One EPA official reasons that "the agency got used to apologizing [for Superfund]" and that "the agency just doesn't think that way."[77] EPA's inability to "sell itself" to Congress has done nothing to improve its image or the perception that the Superfund program is accomplishing anything. Even an environmentalist and strong critic of Superfund acknowledges that "EPA has done a miserable job in selling what they have done well."[78]

Most agree that Superfund is a much better managed program now than during its first eight years. A close observer of the program notes, "Over the past four years, the Superfund program has become better managed at both the political and administrative levels."[79] Nevertheless, many involved in the process complain that EPA's staff is inexperienced. There is high staff turnover, and the best people frequently are lured to consulting firms because of better pay, and they see no success or recognition from the public or Congress. The result is that relatively inexperienced EPA staff are sometimes given considerable authority over site cleanups. This is a source of complaint from environmental groups and the public, which feel that EPA staff are more susceptible to manipulation from PRPs, who they fear may implicitly dangle lucrative job offers for a job "well done," or who at least will not antagonize PRPs for fear of jeopardizing their future career prospects. The lure of future jobs for trained EPA personnel is unmistakable. A *U.S. News & World Report* headline aptly stated "Good Jobs Are Going to Waste,"[80] since the cleanup business is considered to be one of the growth industries of the 1990s. Former OTA official Joel Hirschhorn has said that "the government and private sectors are desperate for competent people."[81]

Other Factors Influencing Superfund

A number of other political dimensions have dictated the genesis and direction of the Superfund program. These include the role of the press, grass-roots environmental groups, congressional oversight, and the influence of pork-barrel politics.

The Press. The 22 September 1980 cover of *Time* showed a human head half-submerged in a pond, the top half normal but the underwater portion a skeleton (along with skeletons of several fish). The not-so-subtle implication: what appears healthy on the surface is actually killing us.[82] Popular television programs in the late 1970s, such as "60 Minutes," "Donahue," and "Today," particularly in the wake of the crisis at Love Canal, helped to both publicize the problem and demonstrate that public officials offered little response. Television programs showing irate citizens and hesitant, noncommittal public officials served only to raise the specter of "hazardous" waste sites everywhere. Uncertainty bred fear, and it appeared that no one could be safe. Suburban refuges from inner city crime could no longer be considered safe from toxic contaminants, hazards that were even found—in the most publicized case, Love Canal— to be seeping into school playgrounds.

But besides widely publicizing the major waste sites discovered in the late 1970s and early 1980s, the national press generally has lost interest in Superfund, other than to report the results of major studies and to show how few sites have actually been removed from the NPL. As one environmental lobbyist said, the issue has become "boring to the press. Editors and reporters say 'this sounds like something we've already done.' "[83] The local press, on the other hand, has been far more active in reporting waste-site listings, cleanup progress, and other significant events that affect local communities. In many respects, the role of the press reflects the roles taken by environmental groups: active local participation yet only sporadic interest from national organizations.

Grass-Roots and Environmental Groups. Much of the political sustenance for a strong Superfund program comes from the efforts of local grass-roots interests. The national Citizens Clearinghouse for Hazardous Waste, an organization founded by former Love Canal activist Lois Gibbs, helps localities generate support for cleanups, coordinates technical assistance, and facilitates other site-specific efforts. Other groups, such as Clean Water Action, perform similar roles. Yet these groups are "national" only in the sense of distributing grass-roots expertise from a central location; their sustenance and energy originate locally. One EPA official said of the role of national environmental groups, "They're out there on the national level in keeping an eye on things, but they are not seen on a site-specific basis."[84] The large national environmental groups have strongly supported Superfund expansion in reauthorization years, including the Sierra Club, Environmental Defense Fund, and others. These groups also have been critical of EPA's progress in site remediation and degree of permanence, and they have pushed strongly for consistent national cleanup standards. Yet for the most part they do not actively support stringent Superfund cleanups on a day-to-day basis for several reasons: other priorities, limited staff, and their dependence on grass-roots organizations to carry on site-specific political lobbying.

When the large national environmental groups do become involved in Superfund reauthorization, they have pushed for as large a trust fund as possible and for the strictest cleanup requirements. Regarding the 1986 reauthorization, one lobbyist said, "Ten billion dollars is not enough to clean up 2,000 sites, but from a political standpoint, *we've gotten as much money as possible now*" [emphasis added].[85] Trade-offs among environmental programs are not part of the political calculus. Another environmental lobbyist told me, "That just isn't the way things work . . .

Our approach is, these are all really great programs, and you get as much resources for them as you can figure out how to get . . . and whether you're working a little too much on Superfund and too little on clean air is somewhat irrelevant."[86]

Local groups had far greater influence, if not in the details of crafting environmental legislation, then in pressuring legislators to do something about the problem of hazardous waste sites and maintaining that pressure. Representative Railsback of Illinois noted that "people in the area are constantly indicating to me that they are worried about how the waste will affect them, their children, their livestock, and their land."[87] The impetus and sustenance for Superfund came from communities like Woburn, Massachusetts, and Times Beach, Missouri, that experienced highly publicized incidents involving hazardous wastes, and who demanded federal action. Congress did seize the issue with EPA's full cooperation, and careers were established and advanced by advocating a huge federal cleanup program. But Superfund stemmed from grass-roots organizations who (in some cases justifiably) mistrusted government officials and reports that told them there was nothing to be worried about.[88] One activist stated, "I think it [SARA] was the best grass-roots environmental campaign that ever was . . . We had the kind of pressure that only grass-roots campaigns can deliver."[89] Of course, the community's response is not monolithic. At some sites the community simply is not particularly concerned, others seek gold-plated cleanup and redevelopment, and still others fight incineration or other cleanup strategies not favored by the community.[90] And while Superfund activists were initially viewed by some as "crazies," today's groups are sophisticated and politically adept. As one EPA official has seen, "they do their homework."[91] Another Washington-based environmental lobbyist acknowledges that "the grass roots interest is higher than ever [while] inside-the-Beltway interest is much lower."[92] Establishing a federal Superfund program was a calculated political decision by the Carter administration and EPA that took advantage of an election-year opportunity to exploit a volatile public concern at the expense of the large and unpopular chemical and petroleum industries.[93] But it is clear that public opinion and the efforts of grass-roots organizations instigated congressional action, not the other way around.

Superfund is less an environmental issue than a public health issue. One environmentalist noted, "This is much more than an environmental issue. The people who care about this issue are concerned whether their kids are playing in playgrounds that have this stuff under the ground and whether it is in their drinking water."[94] One is struck, in reading the floor debate concerning several Superfund bills in 1979–80, how little the discussion reflects traditional environmental concerns. The regard is almost always for the public health impacts, not environmental degradation. Therefore, Superfund appears to be more a response to the public health and property value problems than environmental legislation. What is also striking about the congressional floor debates is how frequently Superfund sites are discussed as equivalents, where every site is equally hazardous. This allowed the passage of a bill that would include large numbers of sites rather than being selective. And the political significance of capitalizing on the peaked public interest in Superfund has not been lost on Superfund's backers. Eric Draper of the National Campaign Against Toxic Hazards said of the first reauthorization, "We had to move out and try to win this most important toxics legislation in a year in which we had advantages like elections."[95] Moreover, environmental groups generally view the problems with Superfund's implementation as primarily political, not technical: "There is no shortage of solutions. The tough question is not how to clean up the mess but how to generate political muscle to put reasonable solutions into action."[96] Another lobbyist told me that environmental groups were too preoccupied by the political scandals of the early 1980s to focus on substantive Superfund issues.[97]

Superfund has been portrayed as a nonincremental victory for poorly organized and poorly funded interests over the well-organized and well-funded industry groups (the Chemical Manufacturers Association, the American Petroleum Institute, the National Association of Manufacturers, and others). William Greider describes Superfund as a singular victory for grass-roots organizations in the 1980s: "While industry and finance generally had their way in the politics of the 1980s, on one important issue they were devastated—the Superfund legislation enacted in 1986 . . . With citizens fully aroused, Congress was enabled to pass a very tough measure that assigns the cleanup costs where they rightfully belong, not to the general taxpayers, but to the specific companies that created the mess. The discredited Reagan White House was in no position to resist. Popular opinion clearly won the day."[98] Vocal members in virtually every congressional district (like the National Education Association, American Association of Retired Persons, and the National Rifle Association) represent a potent political force. Superfund is clearly an unusual grass-roots victory over the special interests of business. Indeed, the strength of environmental groups was so strong that, arguably, the resulting delay in implementing Superfund was the product of two of their "successes": having EPA clean up sites, and getting PRPs to pay for it. Many have argued that pushing for both goals has created long delays and huge transactions costs.[99]

Congressional Oversight. A review by political scientist Joel Aberbach of the general nature of congressional oversight concludes with an analysis that could have been directed specifically at Superfund: "At the level of coordinated review and control of policy and administration, oversight is relatively ineffective. There is an irony here: the weaknesses of the American system in regard to coordinated, centrally directed policymaking and administrative control make it highly responsive to groups or vociferous individuals in the society. As a result, many irritants are responded to, but the response is uncoordinated, and the system can careen along without coordinated direction . . . *The administrative system is at once highly responsive and accountable in the narrow sense, and not well coordinated or centrally controlled in the broad sense.* An easily identified set of central political authorities cannot reasonably be held accountable for its operation"[100] [emphasis added]. Aberbach argues that because (sub)committees are chosen that generally support the program under scrutiny, "once programs are established there are built-in biases in favor of program maintenance," and the oversight that "does take place in an advocacy context . . . shapes how criticisms and events are interpreted."[101]

Legislators have been active both in exposing fraud and abuse of the system in the early 1980s and in detailing how EPA has failed to properly implement Superfund. But relatively little attention has been devoted to fundamental changes in Superfund policy, in terms of either the scope of the problem, liability, financing, or cleanup requirements. In this sense, congressional oversight of Superfund (including numerous reports by the congressional GAO and OTA) has primarily micromanaged the program but has not questioned the intent of the program, nor has it considered the environmental trade-offs involved. Aberbach's conclusion that "congressional oversight probably improves policy at the margins"[102] is true of Superfund as well, in that early EPA mismanagement was exposed. But rather than considering broad changes in the way the legislation is written and its effect on the pace of site remediation, the focus has been to chastise EPA for failing to carry out the letter of the law.

Ironically, the Reagan administration's treatment of Superfund—aimed at preventing a "son of Superfund"—ultimately served to bolster its continuity. The obvious political manipulation of the program and the apparent disregard for congressional intent changed the Superfund program from a cooperative effort between the administration and Congress into a congressionally mandated cleanup program. This is the single most important factor in explaining the significant changes in SARA, compared with CERCLA. The antagonism and distrust between Congress and the EPA, while less apparent today than in the mid-1980s, still pervades their relations. The original CERCLA legislation, given its hurried preparation, represented a reasonable approach to the problem: it enabled EPA to address emergency cleanups (removal actions), to explore the scope of the problem, and to remediate the worst sites, yet it did not set cleanup targets, and it allowed sufficient flexibility for EPA to come to terms with the problem. Had the EPA in the early 1980s been less hostile to the program, the resulting reauthorization would not likely have included the mandatory schedules, strict cleanup standards, and reduced programmatic flexibility. A more responsible EPA could have avoided the subsequent escalation of problems under SARA.

Pork-Barrel Politics? Chapter 6 indicated that allocative pork is apparently not a significant explanation for the pattern of site-specific Superfund expenditures, while chapter 7 showed that the influence of programmatic pork, while significant, was overshadowed by legislators' ideologies. What, then, has been the role of pork-barrel politics in shaping the path of Superfund policy?

It should first be said that the absence of allocative pork found in chapter 6 could change as the program matures. Once the worst sites have been addressed and as funding becomes increasingly scarce, Superfund's opportunity costs will become more apparent. Cleaning up one site will then indicate more obviously that other sites will be deprived of funding and without the compelling justification of high relative site hazards (since some sites would no longer as clearly be worthy of attention). These factors could lead to a program that allocates its funds based on other criteria, such as subcommittee membership support or other political criteria independent of merit. But this is only speculation: there is no systematic evidence to suggest that this form of distributive politics pervaded Superfund policy in the 1980s.

Besides being a new program, what explains the absence of allocative pork? The first reason is that EPA makes cleanup decisions, not Congress. Although some studies have indicated that Congress can dictate agency decision making indirectly,[103] most researchers conclude that the more removed the decision making process is from Congress, the less influential will be distributive politics.[104] Second, the EPA (and Superfund) budget is handled by a congressional appropriations subcommittee whose jurisdiction includes not only EPA, but the Department of Housing and Urban Development, the Department of Veteran's Affairs, NASA, and numerous independent agencies. Consequently, there are many other competing sources of pork that legislators can tap. The results of chapter 6, indicating that subcommittee assignments do not influence Superfund site-specific cleanup decisions, may be due to the fact that committee members have other opportunities to deliver benefits to their constituents besides Superfund cleanups. Third, several persons interviewed suggested that legislators really do not want quick site cleanups if it means anything less than a permanent remedy. Legislators do not want to be associated with a "negotiated settlement" between EPA and PRPs, which could be viewed by constituents as being "bought out" by industry interests. Rather, it is alleged that legislators can even slow up the process by requiring permanent remedies, thereby allowing them to browbeat EPA to their political advantage with respect to constituents.[105] One observer notes, "Superfund has become an enduring political vehicle [to criticize EPA] . . . It continues to be seen as a way to score political points by criticizing the agency [for both environmental and industry groups] . . . When you criticize the agency, you have instant credibility and instant access to publicity . . . You hope that over time a program becomes professionalized, and leaves that kind of political arena [but] Superfund doesn't seem to be able to shake that off."[106] Another summarizes the legislator's perspective: "The problem is a pain. Dealing with riled up citizens, most of whom have never participated in the political process before, and who will trash any outcome except the one they want, is not something your average politician likes to deal with." Moreover, he adds, "Superfund has been insufficiently successful for members to perceive it as good pork."[107] Fourth, the lack of allocative pork may result from the abundance of Superfund money for everybody, at least as it stood in the 1980s, while Congress focused on pushing EPA to get moving. But as the program matures, as noted above, the incentives will begin to change, and the possibility of site-specific pork will arise.

Numerous other explanations contribute as well. The issue is complex, and it may require a significant investment of time and expertise for one legislator to convince EPA that one site is particularly worthy of remedial action. This is particularly difficult since EPA controls any bureaucracy's comparative advantage: program expertise. The judgments of EPA experts, guided by complex health and environmental studies and HRS scores, may be difficult for individual legislators to override. Moreover, even if a legislator is able to convince EPA to take quick action on a specific site, the length of time between influence and result can be considerably longer than the legislative electoral cycles of either two or six years. The ability of the legislator to claim credit therefore relies upon a willingness to expend current political capital for gains that may not accrue for ten years or more; legislators may prefer to direct their attention to other issues with more immediate payoffs. A related issue is that the health effects of the cleanup are highly uncertain, and with EPA reports suggesting that Superfund may be an inefficient way to spend environmental dollars, some legislators may be reluctant to push strongly for cleanups that provide few tangible health benefits. Yet another explanation for the absence of allocative pork is that Superfund is still a relatively new program. Superfund's supporters, including those who support the program because of its potential for future pork, may be more inclined to focus their attention on improving the program's management and political stability rather than reaping immediate political advantages for themselves in the short run. By solidifying Superfund politically and bureaucratically, legislators may feel that the long-run electoral returns will justify the start-up costs. Finally, legislators may be responding self-interestedly to the symbolic appeal of Superfund. The program may represent a litmus test for voters in appraising the broader environmental commitment of their representatives, particularly given the high visibility and political salience of the Superfund program and the public's strong belief that abandoned hazardous waste sites represent one of the most serious environmental problems the country faces. The "winning coalition" depends less on having sites in particular districts cleaned up and more with casting Superfund symbolically as an environmental and public health program that legislators cannot refuse.

The issue of programmatic pork is more complicated, however. Substantial evidence suggests that the *pattern* of development of the Superfund program, and to some extent the specific votes to expand it, was predicated on the notion of distributing resources among as many states as possible. Although the health effects were uncertain, there was never any question that some states had greater hazardous waste problems than others and that representatives from these states were particularly active in securing CERCLA's passage (such as Representative Florio of New Jersey). But despite the unquestioned belief that some states would benefit from a cleanup program more than others, since the level of hazardous waste production varied considerably between them, representatives from states with relatively modest problems were still active (and ultimately successful) in lobbying for a share of the program's resources. Representative Cleveland of New Hampshire offered an amendment that EPA should include on the NPL's worst 100 sites one from each state. (Representative Florio, who could have had no fear that one of New Jersey's sites would be absent from the one hundred worst sites, subsequently forced him to add "to the extent practicable" to the amendment.) This was a rather obvious attempt to spread Superfund resources widely among states, even if environmental and public health threats were not as severe as in other states. As a result, CERCLA requires not only that four hundred sites "shall be designated as the 'top priority among known response targets,'" but also that among the one hundred worst facilities, to the extent practicable one must be from each state.[108] When discussing what this meant, Senator Humphrey of New Hampshire indicated his preference that "the worst hazardous waste site in each State will be taken care of," and that the wording "to the extent practicable" meant that a state may not have a site "serious enough to warrant aggressive Federal involvement . . . or might not desire a Federal presence." Representative Cleveland argued, "I do know that in my own small State of New Hampshire we have specific problems, and they are not large enough or important enough perhaps to make that magic list. But I think we ought to have at least some of them taken care of."[109,110] Humphrey added, "The benefits of this legislation will be available to the residents of every State. After all, it is the residents of every State who will pay to implement this bill . . ."[111]

Naturally, indicating that a site is serious enough to warrant aggressive federal involvement may be substantially different from declaring it one of the one hundred worst sites in the country. The legislation does not therefore compare sites with each other but rather with some vague idea of what constitutes an appropriately "serious" site. Deviating from an allocation of resources based on merit is an obvious instance of spreading the benefits widely to solicit additional political support for a program well beyond its appropriate scale. The distributive political significance was apparent to Representative Maguire of New Jersey: "I feel true sympathy for the Assistant Administrator at EPA who will have to implement decisions on the top 100 sites as he is hounded by 435 Representatives and 100 Senators each with his or her own priority site. It is clear that 535 requests cannot be squeezed into 100 slots."[112]

A sense of "political equity"[113] was instrumental to Superfund's passage, since all legislators could be involved in the program, almost without regard to how hazardous their region's sites were. Other than serving the national public interest, there was no incentive for any legislator to limit the scope of Superfund: the legislator could only (1) limit personal chances of gaining federal cleanup monies; (2) limit other members' chances of obtaining federal cleanup monies (with likely political repercussions); or (3) receive only a small portion of the net benefits of restricting the program compared to the political costs. The only individual incentives to ration cleanup funds were the countervailing pressures from industry groups, which were politically overwhelmed both in 1980 and especially 1986. Leaving the scope of Superfund intentionally vague and open-ended allowed Congress to define a problem from which everyone could benefit. The political implication in 1980 of a "site in every district" was that all legislators could claim credit by having sites cleaned up in their district. Of course, the fact that it usually takes far longer than two years to clean up a site means that legislators with sites in their districts would have to explain why remedial efforts have not been completed. Therefore, the potential for a political handicap arises as well. However, when CERCLA was passed, the expectation was widespread that individual sites could be remediated quickly, so the problem of electoral cycles was not viewed as significant. In addition, legislators can always blame EPA, particularly when they have voted for a multibillion-dollar fund, for failure to properly implement the program.

Moreover, EPA was acutely aware of the congressional interest in receiving a portion of Superfund's substantial resources and was apparently willing to promote the program in order to achieve its own goals of expanding its presence as a public health and cancer-fighting agency.[114] EPA Administrator Costle was not hesitant in promoting the hazardous waste cleanup problem, even if it meant exaggerating its extent: "Every barrel stuck into the ground [is] a ticking time bomb, primed to go off."[115] In a similar fashion, Thomas Jorling, then EPA assistant administrator, testified before Congress, "These wastes are capable of producing the full range of toxic effects in humans including acute poisoning and such chronic responses as carcinogenicity, mutagenicity, and promotion of miscarriages and birth defects."[116] Jorling also said, "We are confronted with perhaps the most serious environmental problem facing the Nation today."[117] He was also careful to note that "we do not have the statutory tools to do the job,"[118] and he is particularly attentive, in his Senate testimony, to the problems of sites in those states represented by committee members.[119]

A preliminary examination suggests that the eventual distribution of Superfund sites is consistent with the political objective of maintaining a high level of congressional support. In a Congress of increasingly fragmented power, this means keeping not just one or two powerful legislators satisfied, but distributing sites over many states and districts. Indeed, by early 1989, forty-five states had at least one site on the proposed NPL, while forty-three had at least one site on the final NPL. By 1991, all fifty states had at least one final NPL site, and twenty states contained twenty or more NPL sites. The six states with the most NPL sites, each with over fifty, accounted for 42 percent (501) of all Superfund sites in 1991, and 35 percent (153) of all House members.[120] Viewed at the congressional district level, the distribution of Superfund sites is nearly as widespread. By the end of 1989, almost two-thirds of all House districts (275) had at least one final NPL site. The number of sites per district is surprisingly uniform as well. Only twenty-nine districts had more than five final NPL sites within their borders, while ninety-eight had just one final site. Much of this is due to the fact that EPA got its list from the states in the first place, rather than systematically identifying the worst sites on its own, which resulted in a more uniform distribution of sites. Nevertheless, the wide distribution of NPL sites means that most legislators opposing Superfund do so at the risk of losing federal monies on an issue of great importance to some of their constituents. The fact that Superfund is sufficiently established that most districts now can benefit from increased funding can serve both Congress and EPA remarkably well. Any attempt to abridge the scope of Superfund could encounter substantial resistance from many members of Congress, rather than only a few select subcommittees (in addition to EPA and grass-roots supporters). The six largest Superfund states command considerable legislative resources and stand to forfeit significant federal expenditures if the Superfund program is curtailed sharply.

Allocating Superfund's cleanup resources widely was simplified by the unassailable notion, at the time, that abandoned hazardous waste sites were everywhere. Virtually all legislators could point to the possibility of a substantial number of sites in their districts or states, even if their states were not major industrial areas. Even potential threats were enough to get the attention of some legislators. Senator Jennings Randolph of West Virginia said, "My State of West Virginia has been spared incidents of the magnitude of those I referred to. But, West Virginia is among the 10 leading States in the production of hazardous substances, so there is always a substantial threat."[121] (Actually, the correlation between the net tons of hazardous waste in a state—production minus exports plus imports—and the number of NPL sites in the state as of 1989 is surprisingly weak.[122]) Consequently, because Superfund's supporters wanted to appeal to a majority of their colleagues and because most of them believed at the time that their districts and states contained abandoned waste sites, the program was easy to expand for political reasons. Prioritizing cleanups and defining "how clean is clean?" were secondary matters.

Besides the congressional intention to distribute resources widely regardless of merit, there is other evidence of self-interested legislative politics in defining key elements of the program. Because the chemical feedstock tax would include the fertilizer industry, senators with strong agricultural interests rose in opposition. Senator Culver of Iowa promoted two amendments (771 and 772) to S. 1480 that would exempt the fertilizer industry from the Superfund tax. He stated, "It is not the intention of this legislation to force responsible firms and industries to pay for those who handle their products irresponsibly" and "the fertilizer companies and farmers themselves have a good record in responding promptly and effectively to spills."[123] He neglected to mention that many chemical companies were hit with the tax regardless of their prior record in responding to spills and dumping waste, although he did acknowledge his political motivation that "the use of fertilizer for agriculture is, of course, of critical importance to Iowa."[124] Senator Dole of Kansas argued that while the effects of the fee on the economy as a whole may be insignificant, the effects on farmers of the fertilizer fee would be particularly acute: "In the case of the agricultural community, we have to consider that any increase in the financial burden on farmers poses real risks. Farming is more sensitive to the ups and downs of the economy, of weather, and of the international situation. Another unpredictable factor is the last thing farmers need."[125] The result is that normal field applications of fertilizer are excluded from Superfund's liability, and fees for fertilizers and chemicals used in making fertilizers are substantially exempted.[126]

Attempts to distribute particularized benefits were not limited to farmers, however. Senator Harry F. Byrd of Virginia submitted an amendment (2611) to S. 1480 to assist small businesses affected by the kepone chemical contamination of Virginia's James River in 1975, by compensating them for capital losses and loss of income. These would include sport and commercial fishing industries and businesses dependent on recreational use of the river.[127] Representative Brown of California, in whose district lies the massive Stringfellow site, preferred that EPA focus on priority sites—one of which assuredly would be Stringfellow. He said that since the proposed $1.2 billion fund was insufficient to remediate all identified sites, "EPA's task, far from one of coming up with a list of sites in need of attention, is one of prioritizing them."[128] Even the chemical industry, which was clearly responsible for a great deal of hazardous waste production and which was an internationally competitive industry, was defended by Representative Moore of Louisiana, a large chemical-producing state: "I think we should all be aware of the result of excessive taxation and our corresponding industrial inability to compete with foreign producers. We have already seen this as is now painfully evident with shoes, automobiles, television sets, steel, and many other items. Meanwhile, the chemical industry has enjoyed a substantial trade surplus of some $5 billion annually, and without the help of this industry, which is one of the few manufacturing exporters we still have left, our trade deficits would be far worse than they are."[129] Representative Moore then went on to show how imposing a fee on nickel would close down a plant—the Port Nickel facility—in Louisiana with a loss of seven hundred jobs. In contrast, Representative Eckhart of Texas, perhaps fearing that his state's petroleum industry would be forced to cover the entire industry tax share, countered, "The chemical industry is sound and does not need to be subsidized."[130]

In a more subtle yet significant way, Congress promoted the pattern of distributive politics by mandating strict cleanup schedules under SARA. By requiring that hundreds of sites either be cleaned up or reach various cleanup stages, legislators could be sure that benefits were distributed widely. Nearly every legislator could be assured of cleanup funds, since NPL sites were in virtually every state and because EPA was compelled to start remedial work at hundreds of sites. Once work begins at Superfund sites or most other projects, it is notoriously difficult to halt completion, regardless of merit, due to the political appeal of "sunk costs," or money spent or committed to a project.[131] Therefore, the 1986 reauthorization that mandated work at hundreds of sites can be seen as a subtle yet effective type of pork that distributes efforts widely to sustain congressional support. By forcing EPA to address many sites on the NPL, legislators could establish a federal presence for eventual cleanup in most districts and states rather than just a few of the worst sites. Also, it is no accident that there is little attention to site discovery by EPA; both Congress and EPA are more interested in ensuring that EPA cleans up those sites on the NPL than in finding new sites. For Congress, finding new sites channels money away from NPL cleanups, while for EPA, site discovery means that they will be berated even further for their poor performance as gauged by the low ratio of sites remediated to those on the NPL.

Finally and as mentioned earlier, Superfund's political appeal to the public can be described in the context of perceived risks. Psychologist Paul Slovic suggests that the degree of control of risk, the dread of risk, the catastrophic potential, its potential fatal consequences, and the inequitable distribution of risks all affect the public's perception of riskiness.[132] Each of these characteristics probably applies to the public's perception of Superfund risks. Although risk experts would call the public's reaction to hazardous waste sites unfounded, the public perception is such that Superfund remains a salient grass-roots political issue. Peter Sandman argues that an "outrage factor" best explains public reactions to risks that are sometimes contrary to the beliefs of experts.[133] Mark Sagoff adds that the *meaning* of risk is at least as important as the magnitude of risk on which experts ordinarily focus their attention.[134] In other words, a qualitative as well as quantitative dimension to risk management exists. In the case of Superfund, the perceptions that hazardous waste sites are a product of corporate greed, that they represent an unwanted and heretofore unrecognized intrusion into hundreds of localities, and that corporations would themselves finance cleanups, help to explain why the public's reaction confounds risks experts. Regardless of the inefficiency and procedural and distributive inequity of the program, continued strong public support—particularly from wealthy communities that are more likely to vote and provide campaign contributions—means that Superfund will most likely remain a politically powerful and enduring program.

Implications for Reforming Superfund

What, then, does this review indicate about the prospects for reform? For one, Superfund was established when inflation was high, productivity was slumping, a conservative Republican president was just elected, and fears abounded over America's ability to compete internationally and to contend with a volatile oil cartel. Consequently, neither poor economic conditions nor a conservative Republican administration is likely to spell Superfund's demise. The above sections argue that Superfund was not an accident, but rather the consequence of a form of political rationality. As a result, the prospects for limiting future Superfund expenditures, when Superfund sites are in every state and most congressional districts, appear remote. Although making the scale of the program consistent with the relative environmental and health risks posed by abandoned hazardous waste sites would represent an important change, convincing members of Congress of its political wisdom is a formidable task. Empirical evidence from chapter 7 suggests that part of legislators' motivations for voting to support or expand Superfund stems from the number of Superfund sites in their states. In addition to current citizen pressures, Douglas Arnold argues that legislators react to voters' "potential preferences" as well.[135] In other words, even if legislators are not currently being pressured to support Superfund and even if there are currently no NPL sites in their district, legislators feel it to be such a significant potential issue to voters that any opposition could be exploited successfully by an opposing candidate.

To summarize, many of the problems of Superfund stem from different sources, making successful policy alternatives all the more difficult to achieve. Although overstating the scale of the hazardous waste site problem derived from a groundswell of grass-roots support for federal action in cleaning up the worst sites, many of the other policy problems with Superfund are traceable to elements of political rationality on the part of Congress and the EPA. Continuing support for Superfund derives from grass-roots and community organizations lobbying individual legislators and EPA regional offices, not from inside the Beltway. Therefore, reforms need to concentrate on bridging the understanding between the beliefs of the public, which views Superfund sites as significant public health and environmental problems, and those of risk experts and EPA generally, who believe otherwise. There appears, however, to be some room for reforming procedural Superfund issues as long as they are not perceived to significantly weaken legislative intent. Indeed, since Congress is not apparently involved in EPA's site-specific cleanup decisions, bureaucratic reform is all the more feasible. Were it the case that Congress dictated bureaucratic policy, bureaucratic reforms could be expected to produce few results. Although there is room to reform cleanup procedures, significant program reforms cannot be achieved without congressional acceptance. However, congressional reforms will be had only with a willing public. In short, although some bureaucratic changes can likely be implemented, more fundamental reforms will depend crucially on direct public support.

As discussed earlier, the public is unlikely to be persuaded by arguments of "acceptable risk" and the like, largely because the public's reaction is related to what they perceive as their lack of *power*, compared with corporate and other opposing interests. The issue involves not just quantitative risks, but people's inability to control outcomes that affect their lives. Many are concerned with excessive corporate power over the political process. Some argue, for example, that it is no accident that the issue of transactions costs looms large in the 1994 reauthorization debate, since insurance companies and other large PRPs have been pushing the issue through advertisements in popular magazines (such as the AIG proposal) and through funded research (such as the Superfund Coalition).[136]

Reforming Superfund therefore does not entail educating the public how to think about risks, but instead placing the public in greater control of making risk management decisions. One problem with the inefficiency of Superfund is that substantial political advantages arise over the uncertainty and fear of waste sites showing up anywhere. Alternative expenditures, such as radon testing, benefit only a segment of the population. Superfund is in part so attractive politically because everyone thinks a waste site could be in his or her backyard. Building the recognition of opportunity costs into the program and involving the public in Superfund decision making are two important components to any Superfund reform. In the final chapter, I propose a reform of the Superfund program that attempts to do just that.

9 Reforming Superfund

Superfund's problems are imposing: affected communities are skeptical, to put it mildly, of the views of risk experts who tell them that many Superfund sites pose insignificant risks; the program is in several respects both inefficient and inequitable; political and public-relations difficulties have limited its effectiveness; and the magnitude of the hazardous waste cleanup problem remains unknown. To complicate matters, responding to Superfund's problems poses a significant dilemma in a representative democracy: many citizens want hazardous waste sites to be cleaned up, but the best available evidence suggests that the health and environmental risks are often marginal. Naturally, this is not the first time that experts and the public have disagreed, but the nature of the debate points to important issues of governance. Should our elected and appointed representatives lead us out of our collective ignorance of the true environmental and health risks, and rechannel Superfund monies where they will do more good? Or could the experts stand to learn something about risk from the public, notably that risk involves more than just the environmental and health hazards involved, and yield to government officials trying to carry out the expressed will of the citizenry through Superfund?

Framing the issue as "the public versus the experts" is ultimately destructive, however, for it allows little recognition—either politically or intellectually—of the merits of the other perspective and therefore no way out of the current policy impasse. As one close observer of the Superfund process aptly states, "The political process has not figured out how to get across the road from the public's perception of this problem to the technocrat's perception of the problem."[1] The "experts versus public" characterization is also destructive because it will not quickly be resolved by new risk assessments or scientific evidence, since the two perspectives focus on different priorities. As Peter Sandman writes, "Technical information, however well taught, is unlikely to change these [risk] priorities because they are not grounded in technical judgments in the first place."[2] Therefore, advocating one perspective over the other produces a political stalemate, a point aggravated by Superfund's entire existence through 1992 under a divided national government with a Democratic Congress and Republican administration. The public will remain unconvinced by risk experts because many individuals view experts (frequently from EPA) as representing a power opposed to their interests in protecting their children's and community's health. The fundamental problem people have with risk assessment and management is not that the concept of opportunity costs is foreign, but that it is believed to represent powerful and opposing interests. Consequently, any efforts at risk communication conveyed in an adversarial process will appear biased, and indeed in many instances it is. Policymakers are forced into an either-or choice between citizens' and experts' views (not to mention those of environmentalists, various industry groups, and so forth), which now results in knock-down drag-out fights over Superfund reauthorization, constant partisan bickering over how Superfund is implemented, and general frustration on the part of virtually everyone involved in actual cleanups.

Too frequently, EPA has treated Superfund as a technical or engineering problem; the EPA official who has been in charge of remedial actions is trained as an engineer, for example.[3] One observer agreed that "the decision process has to be a lot more transparent . . . Approaching it as an engineering problem, they have fundamentally misread what it takes to make the program successful."[4] While states and citizens participate to some extent, Superfund's decision-making process remains excessively bureaucratic. A grass-roots environmental lobbyist argues, "A major failing of Superfund is that communities, who are most affected by the program, are universally left out of the process."[5] Although SARA tried to add components of public participation and established the Technical Assistance Grants program to assist communities, they are not well integrated with Superfund's decision-making process. A close observer notes that public participation is "not intrinsic to the process. It's like they built a car, and then at the end said, 'Oh, yea, we need to add a fin.' "[6]

The only reasonable way to overcome this difference in perspectives is to create institutions that allow the public to be more actively involved in seeking cooperative risk management solutions and that will foster the consideration of public health and the environment alongside legitimate citizen concerns. The technocratic view of risk management is not only excessively limited, but it also fails to enjoin the public in debate over environmental priorities. I argued in chapters 3 and 4 that the concept of opportunity cost is lost in virtually all discussions of Superfund policy, not because the concept is difficult to understand, but because the incentive system created by Superfund encourages it. What I propose here in reforming Superfund is an attempt to bypass the "public versus experts" problem, and in so doing, force communities to face the opportunity costs of expenditures to remediate Superfund sites and force risk experts to see that there is more to risk management than comparing the number of expected cancers avoided. To establish the foundation of the proposed reforms, I first review various rationales for deciding which level of government—federal, state, or local—is most appropriate for financing and implementing environmental programs.

Environmental Federalism

In response to the growing federal share of government expenditures over the past several decades, commentators have again begun calling for a reexamination of federal and state responsibilities in such policy areas as education, infrastructure development and maintenance, health services, housing, community development, and transportation.[7] Programs that span national or state boundaries (acid rain), exhibit nationwide economies of scale (social insurance programs), or are redistributive in nature (food stamps) are thought by some to be best provided at the national or international level, rather than by states or localities.[8] Vice-President Al Gore recognizes the distinction in writing that "my study of the arms race led me to think about other issues, especially the global environment, in a new, more productive way. For example, I began to separate the parts of the environmental issue that were fundamentally local in nature, like hazardous waste sites, from those that represented threats to the entire globe."[9]

One important issue that has received scant attention in the congressional debates over Superfund is the most appropriate level of government to implement the program. I argue below that Superfund was reflexively considered a national problem, and therefore a federal program resulted. In some respects, such as developing technical expertise and prosecuting PRPs, this is appropriate. However, the program has become excessively centralized. State and local implementation of parts of Superfund would in several respects be more appropriate and effective. But before reviewing which characteristics of Superfund are best implemented nationally and locally, I briefly review some principles of environmental federalism that should—but ultimately did not—inform this debate.

Advantages of State and Local Environmental Policies

One advantage of policies implemented by subnational governments is that they can be tailored to the individual characteristics and preferences of the local community. Rather than imposing uniform national standards, states and localities can fashion environmental requirements that best match their needs. Just as some communities favor additional expenditures on schools rather than parks, so too may some communities prefer tighter environmental restrictions, perhaps in exchange for some economic growth, than others. Indeed, prior to national air quality legislation, notably the Clean Air Act of 1970, there was substantial variation in state air quality regulations. Not only can the existing preferences of citizens be better met by subnational governments, but individuals can move to locations that best match their desired combination of local services (including environmental quality), housing prices, local taxes, and so on, commonly known as "voting with your feet."[10] Communities, it is argued, will compete with each other to offer the best package of local amenities and taxes, and in doing so will provide "consumers" with a wide variety of choices. Naturally, the ability to migrate (or "vote") in this manner is predicated not only on an abundance of choices but also on the individual's financial wherewithal to do so.

A further advantage is the presumed ability of local governments to better respond to local needs because they are "closer to the people." Because local officials live in or near the affected communities, know the people who live there, and represent local interests, it is thought that programs appropriate in content and scale are more likely to evolve locally than from federal officials who neither live in the community nor understand local conditions. Quite apart from the advantage of enabling individuals to have significant choices among communities with different local amenities and taxes, the quality of local programs is thought in some cases to be superior as well because of local officials' intimate knowledge of local conditions and capabilities.

A final advantage of local environmental policies is the potential for greater nationwide innovation through local "experiments." While the federal government has but one experience in implementing environmental policy to evaluate, local policies offer variety and therefore the ability to assess which approaches are better and under which conditions they are most successful. If systematically evaluated and shared, hundreds of trial-and-error experiments across the country can yield important insights that would take a single national program hundreds of years to attain. Success in these "laboratories of democracy" provides a public good available to other communities and other levels of government. Thus, subnational environmental policies are advantageous because they can better tailor programs to match local needs, they are closer to the people, and they offer a greater potential for innovation through hundreds of public policy experiments.

Before turning to the advantages of federal environmental policy, it is important to clarify what "local" or "subnational" actually means. Neighborhoods? Towns? Counties? States? Generally speaking, there is no single answer because it depends on the environmental problem in question. A pollutant whose effects are borne entirely within a town should not be regulated nationally, the argument goes, but within that town, according to its preferred trade-off between environmental quality and jobs and other advantages that the local industry may provide. However, if a firm pollutes several surrounding towns as well, say through effluents discharged in a nearby river, then the appropriate jurisdiction for regulating the contaminants would contain all affected areas. Naturally, this principle can extend beyond a few towns to international cooperation, such as debates over acid rain affecting the United States, Canada, and parts of Europe and truly global problems such as stratospheric ozone depletion and global warming. In those instances, it would not serve the self-interest of each country to limit emissions unilaterally, since the costs of limiting emissions would be borne internally, while the benefits mainly accrue to the rest of the world. Therefore it is argued that such limits will not occur, and global cooperation is necessary. Without cooperation, there would be little or no control of pollutants that cross national boundaries. Therefore, the relevant jurisdiction is most appropriately one that can internalize all benefits and costs of pollution control.

Advantages of Federal Environmental Policies

The advantages of national environmental policies follow directly from the disadvantages of local controls. The first is that localities, if left to their own devices, will engage in "destructive competition," excessively sacrificing environmental quality to lure or keep industry and jobs in their region.[11] (Naturally, attracting the jobs and exporting the pollution—downstream, downwind, or down the turnpike—would be even more attractive to the locality. The argument does not rely on interjurisdictional spillovers or externalities, however.) It is argued that in the end, a form of "prisoner's dilemma" prevails, where the collective result is lower environmental quality than any individual jurisdiction would prefer in a cooperative environment.

However, the basis for opposing interjurisdictional competition on these grounds is not straightforward. Barring externalities, localities may be making what they consider to be appropriate decisions trading environmental quality for employment and wages, thereby competing constructively rather than destructively. Depending on current economic conditions, some towns may prefer more or better jobs that industry brings despite the prospect of added pollution. If so, it is not clear that local choices (in the absence of external effects) are necessarily destructive and therefore demand federal intervention.

A further advantage of national environmental policies is said to involve equity. If localities make independent environmental standards decisions, poorer regions will usually be more apt to accept environmental degradation in exchange for jobs than wealthier ones. Therefore, since the result of interjurisdictional competition would be that poorer areas would be those with the worst environmental quality, the argument suggests that uniform national standards would eliminate the inequality. However, depending on how the tighter national requirements are financed, to the extent that national standards are binding and exceed the lowest local standards and fall below those of the highest, neither group may be satisfied by federal control. (Federal regulatory statutes usually allow states to impose stricter standards than their federal counterparts, but not laxer ones.) One community may prefer more jobs and less environmental quality than federal rules permit. To the extent that poorer communities could view themselves as better off by exchanging jobs for environmental quality, national standards could in some respects be viewed as inequitably forcing the environmental priorities of the rich on the poor as well, who have other more pressing social concerns. On the other hand, even if the (oftentimes poor) community prefers to accept the trade-off, the result could be considered inequitable when substantial national benefits (such as lower product prices) are achieved at the expense of a single community accepting, say, hazardous wastes generated mostly by their affluent neighbors.

National financing of environmental programs may, however, be preferable—in terms of vertical equity—to environmental programs financed by local taxes. Progressive taxes are thought to be more easily achieved at the national level than by states, because of migration. For example, imposing highly progressive individual income taxes in Massachusetts may over time drive wealthier individuals to nearby states with lower taxes such as New Hampshire or Connecticut. The same applies to corporations. Corporations and wealthier individuals are more likely to migrate between states rather than internationally in the face of high or progressive taxes in one state (at least from the United States, although smaller countries experience the same problems). Normally, progressive taxes can be accomplished without excessive out-migration only at the national level or in very large states like California. Consequently, environmental programs (or any other, for that matter) financed at the state level are more likely to be neutral or regressive than revenues raised at the federal level with its more progressive income taxes. Naturally, programs financed nationally could be implemented locally, or vice versa, an option, it turns out, that was scarcely considered in the debate over Superfund.

Another advantage of national environmental controls stems not from the interests of localities or individuals directly, but rather from industry. If each state is allowed to impose its own air quality standards for, say, automobile emissions, the implication is that auto manufacturers may have to build cars meeting fifty different emissions levels, obviously an expensive proposition. (While it might be cheaper to build one car meeting the most stringent state's standards, this may itself prove prohibitively expensive.) For this reason, industries (including automobiles) in some cases have lobbied for federal regulations to preempt individual state rules. For example, responding to the prospect of individual state packaging requirements, an industry representative said, "Modifying package designs state by state would be impractical and uneconomical. Distribution would be impossible."[12] Where there are economies of scale, extreme local variation in environmental quality standards may be prohibitively expensive not only to industry but to consumers purchasing their products as well. Other economies of scale may also be present, such as in expertise, information gathering, and other concerns that would be excessively costly if implemented state by state.

One conclusion that can be drawn from the debate over environmental federalism is that the appropriate level of government to implement an environmental program depends on the nature of the pollutant and the degree to which economies of scale can be captured nationally. Accordingly, different pollutants are best regulated by different levels of government. Where pollutants do not cross state boundaries and economies of scale are absent, there appears to be a diminished need for a federal role in implementing environmental programs. Superfund is a program that is appropriately financed nationally, both because past beneficiaries of illegal dumping are numerous and diverse and because federal taxes can be far more equitably raised than state revenues. Nevertheless, Superfund's *implementation* should allow greater local variation and *local control* than is currently permitted.

Federalizing Superfund?

The Superfund program addresses a national responsibility with local environmental and public health implications. The health and environmental impacts of Superfund sites are mostly local or intrastate. Past improper dumping of hazardous wastes benefited millions of Americans in the form of lower product prices and increased shareholder returns, while the costs were concentrated in those communities where improper dumping occurred. The appropriate response should attempt to reverse the past distribution of benefits and costs: cleanup costs should be borne federally, while cleanup benefits should be recognized as essentially local. The "local" nature of the benefits of site remediation naturally vary from site to site. In some cases, small communities or parts of communities are the only beneficiaries of remedial or removal actions, while in others, such as widespread groundwater contamination, the benefits can extend over a much larger area. While there are a few instances of Superfund site hazards crossing state boundaries, for the most part the remedial benefits are concentrated locally. Therefore, while it is in some respects a "national problem," this designation applies only to the number of sites, not to the type of pollution. While financing should remain national, the appropriate jurisdiction to control site cleanups is therefore a subnational government because of the type of pollution, not its prevalence, and the greater ability of smaller governments to understand and respond to local needs.

There is little question that the current level of federal Superfund spending does not mirror the interests of many states. Many states are receiving federal Superfund monies that *they believe* would be better spent addressing other environmental problems. Christopher Daggett, New Jersey's environmental protection commissioner, the state with the most extensive hazardous waste problem (and with the most current NPL sites), has said, "The valid question is, are we spending too much on Superfund? We ought to do a better job of identifying real risks and putting money where they are." Speaking only of environmental problems, Daggett added that better spending alternatives for New Jersey might include greater attention to indoor radon, toxic air pollutants, and pesticide residues on food.[13] If prosperous, densely populated states like New Jersey with many Superfund sites would prefer to direct some of their cleanup funds elsewhere, one can only speculate how poorer states with fewer people exposed would redirect Superfund dollars.

Most commonly for fund-lead sites, the federal government requires that states finance only 10 percent of site remediation costs. Paying ten cents on the dollar, states have little incentive to find cost-effective solutions or to refuse federal Superfund money in the first place. Nevertheless, states do sometimes refuse to pay even the 10 percent share of cleanup costs, a source of significant delay in site remediation. Maryland refused to finance its 10 percent share of a $70 million cleanup of the state's largest site, the Southern Maryland Wood Treatment Plant site, in part because it thought the proposed remedy too expensive, and because the state was hesitant to spend $7 million on one environmental cleanup in the wake of recent layoffs of state workers and the unpopularity of the proposed incineration.[14] In addition, substantial differences can arise between the states and the federal government over which sites should be cleaned up and how. As one grass-roots lobbyist has observed, "Communities want different things at different sites."[15]

The results of a survey I conducted in March 1991 indicated that many state environmental officials believe Superfund spending is currently excessive in relation to other environmental priorities. The survey asked state officials to indicate which of thirty-one environmental problems (taken directly from EPA's 1987 report, *Unfinished Business*) should receive less, more, or about the same levels of funding and regulatory attention.[16] Of the twenty-three states responding to the survey, only six recommended additional federal spending on Superfund, while seven recommended decreased federal funding. Six states called for additional state spending on Superfund, while eight wanted less. In the event of a substantial state budgetary increase, only five of twenty-three states indicated that they would recommend that even a small portion of the monies be devoted to Superfund. (The level of increased spending ranged from 2 percent to a maximum of 15 percent of the significant hypothetical budgetary increase.) Most respondents suggested that additional monies be spent on various air pollution control measures. Therefore, even from the state *environmental* officials surveyed, there is relatively little support for additional Superfund spending. Indeed, more environmental officials recommended reductions in federal and state spending on Superfund than increases.

One of the arguments against state or local environmental policies is that "destructive competition" among jurisdictions may produce excessively lax environmental regulations. This effect does not apply to Superfund, however, because the environmental degradation has already occurred. Localities do not compete for additional jobs in exchange for added pollution with Superfund sites as they do for prospective sources of pollution. There is no competition because Superfund sites are geographically fixed, and therefore localities cannot compete for them in exchange for more jobs. (This can, of course, influence the *current* regulation and siting of hazardous waste sites.) Localities may be pressured by local PRPs to limit cleanup costs in order to preserve local jobs, however. Localities that force costly remediation could be faced with the prospect of a local industry going bankrupt. Therefore, allowing localities to make cleanup decisions themselves may force many of them into difficult bargaining positions with PRPs threatening layoffs.

Despite some of the arguments for local control, there are significant reasons for retaining a federal presence in Superfund policy. Chief among them is the regulatory advantage afforded by Superfund's liability provisions. Individual states may, in the absence of the federal law, engage in forms of destructive competition in trying to lure firms to their states by implementing weak regulations. In addition, there are significant economies of scale in the research of health effects from hazardous wastes that would be, collectively, prohibitively expensive if conducted by fifty states. Finally, although state implementation offers the advantages of experimentation, a federal role in seeking and developing new remedial technologies, if not in applying them, would be far more efficient than duplicative state research. Nevertheless, there remains ample room for state or local control over how Superfund monies are spent.

Why Is Superfund Largely a Federal Program?

The current federal financing of Superfund is appropriate, both because past beneficiaries include most citizens and because revenues can be raised most equitably (in terms of ability to pay) at the federal level. However, implementation is more appropriately a local matter, not a federal one, because localities better understand the problems and choices confronting their own communities and because Superfund site hazards are limited in geographic scope. Why was Superfund established as an exclusively federal program, when the benefits of remedial actions are local?

Judging from congressional debate, there appears to have been little serious discussion of the appropriate level of government at which to implement the program. The principal reason is that Superfund financing and implementation were considered jointly, not as independent factors. Four arguments promoted a federal program. First, because the sites were "everywhere," it was thought to be a national problem that the federal government needed to address. Second, the effects of some sites allegedly crossed state boundaries.[17] Third, it was argued that a comprehensive legal framework was necessary rather than fifty different laws for disposal practices, fees, and so on.[18] Finally, states were judged to be incapable of carrying out such a program. I consider the merits of each of these arguments below.

By far the most common argument for federal intervention involved the scope of the problem. Senator Mitchell of Maine argued that "people have been tragically harmed like this in virtually every State of the Union."[19] Representative Downey of New York noted, "This is a national problem . . . [and] the problem is probably larger, not smaller, than the initial studies have pointed out; given the fact that this is a national problem, it is important to understand that the Federal Government can work."[20] Because every state had a hazardous waste site cleanup problem, it was argued that it was the federal government's responsibility. This argument is difficult to understand in relation to a number of other programs with national interest that are both funded and operated locally. Every state has educational needs, although the federal government plays a relatively minor role. Every community has road repair needs, although these are usually handled at the state or local levels. Every community makes taxing and spending decisions for itself about collecting garbage, improving parks, schools, emergency services, and a host of other issues common to virtually all localities, yet the federal government's role is secondary. Regardless, Superfund's supporters argued that federal intervention was necessary because hazardous waste sites were located in many parts of the country. By treating the entire program as one of either national or state responsibility, the obvious need for some federal role led inevitably to the conclusion that a singular federal role was required.

Stronger arguments for a substantial federal role are economies of scale in expertise and the theoretical possibility of interstate pollution. Representative Downey of New York argued, "It is important that we have one group of experts who can go out and keep an inventory across this country of the problems. Also, some of these problems occur between State lines."[21] One group of experts is clearly easier to assemble and is more efficient than each state hiring its own full-time staff. And in cases where the few sites crossing state boundaries exist, a federal role may be important (although reconciling differences between two or three states is not implausible through state negotiations). However, this still does not address the issues of who should make cleanup decisions, how much money should be spent at each site, how many sites should be remediated, and whether other environmental problems are more important. The arguments that make sense for elements of a federal program were taken as arguments for a federal program from top to bottom with only limited state intervention. That is, a meaningful shared federal and state role was never seriously addressed.

The third argument, that one law regulating hazardous waste disposal is preferable to fifty different state laws, appears to be sound. Representative LaFalce of New York argued, "I think another reason . . . that the States cannot handle it, is that it is a problem that is nationwide in scope and is deserving of a comprehensive legal framework if it is to be attacked and met. We cannot develop a comprehensive legal framework if we allow the States to approach it and work their own wills."[22] A comprehensive legal framework in this regard is appropriate both because of the destructive competition that could ensue by states enacting ever more lenient hazardous waste disposal laws to attract new businesses and because of the prohibitive cost of complying with fifty different regulatory structures for products manufactured and sold in many states.

The problem is that the argument has little or nothing to do with Superfund's remedial cleanups. The regulation of hazardous waste disposal was already being carried out, albeit many argued inadequately, under the RCRA legislation enacted in 1976. Even if states enacted different Superfund cleanup standards, the destructive competition argument for federal intervention does not apply, nor does the argument against different regulations for hazardous waste disposal. Current regulation, either indirectly through Superfund or directly through RCRA, has little effect on abandoned and inactive waste sites (including NPL sites). The regulatory advantages of Superfund, which may be substantial in promoting better current management and disposal of hazardous wastes, do nothing for abandoned sites because the damage has already occurred. Only *future* waste disposal practices can be modified.

The fourth rationale for a federal Superfund program is that states were judged incapable of carrying out such a program, for at least two reasons. First, even large and wealthy states were judged to have insufficient resources to manage such a large problem. Representative Wolff of New York stated, "New York does not have the resources to initiate its own systematic plan for identifying and clean[ing] up its waste sites."[23] Representative Rodino of New Jersey noted, "The scope of the problem is beyond any individual State's capabilities to resolve alone."[24] This was not an appeal to equity—that poor states could not afford such a program—but simply that no state could undertake such a program alone. Second, it was argued that even among states that had large waste site problems, some were not interested in a large Superfund program, nor had they shown an ability to successfully implement one. Representative Florio of New Jersey stated that "many States, quite frankly, are not interested or are not capable of going forward."[25]

The argument that even large states commanded insufficient resources to address the cleanup problem is in certain respects difficult to understand. If large and wealthy states like New York cannot address their own problems, how can fifty combined states address all fifty problems? In this regard, the argument is illogical. Do federal capabilities exceed the pooled resources of the citizens of the fifty states? Moreover, at the time many states were running budget surpluses, while the federal government was reporting record deficits. For example, in 1980 state and local government national income and product accounts finances showed a combined surplus of $25 billion, while the federal government showed a deficit of $60 billion.[26] Therefore, the states could spend the surpluses on cleanups or raise taxes, or the federal government could raise taxes or increase the deficit to finance cleanups. There is no apparent advantage to federal spending over state spending. It can be argued that the federal government should become involved in financing the program for several reasons: that revenues can be raised more progressively, that in lieu of federal involvement destructive competition among states suppresses state tax rates, or finally that nearly all Americans benefited from past improper dumping and therefore should share responsibility for restitution. These arguments never arose, however. The nonsensical argument that the larger federal government could better afford to finance Superfund remained essentially unchallenged, and ultimately prevailed. As discussed in chapter 8, legislators most likely hoped that a disproportionate share of Superfund resources would be directed to their states.

Legislators correctly argued that states were incapable of supporting a complex cleanup program such as Superfund; what was overlooked was the fact that the federal government was scarcely more able. A telling example, both of legislators' high initial expectations for Superfund and of the ability of states to address such problems, involved a 1980 House floor debate between Representatives Florio of New Jersey and Stockman of Michigan. Florio argued that the intention of the proposed legislation was to speed cleanups. As an example, he objected to Stockman's reference to a site in Michigan where the state sued Hooker Chemical and received a $15 million out-of-court consent decree to clean up the site (without any federal involvement and under existing state law).[27] "It took 2 years for the appropriate local agency to respond," said Florio, denouncing the delay. "That is part of what this legislation is all about."[28] By today's standards, two years is remarkably expeditious compared with the decade or more required to remediate many sites. Florio's argument indicates that he believed the Superfund program would enable the federal government to more quickly remediate waste sites, while at the same time his example shows that some states already were capable of addressing certain problems in a timely manner. Michigan has one of the largest Superfund problems, and it is clearly not representative of the ability of other states to act in an equivalent manner. Nevertheless, even before 1980 some states demonstrated a surprising capability by today's standards.

Other legislators argued that the federal government had not demonstrated that it could satisfactorily handle the problem and that states and localities may be able to do a better job. Representative Dannemeyer of California said, "Since when did a Federal regulatory agency ever move quickly on a problem, to wit RCRA, or solve it efficaciously, to wit air and water pollution? And who is to say that State or local government, or even private enterprise, could not do the job in a manner more consistent with the wishes of the local citizenry?"[29] The political problem was that although some legislators were advocating a state-run Superfund program, they were exclusively conservatives using this as a vehicle to promote a small federal fund. Representative Stockman offered an amendment that would create state programs funded by $500 million in federal monies as well as technical assistance. He argued, "Unlike the cases of air emissions, air pollution, and water pollution, where we have pollution crossing State lines and we need a Federal role so that we have equal standards in every State, we are dealing with abandoned, inactive waste sites that were created because of improper disposal in the past. Those sites are not going to go away. They are not going to cross State lines. They are in some State's back yard or some municipality's back yard, and every State and every municipal area has ample power under the State law or the common law to move in those cases where public health is threatened."[30] Senator Helms of North Carolina added, "I have long supported State participation in any Superfund bill dealing with hazardous waste sites. This is both a Federal and a State problem. States have benefited from an industrial location within their borders in salaries to employees, and in State taxes paid by the corporations. Therefore, the burden is not that of the Federal Government to solve problems that could and should have been solved by local and State governments."[31] The motivations were not necessarily to bring cleanups closer to local communities, but rather to reduce the scale of the proposed program. Consequently, the size of the fund and the level of government that would implement the program were implicitly considered jointly rather than as separable options. Because of the ideological positions that each group represented, advocates of a substantial Superfund wanted federal implementation, and those advocating a small fund wanted a state-run program. The middle ground—a large fund implemented by states—was never discussed.

Finally, there were somewhat obvious political reasons for an exclusively federal program to address the program. First, the federal government could not simply give the states a few hundred million dollars and turn its back on the problem. Legislators needed to be seen responding to a problem their constituents wanted the government to act on. In addition, as discussed in chapter 8, legislators from states with large hazardous waste problems had every incentive to portray the problem as national in scope and therefore deserving federal dollars. Doing so meant bringing federal monies to their states. Representative Rodino of New Jersey, for example, urged passage of legislation "to deal with this urgent *national* problem," [emphasis added] one that would certainly attract significant federal resources to his state.

Reforming Superfund

Comprehensive reforms of Superfund must simultaneously address several primary problems identified in earlier chapters: public demands for remediating Superfund risks that experts believe to be relatively small, the substantial transactions costs (both in cleanup delays and money), and program inefficiencies and inequities. Moving toward this end requires more than tinkering with management practices, hiring better staff, and so forth; it requires fundamental reform. The existing Superfund program has committed the federal government to responsibility for cleaning up current NPL sites. Backing away from that commitment, even where remediation is not cost-effective, represents not only an abdication of federal responsibility but is politically unlikely as well. Legislators will not—and indeed politically cannot—turn around and tell their constituents that the site they promised would be cleaned up no longer qualifies under revised federal guidelines.

With the current level of grass-roots public support for Superfund, and financing from a dedicated tax, Congress will be unable to make substantial cuts in funding, as some have advocated. More importantly, cutting Superfund funding would fail to address the risk management issue that is so central to the Superfund debate: what should be done when the public and experts are diametrically opposed on the course of public policy. Cutting Superfund would simply say that the risk experts are right and the public is wrong. As argued earlier, this is both a narrow view of environmental risk management and undemocratic. However, it must also be recognized that reallocating resources committed to Superfund can substantially increase environmental and health benefits. Therefore, the proposed reforms below are intended mostly to allow communities to improve resource allocation rather than redirecting where Superfund resources will be deployed from the national level. I argue that the reforms outlined below substantially increase meaningful public participation, reduce transactions costs, improve both procedural and outcome equity, and can improve efficiency by targeting cleanup monies to the most significant risks. Although various groups will surely view individual parts of this proposal as contrary to their interests, it is possible that the package as a whole can satisfy the necessary conditions for change that each stakeholder requires. Failing that, even individual elements of the proposed reform could substantially improve the cleanup process.

A fundamental reform proposed here is to divide all inactive and abandoned hazardous waste sites (NPL and non-NPL sites) into those closed before 1981 and the remainder. The year 1981 establishes a cutoff year after which firms were aware (or should have been) of Superfund's liability provisions and should have taken appropriate actions to clean up the site. Moreover, older sites generally are further removed from the polluter-pays principle, since current owners and consumers are less likely to be those who previously benefited from past improper dumping. A one-year amnesty period would offer an incentive for any party to disclose the existence of abandoned sites without penalty (unless past dumping was illegal at the time, in which case PRPs would be prosecuted). Any pre-1981 sites discovered after the amnesty period, where PRPs knew of them, should be subject to existing Superfund liability standards but with modified cleanup standards (discussed below). Naturally, the 1981 cutoff year could be changed to 1976, when RCRA was passed; to the mid-1980s, when the constitutionality of Superfund's retroactive liability was upheld in court; or to some other date. The important factor is that the regulatory benefits of Superfund's liability standards be maintained in the future, while simultaneously speeding the cleanup of older inactive sites, to preserve what one environmental lobbyist describes as Superfund's "stunning impact" on current hazardous waste management.[32] Because too little is known about current site risks to the environment and health, EPA should also greatly expand its analytic efforts to determine the hazards posed by various chemicals and wastes found at Superfund sites and the relative risks from other substances as well.

A new National Environmental Restoration Fund (NERF) would be established to finance all pre-1981 site cleanups. The level of NERF funding would be equal to the cost of remediating current pre-1981 NPL sites, plus the cost of remediating any newly discovered pre-1981 sites that qualify for the NPL (those that score over 28.5 on the HRS). The NERF could be financed from general revenues, but political expediency would probably dictate either a broad-based tax or one focused on the chemical, petroleum, and insurance industries. Under the proposed reform, each state would receive that portion of the NERF necessary to remediate the pre-1981 NPL sites within its borders. Each state would then be required to establish a committee of citizen representatives, some of whom live near waste sites, but also including EPA officials, scientists, and others as advisors, to decide how the NERF would be allocated, subject to federal approval. NERF monies could be used for Superfund cleanups, asbestos removal, radon or lead remediation, and any other remedial environmental restoration project. Liability standards for post-1981 sites would be modified to allow for proportional liability, but more importantly, cleanup standards would be changed to require cost-effective levels that take future land-use into account, a departure from the current emphasis on permanence in selecting remedies. This liability scheme would also apply to any future sites discovered (except pre-1981 sites under the amnesty period). Details of each step are explained below.

Pre-1981 Sites: The National Environmental Restoration Fund

The first step for pre-1981 sites is to waive federal liability standards and substitute monies from the newly established NERF to finance site cleanups. To determine the size of the NERF, an estimate would be made of the cost of remediating each current NPL site closed before 1 January 1981 under current cleanup standards. Based on current estimates of NPL site cleanup costs of approximately $30 million each, and approximately 620 pre-1981 NPL sites,[33] this portion of the NERF could be expected to be on the order of $19 billion. Other cost estimates of $40 million per site push the total to nearly $25 billion.

In addition to existing pre-1981 NPL sites, states, communities, PRPs, or individuals could bring to EPA's attention additional sites within the one-year amnesty period without penalty. If the sites exceed the current 28.5 HRS cutoff score, they would be included on the NPL as well and therefore be eligible for NERF funding. This provides an incentive to identify new sites, yet the fact that the 28.5 hurdle must be cleared to qualify for NERF funds would limit the final number of cleanups. This provides the opportunity to identify hazardous waste sites irrespective of a community's past ability to bring the site to the state's attention and limits disparities across states as well, some of which have had far more active site identification programs than others. The intention here is both to identify once and for all (to the extent possible) which sites the federal government has implicitly promised remediation and to actively identify waste sites located in communities that have been less politically active or capable. The result would be a new pre-1981 NPL that includes not only previously identified sites but also any sites not previously recognized by the federal government which would have been sufficiently hazardous to quality for the existing NPL.

The total size of the NERF would be significantly larger than the current trust fund, although (largely because post-1981 sites are not included) far smaller than most estimates of Superfund's ultimate cost. Estimating costs is complicated by the fact that EPA's current guidelines do not sufficiently define appropriate cleanup levels; clearer guidelines would need to be established concerning what "permanent" remediation actually means. Nevertheless, cleanup costs have already been estimated at many sites where Records of Decision (RODs) have been signed. To the $19–25 billion estimated cost of remediating current pre-1981 NPL sites would be added the unknown sum of the cost of remediating any newly qualifying pre-1981 sites. Although the ultimate size of the fund cannot be known until firmer cost estimates for remediating all pre-1981 NPL and newly qualifying sites have been obtained, it is unlikely that the total would exceed $30 billion.

The NERF could be funded in several ways. Ideally, it would be financed from general revenues, both in order to raise the funds most progressively and because the beneficiaries of past improper dumping are so numerous and widespread. Alternatively, a more politically feasible method is to institute an excise tax on insurance claims or on chemical and petroleum products, which would, at least in the short term, be significantly larger than current payments. Finally, a hazardous waste tax could be used to fund the program. However, although the latter method would improve incentives for firms to limit hazardous waste production, it is unlikely to be able to generate sufficient funds, and if sufficiently high, it might encourage "midnight dumping" and other ways of avoiding paying the tax. The most likely result is some combination of general revenues and excise taxes on chemical and petroleum products, not unlike the current funding scheme.

The next step is for each state to be allocated NERF funds corresponding to the total cost of remediating its pre-1981 NPL sites. Some states, such as New Jersey, would receive significant funds, on the order of several billion dollars, while others, such as Nevada, would probably receive far less, perhaps tens of millions of dollars. While this does not necessarily reflect the magnitude of the hazardous waste problem in each state (since NERF funding would not be based on sites scoring below 28.5 on the HRS), it does address the current federal commitment to remediate NPL sites and improves upon the current system by adding the important incentive to identify new sites. Naturally, this would entail significant competition among states for the finite pool of NERF resources, so EPA would need to designate clearly which sites are eligible and which are not. A significant difference from current policy is that NERF monies need not be directed only to NPL sites, but rather to what the newly formed citizen committees believe to be the most pressing environmental and public health risks in each state.

Once the amount each state would receive from the NERF is determined, each state committee would draw up a State Implementation Plan (SIP) for allocating the federal funds. The committees would be chosen by state officials subject to approval from EPA, and would comprise ordinary citizens as well as representatives living near hazardous waste sites, including sites that do not currently qualify for NPL status, and citizens representing remedial efforts for lead, radon, asbestos, and other relevant constituencies. (The scope of participation would depend on the limitations imposed on spending NERF monies.) State environmental officials, scientists, and others would serve as consultants to aid the committee in studying alternative plans for using the federal funds. The committee would then recommend expenditures to the federal EPA through the SIPs. The committee's decisions should be based on significant public participation, not only through representation on the committee itself, but also through a series of public meetings around the state to solicit community reactions to various proposals to allocate the NERF. (Presumably, states would be permitted some flexibility in setting up the committees; however, the federal EPA should ensure that the process and decisions take account of community needs. States could, for example, hold a statewide referendum for voters to approve or disapprove the package of proposed NERF spending.) States would be allowed to spend the money on any remedial environmental efforts, but they would be free to limit expenditures to pre-1981 hazardous waste sites. Regardless, a significant part of the reform is to allow citizens to become more involved in decisions about managing risks and to therefore channel funds to what they feel are the most important needs. The reform is not simply a matter of efficient allocation of funds; it is also a means of fostering public participation—allowing citizens to become involved in a public discussion of social problems.

Upon federal EPA approval, funds would be released to the states, commensurate with the timetables specified in the SIPs. Competitive bidding procedures for remedial contracts would be required. The federal EPA would evaluate each state's progress in reaching its specified goals and could withhold monies if states fail to comply with the agreement, if monies are mismanaged, or the mutual understanding specified in the SIP is violated in any way. EPA's role would be limited to providing information for which economies of scale exist, such as technical advice on cleanup technologies, evaluations of the environmental and health effects of chemicals present at waste sites, and so forth. Accompanying the NERF funds, EPA would provide freely all information, such as risk assessments, health hazard data, or ecological impact assessments, that had been prepared for each site, as well as any available information on all CERCLIS sites. EPA should be encouraged to provide available comparative risk information for Superfund sites, as well as risks from lead paint, radon, and other hazards. States could also request that the federal EPA instead manage the cleanup process, at reasonable cost, when state expertise is lacking. However, the citizen-based committees would in all cases make NERF allocation decisions, and EPA's role would be limited to managing site cleanups.

A "maintenance of effort" provision would be built into each NERF grant, so that states could only use NERF monies for *additional* remedial spending rather than supplanting current spending with NERF funds (and using the freed funds for other purposes). Under this provision, states could not, for instance, spend money previously targeted to state-financed site cleanups for some other purpose (such as road improvements) while NERF monies are substituted. For example, if New Jersey currently spends x million on hazardous waste cleanups, NERF monies could only fund expenditures greater than x million, and similarly for other programs (e.g., lead, radon, or any other permissible NERF expenditures). Nevertheless, NERF funds could be used for administrative costs, additional research, risk assessments, and other purposes deemed necessary by the state committees.

While the state committees would in no way be obligated to use the information provided by EPA or other federal agencies to allocate NERF funds, the committees could finance additional studies comparing risks at sites where existing information is insufficient or unavailable. The shift in decision-making authority alone may make risk assessments more credible, since they would no longer represent a powerful institution's interest. As mentioned earlier, a fundamental problem with communicating site risks now is the feeling of distrust on the part of the public, which feels that EPA and PRPs are trying to impose risk estimates that understate what they believe to be actual site risks. If, however, the state committees were to examine risk estimates of different environmental problems and were given NERF monies to address any remedial environmental and public health problems they saw fit, then the risk assessments may be viewed far more favorably: they would no longer come from an adversary with a proposed agenda to lessen remedial efforts. Even EPA officials acknowledge that in many cases the public simply wants the truth about actual and relative risks. Assistant EPA Administrator Don Clay's experience has showed him that "in many cases, that's all people want— for somebody to tell them the truth about what is going on."[34] Public skepticism will continue to be substantial as long as some outside institution is making cleanup decisions.

Some states naturally will make different expenditure trade-off decisions than others, and that is precisely the point. Instead of being required to adopt a national standard, individual states can choose how the money will be spent within the same resource constraints that (at least implicitly) guide any decision-making process. Each committee will have sufficient funds to remediate all the state's NPL sites, if it chooses, or NERF monies to spend on what it decides are more pressing environmental problems.

Because these individuals ultimately must live in the communities affected by their resource allocation decisions and because external costs and benefits are minimal, who better to decide?

The opportunity costs of committee decisions would be more clearly recognized because of the "zero-sum" allocation problems that each state committee confronts. Providing more money to lead cleanup means that radon, asbestos, Superfund, and other hazards receive less. The fact that resources provided to remediate one risk means they are denied to another forces the committees to consider the relative benefits of spending money in different ways. Proponents of spending money on problem x would need to argue not just that problem x is worthy of attention, but how it is more worthy of attention than problem y. Moreover, instead of the federal government telling the public that x or y is more cost-effective, an unenviable position for elected and appointed federal officials, this reform allows local representatives to reach those decisions themselves. Finally, this reform would eliminate the substantial federal subsidies that from the state's perspective makes Superfund cleanups appear attractive. The town manager in Stratford, Connecticut, for example, welcomed the news that the cleanup of hazardous waste contamination by a previous brake manufacturer would most likely be financed by Superfund. Noting the financial reason for publicizing widespread contamination in the town, he said, "Only the federal government has enough money."[35] By removing what is now a 90 percent federal cost share, states can assess the relative merits of each remedial effort on an equal footing with other remedial environmental programs. From the state's new perspective, a $20 million Superfund cleanup would really cost $20 million instead of the $2 million it costs the state today.

The second fundamental reform of Superfund involves waiving federal Superfund liability for sites closed prior to 1981. This both reduces transactions costs for assigning liability at pre-1981 sites and improves equity in two ways. First, the unfairness of retroactively assigning liability to firms who had dumped properly and legally in the past is removed. Second, the reform eliminates the inequity of forcing current consumers and shareholders to finance present cleanups, which arguably is only achieved regressively. The longer a site has been closed, the less likely that "responsible parties" will be the same people who benefited from the improper dumping in the first place. Finally, Superfund's regulatory impact obviously has no effect on sites closed prior to 1981. As a result, the allegedly significant regulatory advantages of Superfund—which encourage careful handling and disposal of present hazardous wastes—would remain undisturbed.

There would clearly be some litigation over any particular "no-fault" liability cutoff date specified, so transactions costs in this case are not entirely eliminated. The issues include the arbitrariness of 1981 as the particular year, disagreements over when a particular site actually closed, and disputes when some PRPs claim they should not be held liable for cleanup costs because they stopped dumping at a given site prior to 1981 (even though the site continued to operate after 1981). This latter point is particularly troubling, since waste generators may have changed their behavior in the face of CERCLA's existence in 1981 yet could still be held responsible for site cleanups when the dump remained open, even though they discontinued dumping after 1981. While it is theoretically preferable to establish a cutoff date based on when the wastes were dumped, the difficulty in establishing individual dates for individual PRPs may be overwhelming and could eliminate or largely diminish the substantial transactions costs savings achieved by this proposal. Forcing the burden of proof on the PRP to demonstrate that it did not dump since 1981, to waive its liability, may improve the reform's fairness, but it could also cause a series of expensive legal challenges to the policy.

Are the transactions costs savings greater than the new expected transactions costs? It is necessary, of course, first to estimate what the transactions costs savings are likely to be for eliminating liability for pre-1981 sites. Site cleanup costs currently average around $30 million. While estimates vary widely, I will assume here that transactions costs represent 24 percent of costs.[36] With approximately 620 pre-1981 sites (not including newly discovered sites),[37] transactions cost savings would amount to $4.46 billion. To this would be added any future transactions costs avoided for newly qualifying NPL sites, which could easily put the total savings at over $5 billion. This is clearly a "guesstimate," but it is likely that transactions costs are higher for older sites where records are incomplete and PRPs more difficult to locate and prosecute. If cleanup costs or the portion of expenses devoted to transactions costs are higher, which is quite likely, then savings would be even greater. (Naturally, lower percentages, lower cleanup costs, and fewer sites would have the opposite effect.) As mentioned above, while there would be additional transactions costs as a result of these reforms, they are unlikely to come even close to the several billion dollars in cost savings that waiving pre-1981 liability would achieve. It is important to remember that transactions costs savings of even $3 billion would provide enough money to fully remediate approximately one hundred sites or achieve cost-effective cleanups at many more.

Another advantage of these reforms is the greater ability of states to experiment with remedial technologies that the federal government has been hesitant to employ. Further, states would no longer be bound by cumbersome federal procedures and would enjoy greater administrative flexibility in implementing their own Superfund programs. In addition to making alternative expenditure decisions, state committees could opt to provide remedial efforts only where immediate health threats are apparent, and retain the NERF balance (with interest) for future contingencies and cleanups. Superfund and other remedial environmental cleanups would therefore be more carefully tailored to the needs of each state.

Post-1981 Hazardous Waste Sites: A Modified Cleanup Strategy

The most fundamental reforms involve sites that closed prior to 1981; however, significant reforms are required in addressing post-1981 sites as well, to improve the efficiency, speed, and effectiveness of Superfund policy. The first step of the reform is to eliminate the Hazard Ranking System as a method of determining whether sites will be placed on the NPL. As mentioned in earlier chapters, the HRS has two fundamental flaws: the cutoff point for qualifying for the NPL (currently 28.5) is arbitrary, and qualifying for the NPL bears no relationship to whether the site can be cost-effectively remediated.[38] (Not to mention whether the scores are accurately computed, whether the scoring sheets used by field operators accurately reflect site conditions, whether sufficiently trained personnel are performing the assessments, and other problems with the HRS.) The latter fault can have two consequences. First, some sites may not qualify for the NPL although relatively inexpensive measures may reduce modest risks, such as restricting access or providing alternative drinking water supplies. Second, sites may be on the NPL whose remediation is prohibitively costly compared with the reduced environmental and public health risks. Therefore, the existing NPL is, by design, an inappropriate list of target sites to be (even partially) remediated. (HRS scores are relied upon in the allocation of NERF funds for pre-1981 sites so that states are not denied funds they are entitled to under the present system.)

Instead, the statute should require EPA to explicitly compare marginal benefits and costs in making cleanup decisions. This serves two functions. First, it would curb excessive expenditures at some sites, where millions of dollars are used to remediate trivial remaining risks. Second, a comparison of marginal cleanup benefits and costs would expand the number of sites EPA could consider for remedial cleanups; even small sites may qualify for cleanup if modest benefits can be had at even more modest costs. The objective would be to determine at what point increasingly costly remedies no longer provide commensurate current and future environmental and health benefits. Naturally, comparing marginal benefits and costs is not a precise calculation, but simply a means for guiding site-specific analyses and decision making. Part of this process should include greater emphasis on identifying the future land use of the site, including its potential ecological value. A site located in the middle of a commercial center has significant value that should be incorporated in a cost-benefit comparison, and site restoration would ensure productive use of the land. On the other hand, it makes little sense to remediate a site with little future land value to a pristine condition. Finally, EPA should be encouraged to make greater use of mixed funding, where EPA shares in the remedial costs with firms that comply voluntarily, and where future costs are recovered from unwilling firms.[39]

A strengthened emphasis on EPA's current "enforcement-first" strategy should be coupled with "reasonable risk" cleanup standards and reduced tolerance for spending trust fund monies. PRPs should be relatively easy to identify for active sites (or those closed since 1981), and the enforcement-first strategy is particularly compelling since those PRPs should have exercised appropriate care in disposing their hazardous wastes in the wake of CERCLA's passage in December 1980. The existing cleanup trust fund would be maintained for post-1981 sites and would be used mainly to finance "mixed funding" settlements, with far greater attention paid to recovering costs from recalcitrant PRPs. EPA has a great deal of enforcement authority, particularly as modified under SARA, and its use should be encouraged at post-1981 sites. The "stick" EPA can use to convince recalcitrant PRPs to settle is the threat of treble damages should they evade administrative orders requiring cleanups, while the "carrot" is the potential for "mixed funding" settlements (where PRPs can settle with EPA for their share of cleanup costs proportionate to their hazardous waste contribution at the site). Coupled with this could be the possibility of buying out future liability costs for an additional payment. Many PRPs are concerned not only with their current liability but also with any future liability at the site should remediation turn out to be worse than expected. According to several sources close to EPA-PRP negotiations, many firms would be happy to pay a settlement premium, which EPA could base on risk factors from other sites, in exchange for lifetime release from liability. Not only does it encourage PRPs to settle, and therefore expedite site cleanup, but it increases the size of the trust fund for future contingencies and liabilities as well.

Naturally, there would be disputes over the general methodology to employ at each site to determine "reasonable risk" and cost-effectiveness. EPA could request that its independent Science Advisory Board or the National Research Council recommend a general methodology for evaluating cost-effectiveness at post-1981 sites. But while the general outline of performing risk assessments is relatively straightforward, the results of assessments for individual sites are not. This problem plagues current efforts as well. Nevertheless, estimates of the amount of risk remediated should be compared with costs, to determine whether successively more stringent cleanups are worth the costs.

The ongoing Superfund program would therefore require a minimal federal financial contribution with its far greater emphasis on settlements to expedite cleanups. SARA's significant enforcement capabilities would be all the more appealing, since the PRPs would be more easily identifiable and because they were negligent in the face of ample warnings from CERCLA. Settlements should be easier to negotiate, since at many sites cleanup costs would be lower and would depend on cost-effectiveness. The fund would be used primarily to finance cleanups at any "orphan" sites where PRPs cannot be found and to leverage cleanups from PRPs, but this would represent a relatively modest expenditure. The program would operate indefinitely, largely as a revolving fund, and federal contributions for the most part would be limited to administrative expenses to maintain the program.

In addition to the continued federal role in post-1981 sites, the federal government would continue to be involved in Superfund cleanups to the extent that expertise or economies of scale make that necessary. The most important role is the maintenance of Superfund's liability provisions to encourage safe transport and disposal of hazardous wastes. Allowing individual states to set their own standards could lead either to nonexistent standards in some states or to widely varying standards as states compete to retain important industries by promulgating weak standards or loosely enforcing current regulations. Further, perhaps Superfund's greatest (yet unheralded) success, the removal program for emergency spills or cleanups, would remain unchanged and under EPA's control. Finally, EPA should be encouraged to embark on an extensive research program into evaluating the public health and environmental risks of hazardous substances. Results of these studies not only would be used to evaluate cleanup strategies for post-1981 sites under EPA's control but also would be shared with state committees grappling with their own cleanup decisions for pre-1981 sites.

Many of the reforms discussed above could be implemented independent of the others. Liability could be waived for sites closed prior to 1981 without shifting financing or cleanup responsibility to the states. Similarly, site-specific cleanup decisions could be delegated to state committees rather than EPA regional offices without implementing the other reforms. NERF funds could be used only for pre-1981 hazardous waste site cleanups, for any hazardous waste site cleanups, for other remedial environmental problems, or any number of other possibilities. However, plans to reform only Superfund liability—the most likely topic of discussion in the next reauthorization—avoid the serious political and public policy problem of the difference between the perception of risks between the public and risk experts.

Potential Problems in Implementing the Reforms

Reforms of this scale are not without problems, and this is no exception. Critics of fiscal federalism generally have charged that states lack the expertise necessary to implement technically complex programs such as Superfund. However, state governments are far more administratively capable than they were twenty years ago, and there is some evidence to suggest that for Superfund, some states have as much expertise as some EPA regional offices (particularly states with active Superfund programs like Minnesota, New Jersey, and New York).[40] One EPA official noted that "a number of states have very good programs, but the problem is funding."[41] Therefore, some states would need substantial federal assistance to implement their own programs. The federal government must avoid any perception on the part of states that additional Superfund monies can always be had from Congress if their NERF funds are depleted. Further, because citizen committees would be making site-specific decisions, they would not be limited to drawing expertise from state bureaucracies; if state officials were ill-equipped to help the committees with risk decisions, outside help could be solicited. States already have been granted greater authority under the Superfund reauthorization of 1986. Transferring cleanup authority to states would end the current duplication of efforts and would force states to face directly the opportunity costs of spending money on Superfund.

Finally, in most cases states are better able to meet local needs than the federal government, and transferring authority would give rise to greater citizen participation in everything from identifying sites to selecting cleanup remedies. This greater participation at the state level will also foster the recognition that cleanup funds are not inexhaustible and that important choices need to be made. Instead of lobbying EPA and their legislators to permanently remediate their Superfund site, citizens would face the prospect that cleaning up one site may mean that the site in the next town or county will go untreated, or that lead paint or radon problems would be neglected. Faced with these choices, it is likely that greater attention will be paid to cost-effective cleanup strategies, even if it means that the funds will be distributed over more sites—for political reasons as well as cost-effectiveness—than originally intended. Because opportunity costs would become more visible, "clean enough" at many sites may supplant the current political environment where some participants demand the total elimination of risk at the few sites EPA has remediated.

Furthermore, the NERF program could be used in an iterative fashion (although the pitfalls of strategic behavior on the part of the committees could arise). If the state committees devote a significant portion of the NERF funds for Superfund site cleanups, Congress could interpret the result as indicating that even without the institutional mechanisms that favor Superfund cleanups (the 90 percent federal contribution), citizens still believe site cleanups to be the most important remedial environmental hazard. Congress may then choose to expand funding for still more site cleanups. On the other hand, if a large portion of the NERF is dedicated to lead-removal projects, radon remediation, and the like, then the importance of Superfund cleanups is diminished, and there would be little reason to expand Superfund funding for pre-1981 sites. In addition, if citizens decide that the NERF funds could be better spent on other public health or environmental problems, then the political impetus to constantly expand Superfund to provide benefits for communities and, derivatively, to legislators—in short, programmatic pork—would be reduced. The problem with holding out the possibility of more funding for Superfund in front of state committees is that they will be encouraged to spend their NERF funds on Superfund cleanups, knowing that more federal funds are forthcoming. Moreover, fixing a set amount of money for Superfund would diminish the lobbying efforts of legislators from New Jersey, New York, Pennsylvania, and other large Superfund states to expand the program so that their states disproportionately benefit.

A second issue concerns how to handle PRPs who have already made settlement payments for cleanup costs associated with remediating pre-1981 sites. It would appear to be unfair to treat differently those previously complying with Superfund and those resisting. Not only are like situations (pre-1981 sites) treated differently, but PRPs who have complied with Superfund would be punished, while those who dragged their feet through litigation and delay tactics would be rewarded. For these reasons and because relatively few sites have already been remediated, it would seem appropriate to reimburse PRPs for cleanup expenses at pre-1981 sites. Of course, the longer it takes to implement this change, the more expensive the reimbursement (since more pre-1981 sites will have been remediated). Nevertheless, reimbursement costs should be moderate compared with total cleanup costs. However, it is likely that fund-financed cleanups for pre-1981 sites will be more costly than any settlement agreements negotiated by PRPs. Therefore, total cleanup costs may exceed present estimates based in part on PRP-negotiated costs. The downside to reimbursing PRPs is that the PRPs have already admitted guilt, at least under CERCLA, and would appear to be compensated nevertheless. Regardless of which strategy is adopted, neither is central to these Superfund reforms.

A third problem is that eliminating pre-1981 liability would provide no incentive for PRPs to remediate pre-1981 sites voluntarily.[42] However, if the amnesty period in reporting pre-1981 sites without penalty is effective in identifying previously undiscovered hazardous sites, then the issue of voluntary compliance is diminished, since there would, naturally, be fewer unidentified sites. Moreover, the issue of voluntary compliance is commonly associated with the polluter-pays principle, insofar as any PRP who voluntarily remediates a site must be guilty to begin with. Given the unfairness of the current Superfund liability scheme, however, the benefits of supposedly "voluntary" compliance may reflect nothing more than the desire to avoid exorbitant future payments, even for firms that contributed minimally or who had disposed of waste properly in the past.

A further problem involves the future of environmental policy: what sort of precedent does it set when the public is seen to pay for any future environmental problems caused by industry as long as industry can show that the remedial program is sufficiently unfair and inefficient? It suggests to me that we seriously and systematically regulate current pollutants to ensure that future Superfund sites and other problems do not arise. How can we best be sure that hazardous waste sites—or some other insidious form of pollution—do not appear in twenty or thirty years? By studying now which pollutants are most risky, and crafting careful regulations concerning their use, transport, and disposal. A preventative program will almost assuredly be far less expensive and more effective than a remedial program, a point agreed upon by environmentalists and industry alike. And although information upon which to base such decisions will be imperfect, as Vice-President Gore has written in a different context, "We need to act now on the basis of what we know."[43] Spending more time worrying about future problems rather than cleaning up old ones will have large future payoffs in terms of improved environmental quality and public health. This will necessitate improving incentives under the Clean Air and Clean Water Acts, RCRA, TSCA, FIFRA, and other environmental statutes to prevent future environmental debacles.

A fifth potential problem is the uncertain size of the NERF, largely because it is difficult to predict how many newly discovered pre-1981 sites will qualify for the NPL. Congress will be wary of funding an open-ended NERF, as would the industries that may finance the fund, one that could even double existing cost estimates. Nevertheless, I regard it as highly unlikely that the approximately $20 billion fund would be doubled by the addition of newly discovered pre-1981 sites. Moreover, the insurance industry's AIG proposal (see chapter 1) already calls for a fund estimated at $40 billion (although this is coupled with no-fault liability for all Superfund sites, not just pre-1981 sites). Therefore, the political obstacles to a fund in the ballpark of $25 to $30 billion or so appear not to be prohibitive, particularly coupled with a liability waiver at pre-1981 sites. A related political problem is that no well-organized constituency now exists for the alternative NERF expenditures such as radon or lead removal, and therefore only modest political support could be expected.

Finally, because the reforms require that post-1981 sites would be subject to cost-effective cleanup standards, Superfund's regulatory impact on current hazardous waste management may be somewhat diminished. Even under less stringent standards, however, site cleanups would remain sufficiently expensive to compel hazardous waste producers and transporters (in addition to site operators regulated under RCRA) to maintain their careful monitoring of hazardous waste disposal.

Political Feasibility of Reforming Superfund

Some individuals undoubtedly will be made worse off under these proposed reforms. Identifying some of them, a former EPA official notes that "Superfund is a classic lawyer's dream, a classic consultant's dream, a classic fund-raiser's dream, and a classic congressman's dream . . . Too many people have a vested interest in the program."[44] Those who expected their NPL site to be remediated to background conditions may instead see the site partially remediated while the rest of the money goes to other waste sites (or lead abatement or other environmental restoration projects, depending on how NERF monies are expended). Engineering firms expecting the financial rewards of lucrative contracts to remediate waste sites will lose out if state committees choose to allocate the funds differently. Lawyers stand to forfeit significant legal fees because the transactions costs for pre-1981 sites would be virtually eliminated. Therefore, significant wealth transfers are likely to occur in reforming Superfund, and accordingly, political resistance can be expected. I consider in turn below the possible political implications from the perspectives of key Superfund participants.

How would Congress view the proposed reforms? As with any group of diverse individuals, generalizations are misleading. Nevertheless, a few observations may point to greater congressional acceptance than may be expected when control of an important program is shifted substantially from the federal government to states. First, Congress would be appropriating substantial funds for the NERF. Consequently, legislators can defend their actions from criticisms from environmentalists, by contending that Superfund cleanups will proceed more rapidly and that the public has the choice to decide how the remedial funds will be allocated, and from industry, by reminding them that liability for older sites has been eliminated, and that future sites will be subjected to more reasonable cleanup standards. Furthermore, the reforms would enable legislators to tell their constituents they appropriated a substantial fund to clean up hazardous waste sites (and other remedial environmental problems as well) and that constituents now have the opportunity to influence more directly how those funds will be spent. In short, it is politically necessary that the NERF be restricted to restorative environmental projects, so legislators avoid being seen as dismantling the program, yet the greater public participation in allocating the funds ensures that the funds will be spent in accord with the wishes of local interests. Legislators can effectively "sell" these advantages to several important interest groups, most importantly their constituents. Moreover, constituents are likely to believe, rightly or wrongly, that the process will be far more expeditious than current federal efforts have been. It is unlikely that constituents would balk at the control of, say, $500 million to remediate hazardous waste sites or other environmental and public health problems in their state. Surely they will argue that there should be more money, but greater control over cleanups and their pace will most likely be viewed as a countervailing benefit.

Of course, the delegation of authority from the federal government to states may serve to impede program reforms as well. Some have claimed that legislators establish programs such as Superfund for the simple reason that they can serve constituents who are befuddled by a maze of bureaucracy, even though the bureaucratic maze is a product of congressional intent in the first place.[45] This political obstacle might be overcome, since Congress would be seen as responding meaningfully to what is considered by some to be a significant environmental problem; state representatives would then be chiefly responsible for resolving constituent complaints about individual site cleanups.

Every legislator would, however, face the problem of an opposing candidate skewering any decision that appears to condone the notion of "acceptable risk." One commentator notes, "No member could survive the TV ad: 'Your Congressman (or Senator) voted to expose his constituents to cancer. Was your mother's death by cancer preventable? Did the neighbor's child come down with leukemia because of Mr. X's vote? Vote for Joe Blow; he won't let you down.' "[46] Legislators clearly are uncomfortable telling their constituents that partial remediation is enough and that other sites—and other national priorities—demand attention as well. Because Congress would be seen as dedicating a fixed sum of money to address the Superfund problem, and no more, the perception of condoning "acceptable risk" could arise. On the other hand, because allocational decisions would not be in the hands of Congress, legislators could claim, first, that these decisions of risk management are made anyway, although previously behind closed doors, and second, that it is for citizens to decide how the funds will be spent. For pre-1981 sites, the reforms can be viewed as simply the same Superfund program as before, but with the money available faster and with added spending flexibility.

Finally, a number of people interviewed agreed that much of the congressional interest in maintaining Superfund derived not from individual legislators, but from their constituents. Several people interviewed agreed with one conclusion that "there is much more interest outside the Beltway than inside, at least in the last five years or so."[47] While legislators are unlikely to welcome any loss of influence over a major federal program, Superfund has become such a political headache for both Congress and EPA that increased delegation to the states may be as practicable as ever. One said, "I've rarely seen a congressman . . . take a proactive approach to a problem in this area . . . Mostly it's reactive."[48] Indeed, the most recent reauthorization of Superfund in the fall of 1990 underscores the degree of reluctance that major political players bring to engaging in a battle to reform Superfund and provides evidence of the desire to resolve Superfund's problems. Therefore, despite some political problems, it is likely that a number of legislators would view these reforms favorably.

President Clinton, having served as governor of a state with some large and controversial Superfund sites, recognizes some of the problems facing Superfund as well. He has said publicly that "the Superfund has been a disaster. All the money goes to the lawyers, and none of the money goes to clean up the problems that it was designed to clean up."[49] Allowing states greater flexibility in allocating NERF funds may be particularly attractive to a president who recognizes the difficulty states face from federal requirements and restrictions. Local communities similarly can be expected to welcome the added flexibility afforded by the NERF. Many local officials are incensed with federal environmental requirements that they believe are not targeted to the worst problems. Reports by independent state panels in Michigan and Vermont found that large sums of money were spent on relatively small risks, such as exposure to toxic and radioactive wastes, while little was channeled to forest and farmland damage, which were considered to be more important environmental issues.[50] Michael Pompili, an engineer heading the city of Columbus's environmental health division of the Health Department, has said that "this city will not survive without a clean environment." But he then added:

"What bothers me is that the new rules coming out of Washington are taking money from decent programs and making me waste them on less important problems. It kills you as a city official to see this kind of money being spent for nothing."[51]

From EPA's perspective, a bureaucratic problem arises: the agency could view the transfer of authority as a direct threat to the size of its budget, the number of employees, and other organizational factors that would limit the agency's political strength. This much is indisputable. The existing Superfund program is something of an anomaly to the agency, however: a remedial program with a significant public works component residing in a regulatory agency. Superfund is not the first EPA task with elements of a public works program—indeed, the older sewer construction grant program was significantly larger—but the latter was mostly a grants program to states and localities. In addition, EPA has received a great deal of negative publicity regarding Superfund, which has damaged its reputation. Moreover, shifting cleanup decisions for pre-1981 sites to the states does not fundamentally alter EPA's mission to protect public health and the environment. Indeed, it can be argued that EPA would rather prioritize its programs to avoid being overwhelmed with environmental threats ranging from global warming to passive smoking to regulating existing and newly introduced chemicals. Several persons interviewed, including a former EPA official, suggested that EPA knew all along that the results of *Unfinished Business* and *Reducing Risk* would point to an overemphasis on Superfund expenditures in relation to other risks. The point of the reports, they contended, was to slowly shift public opinion—and that of the press—away from chemical scare tactics and toward the most pressing environmental problems. If true, then shifting significant Superfund responsibilities to the states may be seen as consistent with EPA's longer-term interests. Finally, it should be remembered that EPA would continue to have significant responsibilities for the Superfund program, most importantly for post-1981 sites. In addition, for pre-1981 sites it would be involved in approving state implementation plans, coordinating research into health effects and cleanup technologies, and making site-specific cleanup decisions for those states that choose to defer to EPA. Therefore, EPA would still be the central federal institution coordinating Superfund, and it would not forfeit authority or legitimacy to a competing federal agency.

How would states be likely to view the reforms? It can be safely assumed that most states would welcome federal dollars to remediate old and inactive waste sites, even if citizen committees were in control of NERF expenditures. State governments would surely prefer to be able to allocate NERF funds themselves, rather than through citizen committees, and would most likely want greater flexibility in allocating funds to other pressing problems, such as education, health care, general assistance programs, urban aid, and so on. Nevertheless, the flexibility permitted with NERF funds would still allow state problems to be addressed with federal dollars. Governor Booth Gardner of Washington conveys the importance of flexibility to states: "Every time the President [at the time, Bush] meets with governors and legislators he asks, 'If I could do one thing for you, what would you like?' And we always say 'flexibility.'"[52] State representatives could to some extent claim credit for site remediation (or radon programs, lead removal, and so on), advancing their political popularity. Finally, states could choose to request that EPA manage remedial actions using NERF funds, similar to the current system. At worst, the status quo would hold, while at best, additional federal dollars could address the state's most serious environmental and public health threats.

The insurance industry, perhaps the most active corporate interest in Superfund politics, could be expected to strongly support the reforms. First, the industry is released from indirect liability for all pre-1981 sites, so their exposure is lessened considerably. Second, any pre-1981 sites that are not reported to EPA under the amnesty period could, it would seem, be viewed as no fault of the insurance companies, but rather the PRPs themselves. Therefore, insurance company liabilities may be cut in half or more, as well as realizing the benefits of substantially reduced transactions costs. However, it is difficult to see, aside from public relations difficulties, why PRPs would not come forward to volunteer knowledge of the existence of waste sites heretofore unknown. In addition, cleanup costs for post-1981 sites may be reduced as well under new guidelines, further reducing costs to insurers. Of course, the source of NERF monies could raise significant opposition from insurance companies if they were forced to shoulder most of the burden. The insurance industry has already signaled that it intends to be a major player in Superfund's planned 1994 reauthorization, both by its AIG proposal and by recruiting two former House members, Anthony of Arkansas and Eckart of Ohio, to lobby on its behalf.[53]

Potentially responsible parties most often are as concerned about future liability as about present cleanup costs. Consent decrees normally carry "re-opener clauses" that permit subsequent lawsuits should site remediation go awry. It is quite likely that insurance companies and PRPs would be willing to pay significantly more than they do now if they could ensure that they would not be held liable for future contingencies. As one observer close to the process told me, as long as PRPs believe they are paying their fair share and the costs are justified by benefits, corporations "want this out of the way."[54] Thus, as revealed by the AIG plan, a political deal for releasing liability from older sites could be coupled with increased excise taxes on these firms. The problem, discussed at length earlier, is that these added taxes are in part passed on to current consumers (in the form of higher product prices) and to current shareholders (as losses), neither of whom caused the problems in the first place.

For similar reasons, the chemical and petroleum industries could be expected to support the suggested reforms. To the extent that individual companies were PRPs at Superfund sites closed prior to 1981, there would be windfall gains. However, the industry's response may be less favorable if a significant portion of the NERF was funded by raising excise taxes rather than by drawing from general revenues. Mitigating this effect, however, is the knowledge that cleanup standards for post-1981 sites would be based on "reasonable risk" rather than "permanence," thereby lowering future cleanup costs in some cases. Therefore, although carrying out the reforms would most likely require significant financial concessions on the part of the chemical and petroleum industries, both the transactions costs in litigating current cases and the future liability at Superfund sites would be significantly reduced, to the advantage of those industries. If the general business community were forced to shoulder a significant portion of funding the NERF through a general corporation income tax, then opposition would emerge from this constituency as well.

Environmental groups would probably view these reforms as advantageous in some respects, yet problematic in others. They would strongly oppose the absence of uniform cleanup levels, where one state might permanently treat the groundwater at a waste site while another, perhaps opting for an expanded lead remediation program instead, may only provide alternative drinking water supplies to affected residents. Because environmentalists have fought hard in the past for uniform cleanup levels, they would surely find this element of the plan undesirable. Environmentalists could also be expected to oppose the symbolic withdrawal of the polluter-pays principle that apparently undergirds the program for pre-1981 sites. Support by environmentalists would probably hinge critically on the size of the NERF and who finances it. If chemical and petroleum interests finance the NERF, or even the general business community, then environmentalists may support the reform. However, financing from general revenues would likely draw fierce opposition from environmental groups. Finally, environmental groups can be expected to strongly oppose relaxing cleanup standards for post-1981 sites from requiring permanence to allowing "acceptable risk."

Several elements of the plan may win support from national environmental groups, however. First, cleanups may be achieved more quickly, and transactions costs would be significantly reduced for pre-1981 sites;

therefore, a greater portion of funds could be devoted to actual site clean-ups or other remedial environmental activities. Moreover, it would seem antithetical to the interests of environmental groups to oppose cleanup decisions made by state committees that comprised citizen representatives. Finally, environmental groups would support the substantial NERF expenditures to address problems of local concern. Consequently, the proposed reforms may find some strong supporters within the environmental community.

Similarly, elements of the proposed reforms may win support from grass-roots organizations (GROs) connected with Superfund sites, but others will not. GROs would undoubtedly welcome the reduction in transactions costs (allowing faster cleanups) and the generally more co-operative means of allocating resources. The problem, of course, is that although the effort is cooperative at one level—in that a fixed sum of money is targeted to each state—there will be substantial debate within the state over how those monies would ultimately be expended. As a result, GROs that expected full remediation at their sites may decry what they perceive as the lost federal commitment to provide the cleanup. Given the general level of frustration among communities over the current pace of cleanups, however, any change that would expedite *any* actions at Superfund sites may be welcomed. Moreover, disagreements would be channeled through the state committees on which GROs would have representatives. Therefore, although every existing NPL site may not be remediated to background conditions, GROs would at least have had the opportunity to participate in the process of allocating NERF monies. The point is that the decisions would now be made locally rather than by federal officials.

While important political and administrative obstacles stand in the way of such a plan, its significant advantages of fostering innovation, maintaining congressional authority over total expenditures, and promoting allocative efficiency, fairness, and citizen participation may mean that fundamental reforms of this type are feasible. As evidenced by the quiet Superfund reauthorization in 1990, parties lobbying on several sides of the Superfund issue recall the bruising 1986 fight for reauthorization and are, if for no other reason, hopeful that a political resolution is in sight. One industry representative told me that the major Superfund players, both industry and environmental groups, were relieved by the quick 1990 reauthorization of Superfund.[55] Whether they can agree on such substantial reforms is, of course, another matter. Reforming Superfund will require concessions on the part of some groups in return for other advantages, but overall these changes can significantly improve the program. Nevertheless, some remain skeptical that any major changes can occur. A former EPA official says that "Superfund has been the most frustrating program I have ever dealt with, both in and out of government. The administrative procedures are so onerous that radical surgery is the only answer, and I don't see that happening anytime soon."[56]

Conclusions: The Political Economy of Environmental Risks

One of the difficulties in any reform of this type is convincing citizens that the opportunity cost argument is real, that resources freed from Superfund can fund other worthy social goals. Because of the perception that governments waste a significant amount of taxpayer dollars, and perhaps due to a mistrust in government institutions themselves, many citizens believe governments can provide significantly more with the same budget. Why redirect resources from Superfund to radon or lead remediation when both can be had simply by eliminating waste? This dilemma, I believe, motivates a solution that allows people at the grass roots level—in this case the state committees—to decide for themselves how the funds will be allocated. The very real choices that governments confront would then be in the hands of citizen-based committees. The public will be more likely to accept the notions that infinite resources are not available for fully remediating all Superfund sites and that the proposed NERF will not solve every environmental and public health problem, if they are making the choices themselves. This form of delegating risk decisions to state or local committees cannot be applied to all pollutants, however, particularly those that cross political boundaries, such as many forms of air and water pollution. It is, however, ideally suited to Superfund.

A key to reforming Superfund and improving risk management is to more actively engage the public while simultaneously building opportunity costs into the decision-making process. Superfund's adversarial process—where risk experts and the public are at odds over policy—makes risk communication virtually impossible. If the public does not trust risk experts, then the public should decide, armed with adequate funding and an appropriate set of risk-reducing options, what policy course is best. If the committees want to base their spending decisions on a *Newsweek* article rather than on the latest epidemiological and risk assessment information, they are free to do so, but they will also have to justify their choices both to themselves and to their communities. In some instances, like stratospheric ozone depletion, those choices may affect others as well, and local decision making may be inappropriate. But for Superfund sites, lead abatement, radon remediation, and so forth, those suffering the costs, or reaping the benefits, of prudent risk management will be those citizens actually making the decisions. If the risk populists are right, that confronted with the true opportunity costs people still believe that Superfund site risks are more hazardous than other remedial environmental problems, then the proposed reforms will not diminish funding for Superfund site cleanups; state committees will simply dedicate all or most NERF dollars into hazardous waste site cleanups.

The point of allowing a citizen-based committee to make allocative decisions remediating environmental hazards is not that their decisions will be "better" than those of EPA or some other centralized institution, but rather that citizens participate meaningfully in the process, recognize opportunity costs of spending cleanup funds, and finally that they, after all, are the ones who would suffer (or gain) from poor (or good) decisions. The citizen committees therefore have every reason to make allocative decisions that represent their collective interest (to the extent one can be identified among millions of different people with divergent interests and needs). Moreover, that interest can vary from state to state, so that if one state committee prefers to spend all of its money remediating Superfund sites to pristine conditions, so be it. If another wants to spend all of its NERF funds on removing lead paint from inner-city homes, that is its choice. The committees making these important allocative decisions will undoubtedly include citizens representing different interests: those advocating for Superfund cleanups, or asbestos removal, or radon testing and remediation, and so on. The advantage of this institution is that these disparate groups will have to *sit down and talk with each other directly*, rather than currently venting their frustrations through political third parties (usually EPA or their legislators).[57] This does not mean that all participants are going to walk out of meetings overjoyed with the outcome, or that this proposal represents a panacea. As one scholar has written, free citizens will sometimes "recruit agents to represent their interests, fail to reveal their preferences, behave in noncooperative ways, seek to manipulate the terms of debate" and so on.[58] All of these are true, and mistakes will be made. But citizens will at a minimum have been given a chance to participate in meaningful and fair discussions over public policy and will have available to them the best information concerning the environmental and health risks of various remedial problems. There will be no industry interest groups to battle. There will be no "policy elites" involved (unless they are invited). Instead, opposing views on how to spend the money will come from individuals, not unlike themselves, wanting to improve their children's and their community's environment. The nature of the risk communication would be, in this environment, substantially different from that in today's adversarial Superfund process. Risk assessments would not be coupled with a policy preference for cleanups that leave contaminants in the soil where their children play, or any other policy preference (or at least there would be no incentive to do so). Surely risk assessments from some will be predictably different from those of others: the asbestos cleanup industry will produce analyses showing how significant the risks of asbestos exposure are; lead, radon, and hazardous waste cleanup industries will do the same. Only the most naive will take these assessments at face value. Instead, the committees can request experts from EPA, the scientific community, or other independent sources to provide technical information concerning various environmental risks, the costs of remediating them, and so forth. In this manner, risk communication can be conducted in as fair and honest a manner as possible, and most importantly, to best aid the committees in reaching difficult decisions.

The problem is not that the public cannot or does not understand risk assessment or risk management—indeed the concept itself is rather simple—but rather that current policies engender an adversarial process that encourages people to do whatever they can to get federal resources in their community. The policy arguments over risk assessment and cost-benefit analysis do not involve the basic technique, but instead stem from the biased results they are perceived to endorse. One environmentalist said, "The problem I have with risk assessment is that it's not democratic."[59] To be useful, risk assessments must be employed in more public and cooperative, rather than adversarial, forums, where the relationship between technical and populist perspectives can be explored and integrated. The more risk assessments are viewed as ammunition to defend the interests of one interest group, the less useful they will be in public debate. Removing the "politics of blame" from the current Superfund debate can instead allow focusing on the problem at hand. Jan Beyea of the National Audubon Society has said, "Environmentalists need to be very careful to watch their own psychological state. Many of my friends . . . get such a psychological reward from being in the battle, the good guys against the bad guys, that they lose sight of what they are trying to do."[60] Avoiding the good guys–bad guys debate will be central to any efforts at reform. In the instances where risks are concentrated and largely contained—Superfund sites represent one—policies allowing individuals to choose for themselves which risk-reducing policies are best can be workable alternatives.

What I have proposed in this book is not a "middle ground" in the dispute between experts and the lay public over risk management. It is rather "another ground" upon which to rethink our approach to environmental and risk policy. Other institutional ways out of the experts-versus-public bind must be found, not only for remediating hazardous waste dumps but for other public policies concerning risk as well, such as nuclear power and indoor air pollution. One can only hope that Senator George Mitchell's maxim, "doing the right thing is the best politics," will determine the future of Superfund and other programs managing seemingly intractable risks, into the next century. This is but a modest step in that direction.

Appendix

Table A.5.1 Summary Statistics ($N = 3139$)

Dependent variable	Mean	Standard deviation
Number of final NPL sites per county	0.37	1.28

Independent variables	Mean	Standard deviation
Hazardous waste (tons $\times 10^3$)	9965.68	13879.50
Manufacturing (%)	22.02	15.97
College educated (%)	11.48	5.47
Owner-occupied housing (%)	73.18	7.82
New housing units, 1970–80 (%)	33.42	28.78
Median housing value	35295.80	14259.10
Below poverty level (%)	15.78	7.28
Unemployed (%)	8.70	4.12
Nonwhite (%)	11.89	11.89
Population density (per square mile)	227.45	1626.36

Table A.6.1 Variable Definitions

Dependent variables	Definition
Expenditures	Federal outlays on site through 12/31/88 ($000)
Planned obligations	Future federal planned obligations ($000)
Planned cleanup costs	Cost of cleanup estimated from Record of Decision ($000)
Stage of cleanup process	0, if no action as of 12/31/88; 1, if RI/FS completed; 2, if ROD signed; 3, if remedial action started
Removal action?	1, if site removal action performed (else, 0)

Independent variables	Definition
Air HRS score	Air HRS path score (range: 0–100)
GW HRS score	Groundwater HRS path score (range: 0–100)
SW HRS score	Surface water HRS path score (range: 0–100)
State priority?	1, if state-designated priority site (else, 0)
Fund lead?	1, if funded mainly by federal Superfund money (else, 0)
Federal site?	1, if the site is federally owned (else, 0)
Year final NPL	Year site was placed on final NPL
Senate appropriations subcommittee	Number of senators from site's state on Senate Appropriations Subcommittee on HUD/Independent Agencies over last three congresses
Senate authorizing subcommittee	Number of senators from site's state on Senate Subcommittee on Superfund and Environmental Oversight over last three congresses
House appropriations subcommittee	Number of representatives from site's district on House Subcommittee on HUD/Independent Agencies over last three congresses
House authorizing subcommittee	Number of representatives from site's district on House Subcommittee on Transportation, Tourism, and Hazardous Materials over last three congresses

Table A.6.1 (*Continued*)

Independent variables	Definition
Below poverty level (%)	Percentage of county living below the poverty level in 1979
Unemployed (%)	Percentage of county unemployed in 1986
Median housing value ($000)	Median housing value in county in 1980
Nonwhite (%)	Percentage of county residents who are nonwhite in 1984
Owner-occupied housing (%)	Percentage of housing occupied by owners in the county in 1980
College educated (%)	Percentage of county residents who have completed four or more years of college in 1980
District income ($000)	Per capita district income (thousands of 1979 dollars)
County residents since 1975 (%)	Percentage of county residents who have resided in the county for five or more years, beginning in 1975
Sites in EPA region (N)	Number of final NPL sites in the EPA region

Table A.6.2 Sample Statistics (*N* = 788)

Dependent variables	Mean	Standard deviation
Years proposed to final NPL	1.27	0.57
Expenditures ($000)	1,021	2,607
Planned obligations ($000)	8,045	32,750
Stage of cleanup process	1.57	0.95
Removal action?	0.28	0.45
Independent variables		
Air HRS score	8.60	20.81
SW HRS score	14.57	18.43
GW HRS score	62.56	22.51
Priority site?	0.04	0.20
Fund lead?	0.44	0.50
Federal site?	0.04	0.20
Year final NPL	84.32	1.55
Senate appropriations subcommittee	0.74	1.14
Senate authorizing subcommittee	0.34	0.65
House appropriations subcommittee	0.04	0.31
House authorizing subcommittee	0.11	0.47
Below poverty level (%)	10.57	4.68
Unemployed (%)	7.02	3.24
Median housing value ($000)	48.68	17.32
Nonwhite (%)	10.19	10.14
Owner-occupied housing (%)	69.15	8.42
College educated (%)	15.93	6.10
County residents since 1975 (%)	79.01	6.20
Sites in region (N)	117.64	62.41

Table A.7.1 Regression Results on Interest Group Measures of Ideology (absolute value of t-statistics in parentheses)

Variable	SENATE		HOUSE	
	Liberal	*Environmental*	*Liberal*	*Environmental*
Intercept	−235.15(3.86)***	−57.16(0.88)	−48.99(3.54)***	−49.89(3.03)***
Democrat?	41.88(13.00)***	27.78(8.20)***	41.41(26.8)***	32.06(18.5)***
Income (×10⁻³)	3.25(1.07)	−5.88(1.80)*	−2.95(2.46)**	−0.77(0.57)
Unemployed (%)	3.85(3.34)***	0.65(0.47)	1.54(3.73)***	−0.10(0.20)
College (%)	0.96(1.14)	−0.28(0.24)	0.55(2.29)**	1.04(3.92)***
Housing value	0.04(1.98)**	0.02(0.96)	0.02(2.26)**	−0.01(0.80)
Residents since 1975 (%)	2.11(4.03)***	0.33(0.59)	0.624(4.55)***	0.59(3.79)***
Manufacturing share	−90.53(2.58)***	105.09(2.77)***	−4.10(0.26)	48.14(2.71)***
Pop. density (×10⁻⁵)	−317.77(0.30)	1316.73(1.19)	3.84(0.32)	16.75(1.24)
Urban (%)	−0.08(0.41)	0.49(2.31)**	0.20(4.15)***	0.08(1.54)
White (%)	0.48(2.06)**	0.36(1.37)	0.09(1.26)	0.01(0.17)
Southern state?	−0.57(0.10)	−8.03(1.29)	−7.24(3.44)***	−7.24(2.57)**
Western state?	−9.72(1.49)	−19.08(2.74)***	−7.98(2.81)***	−9.05(2.81)***
Observations (*N*)	100	100	427	434
Corrected R^2	0.784	0.687	0.752	0.603

***Significant at 99% level; **95% level; *90% level (two-tailed test).

Table A.7.2 Description of Independent Variables

Independent Variables	Definition
Final NPL sites (N)	Number of final NPL sites in the district/state at the end of calendar year 1988
Chemical share	Share of total state gross domestic product produced by chemical firms (range: 0–100)
Petroleum share	Share of total state gross domestic product produced by petroleum firms (range: 0–100)
Hazardous waste	Tons of net hazardous waste in state in 1985 (amount produced in state plus net imports)
Environmental interests	Portion of state's voting population that is a member of one of the six largest environmental groups in the country (range: 0–1)
Economic ideology	Computed "pure" economic ideology from *National Journal's* liberal ratings on economic issues
Environmental ideology	Computed "pure" environmental ideology from League of Conservation Voters ratings
Democrat?	Democratic legislator, 1; else, 0
Population density	Number of people per square mile in the district/state
Southern state?	1, if the site is in Alabama, Arkansas, Florida, Georgia, Kentucky, Louisiana, Mississippi, North Carolina, Oklahoma, South Carolina, Tennessee, Texas, or Virginia (else, 0)
Western state?	1, if the site is in Arizona, California, Idaho, Nevada, Oregon, Utah, or Washington (else, 0)

Table A.7.3 Sample Statistics

Dependent variables	Mean	Standard deviation
Senate votes[a]		
1	0.84	0.37
2	0.87	0.34
3	0.45	0.50
4	0.39	0.49
5	0.44	0.50
House votes		
1	0.52	0.50
2	0.59	0.49
3	0.52	0.50
Independent variables[b]		
Interests		
# Final NPL sites (state)	29.352	23.701
# Final NPL sites (district)	1.816	2.369
Chemical share	0.019	0.013

Table A.7.3 (*Continued*)

Independent variables	Mean	Standard deviation
Petroleum share	0.005	0.006
Hazardous waste	10,082.100	12,410.000
Environmental interests	0.007	0.003
Ideology[c]		
Economic ideology	0.000	13.740
Environmental ideology	0.220	15.380
Democrat?	0.582	0.494
Control variables		
Population density	2,437.470	7,004.060
Southern state?	0.297	0.457
Western state?	0.161	0.368

[a]A vote supporting Superfund expansion is coded 1, and 0 otherwise.
[b]Independent variable statistics are presented at the district level (i.e., for the House of Representatives); data on Senate variables are available from the author on request.
[c]Ideology statistics are presented for the House of Representatives as of 1985; other data (Senate and/or other years) are available from the author. For the purposes of the statistical study, the variable "Democrat?" is both included and excluded from the definition of ideology.

Notes

Chapter 1. Introduction to Superfund

1. Bruce Yandle, *The Political Limits of Environmental Regulation* (New York: Quorum Books, 1989), 8.
2. *New York Times*, "7 Face U.S. Charges in a Waste Scheme," 14 June 1992, 38.
3. Robert Cameron Mitchell, "Public Opinion and the Green Lobby: Poised for the 1990s?" in Norman J. Vig and Michael E. Kraft, eds., *Environmental Policy in the 1990s* (Washington, D.C.: Congressional Quarterly Press, 1990).
4. U.S. Department of Commerce, Bureau of the Census, *Statistical Abstract of the United States, 1991*, 111th ed. (Washington, D.C., 1991).
5. The Congressional Budget Office estimated that the United States generated 265 million metric tons of hazardous waste in 1983. Congressional Budget Office, *Hazardous Waste Management: Recent Changes and Policy Alternatives* (Washington, D.C.: Government Printing Office, 1985). More recent estimates put the total at over 300 million tons annually.
6. Sixty-seven percent of respondents rated active hazardous waste sites as very serious environmental problems, while 65 percent gave the same rating to abandoned sites. These ratings increased several percentage points from a similar study conducted two years earlier in January 1988. Roper Organization, *Roper Reports 90–2* (New York, N.Y., 1990), 25.
7. Charles A. Wentz, *Hazardous Waste Management* (New York: McGraw-Hill, 1989), 11. U.S. Environmental Protection Agency, "Hazardous Wastes," *Environmental Backgrounder* (Office of Public Affairs, January 1989).
8. Ibid.
9. Congressional Budget Office, *Hazardous Waste Management: Recent Changes*.
10. Ibid.
11. John Tagliabue, "The Legacy of Ashes: The Uranium Mines of Eastern Germany," *New York Times*, 19 March 1991, C4.
12. See, for example, Center for Investigative Reporting and Bill Moyers, *Global Dumping Ground: The International Traffic in Hazardous Waste* (Washington, D.C.: Seven Locks Press, 1990) and the associated documentary aired on PBS's "Frontline."
13. U.S. Environmental Protection Agency, *Environmental Investments: The Cost of a Clean Environment—A Summary*, EPA-230-12-90-084 (Washington, D.C.: December 1990), 3–4. Solid waste regulations are expected to add another $22.3

billion by the year 2000 (in 1986 dollars), and underground storage tanks $3.7 billion.

14. EPA, *Environmental Investments.*

15. U.S. Office of Technology Assessment, *Coming Clean: Superfund Problems Can Be Solved, OTA-ITE-433* (Washington, D.C.: Government Printing Office, October 1989), 27.

16. Milton Russell, E. William Colglazier, and Mary R. English, *Hazardous Waste Remediation: The Task Ahead* (University of Tennessee at Knoxville, Waste Management Research and Education Institute, December 1991), 16, 19, and 22.

17. Thomas P. Grumbly, "Superfund: Candidly Speaking," *EPA Journal* (July/August 1991): 22.

18. EPA, *Environmental Investments, 2–3.*

19. U.S. Environmental Protection Agency, Office of Solid Waste and Emergency Response, *Superfund: A Six Year Perspective,* (Washington, D.C., October 1986), 4.

20. "Congress Clears Superfund Legislation," *1980 Congressional Quarterly Almanac,* 586.

21. The law was subsequently interpreted as requiring strict, joint, and several liability for responsible parties. Strict liability means that even if the party was dumping hazardous wastes legally in the past, it can be found liable if it was dumping wastes that are now considered hazardous. Joint and several liability means that one party may be held legally responsible for the entire cleanup cost even it if dumped only a portion of the waste. In this case, the burden remains with the responsible party to collect from the other negligent parties. And because CERCLA dealt with events occurring before 1980, its provisions apply to events that took place prior to its enactment. The fund established under CERCLA (as amended by SARA) may be used to finance feasibility studies and cleanup efforts while legal procedures are initiated to recover the funds from liable parties.

22. The fund was initially called the Hazardous Substance Response Trust Fund.

23. Marchant Wentworth, lobbyist for Environmental Action, quoted in "Congress Clears Superfund Legislation," *1980 Congressional Quarterly Almanac,* 584.

24. *Congressional Quarterly Almanac, 1980,* 584.

25. For details and various perspectives on that role, see George C. Eads and Michael Fix, eds., *The Reagan Regulatory Strategy* (Washington, D.C.: Urban Institute, 1984); George C. Eads and Michael Fix, *Relief or Reform? Reagan's Regulatory Dilemma* (Washington, D.C.: Urban Institute, 1984); Paul R. Portney, ed., *Natural Resources and the Environment: The Reagan Approach* (Washington, D.C.: Urban Institute, 1984); Jonathan Lash, et al. *A Season of Spoils: The Story of the Reagan Administration's Attack on the Environment* (New York: Pantheon, 1984); and Anne M. Burford with John Greenya, *Are You Tough Enough?* (New York: McGraw-Hill, 1986).

26. Quoted in *Congressional Quarterly Weekly Report,* 17 March 1984, 617.

27. Steven Cohen, "Defusing the Toxic Time Bomb: Federal Hazardous Waste Programs," in Norman Vig and Michael Kraft, eds. *Environmental Policy in the 1980's: Reagan's New Agenda* (Washington, D.C. Congressional Quarterly Press, 1984), 285.

28. Personal interview, October 1991.

29. See Anne M. Burford with John Greenya, *Are You Tough Enough?,* chs. 8 and 9.

30. Quoted in Steven Cohen, "Defusing the Toxic Time Bomb," 288.

31. Personal interview, October 1991.
32. Actually, it would require 1333 years at that rate, but in any event Florio's point is clear. Testimony of James Florio before the Senate Committee on Finance, 99th Cong., 1st Sess., April 25 and 26, 1985 (Washington, D.C.: Government Printing Office, 1986), 273.
33. Testimony of James Florio before the U.S. Senate, Committee on Finance, 99th Cong., 1st Sess., April 25 and 26, 1985 (Washington, D.C.: Government Printing Office, 1986), 270.
34. Quoted in *Congressional Quarterly Weekly Report*, 17 March 1984, 615.
35. Quoted in *Congressional Quarterly Weekly Report*, 17 March 1984, 618.
36. *1984 Congressional Quarterly Almanac*, 309–313.
37. Testimony of EPA Administrator Lee Thomas before the House Ways and Means Committee, 99th Cong., 2d sess., Serial 98–95, 25 July 1984, (Washington, D.C.: Government Printing Office, 1985), 183.
38. Lee Thomas, quoted in Rochelle L. Stanfield, "Superfund Backers Push Big Expansion of Program to Clean up Toxic Wastes," *National Journal* (22 September 1984): 1765.
39. Interview with Winston Porter, "The New Superfund: Protecting People and Their Environment," *EPA Journal* (January/February 1987): 6.
40. Quoted in *1986 Congressional Quarterly Almanac*, 111.
41. Personal interview, August 1991.
42. Both chambers' votes were overwhelming: 386–27 in the House, and 88–8 in the Senate.
43. The fund was renamed the Hazardous Substances Superfund.
44. The fund was to be financed by a 0.1 cent per gallon tax on gasoline and various fuels for boats, trains, and motor vehicles and was set to expire on 31 December 1991 or when revenues reached $550 million.
45. The tax for domestically produced oil was 8.2 cents per barrel, while that for imported oil was 11.7 cents.
46. *1986 Congressional Quarterly Almanac*, 113.
47. CERCLIS stands for the Comprehensive Environmental Response, Compensation and Liabilities Information System.
48. EPA, *A Six Year Perspective*, 6.
49. Jan Paul Acton, *Understanding Superfund: A Progress Report* (Santa Monica, Calif.: Rand Corporation, 1989), 26.
50. The Hazard Ranking System is discussed in greater detail in chapter 4.
51. In addition to "fund" and "enforcement" leads, sites can be designated "state lead," "PRP lead," and "mixed fund lead" as well, depending on who oversees site remediation.
52. States must contribute at least 50 percent of all response costs for sites that are publicly owned or operated, except federal sites for which states contribute the standard 10 percent. These include emergency removals, the RI/FS, remedial design, and remedial action. Of course, PRPs can be held responsible for all cleanup costs.
53. For a more detailed description of the Superfund process, see Environmental Protection Agency, Office of Public Affairs, "The New Superfund: Protecting People and Their Environment," *EPA Journal* (January/February 1987).
54. David J. Hayes and Conrad B. MacKerron, *Superfund II: A New Mandate, A BNA Special Report* (Bureau of National Affairs, 1987), 54.

55. U.S. Environmental Protection Agency, *A Management Review of the Superfund Program: Implementation Plan*, EPA/540/8-89/009 (Washington, D.C., September 1989), 2; and *EPA Journal*, November/December 1991, 5.

56. Personal interview, November 1991.

57. See Charles A. Wentz, *Hazardous Waste Management*, chs. 7 and 8.

58. Joel Hirschhorn, quoted in Rochelle L. Stanfield, "High-Tech Burials," *National Journal* (17 October 1987): 2603.

59. Ibid.

60. The following statistics are drawn from U.S. Environmental Protection Agency, *Superfund NPL Characterization Project: National Results*, EPA/540/8-91/069 (Washington, D.C., November 1991), various tables.

61. Katherine N. Probst and Paul R. Portney, *Assigning Liability for Superfund Cleanups: An Analysis of Policy Options* (Washington, D.C.: Resources for the Future, June 1992), 28.

62. Ibid., 29.

63. Although the 10 percent matching share may sound like a token contribution next to the federal share, in many cases financially strapped states have been reluctant to contribute, thereby holding up remedial progress.

64. U.S. Environmental Protection Agency, *Status of State Involvement in the Superfund Program: FY 80 to FY 89* (Washington, D.C., April 1990), 16.

65. Each Indian tribal government is required under law to be treated as a state.

66. Environmental Protection Agency, Office of Solid Waste and Emergency Response, "State and Local Involvement in the Superfund Program," Publication no. 9375.5-01/FS (Washington, D.C., Fall 1989).

67. EPA, *Status of State Involvement*, 20 and 24.

68. There is some question, however, about how strongly the federal government will enforce state noncompliance. South Carolina and Alabama have threatened to enforce the law because of North Carolina's continued export of hazardous waste to their states, and other states are experiencing similar problems. Ronald Smothers, "Hazardous Waste Battle Pits States against U.S.," *New York Times*, 28 January 1991.

69. The full name is the National Oil and Hazardous Substances Pollution Contingency Plan (40 CFR Part 300). A more complete description of the NCP is provided in chapter 6.

70. These are rare, however. For example, there were only two state-lead removal actions started in fiscal 1988 and one in 1989. EPA, *Status of State Involvement*, 19.

71. Ibid.

72. Figures in this paragraph are from U.S. Environmental Protection Agency, Office of Emergency and Remedial Response, *An Analysis of State Superfund Programs: 50-State Study*, EPA/540/8-89/011, (Washington, D.C., September 1989).

73. Ibid.

74. Sue M. Day, Eiman Zeinelabdin, and Andrew Whitford, *State and Private Sector Cleanups* (Hazardous Waste Remediation Project, University of Tennessee, Knoxville, December 1991), 21.

75. "Hazardous Sites Tax Abilities," *Franklin Union News* (AP report), undated.

76. Superfund chief Bill Hedeman, quoted in *BNA Environmental Reporter* (5 April 1985): 2137–38.

77. Keith Schneider, "Cost of Cleanup at Nuclear Sites Is Raised by 50%," *New York Times*, 4 July 1990, 1.

78. Thomas W. Lippman, "Where 'D and D' Also Could Mean Destruction and Danger," *Washington Post National Weekly Edition*, 31 May 1993, 32.

79. U.S. Office of Management and Budget, *Budget of the United States Government, Fiscal Year 1993* (Washington, D.C.: U.S. Government Printing Office), 1–219; Lippman, "Where 'D and D' Also Could Mean Destruction and Danger."

80. Ibid., 1–225.

81. National Toxic Campaign Fund, *The U.S. Military's Toxic Legacy: America's Worst Environmental Enemy* (Boston, Mass., January 1991). The results of the report were widely publicized, such as "Report Calls Military Nation's Worst Polluter," *New York Times*, 17 March 1991, 24.

82. U.S. OMB, *Fiscal 1993 Budget*, 1–225.

83. Bruce Stutz, "Cleaning Up," *Atlantic* (October 1990): 46; William Sanjour, "In Name Only," *Sierra* (October 1992): 98.

84. Brian Bremmer, "If You Can't Build Weapons, Destroy 'Em," *Business Week* (9 March 1992): 89.

85. Advertisement for *Defense Cleanup*, by Pasha Publications in Arlington, VA. Undated. Received December 1990.

86. Liz Galtney, quoted in Kevin Acker, "Dirty Jobs' Big Rewards," *National Journal* (7 March 1992): 580.

87. Russell, Colglazier, and English, *Hazardous Waste Remediation: The Task Ahead*, 16, 19, and 22.

88. One example of the latter is Hugh Kaufman, a renowned EPA "whistleblower."

89. U.S. General Accounting Office, *Superfund: Extent of Nation's Potential Hazardous Waste Problem Still Unknown*, GAO/RCED-88-44 (Washington, D.C., December 1987).

90. U.S. General Accounting Office, *Superfund Contracts: EPA Needs to Control Contractor Costs*, GAO/RCED-88-182 (Washington, D.C., 29 July 1988).

91. Office of Technology Assessment, *Are We Cleaning Up?: 10 Superfund Case Studies* (Washington, D.C., June 1988), 4.

92. Ibid.

93. Ibid., ch. 1.

94. Senate Subcommittee on Superfund, Ocean and Water Protection. *Lautenberg-Durenberger Report on Superfund Implementation: Cleaning Up the Nation's Cleanup Program* (May 1989), 3.

95. Ibid., 6.

96. Ibid.

97. Ibid.

98. Senate Committee on the Budget, United States Senate, "Management of Superfund," prepared by the Studies and Analysis Group of the Majority Staff, Jim Sasser, Chairman, August 1990, ii.

99. Ibid., 2.

100. Ibid., 5.

101. Both House and Senate versions cut the president's request; the House bill requested $1.63 billion, while the Senate bill asked for $1.616 billion, which was ultimately the amount included for Superfund in the final bill. Congress did, however, increase EPA's overall budget from the president's request of $6.21 billion to a final appropriation of $6.67 billion, mostly due to increases in the construction grants program, to which $600 million was added. *Congressional Quarterly Weekly Report* (7 December 1991): 154.

102. Environmental Defense Fund, Hazardous Waste Treatment Council, National

Audubon Society, National Wildlife Federation, Natural Resources Defense Council, Sierra Club, and U.S. PIRG, *Right Train, Wrong Track: Failed Leadership in the Superfund Cleanup Program* (June 1988), 2.

103. Ibid., 1.
104. Environmental Defense Fund, Hazardous Waste Treatment Council, Friends of the Earth, National Audubon Society, Natural Resources Defense Council, and Sierra Club, *Tracking Superfund: Where the Program Stands* (February 1990), 2.
105. Ibid., 3.
106. *Right Train, Wrong Track,* 45.
107. There was widespread public attention to Love Canal in television news reports, including "Today," "The MacNeil-Lehrer Report," "Sixty Minutes," and "Good Morning America." Marc Landy, "Cleaning up Superfund," *The Public Interest* 85 (Fall 1986):60–61.
108. Fred L. Smith, Jr., "Superfund: A Hazardous Waste of Taxpayer Money," *Human Events* (2 August 1986): 10–11.
109. Robert W. Crandall, "What Ever Happened to Deregulation?" in David Boaz, ed. *Assessing the Reagan Years* (Washington, D.C.: Cato Institute, 1988), 284.
110. Smith, "Superfund: A Hazardous Waste of Taxpayer Money," 10.
111. Ibid., 11.
112. Richard L. Stroup and Jane S. Shaw, "The Free Market and the Environment," *The Public Interest* (Fall 1989): 32, 35.
113. Anne M. Burford with John Greenya, *Are You Tough Enough?*, 106.
114. Paul R. Portney, "Reforming Environmental Regulation: Three Modest Proposals," *Issues in Science and Technology* (Winter 1988): 74–81.
115. Maurice R. Greenberg, Chairman, American International Group, Inc., "Financing the Clean-up of Hazardous Waste: The National Environmental Trust Fund," text of a speech given to the National Press Club, Washington, D.C., 2 March 1989. Advertisements advocating this concept have appeared frequently in the print media as well.
116. Ibid., 4.
117. Acton, *Understanding Superfund: A Progress Report*, 61.
118. Quoted in Teresa Austin, "Superfund: New Leadership, Old Problems," *Civil Engineering* (March 1993): 46.
119. Ibid., 16.
120. See EPA, *A Six Year Perspective*, 1–2.
121. Personal interview, August 1991.
122. Bruce Diamond, quoted on National Public Radio, October 1991.
123. Personal interview, August 1991.
124. Personal interview, November 1991.
125. Personal interview, August 1991.
126. Quoted in William K. Burke, "The Booming Business in Waste," *E: The Environmental Magazine* (May/June 1993): 43.
127. Daniel Mazmanian and David Morrell, "The Elusive Pursuit of Toxics Management," *The Public Interest* (Winter 1988): 89.
128. Personal interview, November 1991.
129. Personal interview, October 1991.
130. Jerry L. Mashaw and David L. Harfst, *The Struggle for Auto Safety* (Cambridge, Mass.: Harvard University Press, 1990), 215.

131. These problems plague most of the new "social" regulatory agencies, such as NHTSA, OSHA, CPSC, and EPA. See, for example, Mashaw and Harfst.

Chapter 2. Assessing Risks

1. Mary Douglas and Aaron Wildavsky, *Risk and Culture* (Berkeley, Calif.: University of California Press, 1982), 10.
2. Reported in Dale Hattis and David Kennedy, "Assessing Risks From Health Hazards: An Imperfect Science," *Technology Review* (May/June 1986), reprinted in Theodore S. Glickman and Michael Gough, *Readings in Risk* (Washington, D.C.: Resources for the Future, 1990), 160.
3. Wesley Blixt, "NRC Asks Nuclear Plant Tests," *Franklin Union News*, 23 July 1991, 1.
4. Baruch Fischhoff, et al., *Acceptable Risk* (Cambridge: Cambridge University Press, 1981), 81.
5. A good summary of scientific disagreements involving chemical cancer risks can be found in John D. Graham, Laura C. Green, and Marc J. Roberts, *In Search of Safety* (Cambridge, Mass.: Harvard University Press, 1988). See also National Research Council, *Risk Assessment in the Federal Government: Managing the Process* (Washington, D.C.: National Academy Press, 1983).
6. Samuel M. Cohen and Leon B. Ellwein, "Cell Proliferation and Carcinogenesis," *Science* (31 August 1990): 1007–11.
7. Joel Brinkley, "Animal Tests as Risk Clues: The Best Data May Fall Short," *New York Times*, 23 March 1993, A16.
8. Ibid.
9. "Academy Splits on Risk," *Science* (5 February 1993): 759.
10. I mean by this that the deviation in observed cancer from the test group to the control group is not likely to arise from chance. Generally, biologists and social scientists use a somewhat arbitrary threshold of 95 percent, meaning that with certain assumptions there is only a 5 percent chance that the observed difference is a result of an unusual observed sample.
11. High animal doses are necessary because although it is possible, and indeed scientifically preferable, to increase the number of animals studied and lower the dose to each, managing such an effort becomes prohibitively expensive. For example, to detect a cancer with a relatively high potency of one case in 10,000, one would need at least 10,000 test animals, at a cost of several hundred dollars per animal (depending on the type of animal, the duration of the experiment, and so on). As a result, generally fewer than a thousand animals are tested at once, and are divided into several smaller groups for varying—and necessarily higher—chemical doses in order to produce the expected reaction.
12. Cohen and Ellwein, "Cell Proliferation and Carcinogenesis," 1009.
13. Ibid.
14. Graham, Green, and Roberts, *In Search of Safety*, 153.
15. Humans are approximately 2500 times the weight of mice, but have only 184 times the surface area. (Surface area is more commonly used.) Lester Lave, ed. *Quantitative Risk Assessment in Regulation* (Washington, D.C.: The Brookings Institution, 1982), 42.
16. Graham, Green, and Roberts, *In Search of Safety*, 166–67.
17. Elizabeth Anderson, Paul Chrostowski, and Judy Vreeland, "Risk Assessment Issues Associated with Cleaning Up Inactive Hazardous Waste Sites," pp. 15–34

in Howard Kunreuther and Rajeev Gowda, eds. *Integrating Insurance and Risk Management for Hazardous Wastes* (Boston: Kluwer Academic Publishers, 1990), 20.

18. Graham, Green, and Roberts, *In Search of Safety*, 182.
19. Actually, epidemiological studies may still require extrapolation from high doses to low doses. For example, workers exposed to benzene may be exposed to much higher levels than the general population. Thus, the results of an epidemiological study of such workers would need to be adjusted accordingly, with some of the same problems that occur with bioassays (except that the significant interspecies problems are avoided.)
20. On the current state of pollution monitoring in the United States, see Clifford S. Russell, "Monitoring and Enforcement," pp. 243–74 in Paul R. Portney, ed., *Public Policies for Environmental Protection* (Washington, D.C.: Resources for the Future, 1990).
21. David Ozonoff, Boston University School of Public Health, quoted in Hattis and Kennedy, "Assessing Risks from Health Hazards," 158.
22. Joel Brinkley, "Animal Tests as Risk Clues," A16.
23. Ibid.
24. Michael Gough, "Estimating Cancer Mortality," *Environmental Science and Technology* (1989): 925–30.
25. John D. Graham, "Improving Chemical Risk Assessment," *Regulation* (Fall 1991): 14.
26. James Wilson, discussant's comments in Kunreuther and Gowda, eds. *Integrating Insurance*, 37.
27. Philip H. Abelson, "Diet and Cancer in Humans and Rodents," *Science* (10 January 1992): 141.
28. Michael Gough, "Environmental Epidemiology: Separating Politics and Science," *Issues in Science and Technology* (Summer 1987): 24.
29. The phrase "popular epidemiology" is taken from Phil Brown and Edwin J. Mikkelsen, *No Safe Place: Toxic Waste, Leukemia, and Community Action* (Berkeley: University of California Press, 1990), ch. 4.
30. Richard B. Belzer, "The Peril and Promise of Risk Assessment," *Regulation* (Fall 1991): 47.
31. The expected value is the 50th percentile estimate of risk, where the researcher is just as likely to overstate as understate the true risks. The 95th percentile upper bound suggests that only a 5 percent chance exists that the risk is greater than that reported and a 95 percent chance that the risk is overstated.
32. These are drawn from the summary found in Robert C. Paehlke, *Environmentalism and the Future of Progressive Politics* (New Haven: Yale University Press, 1989), 30–32.
33. Paul Slovic, "Perception of Risk," *Science* (April 1987): 283–84.
34. Ibid., 283.
35. Graham, Green, and Roberts, *In Search of Safety*, 205.
36. Fischhoff, et al., *Acceptable Risk*, 81.
37. Adam M. Finkel, science of risk forum contributor, *EPA Journal* (March/April 1991): 38.
38. Personal interview, June 1990.
39. Sheila Jasanoff, "Complete Separation of the Two Processes is a Misconception," *EPA Journal* (January/February/March 1993): 37.

40. Jasanoff, "Complete Separation," 36.
41. H. W. Lewis, *Technological Risk* (New York: W. W. Norton, 1990), 112–13.
42. Brinkley, "Animal Tests as Risk Clues."
43. Belzer, "Peril and Promise," 48.
44. This point is also made by Aaron Wildavsky, "Richer is Safer," *The Public Interest* (Summer 1980): 23–39.
45. Lois Swirsky Gold, et al., "Rodent Carcinogens: Setting Priorities," *Science* (9 October 1992): 265.
46. See John H. Weisburger, letter to the editor, "The Alar Case," *Issues in Science and Technology* (Summer 1991): 18.
47. Timothy Egan, "Apple Growers Bruised and Bitter after Alar Scare," *New York Times*, 9 July 1991, 1.
48. In technical terms, Type I errors are minimized, while Type II errors become increasingly likely.
49. Lewis, *Technological Risk*, 115–6.
50. Ibid, 115, 117.
51. John Morrall, "Review of the Record," *Regulation* (November/December 1986): 32.
52. Letter in *Issues in Science and Technology* (Summer 1991): 18.
53. Quoted in *New York Times*, 19 August 1991, A11.
54. This draws on Mark Rushevsky's *Making Cancer Policy* (Albany: State University of New York Press, 1986). The quotes are from pages 125 and 129.
55. Quoted in Rushevsky, *Making Cancer Policy*, 134–35.
56. Graham, Green, and Roberts, *In Search of Safety*, 188.
57. Francis M. Lynn, "The Interplay of Science and Values in Assessing and Regulating Environmental Risks," *Science, Technology, & Human Values* (Spring 1986): 45–46. See also Thomas M. Dietz and Robert W. Rycroft, *The Risk Professionals* (New York: Russell Sage Foundation, 1987).
58. The primary EPA publications for conducting risk analyses include *Risk Assessment Guidance for Superfund, Volume I, Human Health Evaluation Manual*, and *Volume II, Environmental Evaluation Manual*.
59. EPA wisely expresses risk numbers only to one significant figure (e.g., 3.3×10^{-5} is two significant figures; 3×10^{-5} is one) so as not to deceive with false precision. Ibid., vol. I, 8–12. In other ways, however, such as presenting single point estimates for site risks, the same caution is not always exercised.
60. The degree of conservatism depends on the independence of the individual statistical relationships, however, so the cumulative impact of multiplying several 95th percentile estimates will vary from site to site.
61. For example, one Superfund site, Western Processing in Kent, Wash., contained eighty-three EPA priority pollutants in the soil and fifty-seven in the groundwater. David Lincoln, "The Assessment of Risk at Superfund Sites," *Environmental Progress* (November 1987): 216.
62. U.S. Environmental Protection Agency, *Risk Assessment Guidance for Superfund: Volume I; Quick Reference Fact Sheet*, 9285.7-01/FS (April 1990), 3.
63. Ibid.
64. Paul R. Portney and Alan J. Krupnick, *The Benefits and Costs of Superfund Cleanups: An Information Assessment (Coalition on Superfund: September 1989)*, 47.
65. Graham, Green, and Roberts, *In Search of Safety*, 177.
66. Ibid.

67. Tamara L. Sorell, "Common Methodological Flaws in Risk Assessment," pp. 229–35 in B. J. Garrick and W. C. Gekler, eds. *The Analysis, Communication, and Perception of Risk* (New York: Plenum Press, 1991).

68. Ibid., 232.

69. Carolyn B. Doty and Curtis C. Travis, "The Superfund Remedial Action Decision Process: A Review of Fifty Records of Decision," *JAPCA Journal* 39 (December 1989): 1535–43.

70. This does not mean that, at the highest extreme, one out of every 100 people living around the site is likely to contract cancer as a result of the Superfund site. One recent newspaper article, for example, reported that consultants estimated the cancer risk from soil vapors at a particular site to be 1 in 10,000 (10^{-4}), which the article cited as "meaning one cancer death for every 10,000 residents." Elliot Diringer, "How Toxic Cleanups Bog Down," *San Francisco Chronicle*, 31 May 1991, A4. Many people are only slightly exposed or not exposed at all to the risks, and cancer risk estimates frequently refer to seventy years of consistent exposure, for the most sensitive person, using the most conservative estimates. These sorts of exaggerations fuel the fear of Superfund sites and other chemical risks, and mask differences between what in some cases are serious public health threats with sites that pose little threat to human health or the environment.

71. Doty and Travis, "Superfund Remedial Action," 1536.

72. National Research Council, *Environmental Epidemiology: Public Health and Hazardous Waste Sites* (Washington, D.C.: National Academy Press, 1991), 1.

73. Daniel Patrick Moynihan, "A Legislative Proposal: Why Not Enact a Law That Would Help Us Set Sensible Priorities?" *EPA Journal* (January/February/March 1993): 47.

74. Jasanoff, "Complete Separation," 35.

75. Jonathan Lash, "Should We Set Priorities Based on Risk Analysis?" *EPA Journal* (March/April 1991): 19.

76. Stephen Klaidman, *Health in the Headlines: The Stories behind the Stories* (New York: Oxford University Press, 1992).

77. Sheldon Krimsky and Alonzo Plough, *Environmental Hazards: Communicating Risks as a Social Process* (Dover, Mass.: Auburn House, 1988), 300.

Chapter 3. Managing Risks

1. Marc K. Landy, Marc J. Roberts, and Stephen R. Thomas, *The Environmental Protection Agency: Asking the Wrong Questions* (New York: Oxford University Press, 1990), 251.

2. William E. Schmidt, "In Missouri, a Battle over Burying a Toxic Town," *New York Times*, 30 May 1990.

3. *New York Times*, "U.S. Health Aide Says He Erred on Times Beach," 26 May 1991, 20.

4. Ibid.

5. Ibid.

6. Ibid.

7. Quoted in Keith Schneider, "New View Calls Environmental Policy Misguided," *New York Times*, 21 March 1993, 30.

8. The figures are derived from "Rescission of the Passive Restraints Standard: Costs and Benefits", Case Program #C16-82-562.2, J. F. Kennedy School of Government, 1989. This example is only illustrative, and is not intended to be a full accounting of the benefits and costs of mandatory airbags. There is considerable

debate over these effects, however. (See, for example, Sam Peltzman, "The Effects of Automobile Safety Regulation," *Journal of Political Economy* (1975), and more recently Robert S. Chirinko and Edward P. Harper, Jr., "Buckle Up or Slow Down?" *Journal of Policy Analysis and Management* (Spring 1993): 270–96). Nevertheless, policymakers were confronted with this information and decided against a policy that they believed would have had the impacts described.

9. The "populist" perspective is a label for several nonrational perspectives, variously termed cultural, psychometric, and populist. I have borrowed this term from K. S. Shrader-Frechette's use of the term "antipopulists" to describe what I have here termed "rationalists," in *Risk and Rationality: Philosophical Foundations for Populist Reforms* (Berkeley: University of California Press, 1991).

10. Morrall, "Review of the Record," 30. Another study that reached similar results is John D. Graham and James W. Vaupel, "Value of a Life: What Difference Does It Make?" *Risk Analysis* (1981): 89–95.

11. U.S. Office of Management and Budget, *U.S. Government Budget, Fiscal Year 1992*, table C-2, pt. 2, (Washington, D.C.: Government Printing Office, 1991), 370.

12. Bruce N. Ames, Renae Magaw, and Lois S. Gold, "Ranking Possible Carcinogenic Hazards," *Science* 236 (17 April 1987), reprinted in Glickman and Gough, *Readings in Risk*, 78. See also the comments from Samuel S. Epstein and Joel B. Swartz, "Carcinogenic Risk Estimation," *Science* (20 May 1988): 1043–45, and the response by Ames and Gold, ibid., 1045–47.

13. Richard D. Pollack, "The Science of Cancer," *The Public Interest* (Winter 1992), 129.

14. Ames, Magaw, and Gold, "Ranking Possible Carcinogenic Hazards," 86.

15. Quoted in Dick Thompson, "The Danger in Doomsaying," *Time*, 9 March 1992, 61.

16. Richard Doll and Richard Peto, *The Causes of Cancer* (Oxford: Oxford University Press, 1981). For a different perspective, see Samuel S. Epstein, *The Politics of Cancer* (New York: Anchor/Doubleday, 1979).

17. Brian E. Henderson, Ronald K. Ross, and Malcolm C. Pike, "Toward the Primary Prevention of Cancer," *Science* (22 November 1991): 1137.

18. Michael Gough, "How Much Cancer Can EPA Regulate Away?" *Risk Analysis* 10 (1990): 1–6.

19. Ames, Magaw, and Gold, "Ranking Possible Carcinogenic Hazards," 86.

20. Viewed another way, a $413,000 present investment would be exhausted after thirty years of payments of $30,000 annually, assuming an interest rate of 6 percent.

21. Peltzman, "Effects of Automobile Safety Regulation."

22. There are a number of assumptions required to make this inference, including that workers perceive the true relative risks of different jobs and that they are mobile. These studies depend on a labor market being in competitive equilibrium, where given the "price" of risk, no one prefers to switch jobs.

23. Michael J. Moore and W. Kip Viscusi, "Doubling the Estimated Value of Life," *Journal of Policy Analysis and Management* (Spring 1988): 476–90. A survey shows that the value per statistical life saved ranges from $1.6 million to $8.5 million in 1986 dollars. See Ann Fisher, Lauraine G. Chestnut, and Daniel M. Violette, "The Value of Reducing Risks of Death: A Note on New Evidence," *Journal of Policy Analysis and Management* (Winter 1989): 96.

24. Wildavsky, "Richer is Safer."

25. Ralph L. Keeney, "Mortality Risks Induced by Economic Expenditures," *Risk Analysis* (1990): 147–59.

26. Keeney, "Mortality Risks," 154.

27. The U.S. Office of Management and Budget has tried to incorporate this thinking into occupational health and other regulations issued by the Labor Department. OMB argued that because the cost of a proposed regulation was $163 million, 22 additional deaths would result from lowered incomes ($163/7.5 = 22), compared with an expected 8 to 13 annual deaths prevented by the regulation. OMB later withdrew from its demands, after criticism from a number of senators, one of whom called it "a bit off the wall," and another spoke of the "absurd and twisted thinking that less protection saves lives." Adam Clymer, "OMB Retreats on Work-Health Issue," *New York Times*, 30 March 1992, A8.

28. W. Henson Moore, quoted in Paul Slovic, Mark Layman, and James H. Flynn, "Risk Perception, Trust, and Nuclear Waste: Lessons from Yucca Mountain," *Environment* (April 1991): 8.

29. Sheldon Krimsky and Dominic Golding, "Reflections," in Sheldon Krimsky and Dominic Goldings, eds., *Social Theories of Risk* (Westport, Conn.: Praeger, 1992), 355–56.

30. National Research Council, *Improving Risk Communication* (Washington, D.C.: National Academy Press, 1989), 3.

31. Krimsky and Golding, *Social Theories*, 358.

32. Shrader-Frechette, *Risk and Rationality*.

33. Shrader-Frechette, *Risk and Rationality*, 20.

34. Burton Weisbrod, "Income Redistribution Effects and Benefit-Cost Analysis," pp. 177–209 in Samuel B. Chase, Jr., ed. *Problems in Public Expenditure Analysis* (Washington, D.C.: The Brookings Institution, 1968).

35. Baruch Fischhoff et al., *Acceptable Risk*, 28.

36. Peter Sandman, "Risk Communication: Facing Public Outrage," *EPA Journal* (November 1987): 21–22.

37. Slovic, Layman, and Flynn, "Risk Perception," 30.

38. Krimsky and Plough, *Environmental Hazards*, 302.

39. Krimsky and Plough, *Environmental Hazards*, 303.

40. Sheldon Krimsky, "Risk Analysis and Public Policy," letter in *Environment* (March 1993): 41.

41. Krimsky and Plough, *Environmental Hazards*, 303.

42. Ibid., 302–3.

43. Ibid., 306.

44. Shrader-Frechette, *Risk and Rationality*, 13.

45. For an insightful critique, see Richard N.L. Andrews, "Risk Assessment: Regulation and Beyond," pp. 167–86 in Vig and Kraft, eds. *Environmental Policy in the 1990s*.

46. The risks of these activities are drawn from Fischhoff et al, *Acceptable Risk*, 81.

47. *Congressional Quarterly Weekly Report*, 20 January 1990, 142.

48. *New York Times*, 16 July 1991, A18, letter to editor. This is highly questionable in light of the evidence presented by Doll and Peto, however.

49. Ibid.

50. Quoted in *Congressional Quarterly Weekly Report*, 20 January 1990, 143.

51. Philip Shabecoff, *A Fierce Green Fire: The American Environmental Movement* (New York: Hill and Wang, 1993), 220.

52. Ibid., 219.

53. John W. Ellwood and Eric M. Patashnik, "In Praise of Pork," *The Public Interest* (Winter 1993): 19–33.

54. Lawrie Mott, "Should We Set Priorities Based on Risk Analysis?" *EPA Journal* (March/April 1991): 21.

55. Maureen L. Cropper and Paul R. Portney, "Discounting Human Lives," *Resources* (Summer 1992): 1–4.

56. Robert N. Bellah et al., *The Good Society* (New York: Alfred A. Knopf, 1991), 117.

57. Ibid.

58. Steven Kelman, "Cost-Benefit Analysis: An Ethical Critique," *Regulation* (1981).

59. Mark Sagoff, *The Economy of the Earth* (Cambridge: Cambridge University Press, 1988), 53.

60. Ibid., 45.

61. Ibid., 60.

62. Murray Edelman, *The Symbolic Uses of Politics* (Urbana: University of Illinois Press, 1964).

63. Sagoff, *Economy of the Earth*, 35.

64. For an account of the role of local interests in shaping the provisions of the 1977 amendments to the Clean Air Act, see Bruce A. Ackerman and William T. Hassler, *Clean Coal/Dirty Air* (New Haven: Yale University Press, 1981).

65. Robert W. Crandall, *Controlling Industrial Pollution* (Washington, D.C.: The Brookings Institution, 1983).

66. Sagoff, *Economy of the Earth*, 213.

67. Robert Bellah et al., *Good Society*, 119.

68. Jonathan Lash, quoted in Leslie Roberts, "Counting on Science at EPA," *Science* 249 (10 August 1990): 618.

69. This section draws on my doctoral dissertation, "The Use of Cost-Benefit Analysis in the Federal Government," University of California at Berkeley, Graduate School of Public Policy (December 1988).

70. U.S. Department of Transportation, *Guidance for Regulatory Evaluations: A Handbook for DOT Benefit-Cost Analysis* (Washington, D.C.: rev. April 1984), 22.

71. Steven Kelman, "Economists and the Environmental Muddle," *The Public Interest* (Summer 1981): 106–23.

72. Kelman, "Economists and the Environmental Muddle," 110.

73. See David L. Weimer and Aidan R. Vining, *Policy Analysis: Concepts and Practice* (Englewood Cliffs, N.J.: Prentice-Hall, 1989), ch. 12.

74. Cass Sunstein, *The American Prospect* (Spring 1993): 12–13.

75. Mancur Olson, *The Logic of Collective Action* (Cambridge, Mass.: Harvard University Press, 1965).

76. National Research Council, *Improving Risk Communication*, 6.

77. Slovic, Layman, and Flynn, "Risk Perception," 30.

78. Susan G. Hadden, *A Citizen's Right to Know: Risk Communication and Public Policy* (Boulder, Colo.: Westview Press, 1989), 16.

79. William K. Reilly, "The Next Environmental Policy: Preventing Pollution," *Domestic Affairs* (Summer 1991): 93.

Chapter 4. Is Superfund an Effective Use of Environmental Resources?

1. Personal interview, October 1991.

2. "Welfare effects" include recreation, soiling and material damages, property damages, and aesthetic losses (such as impaired visibility).

3. U.S. Environmental Protection Agency, Office of Policy, Planning and Evaluation, *Unfinished Business: A Comparative Assessment of Environmental Problems: Overview Report, Volume I* (February 1987), xiv.

4. Ibid., 75.

5. Ibid., 76.

6. Personal interview, October 1991.

7. EPA's Science Advisory Board includes mostly non-EPA environmental experts, and was chaired by Raymond Loehr, a professor of civil engineering, and Jonathan Lash, an environmental lawyer who was then secretary of natural resources for Vermont.

8. Frederick Allen, quoted in Leslie Roberts, "Counting on Science at EPA," 616.

9. Leslie Roberts, "Counting on Science at EPA," 616–18.

10. U.S. Environmental Protection Agency, Science Advisory Board, *Reducing Risk: Setting Priorities and Strategies for Environmental Protection*, SAB-EC-90-021 (September 1990), 7.

11. Ibid., 13. A Strategic Options subcommittee examined ways to reduce environmental risks.

12. Ibid., 13–14.

13. Ibid., 17, 22.

14. William K. Reilly, "Next Environmental Policy," 73–98.

15. Letter to the editor, *New York Times*, 21 April 1993, A22.

16. Personal interview, September 1991.

17. Marlise Simons, "West Offers Plan to Clean Up East," *New York Times*, 4 May 1993, A13.

18. U.S. Department of Health and Human Services, Agency for Toxic Substances and Disease Registry, *ATSDR Biennial Report to Congress, Volume 2* (Atlanta, Georgia, December 1988), 57.

19. An Office of Technology Assessment study estimated that the cost per life saved at Superfund sites averaged around $5 million considering only cancer risks, though they admit that the cost "varies greatly from site to site." OTA assumed 5,000 people exposed at each site, risk reductions from 10^{-3} to 10^{-6}, and a cleanup cost of $25 million. U.S. Office of Technology Assessment, *Coming Clean*, 25–26. While one can quibble with the exposure and risk figures used by OTA, the real problem is that the *average* cost is not particularly relevant since it obscures the fact that some sites are far riskier than others. OTA does recommend that high-risk sites be cleaned up first, but validating the cost-effectiveness of the program based on average risks misses the point (which OTA stresses in other contexts) that sites are dramatically different and should be evaluated individually.

20. Personal interview, October 1991.

21. See discussion of the Cropper and Portney study in chapter 3.

22. Keith Schneider, "In Arkansas Toxic Waste Cleanup, Highlights of New Environmental Debate," *New York Times*, 2 November 1992, B11.

23. Quoted in Keith Schneider, "New View Calls Environmental Policy Misguided," *New York Times*, 21 March 1993, 30.

24. Personal interview, November 1991.

25. This does not include any "existence values" that some people may hold for the knowledge that, say, groundwater is uncontaminated, even though they will never use it. Therefore, appropriate compensation may be higher.

26. Quoted in Schneider, "New View Calls," 30.

27. Lewis, *Technological Risk*, 247–49.

28. A picocurie is a measure of the radioactivity in a picogram (10^{-12} grams) of radium, or the amount of a radionuclide necessary to produce 2.2 radioactive decays per minute. Thus, 0.25 picocuries of radon is the radiation equivalent of 0.00000000000025 grams of radium. William Nazaroff and Kevin Teichman, "Indoor Radon," *Environmental Science and Technology* (1990): 775.

29. Warren E. Leary, *New York Times*, 2 February 1991, 10.

30. Nazaroff and Teichman, "Indoor Radon," 775.

31. U.S. Environmental Protection Agency, *A Citizen's Guide to Radon* (Washington, D.C., August 1986), 4.

32. Joseph E. Henderson, Jr., "The Threat of Indoor Radon," *Journal of Property Management* (July/August 1986): 44.

33. EPA, *Citizen's Guide to Radon*, 11.

34. Ibid., 12.

35. Philip H. Abelson, "Radon Today: The Role of Flimflam in Public Policy," *Regulation* (Fall 1991): 95.

36. Ibid., 98.

37. Margo T. Oge and William H. Farland, "Radon Risk in the Home," letter to the editor, *Science* (6 March 1992): 1194.

38. Jonathan M. Samet, "Radon Risks," letter in *Issues in Science and Technology* (Spring 1993): 17.

39. Roper Organization, *Roper Reports* 90–2, 27. The only problem receiving a lower percentage was radiation from microwave ovens, where 13 percent considered the risk very serious.

40. Ibid.

41. *New York Times*, "Radon in Jersey Poses Grave Risk," 1 October 1989, 41.

42. Nazaroff and Teichman, "Indoor Radon," 778.

43. Ibid.

44. Number 100-1047 on H.R. 2837.

45. Anthony V. Nero, Jr., "A National Strategy for Indoor Radon," *Issues in Science and Technology* (Fall 1992): 33.

46. The EPA has stated publicly, "We do not believe that EPA regulatory intervention beyond guidance would prove warranted given the localized nature of radon problems and the need for States and localities to tailor their programs to specific areas." See *Radon Contamination: How Federal Agencies Deal With It*, Hearing before the Senate Subcommittee on Superfund and Environmental Oversight, 100th Cong., 2d Sess. (Washington, D.C.: Government Printing Office), 18 May 1988, 69.

47. Keith Schneider, "How a Rebellion over Environmental Rules Grew from a Patch of Weeds," *New York Times*, 24 March 1993, A16.

48. Keith Schneider, "EPA Proposes Costly Rules to Curb Radon Health Threat in New Houses," *New York Times*, 7 April 1993, A16.

49. Statement of Dr. James O. Mason, CDC, *The Administration's Strategy to Reduce Lead Poisoning and Contamination*, A Hearing before the Senate Subcommittee on Environment and Public Works (Washington, D.C.: Government Printing Office, 21 February 1991), 11.

50. *Administration's Strategy*, 87.

51. U.S. Department of Health and Human Services, Centers for Disease Control, *Preventing Lead Poisoning in Young Children* (Atlanta, Ga., October 1991), 9.

52. Ibid., 89.

53. Ibid., 8.

54. Statement of Dr. James O. Mason of CDC, *Administration's Strategy*, 87.

55. U.S. Department of Housing and Urban Development, Office of Policy Development and Research, *Comprehensive and Workable Plan for the Abatement of Lead-based Paint in Privately-Owned Housing: A Report to Congress*, HUD-PDR-1295 (Washington, D.C., January 1991), 2–2. See also K. R. Mahaffey, "Nutritional Factors in Lead Poisoning," *Nutrition Review* (1981): 353–62.

56. HUD, *Comprehensive Plan*, 2–2.

57. Airborne lead is no longer the widespread problem that it once was, and is only considered a problem in localized areas such as those near industrial sources. While these "point sources" can contribute significantly to increased lead levels in the blood of people near the source, they are not considered a major source of the overall problem. CDC, *Preventing Lead Poisoning*, 23.

58. HUD, *Comprehensive Plan*, 2–12; CDC, *Preventing Lead Poisoning*, chap. 3.

59. It can also be inhaled in the form of dust, although this does not seem to be as significant a contributor as hand-to-mouth contact. CDC, *Preventing Lead Poisoning*, 20; HUD, *Comprehensive Plan*, 2–17. The dust can be generated by the natural chalking process that paint goes through, by paint chips falling to the ground, from lead-based paint on friction surfaces like windows, and others. HUD, *Comprehensive Plan*, 3–12; CDC *Preventing Lead Poisoning*, 4, 18.

60. CDC, *Preventing Lead Poisoning*, 19.

61. Ibid., 20.

62. Herbert Needleman and C. A. Gatsonis, "Low Level Exposure and the IQ of Children," *JAMA* (1990): 673–78. See also H. L. Needleman et al., "The Long-Term Effects of Exposure to Low Doses of Lead in Childhood," *New England Journal of Medicine* (1990): 83–88. There is, however, controversy surrounding Needleman's findings. See, for example, "Lead Study Challenge," letter to the editor, *Science* (14 February 1992): 783; and Joseph Palce, "Get-the-Lead-Out Guru Challenged," *Science* (23 August 1991): 842.

63. HUD, *Comprehensive Plan*, 2–7.

64. Statement of Dr. James Mason of CDC, *Administration's Strategy*, 88.

65. Statement of William K. Reilly, *Administration's Strategy*, 46.

66. HUD, *Comprehensive Plan*, 2–17.

67. "California Finds Lead Exposure Could Affect 1 of 5 Children," *New York Times*, 3 September 1991, C10.

68. CDC, *Preventing Lead Poisoning*, 65.

69. HUD, *Comprehensive Plan*; Mark R. Farfel and J. Julian Chisolm, Jr., "Health and Environmental Outcomes of Traditional and Modified Practices for Abatement of Residential Lead-based Paint," *American Journal of Public Health* (October 1990): 1243–44.

70. For a thorough discussion of various abatement methods, see U.S. Department of Housing and Urban Development, Office of Policy Development and Research, *The HUD Lead-based Paint Abatement Demonstration (FHA)* (Washington, D.C., August 1991).

71. Statement by John C. Weicher of HUD, *Administration's Strategy*, 128.

72. Statement by Dr. James Mason of CDC, *Administration's Strategy*, 91.

73. Jane E. Brody, "Lead-Poisoning Harm Held to be Partly Reversible," *New York Times*, 8 April 1993, A18.

74. CDC, *Preventing Lead Poisoning*, 18–19; R. L. Bornschein, P. A. Succop, and K. M. Krafft, "Exterior Surface Dust Lead, Interior House Dust Lead and Childhood Lead Exposure in an Urban Environment," in D. Hemphill, ed. *Trace Sub-*

stances in *Environmental Health* (Columbia: University of Missouri, 1986), 322–32; J. J. Chisholm, E. D. Mellits, and S. A. Quaskey, "The Relationship Between the Level of Lead Absorption in Children and the Age, Type and Condition of Housing," *Environmental Resources* 25 (1981): 449–56.

75. HUD, *Comprehensive Plan*, xix.

76. Ibid., 4–12.

77. Ibid., 4–12.

78. The testing industry is estimated to be currently capable of testing a maximum of 500,000 units per year. HUD, *Comprehensive Plan*, xx.

79. CDC, *Preventing Lead Poisoning*, 77.

80. HUD, *Comprehensive Plan*, 4–19.

81. U.S. Department of Health and Human Services, Centers for Disease Control, *Strategic Plan for the Elimination of Childhood Lead Poisoning* (February 1991), app. II.

82. In October, 1991, CDC lowered the blood level at which intervention is recommended from 15 μg/dl to 10 μg/dl. CDC, *Preventing Lead Poisoning*, 1. This level has been lowered steadily from 40 μg/dl in 1970, and 25 μg/dl in 1985. Ibid., 8.

83. Jonathan H. Adler, "Is Lead a Heavy Threat?" *Regulation* (Fall 1992): 13–15.

84. Michael Weisskopf, "Strategy on Lead Turns out Not to Be Blitzkrieg," *Washington Post*, 25 October 1991, A25.

85. Philip J. Hilts, "Lower Lead Limits Are Made Official," *New York Times*, 8 October 1991, C3.

86. U.S. Government Printing Office, *Budget of the United States Government, Fiscal Year 1992* (Washington, D.C.: 1991), II–30, II–31.

87. Vernon Houk, quoted in Philip Hilts, "White House Shuns Key Role on Lead Exposure," *New York Times*, 24 August 1991, 14.

88. For a story of the scientific controversy, see Joseph Hooper, "The Asbestos Mess," *New York Times Magazine*, section 6 (25 November 1990), 38–53.

89. Ibid.

90. See Michael Gough, "Uncle Sam Flunks Asbestos Control in Schools," *Issues in Science and Technology* (Spring 1988): 81.

91. Steven Labaton, "Moves to Speed Asbestos Cases," *New York Times*, 2 May 1991, D2.

92. See, for example, the testimony of Linda Fisher, assistant administrator for pesticides and toxic substances, before the Senate Subcommittee on Toxic Substances, Environmental Oversight, Research and Development, Senate Hearing 101-835 (26 April 1990), 75–77.

93. Gough, "Uncle Sam Flunks," 85.

94. U.S. Office of Management and Budget, *Budget of the United States Government, Fiscal Year 1992*, 1015.

95. Charlotte Twight, "Regulation of Asbestos: The Microanalytics of Government Failure," *Policy Studies Review* 10 (Fall 1990):19.

96. *Unfinished Business in New England: A Comparative Assessment of Environmental Problems, Public Health Risk Work Group Report* (December 1988), 93.

97. See, for example, Health Effects Institute-Asbestos Research, *Asbestos in Public and Commercial Buildings: A Literature Review and Synthesis of Current Knowledge* (Cambridge, Mass.: HEI-AR, 1991). In addition, the study notes that "it is almost certain that the overall excess of cases [of lung cancer] that could be attributed to asbestos exposure in buildings will be relatively small and probably undetectable" (Ibid., 8–2).

98. Ibid., 1–12.
99. This section draws on my article "Superfund Expenditures and Cleanup Priorities: Distributive Politics or the Public Interest?" *Journal of Policy Analysis and Management* (Fall 1990): 455–83.
100. Considerable controversy has surrounded the HRS scores, causing Congress in 1986 under SARA to require EPA both to revise the system by including other migration pathways and to consider the impact of a cutoff point other than 28.5 for NPL eligibility. The revised HRS system issued in December 1990 (Federal Register 51532 (vol. 55, no. 241, 14 December 1990)) significantly revises the algorithms that are used to calculate the scores for each pathway. In addition, the new HRS weighs ecological (as opposed to human health) risks more highly. The proposed new formula uses a root-mean-square method rather than the normalization method used previously.
101. Sites that states designate as their highest "priority" are exempted from the 28.5 cutoff, although fewer than ten sites fall into this category.
102. This is required under Section 105 of CERCLA. Fred Smith has noted in an interview and in print the congruence between the initial number of Superfund NPL sites and the number of congressional districts. Smith, "Superfund: A Hazardous Waste," 11.
103. Office of Technology Assessment, *Coming Clean*, 122.
104. U.S. Environmental Protection Agency, *Field Test of the Proposed Revised Hazard Ranking System (HRS)*. EPA/540/P-90/001 (Washington, D.C., May 1990), 5–27.
105. This has been changed in the revised HRS, where the population cap was eliminated.
106. Personal interview, May 1990.
107. Office of Technology Assessment, *Coming Clean*, 118.
108. Office of Technology Assessment, *Coming Clean*, 114.
109. Personal interview, October 1991.
110. Bernard J. Reilly, "Stop Superfund Waste," *Issues in Science and Technology* (Spring 1993): 58.
111. Jack Schramm, discussant's remarks in Kunreuther and Gowda, eds. *Integrating Insurance*, 98.
112. Quoted in Keith Schneider, "New View Calls," 30.
113. EPA's classification system includes B1 chemicals (where limited human data are available), B2 chemicals (sufficient animal evidence but no human evidence), class D chemicals, which are not classifiable as to human carcinogenicity, and finally class E chemicals, where evidence suggests they are noncarcinogenic. Environmental Protection Agency, *Risk Assessment Guidance for Superfund, Volume 1, Human Health Evaluation Manual (Part A)* (December 1989), 7–11.
114. Thomas P. Grumbly, "Superfund: Candidly Speaking," 21.
115. Gary H. McClelland, William D. Schulze, and Brian Hurd, "The Effect of Risk Beliefs on Property Values: A Case Study of a Hazardous Waste Site," *Risk Analysis* (1990): 485–97. Others have found, however, that upon remediating Superfund sites around Houston, property value declines vanished. Janet E. Kohlhase, "The Impact of Toxic Waste Sites on Housing Values," *Journal of Urban Economics* (July 1991): 1–26.
116. Robert M. Brandon, director of Citizens/Labor Energy Coalition, quoted in Stanfield, "Superfund Backers Push Big Expansion," 1764.

117. Douglas W. Wolf and Linda E. Greer (both from NRDC), letter in the *New York Times*, 11 September 1991, A26.
118. Reilly, "Next Environmental Policy," 79.
119. *New York Times*, "U.S. Has New Plan against Smoking," 5 October 1991, 6.
120. Andrew Pollack, "Both Heart Drugs Are Effective; Doctors Prescribe the Costly One," *New York Times*, 30 June 1991, 1.

Chapter 5. Environmental Equity and Superfund

This chapter draws on the material from my article, "Environmental Policy and Equity: The Case of Superfund," *Journal of Policy Analysis and Management* (Spring 1993): 323–43. Copyright 1993 by the Association for Public Policy Analysis and Management.

1. Felicity Barringer, "In Capital, No. 2 River is a Cause," *New York Times*, 1 December 1991, 24; John H. Cushman, Jr., "Environmental Hazards to Poor Gain New Focus at EPA," *New York Times*, 21 January 1992, C4.; and Peter T. Kilborn, "Dying Town Considers Salvation in a Landfill," *New York Times*, 6 October 1991, 20.
2. Keith Schneider, "Minorities Join to Fight Toxic Waste," *New York Times*, 25 October 1991, A20.
3. NPR's program "Fresh Air" aired on 29 January 1992, and featured interviews with Robert Bullard, a University of California at Riverside sociologist who claims that poor and minority communities are discriminated against in hazardous waste siting, and Robert Wolcott, head of EPA's committee that studied the issue of race and environmental quality. The "MacNeil-Lehrer NewsHour" program was aired 11 February 1992.
4. U.S. Environmental Protection Agency, Office of Policy, Planning, and Evaluation, *Environmental Equity: Reducing Risk for All Communities* (Washington, D.C.: U.S. EPA, June 1992).
5. Kilborn, "Dying Town," 20.
6. James T. Hamilton, "Politics and Social Costs: Estimating the Impact of Collective Action on Hazardous Waste Facilities," *RAND Journal of Economics* (Spring 1993): 101–25.
7. United Church of Christ, Commission for Racial Justice, *Toxic Waste and Race in the United States*, A National Report on the Racial and Socio-Economic Characteristics of Communities with Hazardous Waste Sites, 1987, xiii and xv.
8. Ibid.
9. U.S. General Accounting Office, *Siting of Hazardous Waste Landfills and Their Correlation with Racial and Economic Status of Surrounding Communities* (Washington, D.C.: General Accounting Office, 1983).
10. Robert D. Bullard, *Dumping in Dixie: Race, Class, and Environmental Quality* (Boulder: Westview Press, 1990).
11. Clean Sites, Inc., *Hazardous Waste Sites and the Rural Poor: A Preliminary Assessment* (Alexandria, Va., March 1990).
12. Jay M. Gould, *Quality of Life In American Neighborhoods: Levels of Affluence, Toxic Waste, and Cancer Mortality In Residential Zip Code Areas* (Boulder: Westview Press, 1986).
13. John A. Hird, "Do Environmental Pollutants Disproportionately Affect the Poor and Racial Minorities?" February 1993, mimeographed.

14. Senator David Durenberger, "A Dissenting Voice," *EPA Journal* (March/April 1991): 50.
15. For an excellent discussion of the use of equity in public policy, see Deborah A. Stone, *Policy Paradox and Political Reason* (Glenview, Ill.: Scott-Foresman, 1988), chap. 2.
16. One exception is Clean Sites, Inc., *Hazardous Waste Sites*, which evaluated the effects of RCRA and Superfund sites on residents of rural poor counties, where groundwater contamination is particularly critical. See also Paul R. Portney, contributor to "Who Should Pay?" *EPA Journal* (July/August 1991): 37–38, for a discussion of the relationship between Superfund policy and equity.
17. U.S. Office of Management and Budget, *Fiscal 1993 Budget*, 1–219. See also, Lawrence J. Haas, "Never Say Die," *National Journal* (28 March 1992): 755–57, stating that the fiscal year 1993 budget calls for eliminating over 4,000 federal projects and programs.
18. U.S. Senate, Committee on Environment and Public Works, *A Legislative History of the Comprehensive Environmental Response, Compensation, and Liability Act of 1980, Volume I*. Serial no. 97-14 (Washington, D.C.: Government Printing Office, 1983), 153.
19. U.S. Senate, *A Legislative History, Volume 2*, 288.
20. Forcing greater reductions would cost more in resources than the benefits of the cleaner air, while to do less (such as a free nonregulated market) would mean that environmental and health benefits in excess of costs were not being realized. A good introduction to environmental economics can be found in Tom Tietenberg, *Environmental and Natural Resources Economics*. 2d ed. (HarperCollins, 1988); a more advanced treatment is William J. Baumol and Wallace E. Oates, *The Theory of Environmental Policy*, 2d ed. (Cambridge: Cambridge University Press, 1988).
21. Probst and Portney, *Assigning Liability*, 28.
22. Personal interview, September 1991.
23. Love Canal is a celebrated example where the Hooker Chemical Company warned the local school board, which bought their property for $1, about the underground chemical wastes contained on the property. Nevertheless, although the board approved construction of a new school on the property, Hooker was ultimately held liable for the spread of contaminates. Landy, Roberts, and Thomas, *Environmental Protection Agency*, ch. 5.
24. Personal interview, September 1991.
25. Personal interview, August 1991.
26. Personal interview, September 1991.
27. See the testimony of F. Henry Habicht II, then assistant attorney general in the Justice Department, before the Senate Environment and Public Works Committee, "Insurance Issues and Superfund," Senate Hearing 99-61 (3 April 1985), 8, 13–14.
28. Ibid.
29. Keith Schneider, "Industries and Towns Clash over Who Pays to Tackle Toxic Waste," *New York Times*, 18 July 1991, A14.
30. Reported in Alfred R. Light, "A Defense Counsel's Perspective on Superfund," *Environmental Law Reporter* (July 1985): 10204. A different perspective can be found in Thomas S. Ulen, Mark A. Hester, and Gary V. Johnson, "Minnesota's Environmental Response and Liability Act: An Economic Justification," *Environmental Law Reporter* (April 1985): 10109–15.
31. The study's results were provided in the testimony of John C. Butler, III, *Insurance*

Issues and Superfund: Hearing Before the Committee on Environment and Public Works, U.S. Senate (3 April 1985), 118.

32. Jan Paul Acton and Lloyd S. Dixon, *Superfund and Transaction Costs: The Experience of Insurers and Very Large Industrial Firms* (Santa Monica, Calif.: RAND, 1992).

33. Representative Harsha, quoted in Carroll E. Dubuc and William D. Evans, Jr., "Recent Developments under CERCLA: Toward a More Equitable Distribution of Liability," *Environmental Law Reporter* (June 1987): 10198.

34. Buraff Publications, *Real Estate/Environmental Liability News*, Washington, D.C., undated.

35. Bill Roberts, forum contributor to "Who Should Pay?" *EPA Journal* (July/August 1991): 39.

36. Personal interview, September 1991.

37. Peter S. Menell, "The Limitations of Legal Institutions for Addressing Environmental Risks," *Journal of Economic Perspectives* 5 (Summer 1991): 93–113.

38. Personal interview, October 1991.

39. Robert M. Brandon, director of Citizens/Labor Energy Coalition, quoted in Stanfield, "Superfund Backers Push Big Expansion," 1766.

40. U.S. Office of Management and Budget, *Fiscal 1992 Budget*, 4–1013.

41. Douglas W. McNiel, Andrew W. Foshee, and Clark R. Burbee, "Superfund Taxes and Expenditures: Regional Redistributions," *Review of Regional Studies* (Winter 1988): 4–9.

42. Ibid., 8.

43. Jacques Steinberg, "A Mercury Cleanup Leaves Disruption and Fear," *New York Times*, 13 April 1993, B1.

44. Only about one-fourth of chemical industry output is sold as final goods to consumers, although sales by the industry end up in literally thousands of consumer products. Michael L. Dertouzos, Richard K. Lester, Robert M. Solow, and the MIT Commission on Industrial Productivity, *Made in America: Regaining the Productive Edge* (New York: HarperPerennial Edition, 1990), 189.

45. Probst and Portney, *Assigning Liability*, app. B and D.

46. Shrader-Frechette, *Risk and Rationality*, 120.

47. The study's author notes that "there appears to be no anticipation effect; consumers did not internalize the dangers until confronted with federal government documentation and ensuing publicity." Kohlhase, "Impact of Toxic Waste," 11. Other studies have found property value declines related to proximity to hazardous waste sites. See Kusum Ketkar, "Hazardous Waste Sites and Property Values in the State of New Jersey," *Applied Economics* (1992): 647–59.

48. For different perspectives on the latter point, see Kohlhase, "Impact of Toxic Waste," and Ketkar, "Hazardous Waste Sites."

49. Slovic, "Perception of Risk," 283.

50. Theodore J. Lowi, "Risks and Rights in the History of American Governments," *Daedalus* (Fall 1990): 18.

51. The county-level socioeconomic data are from the U.S. Census's *County and City Data Book, 1988* on CD-ROM. Superfund site data were provided by EPA.

52. *Superfund Week* (26 March 1993): 1.

53. This is not to minimize the contamination at Rye Brook, which will cost $2.2 million to remediate and has caused significant disruption to the lives of those affected; the site serves only as an example of geographically limited contamination. Steinberg, "Mercury Cleanup," *New York Times*, 13 April 1993, B1.

54. Because over 80 percent of counties do not contain any NPL sites, the dependent variable contains many zero observations; therefore, Tobit is the appropriate estimator, since estimating the model using ordinary least squares would produce inconsistent estimates and coefficients that are usually biased toward zero compared with the maximum likelihood estimator. The estimates reported are robust across different model specifications; ordered probit estimates were similar in direction and significance. William H. Greene, *Econometric Analysis* (New York: Macmillan), 729–30. Ordered probit results are available from the author on request. The statistical package Stata was used for estimation.

55. Because there are different ways to define "disproportionately" and "many," these two questions are distinct.

56. The averages for poverty, unemployment, median housing value, and percentage nonwhite are 9.04, 6.00, $56,887, and 12.11, respectively.

57. The average percentages for each category were: 9.41 for poverty, 6.40 for unemployment, 9.61 for nonwhites, and $48,369 was the median housing value. These are all significantly different from the county averages.

58. The t-statistics for these coefficients are -13.56 (poverty), -6.28 (unemployment), 15.67 (median housing value), and -2.84 (nonwhite), all of which indicate strong statistical significance. Negative values indicate an inverse correlation between the measure and the number of NPL sites in the county.

59. Kevin Phillips, *The Politics of Rich and Poor* (New York: Random House, 1990).

Chapter 6. How EPA Allocates Superfund's Resources

This chapter draws on my earlier article, "Superfund Expenditures and Cleanup Priorities: Distributive Politics or the Public Interest?" *Journal of Policy Analysis and Management* (Fall 1990): 455–83. Copyright 1990 by the Association for Public Policy Analysis and Management.

1. See, for example, Arthur Maass, *Muddy Waters: The Army Engineers and the Nation's Rivers* (Cambridge, MA: Harvard University Press, 1951); John A. Ferejohn, *Pork Barrel Politics: Rivers and Harbors Legislation, 1947–1968* (Stanford, Calif.: Stanford University Press, 1974); and John A. Hird, "The Political Economy of Pork: Project Selection at the U.S. Army Corps of Engineers," *American Political Science Review* (June 1991): 429–56.

2. Peter Kerr, "New Jersey Debate: Long on Quips, Loose on Facts," *New York Times*, 27 September 1989, B1.

3. CERCLA never directs the language to EPA specifically, but rather to the president, although the legislative history makes it clear that EPA was intended to carry out its provisions. President Carter issued an Executive Order giving Superfund responsibility to EPA in January 1981.

4. See *Federal Register*, vol. 55, no. 46, Thursday, 8 March 1990, pt. II, Environmental Protection Agency.

5. ARARs are a statutory requirement as well, under CERCLA section 121(d).

6. EPA's *Overview of ARARs* (Publication 9234.2-03/FS) lists the six possible waivers of ARARs, and examples of each.

7. 300.430(f)(1)(ii)(D).

8. For example, Senator Stafford of Vermont said that "such intangible or long-term benefits must be considered in weighing whether a particular response or cost is appropriate," but then added that in protecting the public health and welfare interests, "the President is not to be constrained by a rigid or inflexible construc-

tion of this language concerning cost effectiveness or considering costs or bene-
fits." (U.S. Senate Committee on Environment and Public Works, *A Legislative History of CERCLA, Volume 3*, Serial no. 97-14, 346.) However, Stafford's earlier comments to Senator Helms of North Carolina appear to advocate a cost-
benefit approach. Helms: "My concern is, first, that there be adequate direction
in the bill that under the contingency plan cost benefit analysis will be applied
to determine whether and when action should be taken to remove hazardous
substances or to remedy or otherwise respond to releases. . . ." Stafford's response: "The Senator is correct that considerations of the relationship between
the costs and the benefits of a particular response action are an essential part of
both the national contingency plan, to be developed under section 105, and the
selection of remedial and response actions under section 104. We intend that priorities be set for expenditures from the fund, and that such expenditures be made
in those situations which most present a threat. The fund should not be used to
clean up or remedy any and every discharge." (U.S. Senate Committee on Environment and Public Works, *A Legislative History of CERCLA, Volume 1*, Serial No.
97-14, 768.)

9. "Community" is broadly defined to include all interested parties, such as the affected locality and PRP's. See *Federal Register*, vol. 55, no. 46 (8 March 1990),
8723.

10. 300.430(e)(2)(i)(A). The proposed NCP defined acceptable exposure levels between 10^{-4} and 10^{-7}, but the latter figure was changed to 10^{-6} in the final version
of the rule.

11. Environmental Defense Fund, Hazardous Waste Treatment Council, National Audubon Society, National Wildlife Federation, Natural Resources Defense Council,
Sierra Club, and U.S. PIRG, *Right Train, Wrong Track*, (June 1988).

12. Grumbly, "Superfund: Candidly Speaking," 21.

13. Personal interview, October 1991.

14. Doty and Travis, "Superfund Remedial Action," 1535–43.

15. Ibid., 1538.

16. Ibid., 1543.

17. Shreekant Gupta, George Van Houtven, and Maureen L. Cropper, "Cleanup Decisions under Superfund: Do Benefits and Costs Matter?" *Resources* (Spring 1993):
13–17.

18. Those familiar with the Delphi technique will recognize that EPA's version is
highly "modified," in large part because those involved are not anonymous to the
others, and because the process is not iterative in the sense that a true Delphi
method would be. The process is more accurately described as a group of experts
hashing out a group consensus.

19. The concept of a "fair-share" was developed by Wildavsky for understanding
budgeting among several agencies, but it can be applied to several divisions or
units within an agency as well. See, most recently, Aaron Wildavsky, *The New Politics of the Budgetary Process*, 2d ed. (New York: HarperCollins, 1992), 87–
88.

20. At the time, the range was from 29 to 199 final NPL sites in each region.

21. Robert P. Inman, "Federal Assistance and Local Services in the United States: The
Evolution of a New Federalist Fiscal Order," pp. 33–74 in Harvey S. Rosen, ed.
Fiscal Federalism: Quantitative Studies (Chicago: University of Chicago Press,
1988), 51.

22. They include David R. Mayhew, *Congress: The Electoral Connection* (New Ha-

ven: Yale University Press, 1974); Morris P. Fiorina, *Congress: Keystone of the Washington Establishment* (New Haven: Yale University Press, 1977) and *Representatives, Constituencies, and Roll Calls* (Lexington, Mass.: Lexington, 1974); David A. Stockman, "The Social Pork Barrel," *The Public Interest* (Spring 1975): 3–30; R. Douglas Arnold, *Congress and the Bureaucracy: A Theory of Influence* (New Haven: Yale University Press, 1979); Barry R. Weingast, Kenneth A. Shepsle, and Christopher Johnsen, "The Political Economy of Benefits and Costs: A Neoclassical Approach to Distributive Politics," *Journal of Political Economy* (August 1981): 642–64; Barry R. Weingast and Mark J. Moran, "Bureaucratic Discretion or Congressional Control? Regulatory Policymaking by the Federal Trade Commission," *Journal of Political Economy* (October 1983): 765–800; and Bruce Bender, "An Analysis of Congressional Voting on Legislation Limiting Congressional Campaign Expenditures," *Journal of Political Economy* (October 1988): 1005–21. Other studies have, however, found relatively little congressional influence, including John R. Gist and R. Carter Hill, "Political and Economic Influences on the Bureaucratic Allocation of Federal Funds: The Case of Urban Development Action Grants," *Journal of Urban Economics* (September 1984): 158–72; and Michael J. Rich, "Distributive Politics and the Allocation of Federal Grants," *American Political Science Review* (March 1989): 193–213.

23. Fiorina, *Congress,* 1977, argues that the apparent decline in "marginal" districts (where the election outcome is likely to be close) is a result of legislators' increasing concerns with servicing their districts with pork and other favors as opposed to their stands on national issues. Excessive reliance on national issues, Fiorina claims, will produce marginal districts because "for every voter a congressman pleases by a [national] policy stand, he will displease someone else" (pp. 36–37). Obviously, this depends on the issue in question. For example, many legislators have taken strong stands on the abortion issue, a national issue that is bound to anger a number of constituents. This may be due in part, however, to a legislator's ability to target congressional mailings that stress certain issues to a subset of their constituency. See, for example, Hedrick Smith, *The Power Game: How Washington Works* (New York: Random House, 1988).

24. Randall L. Calvert, Mark J. Moran, and Barry R. Weingast, "Congressional Influence over Policy Making: The Case of the FTC," pp. 493–522 in Mathew D. McCubbins and Terry Sullivan, eds. *Congress: Structure and Policy* (Cambridge: Cambridge University Press, 1987).

25. On the whole, legislators' preferences probably reflect both political and public interest objectives. Legislators still may be preoccupied by reelection goals but, having sufficiently satisfied their constituencies, may pursue public objectives, which may include efficiency or equity in federal programs.

26. For example, suppose it is decided that another military base is necessary for national security, where national benefits exceed cost. Assume that it makes no difference strategically if it is located in South Dakota, Montana, North Dakota, or Idaho, and that each base could be constructed and maintained at equal cost. If the base is awarded to North Dakota because of a particularly influential legislator, should the outcome be characterized as pork? Past studies testing for pork implicitly accepted this condition as evidence of pork, even though there is no efficiency loss. (In this example, there was no efficiency loss by assumption. In previous research, efficiency has not been included in the attributes of the projects studied when testing for pork.) There may, however, be reasons involving equity for locating the project in one state or another, such as the needs of a particularly

depressed region. The problem of a political process replete with pork is not evident without the knowledge of the project's merits. Hird, "Political Economy of Pork," 1991.

27. Congressional appropriations and oversight committees provide one means by which legislators register their preference for projects beneficial to their constituency. Legislators can to some extent choose committee assignments that reflect constituency interests. (Kenneth A. Shepsle, *The Giant Jigsaw Puzzle: Democratic Committee Assignments in the Modern House* (Chicago: University of Chicago Press, 1978). Consequently, agriculture committees tend to be dominated by legislators from farming districts, merchant marine and fisheries committees by representatives of coastal districts, and so on. Under this interpretation, legislators select committee assignments (and indirectly projects) based on reelection goals and so choose committees they feel can provide the greatest net benefits to their districts, which improves their chances for reelection.

28. See, for example, Bernard Ashball, *The Senate Nobody Knows* (New York: Doubleday, 1978); and Elizabeth Drew, *Senator* (New York: Simon & Schuster, 1979). Of course legislators may pursue their careers to fulfill other desires as well, such as prestige and power that may be incorporated into a model of self-interest. For example, Anthony Downs notes: "Thus politicians in our model never seek office as a means of carrying out particular policies; their only goal is to reap the rewards of holding office *per se*. They treat policies purely as means to the attainment of their private ends, which they can reach only by being elected." Anthony Downs, *An Economic Theory of Democracy* (New York: Harper & Row, 1957), 28.

Steven Kelman argues that "Americans are split on the question of whether congressmen should vote their own best judgment or the opinion of the majority in the district," and cites survey findings that between one-third and one-half of people think legislators should vote their own judgment. Steven Kelman, *Making Public Policy: A Hopeful View of American Government* (New York: Basic Books, 1987), 61–62. Kelman presumably views the legislators' best judgment as distinct from their interest in being reelected. Kelman notes as further evidence of a lack of congressional interest in pork that the most sought after committees are those dealing with broad national issues, which do not normally include public works projects.

29. Ferejohn, *Pork Barrel Politics*.

30. See Arnold, *Congress and the Bureaucracy*, 81–91 for a discussion of other problems in Ferejohn's analysis.

31. Starting with Arnold.

32. Calvert, Moran, and Weingast, "Congressional Influence," 496.

33. For example, Rich, "Distributive Politics." Arnold does mention the possibility of doing so (*Congress and the Bureaucracy*, 89), but appropriate data were apparently unavailable for his empirical studies. This problem, the paucity of observable decisions that incorporate explicit measures of social merit, clearly limits the model's applicability to a wide variety of policy applications. However, creative ways can be found to incorporate, if not explicit cost-benefit analyses, then at least some approximation of the project's social merit.

34. Some studies have employed variables measuring the economic characteristics of the region, but not the economic impact of the project itself. For example, economist Robert Crandall employs a logistic model to test the effects of local pollution and economic conditions on congressional voting patterns concerning environmental policy issues. (Crandall, *Controlling Industrial Pollution*, ch. 7.) He in-

cludes a number of measures of the regional characteristics, including income, income growth, percentage of "natural lands," and water and air pollution variables. His argument that "rapidly growing states with large amounts of federal lands send representatives to Washington who vote against major environmental measures" (p. 117) would be more persuasive had the economic impacts on each of the states of the various legislative proposals been included explicitly in his model (e.g., the efficiency and equity consequences). (Crandall also acknowledges the potential importance of other determinants of congressional voting. Ibid., 119, 121.) In all fairness, however, such variables are used in the many instances where a program's geographic benefits and costs are not estimated and where, in Crandall's case, the impacts are broadly known (in this case, to benefit eastern states with high-sulfur coal at the expense of low-sulfur coal western states).

35. For an insightful critique of studies claiming to find congressional influence, see Terry M. Moe, "An Assessment of the Positive Theory of 'Congressional Dominance,' " *Legislative Studies Quarterly* (November 1987): 475–520.

36. See, for example, Ferejohn, *Pork Barrel Politics.*

37. This distinction is made in greater detail in Hird, "Political Economy of Pork."

38. See, for example, Stockman, "Social Pork Barrel."

39. Fiorina, *Congress: Keystone.*

40. Bruce Yandle, *Political Limits*, 119.

41. Anne M. Burford with John Greenya, *Are You Tough Enough?* (New York: McGraw-Hill, 1986), 107.

42. By far the largest component of Superfund receipts is derived from excise taxes on petroleum and chemical products. Between fiscal years 1981 and 1989, excise taxes were on average about two-thirds of Superfund receipts, while general revenues represented less than 10 percent. SARA dramatically increased the excise taxes on petroleum (from 0.79 cents to 8.2 cents per barrel of domestic and 11.7 cents per barrel of imported petroleum) and slightly increased the taxes on feedstock chemicals (Section 201). In addition, an environmental tax on corporate alternative minimum taxable income was added under SARA. As a result, annual excise tax revenues tripled between fiscal years 1985 and 1987, from $270 million to over $830 million, and rising by 1989 to almost $1.2 billion.

43. Landy, "Cleaning up Superfund," 58–71.

44. Personal interview, July 1991.

45. Indeed, one interviewee told of a small consulting firm started up by two former MITRE (the firm that developed and implements the HRS) employees that advises states and private parties how to keep their sites off the NPL. One technique is to perform limited site cleanups to ensure that the HRS score will be below 28.5 and therefore will not qualify for the NPL. If the HRS score were risk-based, this might encourage good public policy, since firms would see it in their self-interest to clean up the site when marginal social benefits exceed cleanup costs. Because this is not the case, the limited cleanups are inefficient either because cleanup costs are still too high relative to risks or because the sites are not sufficiently remediated although they score below 28.5.

46. For example, by early 1989, eighteen Alternative Remedial Contracts Strategy awards were made for a total of $2.7 billion over a ten-year period, and five remedial planning contracts had been awarded for over $600 million for four- to five-year periods. The three largest firms receiving these contracts accounted for nearly 50 percent of the total $3.3 billion awarded, with the top nine firms receiving 85 percent.

47. This formulation of legislative incentives should not be confused with Pitney's term "bile barrel politics." Pitney was referring to siting new facilities that impose large costs on localities for the benefit of the larger public, such as prisons, nerve gas facilities, and the like. John J. Pitney, Jr., "Bile-Barrel Politics: Siting Unwanted Facilities," *Journal of Policy Analysis and Management* (Spring 1984): 446–48. This type of distributive politics differs, however, in that the localities are trying to receive federal assistance to clean up an existing site, rather than prohibiting its introduction to the region.

48. Milton R. Copulos, "Why the Superfund Pork Barrel Deserves a Veto," (Washington, D.C.: The Heritage Foundation, 9 October 1986), Executive memorandum #136, partially reprinted in Lewis K. Uhler, *Setting Limits: Constitutional Control of Government* (Washington, D.C., Regnery Gateway, 1989), 73.

49. See Hird, "Superfund Expenditures," table 1 for estimation results.

50. Another way to determine empirically whether Congress influenced agency behavior is to examine changes in the relevant committee assignments and link them with changes in agency behavior. This methodology is difficult to employ with the Superfund program both because it is so new and (not unrelated) because there was little change in the composition of the Superfund subcommittees between 1981 and 1989. The changes that have been made in subcommittee chairs have been as much a result of majority party shifts in the Senate as changes within parties.

51. See, for examples, Maass, "Muddy Waters"; Robert H. Haveman, *Water Resource Investment and the Public Interest* (Nashville: Vanderbilt University Press, 1965); Elizabeth Drew, "Dam Outrage: The Story of the Army Engineers," *Atlantic* (April 1970): 51–62; and Daniel A. Mazmanian and Jeanne Nienaber, *Can Organizations Change? Environmental Protection, Citizen Participation, and the Corps of Engineers* (Washington, D.C.: The Brookings Institution, 1979).

52. Eight sites from Puerto Rico were not included in the statistical analysis because of Puerto Rico's unique national political representation. Missing data for three sites reduced those evaluated to 788.

53. The pathways include air, groundwater, and surface water. Although the biases in these scores were noted in chapter 4, they still represent the most consistent and objective measure of the impact of Superfund sites on the affected population. As mentioned earlier, the scores measure not only toxicity, but potential population exposure as well. Measures of the economic benefits and costs of site cleanup, the number of people affected by the hazard, and the toxicity of the material would improve the empirical representation of the public benefit (B). However, because benefit-cost calculations are not required for NPL sites, the HRS scores most closely represent the relevant considerations.

54. The Senate subcommittees dealing chiefly with Superfund are the Appropriations Subcommittee on HUD and Independent Agencies, and the Environment and Public Works Subcommittee on Superfund and Environmental Oversight. On the House side, the subcommittees are the Appropriations Subcommittee on HUD and Independent Agencies, and the Energy and Commerce Subcommittee on Transportation, Tourism, and Hazardous Materials. The names of certain subcommittees changed slightly over the three terms in question.

Since the primary congressional influence over site cleanup priorities could have extended over three congressional terms (1983–84, 1985–86, 1987–88), the number of representatives serving on the relevant Superfund committees over the three terms was aggregated into one variable. For instance, if one representative from the site's district served on the relevant subcommittee for all three terms, the variable would be coded 3. Thus, unit increments in the congressional variables represent not just the addition of one committee member, but one member for one term. While this makes modeling simpler, it should be noted that, at least theoretically, the impact of a key representative serving for one term may be diluted by the averaging involved. However because in this case the committee membership was relatively stable over the three terms, intertemporal variation should not be significant.

55. This follows political scientist Douglas Arnold's research.

56. Admittedly, better measures probably are available to measure the degree of local political demand for site cleanup. One such variable may be the degree of media coverage the site receives. However, since national indices are available for only a handful of newspapers and televisions stations, these indicators would be skewed toward major metropolitan areas and only the most nationally prominent sites (such as Love Canal, Times Beach, and Stringfellow).

57. Although the algorithm supposedly factors the affected population into the HRS scores, because of the uncertain relationship between population and HRS scores established above, I also tested the model with a variable for population density. In each case, the coefficient was insignificant and had only a negligible impact on the other estimated coefficients.

58. The R^2 for the regression with 400 observations (between 1984 and 1987) was 0.523. The specific estimation results are available from the author.

59. Independent analyses showed that the separate HRS pathway scores better explained the variation in both expenditures and planned obligations than did the composite HRS score, and better than first derivatives of HRS scores with respect to each pathway. Decision makers may have been taking into account (either implicitly or explicitly) the biases inherent in calculating the total HRS score by placing varying emphasis on each of the pathways.

60. Various specifications, including only the subcommittee chairs, House and Senate leadership positions (e.g., majority leaders), and full appropriations and authorization committee membership, turned up no significant congressional committee influence over either past expenditures or future planned obligations.

61. The specific results are available from the author. There were 194 observations, with an R^2 of 0.206.

62. Each additional point in the surface water pathway score was associated with an increase in approximately $203,000 in cleanup costs. The influence of the groundwater pathway was significant at the 99+% level of confidence and was associated with an increase of about $101,000 in ROD costs. The air pathway was statistically significant at only the 90% level ($t=1.89$), and contributed about $88,000 for each point increase.

63. The ordered probit model was used because it assesses qualitative differences between different stages reached in the cleanup process, and because it could model the entire process—all three cleanup stages—jointly. The empirical estimates provided by the ordered probit model are similar in sign and significance to separate binary logit and probit estimates for each stage (available from the author), so the coefficients are robust across different model specifications. Data limitations and the unique structural features of this process precluded modeling the process as a survival or proportional hazards model. The principal data limitation is that the length of time between each stage of the process is unknown, so the dependent variable in survival models, the duration of time in the queue, could

not be specified. Importantly, sites do not enter the process at the same time (i.e., they are added to the NPL in different years), so even if the duration were available, it would represent different starting periods for each site.

64. It should be noted that the interpretation of ordered probit results is not straightforward. Unlike binomial logit or probit, increases in an independent variable (where the coefficient is positive) signify only that the probability of the dependent variable being zero is diminished, and the probability of the dependent variable with the highest value (in this case, 3) has increased. Marginal changes for intermediate steps (in this case, the probability of a site reaching stage 1 or stage 2) are ambiguous. See Greene, *Econometric Analysis*, 705.

65. These estimation results are available from the author.

66. This hypothesis was suggested to me in an interview with a former EPA official, John Campbell.

67. A series of J-tests was used to determine which of the two independent models, public interest or distributive politics, better fit the Superfund data for each of the dependent variables analyzed in table 6.1. The distributive politics model (H_0) included the four congressional committee assignments, as well as the control variables, while the public interest model (H_1) included the three HRS pathway scores plus the income variable representing equity. (Said another way, the distributive politics model was identical to those estimated in table 6.1 except that the HRS scores and income variable were omitted, while the congressional committee variables were omitted for the public interest model.) To conduct the J-test, the decision on whether or not a remedial action had started on the site, for example, was regressed (using logit analysis) on the distributive politics model, and the predicted probabilities saved. Then, the same dependent variable was regressed on the public interest model with the predicted probabilities included from the distributive politics regression. In each case, the coefficient on the predicted probabilities variable was not significantly different from zero, implying that the distributive politics model did not add explanatory power to the public interest model (could not reject H_1). The procedure then was reversed, and the t-statistic on the public interest predicted probabilities allowed the rejection of H_0, the distributive politics model. In each case, the public interest model dominated the distributive politics model.

68. Personal interview, September 1991.

69. This hypothesis (of Florio directing resources to his district) was rejected by using a dummy variable for Florio's first district in New Jersey; the results are available from the author.

Chapter 7. Why Have Legislators Voted to Expand Superfund?

This chapter is drawn from my "Congressional Voting on Superfund: Self-Interest or Ideology?" *Public Choice* 77 (1993): 333–57. By permission of Kluwer Academic Publishers.

1. An alternative perspective on pork that illuminates its potential benefits is provided in Ellwood and Patashnik, "In Praise of Pork," 19–33.

2. Weingast, Shepsle, and Johnsen, "Political Economy of Benefits and Costs," 642–64.

3. A more comprehensive review can be found in Arnold, *Congress and the Bureaucracy*; Calvert, Moran, and Weingast, "Congressional Influence," pp. 493–522 in McCubbins and Sullivan, eds. *Congress: Structure and Policy*. See Terry M. Moe,

"The Politics of Bureaucratic Structure," pp. 267–329 in John E. Chubb and Paul E. Peterson, eds. *Can the Government Govern?* (Washington, D.C.: The Brookings Institution, 1989) for an indictment of the view that government behavior is explained by congressional self-interest. See Sam Peltzman, "The Economic Theory of Regulation after a Decade of Deregulation," pp. 1–41 in Martin Neil Baily and Clifford Winston, eds., *Brookings Papers on Economic Activity: Microeconomics* (Washington, D.C.: The Brookings Institution, 1989) for a defense of self-interest in federal regulation. Jane J. Mansbridge, ed. *Beyond Self-Interest* (Chicago: University of Chicago Press, 1990) provides critiques and alternative models to strict self-interest in a variety of fields.

4. Bender, "Analysis of Congressional Voting," 1005–21.
5. Ibid., 1016.
6. See, for example, Larry Sabato, "Real and Imagined Corruption in Campaign Financing," pp. 155–79 in A. James Reichley, ed. *Elections American Style* (Washington, D.C.: The Brookings Institution, 1987) and Norman Ornstein, "The Permanent Democratic Congress," *The Public Interest* 100 (Summer 1990): 24–44.
7. Logrolling plagues the second approach outlined below as well.
8. However, it should be noted that other social scientists, notably economists, frequently invoke separability assumptions built into demand equations, e.g., that the price of automobiles has an insignificant effect on the demand for wood products. Thus, it is not unusual that political scientists would apply similar assumptions in analyzing the behavior of legislators as economists do with consumers.
9. Kau and Rubin attempt to incorporate the effects of logrolling in their analysis, assuming that its effects will be evidenced in other roll-call votes. James B. Kau and Paul H. Rubin, "Self-Interest, Ideology, and Logrolling in Congressional Voting," *Journal of Law and Economics* (October 1979): 365–84.
10. Joseph P. Kalt and Mark A. Zupan, "Capture and Ideology in the Economic Theory of Politics," *American Economic Review* (June 1984): 279–300.
11. Kau and Rubin, "Self-Interest."
12. These include Ackerman and Hassler, *Clean Coal, Dirty Air*; Crandall, *Controlling Industrial Pollution*; several examples cited in Yandle, *Political Limits*; and Peter Pashigian, "Environmental Regulation: Whose Self-Interests Are Being Protected?" *Economic Inquiry* 23 (October 1985): 551–84.
13. Kau and Rubin, "Self-Interest"; Kalt and Zupan, "Capture and Ideology"; and Joseph P. Kalt and Mark A. Zupan, "The Apparent Ideological Behavior of Legislators: Testing for Principal-Agent Slack in Political Institutions," *Journal of Law and Economics* 33 (April 1990): 103–31.
14. Sam Peltzman, "Constituent Interest and Congressional Voting," *Journal of Law and Economics* 27 (April 1984): 181–210.
15. Kalt and Zupan, "Capture and Ideology," 1990.
16. As in many studies, data on the means are substituted for data on medians, in large part because the former is far more commonly reported.
17. Results for other years are not printed here due to space constraints but are available from the author on request.
18. In doing so, the multicollinearity problems inherent in the simple ideology measure as an explanatory variable of roll-call votes should be eliminated.
19. Several lopsided votes were not analyzed because the distinctions between legislators' attributes and their voting patterns could not be uncovered statistically. "Lopsided" here is defined roughly as 90 percent or more of votes in one direction.

The definition still allows the inclusion of votes that were not particularly close (Senate votes 1 and 2).

20. HRS scores are not used in place of the number of sites in each district for two primary reasons. First, there is no straightforward way to aggregate HRS scores across sites. For example, if in a legislator's district there are 4 sites with HRS scores of 20, 45, 65, and 80, what is the appropriate aggregate measure? The mean? Median? Highest or lowest score? Capturing this in one variable is potentially misleading. Second, and more importantly, the implicit assumption, that all sites have the same "scores" and are thus weighted (counted) uniformly, is far more reasonable politically. The pressure exerted on a legislator to help constituents clean up a Superfund site is for the most part irrespective of the HRS score, and has more to do with the ability of residents to organize effectively, their general level of environmental awareness, and so on. A well-publicized abandoned hazardous waste dump in a legislator's district is no less politically palpable because its HRS score is 35 rather than 60. Residents' demands for action for the most part contradict the opinions of risk experts who contend that risks are small in the first place. Thus, the number of sites in the district or state better represents the political motivation than would HRS scores.

21. Kingdon offers four reasons for legislators from the same state voting in concert. First, the representative may simply know other state representatives better and may place greater trust in them. Second, a state's interest may be involved, in this case groundwater contamination, which may affect multiple districts. Third, a strong state delegation may aid the legislator's bargaining position in intra-House disputes. Finally, it may be particularly useful in constituency relations, especially in explaining one's voting record; a "solid" delegation may induce opponents to restrain their criticism. John W. Kingdon, *Congressmen's Voting Decisions* (Ann Arbor: University of Michigan Press, 1973).

In addition, former Representative Florio from New Jersey provides a good example of a legislator trying to expand his appeal from his district to the state. Even though Florio is widely credited with being the "father" of Superfund, evidence suggests that he did not direct cleanup resources disproportionately to his district. Instead, he was able to expand his appeal beyond his district by being a visible proponent of a program important to New Jersey voters. His documented claim as an environmentalist was an important ingredient in his successful bid for state governor.

22. I want to thank Mark Zupan for kindly providing me with these data.

23. Multicollinearity problems were relatively insignificant for nearly all linear relationships (i.e., $\rho < = 0.40$). The exceptions include: "pure" liberal and environmental ideology scores were positively correlated for both the Senate ($\rho = 0.48$) and the House ($\rho = 0.44$), and environmental interests were negatively correlated with Southern states ($\rho = -0.56$) and the share of the state's economy devoted to chemical industries ($\rho = -0.46$). In addition, the number of sites in the state is positively correlated with population density ($\rho = 0.48$), and a state's net hazardous waste production is positively correlated with Southern states.

24. It should be noted up front that the correlations noted below do not necessarily confirm the behavioral assumptions underlying the specification of the model.

25. The statistical confidence in the number of sites in the district is weaker than that in the state, however.

26. These results are available from the author on request.

27. It should be noted that the model overall is by far the least effective in explaining the variation in House vote 3, with a likelihood ratio statistic (0.294) less than half that of any other vote (in either chamber).

28. The data were simply stacked on top of each other, with the dependent variable representing the sum of the three pooled votes (with 1 designating a vote to support Superfund expansion, and 0 otherwise).

29. See Peter Kennedy, *A Guide to Econometrics*, 2d ed. (Cambridge, Mass.: MIT Press, 1985) for a more thorough explanation of the technique.

30. The individual logit results and J-tests are available from the author by request.

Chapter 8. The Political Rationality of Superfund

1. Some in industry also fear, however, that a wide-ranging public discussion of the program could lead to still higher taxes.

2. This *can* be viewed as self-interested, since removing the waste would add the possibility of additional exposure during transport, the possibility of an accident, etc. However, many local residents also believe that the waste should not be dumped on some unsuspecting town, similar to the position they find themselves in. See Lois Marie Gibbs, *Love Canal: My Story* (Albany: State University of New York Press, 1982).

3. See, for example, the *Lautenberg-Durenberger Report*.

4. There are, of course, more specific problems with the program, such as the lack of adequately trained EPA personnel managing site cleanups. These problems, while significant, derive from the more fundamental problems outlined above.

5. *Congressional Record*, 19 September 1980.

6. *Congressional Record*, 24 November 1980.

7. Ibid.

8. Ibid.

9. *Congressional Record*, 23 September 1980.

10. Ibid.

11. *Congressional Record*, 24 November 1980.

12. Ibid.

13. Testimony of Thomas C. Jorling, Assistant Administrator, Water and Waste Management, Environmental Protection Agency, Before the Subcommittees on Environmental Pollution and Resource Protection, Committee on Environment and Public Works, U.S. Senate (20 June 1979). (Written responses to questions by Senator Stafford.) Prepared statement of Thomas C. Jorling before the same committee.

14. Statement of Senator Culver, Introducing S. 1480. *Congressional Record*, 11 July 1979.

15. Jorling testimony. Written response to question of Senator Stafford.

16. Jorling testimony. Written response to question of Senator Culver.

17. Personal interview, Spring 1990.

18. *Congressional Record*, 24 November 1980.

19. Senate Report no. 96-848; Environmental Emergency Response Act, Report of the Committee on Environment and Public Works, U.S. Senate (Government Printing Office, Washington, D.C.: 11 July 1980), 119–20.

20. *Congressional Record*, 19 September 1980.

21. Senate Report no. 96-848, 118.

22. *Congressional Record*, 19 September 1980.

23. *Congressional Record*, 23 September 1980.

24. This view was shared by most of the individuals I interviewed for this project.
25. Jorling testimony, prepared statement.
26. Ibid.
27. *Congressional Record*, 24 November 1980.
28. *Congressional Record*, 3 December 1980.
29. Ibid.
30. Ibid.
31. Senator Mitchell stated publicly that the threat of a filibuster came from opponents of S.1480. *Congressional Record*, 24 November 1980.
32. National Research Council, *Environmental Epidemiology.*
33. Ibid, 7.
34. Personal interview.
35. Quoted in Burke, "Booming Business," 41.
36. The transaction cost share is a statistically significant 34 percentage points lower for single-PRP sites than for multiple-PRP sites. Acton and Dixon, *Superfund and Transaction Costs*, 52.
37. Ibid.
38. Eugene R. Anderson and Robert M. Horkovich, "Why Insurance Companies Say No," *New York Times*, 3 May 1992, F13.
39. Richard K. Schoepperle, "A Hole in Their Argument," Letters, *New York Times*, 17 May 1992, F11.
40. For the 29 sites evaluated as a test for the proposed HRS scoring, EPA concludes "site scores were generally higher under the proposed HRS than under the current HRS. Only two sites scored 51 or above under the current HRS; 16 scored 51 or above under the proposed HRS." U.S. Environmental Protection Agency, *Field Test of the Proposed Revised Hazard Ranking System (HRS)*, EPA/540/P-90/001 (Washington, D.C., May 1990), 6–12.
41. The HRS is not intended to prioritize cleanups, but only to determine eligibility for the NPL.
42. U.S. General Accounting Office, *EPA's Inventory of Potential Hazardous Waste Sites Is Incomplete* (Washington, D.C., 26 March 1985).
43. "An Interview with Don Clay," *EPA Journal* (July/August 1991): 15.
44. Ibid.
45. Quoted in Burke, "Booming Business," 40.
46. See Grumbly, "Superfund: Candidly Speaking," 19–22.
47. Ibid., 21.
48. Gibbs, *Love Canal*, 106.
49. *Congressional Record*, 19 September 1980.
50. *Congressional Record*, 23 September 1980.
51. Ibid.
52. Jorling testimony.
53. *Congressional Record*, 19 September 1980.
54. *Congressional Record*, 23 September 1980.
55. *Congressional Record*, 18 September 1980.
56. *Congressional Record*, 19 September 1980.
57. *Congressional Record*, 23 September 1980.
58. Jorling testimony, prepared statement.
59. Senate Report No. 96-848; Environmental Emergency Response Act, Report of the Committee on Environment and Public Works, U.S. Senate (Washington, D.C.: U.S. Government Printing Office, 11 July 1980), 71–72.

60. Grumbly, "Superfund: Candidly Speaking," 20.
61. See John J. Lyons, "Deep Pockets and CERCLA: Should Superfund Liability Be Abolished?" *Stanford Environmental Law Journal* (1986–87): 271–344, for a discussion of the political obstacles to broadening CERCLA's tax base and eliminating the liability scheme.
62. *San Francisco Chronicle*, "Toxic Cleanup a Bonanza for the Legal Profession," 29 May 1991, A4.
63. Ibid.
64. Personal interview, October 1991.
65. See McClelland, Schulze, and Hurd, "Effect of Risk Beliefs," 495.
66. Glenn Paulson, *The Goals and Indicators of Progress in Superfund: Report I-1, The Goals of Superfund*, submitted to the Coalition on Superfund (Illinois Institute of Technology, September 1989), 7.
67. Quoted in William Greider, *Who Will Tell the People* (New York: Simon and Schuster, 1992), 56.
68. Dietz and Rycroft, *The Risk Professionals*.
69. Waste Management Research and Education Institute, *The Superfund Process: Site-Level Experience* (Knoxville: University of Tennessee, December 1991).
70. Gibbs, *Love Canal*, 148.
71. "Questions the Public Is Asking: An Interview With Don Clay," *EPA Journal* (July/August 1991): 17.
72. Personal interview, September 1991.
73. Lew Crampton, quoted in Burke "Booming Business," 42.
74. Quoted in Burke, "Booming Business," 43.
75. Personal interview, October 1991.
76. Personal interview.
77. Personal interview, November 1991.
78. Personal interview, October 1991.
79. Grumbly, "Superfund: Candidly Speaking," 22.
80. Amy Saltzman, "Good Jobs Are Going to Waste," *U.S. News & World Report* (12 September 1988): 70.
81. Ibid.
82. This is also mentioned on the House floor by Representative Rinaldo of New Jersey, *Congressional Record*, 19 September 1980.
83. Personal interview, June 1990.
84. Personal interview, September 1991.
85. Linda Greer, formerly of EDF, quoted in Stanfield, "Superfund Backers Push Big Expansion," 1765.
86. Personal interview, June 1990.
87. *Congressional Record*, 19 September 1980.
88. There is, however, some doubt as to the severity of the health impacts even at the much-publicized Love Canal site. See Landy, Roberts, and Thomas, *The Environmental Protection Agency*, chap. 5.
89. Personal interview, October 1991.
90. Personal interview, November 1991.
91. Personal interview, September 1991.
92. Personal interview, Spring 1990.
93. Landy, Roberts, and Thomas, *The Environmental Protection Agency*.
94. Robert M. Brandon, director of Citizens/Labor Energy Coalition, quoted in Stanfield, "Superfund Backers Push Big Expansion," 1763.

95. Quoted in Stanfield, "Superfund Backers Push Big Expansion," 1762.
96. John T. O'Connor, National Campaign Against Toxic Hazards, quoted in Stanfield, "Superfund Backers Push Big Expansion," 1763–64.
97. Personal interview, June 1990.
98. Greider, *Who Will Tell the People*, 42.
99. EPA officials, however, argue that only minor delays are caused by PRP-financed cleanups. Personal interview, October 1991.
100. Joel D. Aberbach, *Keeping a Watchful Eye: The Politics of Congressional Oversight* (Washington, D.C.: The Brookings Institution, 1990), 201.
101. Ibid., 199.
102. Ibid., 198.
103. Calvert, Moran, and Weingast, "Congressional Influence," pp. 493–522 in McCubbins and Sullivan, eds. *Congress: Structure and Policy.*
104. R. Douglas Arnold, "Legislators, Bureaucrats, and Locational Decisions," pp. 523–548 in McCubbins and Sullivan, eds. *Congress: Structure and Policy.*
105. On this general point, see Fiorina, *Congress: Keystone of the Washington Establishment.*
106. Personal interview, October 1991.
107. Personal interview, October 1991.
108. Section 105(8)(B).
109. *Congressional Record*, 23 September 1980.
110. Cleveland also tellingly states that his amendment stems from his experiences on the House Public Works and Transportation Committee, which is notorious for pork-barrel politics: "When we have programs such as this, we always tried to have each State qualify for at least a part of the program." *Congressional Record*, 23 September 1980. It comes as no surprise to political scientists that the effort to spread resources widely is not unique to Superfund.
111. *Congressional Record*, 24 November 1980.
112. *Congressional Record*, 23 September 1980.
113. See R. Douglas Arnold, "Legislators," 542.
114. Landy, Roberts, and Thomas, *The Environmental Protection Agency*, 1990.
115. *Time* (22 September 1980): 58.
116. Jorling testimony, prepared statement.
117. Jorling testimony.
118. Jorling testimony.
119. Jorling was particularly careful to mention that the Chairman's state (Iowa) had a particularly noxious waste site. Jorling testimony.
120. The states are, in descending order, New Jersey, Pennsylvania, California, New York, Michigan, and Florida.
121. *Congressional Record*, 24 November 1980.
122. While it is a positive correlation, it is not statistically significant at normal confidence levels. Simple regression estimates yield the following results: (# NPL sites) = 13.26 + 0.00047 (hazardous waste)(t = 1.74). The adjusted R^2 is just 0.04.
123. *Congressional Record*, 10 December 1979.
124. Ibid.
125. *Congressional Record*, 24 November 1980.
126. Section 211.
127. *Congressional Record*, 30 September 1980.
128. *Congressional Record*, 19 September 1980.

129. Ibid.

130. Ibid.

131. Robert D. Behn, "Policy Analysis and Policy Politics," *Policy Analysis* (1981).

132. Slovic, "Perception of Risk."

133. Peter M. Sandman, "Two-Way Environmental Education," *EPA Journal* (September/October 1991): 39–41.

134. Mark Sagoff, Forum contributor to "Should We Set Priorities Based on Risk Analysis?" *EPA Journal* (March/April 1991): 30.

135. R. Douglas Arnold, *The Logic of Congressional Action* (New Haven: Yale University Press, 1991).

136. See, generally, Greider, *Who Will Tell the People.*

Chapter 9. Reforming Superfund

1. Personal interview, October 1991.

2. Sandman, "Two-Way Environmental Education."

3. As of the fall of 1992.

4. Personal interview, October 1991.

5. Personal interview, October 1991.

6. Personal interview, October 1991.

7. Alice M. Rivlin, *Reviving the American Dream* (Washington, D.C.: The Brookings Institution, 1992).

8. Edward M. Gramlich, "The Economics of Fiscal Federalism and Its Reform," pp. 152–74 in Thomas R. Schwartz and John E. Peck, eds., *The Changing Face of Fiscal Federalism* (Armonk, N.Y.: M. E. Sharpe, 1990).

9. Al Gore, *Earth in the Balance: Ecology and the Human Spirit* (Boston: Houghton Mifflin, 1992), 7.

10. In his classic article, Charles Tiebout showed that under some fairly restrictive conditions, such as costless migration and sufficient variation in services and prices, local government variations could yield an efficient allocation of public goods. "A Pure Theory of Local Expenditures," *Journal of Political Economy* (October 1956): 416–24.

11. John H. Cumberland, "Efficiency and Equity in Interregional Environmental Management," *The Review of Regional Studies* (1980): 1–9.

12. John Holusha, "Some Corporations Plead for the Firm Hand of Uncle Sam," *New York Times*, 24 February 1991, E6.

13. Robert Hanley, "Superfund Sites Lose New Jersey Priority," *New York Times*, 7 November 1989, B1. Naturally, Daggett's comments are made in the context of a large federal Superfund program and a relatively small federal radon program, so his comments do not necessarily imply that more money should be spent on Superfund than radon, air toxics, etc. Nevertheless, the environmental representative for the state hardest hit by hazardous waste problems at a minimum appears to believe that any *additional* money would be better spent elsewhere, implying that Superfund should not be expanded before several other programs.

14. "Maryland Refuses to Fund Largest NPL Site," *Superfund* (Arlington, Va.: Pasha Publications, 15 May 1992), 3.

15. Personal interview, October 1991.

16. More detailed information is available from the author on request.

17. Representative Downey of New York, *Congressional Record*, 23 September 1980.

18. Representative LaFalce of New York, *Congressional Record*, 23 September 1980.

19. *Congressional Record*, 24 November 1980.

20. *Congressional Record*, 23 September 1980.
21. Ibid.
22. Ibid.
23. Ibid.
24. *Congressional Record*, 19 September 1980.
25. *Congressional Record*, 23 September 1980.
26. Combined state surpluses rose through the mid-1980s, while federal deficits rose substantially over the same period. *Economic Report of the President* (Washington, D.C.: Government Printing Office, February 1992), 389. Many state surpluses evaporated by the early 1990s, however.
27. *Congressional Record*, 23 September 1980.
28. Ibid.
29. *Congressional Record*, 3 December 1980.
30. *Congressional Record*, 23 September 1980.
31. *Congressional Record*, 24 November 1980.
32. Personal interview, June 1990. Although it can be argued that these regulatory impacts should be incorporated into RCRA, until then Superfund's liability scheme continues, albeit crudely, to check hazardous waste disposal abuses. As it now stands, RCRA corrective actions apply only to current *owners* of landfills. Generators and transporters are not included, so the added incentive to monitor the disposal or hazardous wastes is removed.
33. According to an EPA/RFF survey, about 52 percent (369/708) of sites were closed prior to 1981; 52 percent of the roughly 1200 current NPL sites equals approximately 620 sites. Probst and Portney, *Assigning Liability*, 28.
34. "Questions the Public Is Asking: An Interview With Don Clay," *EPA Journal* (July/August 1991): 17.
35. Quoted in "U.S. Calls 15 Stratford Sites Hazards," *New York Times*, 28 May 1993, B6.
36. This figure is the lower end of a range of estimates in the testimony of John C. Butler III. *Insurance Issues and Superfund: Hearing Before the Committee on Environment and Public Works*, U.S. Senate (3 April 1985), 118. The RAND study results put transactions costs significantly higher than 24 percent of total costs.
37. Approximately 1200 NPL sites times 52 percent (see Probst and Portney, *Assigning Liability*).
38. For a discussion, see Office of Technology Assessment, *Coming Clean*, chap. 2.
39. This is a position advocated by Thomas P. Grumbly, "Superfund."
40. This is, at least, the view of some state officials interviewed.
41. Personal interview.
42. Probst and Portney, *Assigning Liability*, 38.
43. Gore, *Earth in the Balance*, 37.
44. Personal interview.
45. See Fiorina, *Congress: Keystone of the Washington Establishment*.
46. Jack Clough, "A Legislative Perspective on an Integrated Waste Management Strategy," pp. 317–26 in Kunreuther and Gowda, eds. *Integrating Insurance*, 324.
47. Personal interview, October 1991.
48. Personal interview, October 1991.
49. Quoted in David E. Rosenbaum, "President Presses Business Leaders on Tax-Rise Plan," *New York Times*, 12 February 1993, A24.
50. Schneider, "How a Rebellion."
51. Quoted in Schneider, "How a Rebellion."

52. Quoted in Martin Tolchin, "White House Reassures Hard-Pressed Governors," *New York Times*, 3 February 1991, 18.
53. Peter H. Stone, "From the K Street Corridor," *National Journal* (27 February 1993): 524.
54. Personal interview, October 1991.
55. Personal interview, July 1991.
56. Quoted in Austin, "Superfund: New Leadership," 48.
57. For a discussion of the advantages of cooperationist institutions, see Steven Kelman, "Adversary and Cooperationist Institutions for Conflict Resolution in Public Policymaking," *Journal of Policy Analysis and Management* (Spring 1992): 178–206.
58. Laurence E. Lynn, Jr., Review in *Journal of Policy Analysis and Management* (Winter 1992): 137.
59. Personal interview, October 1991.
60. Quoted in Theodore Roszak, "Green Guilt and Ecological Overload," *New York Times* (op-ed), 9 June 1992, A27.

Acknowledgments

I would like to thank especially the dozens of busy individuals who gave their valuable time to be interviewed for this project, from a former Senator to current EPA officials, industry representatives, environmental lobbyists, grass-roots representatives, attorneys, and others connected in some way to Superfund policy. Two former undergraduates from the University of Massachusetts, Jon Levine and Alan Rose, provided first-rate research assistance, as did Brooke Raasch and Jeremy Arkes; graduate student Mike Reese read the entire manuscript several times and provided outstanding research assistance and criticism. For reading, commenting, and generally improving parts of the evolving manuscript, I would like to thank Lee Friedman, Bob Hahn, Winston Harrington, Bob Nakosteen, Paul Portney, Sharon Tracey, anonymous referees, and seminar participants at Georgetown, Rochester, and Syracuse Universities. Finally, for financial support I am indebted to the dean of Social and Behavioral Sciences, the Graduate School, and the Massachusetts Institute for Social and Economic Research, all at the University of Massachusetts at Amherst.

Index

About the Author

John A. Hird is currently Assistant Professor of Political Science at the University of Massachusetts at Amherst, and Faculty Fellow, Massachusetts Institute for Social and Economic Research. He received his Ph.D. in public policy from the University of California at Berkeley and has previously served as Economist with the Council of Economic Advisers and as Research Fellow in Governmental Studies at the Brookings Institution. In September 1992 he was awarded the first annual Miriam Mills Award for an outstanding contributor to public policy studies under age thirty-five by the Policy Studies Organization.